With an excellent new chapter on troubleshooting, this text remains the best-value and most easily accessible textbook for students taking a Management or Accounting degree. Thoroughly recommended.

Richard Hull, Senior Lecturer in Management, Newcastle University Business School, UK

The new edition of Collis & Hussey builds on the strengths of previous editions, providing a clear and accessible foundation for undergraduate and postgraduate management students in undertaking research. The authors combine a sound approach to research methods with a sympathetic understanding of the practical problems regularly faced by students new to individual research. The book is helpful for students working alone (particularly the chapters on collecting and analysing data, expanded for this edition) and for formal research methods courses.

Christopher Napier, Professor of Accounting, School of Management, Royal Holloway, University of London, UK

Collis and Hussey take the beginning researcher by the hand and lead them sympathetically and lucidly through the academic maze.

Peter Walton, Professor of Accounting, Accounting and Finance Research Unit, The Open University, UK

Finding a rigorous overview of the variety of research approaches can be difficult, but a broad grounding is essential if students are to make sensible choices about the relevant approach needed to answer their particular research questions. Collis and Hussey not only provide this starting point but also give signposts to the more detailed literature that will allow students to focus successfully.

Jane Broadbent, Deputy Vice-Chancellor and Professor of Accounting, Roehampton University, UK

I have used Collis and Hussey's *Business Research: A Practical Guide for Undergraduate & Postgraduate Students* since the first edition was published in 1997. Research methods is an impenetrable topic for most students, especially undergraduates, and at the time this book filled a gap in the market, with its readable style and accessible format. I am delighted to see the third edition in updated form with progress tests and activities and a focus on the practical issues that students face when approaching a research project for the first time. The main strength of the work remains the strong student focus, helping them to make sense of the different referencing systems, and copious tips and advice on all aspects of preparing a dissertation or thesis. It is also extremely useful for students preparing their research proposal, which is a key component for the successful completion of any project. The inclusion of screen shots and output files from the latest version of *SPSS* (16.0) is also a very helpful feature of the third edition.

Professor Neil Marriott, Dean, Winchester Business School and Hoare Chair of Business, UK

This is a good introductory book to business research methods. It manages to make very accessible a subject that is, at the same time, important for business students and difficult for them to grasp. The book is user-friendly, and the troubleshooting session at the end is a must for students in difficulties with their research projects.

Gilberto Montibeller, Department of Management, London School of Economics, UK

Praise for the second edition of *Business Research:*

Comprehensive, clarifying, convincing … from front to back this book offers everything that the research student requires. Practical help is accompanied by a clear analysis of theoretical concepts. If you have struggled with research in the past this book will be a good companion for your research projects in the future.

Elizabeth Mantzari, PhD student, University of Essex, UK

Business Research by Collis and Hussey offers a coherent, extremely well thought out and stimulating book on research in business. Activities and progress tests allow the text to be used in class, and also, can be used to refine one's 'knowledge' individually. I especially enjoyed the section 'Making Academic Decisions', as having recently joined a university at postgraduate level I think the majority of my recent troubles and woes would have been made less dramatic had I read it before I arrived. I have already recommended the book to many of my colleagues teaching both undergraduate and postgraduate students. An excellent book, which can be used as a checklist for experienced researchers, or treated as a 'sacred text' by students new to research.

Simon Parker, Postgraduate Assistant Researcher, Lincoln Business School, UK

I purchased your book some time ago and am now in the throes of a dissertation at Sheffield University. I just wanted to say thank you for writing such a wonderful book that explains everything really logically and is also inspiring and interesting! Yes, I never thought I would say that about research methods! It's worth every penny!

Donna O'Brien, nearly-finished dissertation student, Sheffield University, UK

Jill Collis & Roger Hussey

WITHDRAWN

Business Research

A Practical Guide for Undergraduate & Postgraduate Students

THIRD EDITION

palgrave
macmillan

First edition 1997
Reprinted 9 times
Second edition 2003
Reprinted 10 times
Third edition 2009
First Published 1997 by
PALGRAVE MACMILLAN

Palgrave Macmillan in the UK is an imprint of Macmillan Publishers Limited, registered in England, company number 785998, of Houndmills, Basingstoke, Hampshire RG21 6XS.

Palgrave Macmillan in the US is a division of St Martin's Press LLC, 175 Fifth Avenue, New York, NY 10010.

Palgrave Macmillan is the global academic imprint of the above companies and has companies and representatives throughout the world.

Palgrave® and Macmillan® are registered trademarks in the United States, the United Kingdom, Europe and other countries.

ISBN-13: 978–1–4039–9247–5
ISBN-10: 1–4039–9247–9

This book is printed on paper suitable for recycling and made from fully managed and sustained forest sources. Logging, pulping and manufacturing processes are expected to conform to the environmental regulations of the country of origin.

A catalogue record for this book is available from the British Library.

A catalog record for this book is available from the Library of Congress.

10 9 8 7
18 17 16 15 14 13 12

Printed in China

Contents

List of figures

List of tables

List of boxes

Preface to the Third Edition

The success of the previous editions of *Business Research* has led to the development of this fully revised and expanded third edition. However, the aim remains unchanged and that is to provide practical guidance to students and others conducting research in business and management disciplines. The book retains the successful format of the earlier editions, but the design has been improved to better meet the needs of students and those responsible for teaching research methods. To reinforce learning, reflective and practical activities are now included at the end of each chapter, and lecturers are provided with PowerPoint presentations covering the main learning outcomes.

Each chapter is clearly structured around a particular topic and the different aspects are simply described and explained. Many first time researchers find the language of research off-putting. Therefore, new terms are introduced gradually and the glossary provides clear explanations. Existing users will find the third edition retains the familiarity of the original and will notice the expansion of some chapters and the insertion of new chapters. The success of the book in different countries has led to a more international perspective. The range of literature now available via e-resources, together with the widespread use of user-friendly software for data analysis, provided the impetus for other revisions.

Undergraduate and postgraduate students on taught courses often need to complete their research within a tight time frame. Consequently, they have to balance the conceptual demands of the subject with pressing practical considerations. On the other hand, doctoral students generally have more time, but need to develop greater knowledge of the conceptual aspects of research. For all students, the main problem is how to find the most efficient and effective way of collecting, analysing and presenting data while maintaining academic rigour. The studies we have referenced to illustrate the methods covered in this book were chosen for their richness and variety of approach rather than because they are classic studies.

Business Research offers a succinct and accessible guide to research methods, which makes it an ideal core text. Students and lecturers will find that the chapters follow the typical pattern of the research process, from the design of the project to the writing-up stage. The practical activities and references to further reading can be used for independent study or as basis for group work. At any time, students can refer to the 'Troubleshooting' chapter for advice. Indeed, despite the new materials included in this edition, the book is still small enough to carry around as a constant source of reference.

JILL COLLIS
Kingston University, UK

ROGER HUSSEY
University of Windsor, Canada

Acknowledgements

We are grateful to all our colleagues in the UK, Canada and abroad, and the many cohorts of students who have kindly commented on previous editions of this book. We would also like to thank SPSS Inc. for allowing us to reproduce their screen images, which has enabled us to improve our practical guide to statistical methods in this edition.

We are indebted to our editorial team headed by Martin Drewe and Linda Norris for their forbearance and support in preparing the third edition. Finally, we are deeply indebted to Sir Timothy John Berners-Lee for the gift of the World Wide Web, which allows this transatlantic duo to continue writing together and communicate with their publishers without leaving their desks!

Every effort has been made to trace all copyright holders, but if any have been inadvertently overlooked, the publishers will be pleased to make the necessary arrangements at the first opportunity.

1

Understanding research

Learning objectives

When you have studied this chapter, you should be able to:

- explain the nature and purpose of research

- classify different types of research

- identify the main stages in the research process

- identify the characteristics of a good research project.

1.1 INTRODUCTION

Whether you are merely at the stage where you are contemplating carrying out business research or you have already begun planning your study, you will find this chapter useful for clarifying your initial thoughts. We start by examining the nature and purpose of academic research that focuses on business issues and the different ways in which studies can be categorized. We also look at the general differences between undergraduate, postgraduate and doctoral research projects before going on to discuss what makes a good project.

1.2 NATURE AND PURPOSE OF BUSINESS RESEARCH

Although *research* is central to both business and academic activities, there is no consensus in the literature on how it should be defined. One reason for this is that research means different things to different people. However, from the many definitions offered, there is general agreement that research is:

- a process of enquiry and investigation
- systematic and methodical, and
- increases knowledge.

Looking at the *nature* of research, this tells us that researchers need to use appropriate methods for collecting and analysing research data, and to apply them rigorously. It tells us that the *purpose* of research is to investigate a research question with a view to generating knowledge. The research question you investigate will relate to a particular problem or issue that you identify from studying a particular topic. Research is much more than mere speculation or assumptions about business events, transactions and activities. You will need to study your chosen topic and the choice of research methods. Students need to meet the criteria that relate to their degree programme, and all researchers will need to meet the standards expected by their institutions and/or funding body.

A research project offers both undergraduate and postgraduate students an opportunity to identify and select a research problem and investigate it independently under the guidance of a supervisor. It allows you to apply theory to or otherwise analyse a real problem, or to explore and analyse more general issues. It also enables you to apply techniques and procedures to illuminate the problem and contribute to our greater understanding of it or to generate solutions. Thus, the typical objectives of research can be summarized as follows:

> **KEY DEFINITIONS**
>
> Research is a systematic and methodical process of enquiry and investigation with a view to increasing knowledge.

- to review and synthesize existing knowledge
- to investigate some existing situation or problem
- to provide solutions to a problem
- to explore and analyse more general issues
- to construct or create a new procedure or system
- to explain a new phenomenon
- to generate new knowledge
- a combination of any of the above.

Our summary illustrates that research is purposeful, as it is conducted with a view to achieving an outcome. The nature of that outcome will depend on the type of research you are conducting and the level at which you are operating. The outcome may be presented in the form of a *dissertation* for an undergraduate or taught Master's degree or for a Master of Philosophy (MPhil). Alternatively, it is likely to take the form of a *thesis* for a doctoral degree such as Doctor of Business Administration (DBA) or Doctor of Philosophy (PhD). Academic research can also be conducted for the purpose of publishing the study as a book or an article in an academic journal or for consultancy purposes. This book focuses primarily on the needs of students carrying out some form of business research for a qualification and those pursuing academic careers.

Types of enterprise to research include small and medium-sized enterprises (SMEs), businesses with limited liability (such as companies), and organizations in the not-for-profit or public sectors. The focus in the media is mainly on big business, yet 99% of businesses are small or medium-sized enterprises (SMEs) and you may find yourself employed by one or even starting one. Whatever type of entity you choose as the focus of your research, you will find a wide range of issues to investigate.

The typical users of business research are:

> **KEY DEFINITIONS**
>
> A discourse is 'a lengthy treatment of a theme'.
>
> A dissertation is a 'detailed discourse, esp. as submitted for academic degree'.
>
> A thesis is a 'dissertation, esp. by candidate for a higher degree'.
>
> (*Oxford Compact Dictionary & Thesaurus*, 1997, pp. 211, 216 and 801 respectively)

- The government – for developing/monitoring policies, regulations and so on
- Owners, managers and business advisers – for keeping up to date with new ideas and specific developments in business
- Management – for developing internal policies and strategies (for example comparing research results relating to their own business with those with previous periods, their competitors and/or industry benchmarks)
- Academics – for further research and educational purposes.

1.3   CLASSIFYING RESEARCH

As there are many ways of *classifying research*, it can be bewildering at first. However, studying the various characteristics of the different types of research helps us to identify and examine the similarities and differences. Research can be classified according to the:

- *purpose* of the research – the reason why it was conducted
- *process* of the research – the way in which the data were collected and analysed
- *logic* of the research – whether the research logic moves from the general to the specific or vice versa
- *outcome* of the research – whether the expected outcome is the solution to a particular problem or a more general contribution to knowledge.

For example, the aim of your research project might be to describe a particular business activity (purpose) by collecting qualitative data that are quantified and analysed statistically (process), which will be used to solve a business problem (outcome). Table 1.1 shows the classification of the main types of research according to the above criteria.

TABLE 1.1 Classification of main types of research

Type of research	Basis of classification
Exploratory, descriptive, analytical or predictive research	Purpose of the research
Quantitative or qualitative research	Process of the research
Applied or basic research	Outcome of the research
Deductive or inductive research	Logic of the research

1.3.1 EXPLORATORY, DESCRIPTIVE, ANALYTICAL AND PREDICTIVE RESEARCH

If we are classifying research according to its *purpose*, we can describe it as being exploratory, descriptive, analytical or predictive. At the undergraduate level, research is usually exploratory and/or descriptive. At postgraduate or doctoral level it is always analytical or predictive. Table 1.2 shows this classification in increasing order of sophistication and gives examples. One drawback of increasing the level of sophistication in research is that the level of complexity and detail also increases.

TABLE 1.2 Examples of research classified by purpose	
Type of research	**Example**
Exploratory	An interview survey among clerical staff in a particular office, department, company, group of companies, industry, region and so on, to find out what motivates them to increase their productivity (that is, to see if a research problem can be formulated).
Descriptive	A description of how the selected clerical staff are rewarded and what measures are used to record their productivity levels.
Analytical	An analysis of any relationships between the rewards given to the clerical staff and their productivity levels.
Predictive	A forecast of which variable(s) should be changed in order to bring about a change in the productivity levels of clerical staff.

Exploratory research is conducted into a research problem or issue when there are very few or no earlier studies to which we can refer for information about the issue or problem. The aim of this type of study is to look for patterns, ideas or hypotheses, rather than testing or confirming a hypothesis. A *hypothesis* is a proposition that can be tested for association or causality against empirical evidence. *Empirical evidence* is data based on observation or experience, and *data**** are known facts or things used as a basis for inference or reckoning. In exploratory research, the focus is on gaining insights and familiarity with the subject area for more rigorous investigation at a later stage.

* This term is a Latin plural noun, the singular of which is 'datum'.

Typical techniques used in exploratory research include case studies, observation and historical analysis, which can provide both quantitative and qualitative data. Such techniques are very flexible as there are few constraints on the nature of activities employed or on the type of data collected. The research will assess which existing theories and concepts can be applied to the problem or whether new ones should be developed. The approach to the research is usually very open and concentrates on gathering a wide range of data and impressions. As such, exploratory research rarely provides conclusive answers to problems or issues, but gives guidance on what future research, if any, should be conducted.

Descriptive research is conducted to describe phenomena as they exist. It is used to identify and obtain information on the characteristics of a particular problem or issue. Descriptive research goes further in examining a problem than exploratory research, as it is undertaken to ascertain and describe the characteristics of the pertinent issues. The following are examples of research questions in a descriptive research study:

- What is the absentee rate in particular offices?
- What are the feelings of workers faced with redundancy?
- What are the qualifications of different groups of employees?
- What type of packaging for a box of chocolates do consumers prefer?

- What information do consumers want shown on food labels?
- Which car advertisements on television do men and women of different ages prefer?
- How many students study accounting in China compared with students in Australia?
- How do commuters travel to work in capital cities?

You will notice that many of these questions start with 'what' or 'how' because the aim is to describe something. However, further clarification would be required before the study could begin. For example, we cannot ask everyone in the world about which car advertisements or chocolate box packaging they prefer. Even a study that compared the number of students studying accounting in China and Australia requires clarification of the type of students (for example age, sex and nationality) and what is studied (for example level/stage in the course, main subjects covered and qualification). Therefore, even in a descriptive study, you must spend time refining your research questions and being specific about the phenomena you are studying. We will explain how this can be achieved in later chapters.

Analytical or *explanatory research* is a continuation of descriptive research. The researcher goes beyond merely describing the characteristics, to analysing and explaining why or how the phenomenon being studied is happening. Thus, analytical research aims to understand phenomena by discovering and measuring causal relations among them. For example, information may be collected on the size of companies and the levels of labour turnover. A statistical analysis of the data may show that the larger the company the higher the level of turnover, although as we will see later, research is rarely that simple. An important element of explanatory research is identifying and, possibly, controlling the *variables* in the research activities, as this permits the critical variables or the causal links between the characteristics to be better explained. A variable is a characteristic of a phenomenon that can be observed or measured.

Predictive research goes even further than explanatory research. The latter establishes an explanation for what is happening in a particular situation, whereas the former forecasts the likelihood of a similar situation occurring elsewhere. Predictive research aims to generalize from the analysis by predicting certain phenomena on the basis of hypothesized, general relationships. Thus, the solution to a problem in a particular study will be applicable to similar problems elsewhere, if the predictive research can provide a valid, robust solution based on a clear understanding of the relevant causes. Predictive research provides 'how', 'why' and 'where' answers to current events and also to similar events in the future. It is also helpful in situations where 'what if' questions are being asked. The following are examples of research questions in a predictive research study:

> **KEY DEFINITIONS**
>
> Data are known facts or things used as a basis for inference or reckoning.
>
> Empirical evidence is data based on observation or experience.
>
> A hypothesis is a proposition that can be tested for association or causality against empirical evidence.
>
> A variable is a characteristic of a phenomenon that can be observed or measured.

- In which city would it be most profitable to open a new retail outlet?
- Will the introduction of an employee bonus scheme lead to higher levels of productivity?
- What type of packaging will improve the sales of our products?
- How would an increase in interest rates affect our profit margins?
- Which stock market investments will be the most profitable over the next three months?
- What will happen to sales of our products if there is an economic downturn?

1.3.2 QUANTITATIVE AND QUALITATIVE RESEARCH

Looking at the approach adopted by the researcher can also differentiate research. Some people prefer to take a *quantitative* approach to addressing their research question(s) and design a study that involves collecting quantitative data (and/or qualitative data that can be quantified) and analysing them using statistical methods. Others prefer to take a *qualitative* approach to addressing their research question(s) and design a study that involves collecting qualitative data and analysing them using interpretative methods. As you will see in later chapters, a large study might incorporate elements of both as their merits are often considered to be complementary in gaining an understanding in the social sciences.

Referring to a research approach as quantitative or qualitative can be misleading, as a researcher can design a study with a view to collecting qualitative data (for example published text or transcripts of interviews) and then quantifying them by counting the frequency of occurrence of particular key words or themes. This allows researchers to analyse their data using statistical methods. On the other hand, a researcher can collect qualitative data with the intention of analysing them using non-numerical methods, or collect data that are already in numerical form and use statistical methods to analyse them. In this chapter, we will continue to refer to quantitative and qualitative approaches, but we will discuss alternative terms you may wish to use later in the book.

Some students avoid taking a quantitative approach because they are not confident with statistics and think a qualitative approach will be easier. Many students find that it is harder to start and decide on an overall design for a quantitative study, but it is easier to conduct the analysis and write up the research because it is highly structured. Qualitative research is normally easier to start, but students often find it more difficult to analyse the data and write up their final report. For example, if you were conducting a study into stress caused by working night shifts, you might want to collect quantitative data such as absenteeism rates or productivity levels, and analyse these data statistically. Alternatively, you might want to investigate the same question by collecting qualitative data about how stress is experienced by night workers in terms of their perceptions, health, social problems and so on.

There are many arguments in the literature regarding the merits of qualitative versus quantitative approaches, which we will examine later on in the book. At this stage, you simply need to be aware that your choice will be influenced by the nature of your research project as well as your own philosophical preferences. Moreover, you may find that the access you have been able to negotiate, the type of data available and the research problem persuade you to put your philosophical preferences to one side.

KEY DEFINITIONS

Applied research describes a study that is designed to apply its findings to solving a specific, existing problem.

Basic (or pure) research describes a study that is designed to make a contribution to general knowledge and theoretical understanding, rather than solve a specific problem.

1.3.3 APPLIED AND BASIC RESEARCH

A standard classification of research divides projects into *applied research* and *basic research*. Applied research is a study that has been designed to apply its findings to solving a specific, existing problem. It is the application of existing knowledge to improve management practices and policies. The research project is likely to be short term (often less than 6 months) and the immediacy of the problem will be more important than academic theorizing. For example, you might be investigating the reorganization of an office layout, the improvement of safety in the workplace or the reduction of wastage of raw materials or energy in a factory process. The output from this type of research is likely to be a consultant's report, articles in professional or trade magazines and presentations to practitioners.

When the research problem is of a less specific nature and the research is being conducted primarily to improve our understanding of general issues without emphasis on its immediate application, it is classified as basic or pure research. For example, you might be interested in whether personal characteristics influence people's career choices. Basic research is regarded as the most academic form of research, as the principal aim is to make a contribution to knowledge, usually for the general good, rather than to solve a specific problem for one organization.

Another example of applied research that is conducted in academic institutions often goes under the general title of *educational scholarship* (or *instructional research* or *pedagogic research*). This type of study is concerned with improving the educational activities within the institution and the output is likely to be case studies, instructional software or textbooks.

Basic research may focus on problem solving, but the problem is likely to be theoretical rather than practical. The typical outcome of this type of research is knowledge. Basic research may not resolve an immediate problem, but will contribute to our knowledge in a way that may assist in the solution of future problems. The emphasis, therefore, is on academic rigour and the strength of the research design. The output from basic research is likely to be papers presented at academic conferences and the articles published in academic journals.

1.3.4   DEDUCTIVE AND INDUCTIVE RESEARCH

Deductive research is a study in which a conceptual and theoretical structure is developed and then tested by empirical observation; thus, particular instances are deduced from general inferences. For this reason, the deductive method is referred to as moving from the general to the particular. For example, you may have read about theories of motivation and wish to test them in your own workplace. This will involve collecting specific data of the variables that the theories have identified as being important.

Inductive research is a study in which theory is developed from the observation of empirical reality; thus, general inferences are induced from particular instances, which is the reverse of the deductive method. Since it involves moving from individual observation to statements of general patterns or laws, it is referred to as moving from the specific to the general. For example, you may have observed from factory records in your company that production levels go down after two hours of the shift and you conclude that production levels vary with length of time worked.

All the different types of research we have discussed can be helpful in allowing you to understand your research and the best way to conduct it, but do not feel too constrained. It is important to recognize that one particular project may be described in a number of ways, as it will have purpose, process, logic and outcome. For example, you may conduct an applied, analytical study using a quantitative approach. In a long-term project, you may wish to use qualitative and quantitative approaches, deductive and inductive methods, and you will move from exploratory and descriptive research to analytical and predictive research. The key classifications we have examined can be applied to previous studies that you will review as part of your research and you can use these typologies to describe your own study in your proposal and later on in your dissertation or thesis.

> **KEY DEFINITIONS**
>
> **Deductive research** describes a study in which a conceptual and theoretical structure is developed which is then tested by empirical observation; thus particular instances are deducted from general inferences.
>
> **Inductive research** describes a study in which theory is developed from the observation of empirical reality; thus general inferences are induced from particular instances.

1.4   ACADEMIC LEVELS OF RESEARCH

The *academic level* of your research in terms of the sophistication of the research design and duration of the project will depend on your reasons for undertaking it. The requirements for undergraduates are very different from those for postgraduate students and doctoral students. However, the basic principles, issues and practicalities are the same.

1.4.1   UNDERGRADUATE LEVEL

If you are an undergraduate student, you may be required to undertake a research project as part of a course or it may even be a complete course. You are normally expected to be familiar with the main concepts and terms as explained in this book and undertake one or more of the following activities:

- Design a research project – On some courses you will be expected to design a research project and then write a report that explains the rationale for your chosen design and describes its strengths and weaknesses.
- Write a research proposal – A research proposal requires you to design a project as above, but also to include a preliminary review of the literature.
- Conduct a research project – In many cases you will be required not only to design a project and write a proposal, but also to do some actual research. This would entail writing a review of the literature and also collecting and analysing existing data or new data (for example from interviews or a questionnaire survey). In some cases, you may be allowed to base your entire project on a critical literature review, where you will analyse the literature on a chosen topic and draw conclusions. In all cases, you will be required to write a research report, which may be called a dissertation or thesis.

1.4.2   POSTGRADUATE AND DOCTORAL STUDENTS

If you are on an MBA programme or a specialized Master's programme, you will normally be expected to design a research project, write a proposal, conduct the study and write a report (which may be called a dissertation or thesis). In some cases, you may find that you are allowed to conduct a critical literature review only, where you will be expected to analyse and synthesize the literature on a chosen topic and draw conclusions. The processes are very similar to undergraduate research, but a more comprehensive approach is needed and higher quality of work will be required.

If you are doing a Master's degree by research or a doctorate, the intensity of the research will be much greater and you will need to read this book thoroughly and the recommended reading that is relevant to your subject. It is important to remember that, at this level, the country in which you are studying and the expectations of your institution will have a significant influence on the process and outcome of your research.

1.4.3   ACADEMIC RESEARCHERS

If you are seeking an academic post, looking for promotion or engaged in research as part of your job, this book will reinforce your knowledge or give you a new perspective on a particular issue you have not considered previously, and help you to write conference papers and journal articles.

1.5   OVERVIEW OF THE RESEARCH PROCESS

Whatever type of research or approach is adopted, there are several fundamental stages in the *research process* that are common to all scientifically based investigations. The simplified diagram shown in Figure 1.1 illustrates a traditional and highly structured view of the research process.

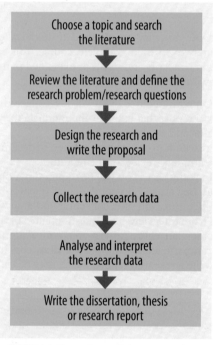

Choose a topic and search the literature

↓

Review the literature and define the research problem/research questions

↓

Design the research and write the proposal

↓

Collect the research data

↓

Analyse and interpret the research data

↓

Write the dissertation, thesis or research report

FIGURE 1.1 Overview of the research process

This model presents research as a neat, orderly process, with one stage leading logically on to the next stage. However, in practice, research is rarely like that. For example, failure at one stage means returning to an earlier stage and many stages overlap. Thus, if you were unable to collect the research data, it may be necessary to revise your definition of the research problem or amend the way you conduct the research. This is often a good reason for conducting some exploratory research before commencing a full project.

We will look briefly at each stage in the research process now to give you an overview of the nature of research, but greater detail is provided in the subsequent chapters.

1.5.1   THE RESEARCH TOPIC

The starting point is to choose a *research topic*, which is a general subject area that is related to your degree if you are a student or your discipline if you are an academic. You may find a research topic suggests itself as a result of your coursework, job, interests or general experience. For example, you may be interested in the employment problems of minority groups in society, the difficulties of funding small businesses, what makes managers successful, or the commercial sponsorship of sport.

1.5.2   THE LITERATURE

Once you have chosen a general topic, you need to search the literature for previous studies and other relevant information on that subject and read it. By exploring the existing body of knowledge, you should be able to see how your topic is divided into a number of different areas that will help you focus your ideas on a particular research problem.

1.5.3   THE RESEARCH PROBLEM

All students experience some difficulty in narrowing down their general interest in a research topic to focus on a particular *research problem* or issue that is small enough to be investigated. This is often referred to as defining the research problem and leads on to setting the *research question(s)*. The classic way in academic research to identify a research problem is to consider the literature and identify any gaps, as these indicate original areas to research. You will also find that many academic articles incorporate suggestions for further research in their conclusions. If you have conducted an undergraduate dissertation already, that subject area may lead you to your Master's or doctoral research questions. If you are an academic, you may also have conducted previous academic or consultancy research that suggests research questions for your present study. You will need to focus your ideas, decide the scope of your research and set parameters. For example, perhaps your study will investigate a broad financial issue, but focus on a particular group of stakeholders, size of business, industry, geographical area, or period of time.

1.5.4   THE RESEARCH DESIGN

The starting point in *research design* is to determine your research *paradigm*. A research paradigm is a framework that guides how research should be conducted, based on people's philosophies and assumptions about the world and the nature of knowledge. Your overall approach to the entire process of the research study is known as your *methodology*. Although, in part, this is determined by the research problem, the assumptions you use in your research and the way you define your research problem will influence the way you conduct the study.

> **KEY DEFINITIONS**
>
> A methodology is an approach to the process of the research encompassing a body of methods.
>
> A paradigm is a framework that guides how research should be conducted, based on people's philosophies and their assumptions about the world and the nature of knowledge.

1.5.5   COLLECTING RESEARCH DATA

There are a variety of ways in which you can collect research data and we look at the main *methods of data collection* later in Chapters 8 and 10. Because of the many differences between quantitative and qualitative methods, these are explained in separate chapters. If you have a quantitative methodology, you will be attempting to measure variables or count occurrences of a phenomenon. On the other hand, if you have a qualitative methodology, you will emphasize the themes and patterns of meanings and experiences related to the phenomena.

1.5.6   ANALYSING AND INTERPRETING RESEARCH DATA

A major part of your research project will be spent analysing and interpreting research data. The main *methods of data analysis* used will depend on your research paradigm and whether you have collected quantitative or qualitative data. We will be looking at this in more detail in Chapters 9, 11 and 12. It is important to realize, however, that although data collection and data analysis are discussed separately in this book, the stages are sometimes simultaneous. You should not make decisions about your data collection methods without also deciding which analytical methods you will use.

1.5.7   WRITING THE DISSERTATION OR THESIS

It is at the writing-up stage that many students experience problems, usually because they have left it until the very last minute! It is important to start writing up your research in draft as soon as you start the early stages of the project, and continue to do so until it is completed. To a large extent, the stages outlined above will be captured in the structure of your dissertation or thesis. It is valuable at the outset to consider a possible structure, as it will give you an idea of what you are aiming for and Table 1.3 shows a typical structure. The title should be descriptive but not lengthy. Remember that any planned structure will have the disadvantage of making the research process look much more orderly than it really is. Although all research reports differ in structure according to the problem being investigated and the methodology employed, there are some common features.

TABLE 1.3 Indicative structure of a dissertation or thesis	% of report
1. Introduction	
– The research problem or issue and the purpose of the study	
– Background to the study and why it is important or of interest	
– Structure of the remainder of the report	10
2. Review of the literature	
– Evaluation of the existing body of knowledge on the topic	
– Theoretical framework (if applicable)	
– Where your research fits in and the research question(s) and propositions or hypotheses, if applicable	30
3. Methodology	
– Identification of paradigm *(doctoral students will need to discuss)*	
– Justification for choice of methodology and methods	
– Limitations of the research design	20
4. Findings/Results *(more than one chapter if appropriate)*	
– Presentation and discussion of the analysis of your research data/statistical tests and their results	30
5. Conclusions	
– Summary of what you found out in relation to each research question you investigated	
– Your contribution to knowledge	
– Limitations of your research and suggestions for future research	
– Implications of your research for practice or policy (if appropriate)	10
	100
References *(do not number this section)*	
– A detailed, alphabetical (numerical, if appropriate) list of all the sources cited in the text	
Appendices	
– Detailed data referred to in the text, but not shown elsewhere	

1.6   DEVELOPING A RESEARCH STRATEGY

Research is a time-consuming and expensive activity and therefore you will need to develop a *research strategy* to ensure you meet your objectives. A humorous view of the challenges facing researchers is shown in Figure 1.2. However, this map was drawn in 1969 and in the intervening years many techniques and methods have been developed that help researchers overcome the difficulties depicted in this cartoon.

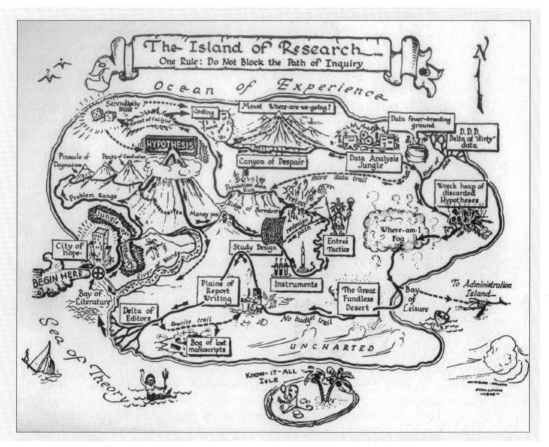

FIGURE 1.2 Island of research
Source: Agnew and Pyke (1969, frontispiece).

Although a few lucky individuals are in a position to conduct studies purely out of interest, most require some definite outcomes. This may be a dissertation or thesis that gets you a good grade as a student, transferable skills that improve your employability or a journal publication that will help you further your academic career. The main steps are:

- Getting organized
- Identifying your desired outcome(s)
- Choosing a research topic
- Determining the research problem/question(s)
- Drawing up a detailed table of contents
- Establishing a timetable or schedule
- Being serious about writing.

These aspects will be discussed in depth throughout this book, but so that you can start developing your research strategy straightaway, we give some helpful pointers now.

1.6.1   GETTING ORGANIZED

You will not be successful in doing research if you are not organized. We can all think of exceptions of brilliant researchers who ignore this rule but, for most of us, success depends on being administratively competent. This entails having a good filing system, dating and recording all your research activities and committing everything to paper or computer. At this stage, you need to work out how much time you have, what financial resources you need and what physical resources you have in terms of computer hardware and software and any other technology. You will also need to draw up a list of contacts, groups and institutions that may be helpful. They may be able to help by offering advice and guidance, allowing you access to facilities such as a library or to collect data, or by assisting you in some way to achieve your desired outcomes.

1.6.2   IDENTIFYING THE OUTCOME(S)

You need to be specific when identifying the outcome(s) of your research. It is not sufficient to say that you want a high grade for your research project or to publish in one of the top academic journals. If you want to get the top grades for your dissertation or thesis, you need to understand the requirements you have to satisfy, and these are discussed in Chapter 2. If you want your work to be published, you need to read articles in the journal you have chosen and understand the editorial policy. We offer advice on this in Chapter 13.

1.6.3   CHOOSING A RESEARCH TOPIC

There is often a conflict between what you would like to do and what is feasible. The level of research and the outcome you desire will frequently determine the research you will conduct. You may be very interested in the history of sea bathing, but this may not be suitable if the particular aspect of sea bathing you choose is not relevant to your degree programme. If you are pursuing an academic career, you will need to think whether the topic you choose will provide you with a research niche upon which to build an impressive reputation. At the other end of the scale, the time constraints you face on a Bachelor's or Master's programme make it unlikely that you will be able to conduct a large survey of the opinions of directors of the world's top companies. Even a seasoned researcher with an enviable reputation would find such a project a challenge. Your research must be feasible and lead to your expected outcome(s).

1.6.4   DETERMINING THE RESEARCH PROBLEM/QUESTION(S)

Do not focus solely on the immediate outcome(s) of your research only, but think about how you might be able to develop your work. For example, if you are a student, you might want to examine an issue in a particular industry where you hope to find employment when you graduate. For those pursuing research to further their careers, there is a good argument for choosing an issue that will help you to build a reputation and become one of the experts in a particular field.

1.6.5   BEING SERIOUS ABOUT WRITING

You will be judged by your ability to communicate, particularly your written output; a poorly crafted dissertation, thesis, conference paper or article can destroy what may have been a well-designed and carefully executed study. We give considerable guidance on writing in the later chapters but the immediate advice is to start writing notes and drafts now and to continue to write, review and revise your work so that your final draft will represent the highest quality in terms of substance, structure, grammar and spelling.

1.7   CHARACTERISTICS OF GOOD RESEARCH

KEY DEFINITIONS

Methodological rigour refers to the appropriateness and intellectual soundness of the research design and the systematic application of the research methods.

Many of the characteristics of good research can be developed by adopting a methodical approach. *Methodological rigour* is very important and this term refers to the appropriateness and intellectual soundness of the research design and the systematic application of the methods used. Therefore, it requires a careful, detailed, exacting approach to conducting the research.

The characteristics of a good research project vary according to the philosophical assumptions that underpin your research. These assumptions are discussed later in Chapter 4 and are very important at all academic levels. A soundly based research design should allow a degree of flexibility to enable you to pursue new developments in the topic if they are relevant to the study and you have sufficient time. In subsequent chapters, we will explain how this can be achieved. At this stage, it is useful to have an overview of what makes a good research project. Therefore, Table 1.4 compares the main characteristics of good and poor projects.

TABLE 1.4 Characteristics of good and poor research projects

Criteria	Poor project	Good project
Research problem and scope	Unclear and unfocused	Sharply focused Related to academic debate
Literature review	A list of items Relevance unclear Little or no evaluation Research questions missing, impractical or unfocused	Critical evaluation of relevant, up-to-date literature Linked to focused, feasible research questions
Methodology	Little appreciation of research design No justification of choice Not linked to the literature	Cohesive design Excellent review of research design options Linked to the literature
Analysis and discussion	Unclear findings, unrelated to research questions Little or no attempt to discuss in relation to literature review	Clear findings discussed in an analytical manner that generates new knowledge and insight Linked to the literature
Conclusions	Some conclusions but not linked to research questions Implications and limitations of results not addressed	Conclusions clearly linked to research questions Attention given to implications and limitations
Referencing	Plagiarism through omission or inadequate referencing	All sources cited in the text and full bibliographic details listed at the end
Communication	Difficult to follow Many spelling and grammar mistakes	Clear flow of ideas Appropriate spelling and grammar

1.8   CONCLUSIONS

This chapter has examined the purpose and nature of research, and the ways in which it can be classified. We have given an overview of the different types of research and the factors that need to be considered at various levels. A research project offers an opportunity to identify and select a research problem to investigate independently under the guidance of a supervisor. It gives you the opportunity to apply theory or otherwise analyse a real business problem or issue. Your research needs to be systematic and methodical and your study will illuminate the problem or issue and contribute towards our greater understanding of it. To ensure you are satisfied with your research and achieve the outcomes you desire, you must develop a research strategy. The most important part of that strategy from the onset is to start writing. You should make sure that you keep careful records to ensure that other people's contribution to knowledge is not confused with yours.

ACTIVITIES

1. Select two academic journals from your discipline in the library and construct a table that classifies articles according to whether the research is exploratory, descriptive, analytical or predictive.

2. Construct a second table that classifies the same articles according to whether the research is quantitative or qualitative.

3. Now construct a third table that classifies the same articles according to whether the research is applied or basic.

4. Finally, construct a table that classifies the same articles according to whether the research is deductive and inductive.

5. Reflect on the results shown in your four tables and write notes on similarities and differences in these classifications. Summarize your notes in the form of a diagram.

PROGRESS TEST

Complete the following sentences:

1. Research is a process of enquiry and investigation that is conducted in a systematic and methodical way with a view to increasing _____.

2. A study in which theory is developed from the empirical evidence is known as _____ research.

3. A study in which theory is tested against empirical evidence is known as _____ research.

4. An idea or proposition that can be tested against empirical evidence is called a _____.

5. Empirical evidence is data based on experience or _____.

Are the following statements true or false?

6. A research paradigm is a lengthy treatment of a theme that is submitted for an academic degree.

7. Descriptive research can take a quantitative or qualitative approach.

8.   A qualitative approach to research does not require IT skills.

9.   An exploratory study is always used to test or confirm a hypothesis.

10.   Research that has been designed to resolve a specific problem is known as applied research.

Multiple choice questions:

11.   The result of building up information from other information is known as:
    a) an analysis
    b) a dialysis
    c) a synopsis
    d) a synthesis

12.   The result of setting out a reasoned argument in steps is known as:
    a) a comparison
    b) a debate
    c) an evaluation
    d) an evasion

13.   The classification of studies into exploratory, descriptive, analytical or predictive research is based on:
    a) the logic of the research
    b) the outcome of the research
    c) the process of the research
    d) the purpose of the research

14.   The classification of studies into applied or basic research is based on:
    a) the logic of the research
    b) the outcome of the research
    c) the process of the research
    d) the purpose of the research

15.   Inductive research seeks to:
    a) classify theory
    b) confirm theory
    c) develop theory
    d) test theory

2

Making academic decisions

Learning objectives

When you have studied this chapter, you should be able to:

- understand the general entry requirements for degree programmes

- understand the general standards for research at different levels

- choose a university or college

- consider issues relating to your future employability

- choose a supervisor for your research.

2.1 INTRODUCTION

Although you may be thinking hard about your research already, if your research is going to be a means of achieving an academic qualification, you will need to look at the academic regulations and procedures at an early stage. Even if you are writing an internal consultancy report, you will need to consider the terms of reference. As the academic requirements can vary from one institution to another, we only provide a general guide, but this chapter should alert you to the main points. We also advise on choosing an academic institution and supervisor and examine how your choices can enhance your employability.

2.2 GENERAL ENTRY REQUIREMENTS FOR DEGREE PROGRAMMES

In this section, we explain the general entry requirements for undergraduate and postgraduate degree programmes in business and management and the standards expected in the associated research report, known as a *dissertation* or *thesis*. There are no hard and fast rules and this is largely a matter of convention. Of course, the detailed requirements will be defined by your university or college, the type of research you are undertaking and whether it is going to be submitted in whole or part assessment of your degree. When you have completed your research, you will write it up and it will be assessed. There may also be an oral examination.

Table 2.1 shows the main degrees and corresponding name of the associated research report. The degrees are shown in ascending order, starting with the undergraduate degrees and ending with the doctorates, which are the highest of the postgraduate degrees. This concentrates on research reports that are an important part of an award (such as a Bachelor's degree, taught Master's degree or DBA), or those that lead directly to an award (such as an MPhil or PhD). However, you might also be conducting research as part of an assignment (for example for course work on a degree programme) or a consultancy project. In such cases, the regulations may be fairly loose or non-existent and you will need to establish *terms of reference* for your project. These allow you to establish:

KEY DEFINITIONS
A discourse is 'a lengthy treatment of a theme'.
A dissertation is a 'detailed discourse, esp. as submitted for academic degree'.
A thesis is a 'dissertation, esp. by candidate for a higher degree'.
(*Oxford Compact Dictionary & Thesaurus*, 1997, pp. 211, 216 and 801 respectively)

- the purpose of the research
- the scope of the study
- the research question(s) to be addressed
- the nature of the research (for example whether it will be exploratory, descriptive or analytical, and whether you are expected to make recommendations as well as draw conclusions from your findings).

The terms of reference need to be negotiated with the person requesting or commissioning the research and it will be your responsibility to ensure that your research fulfils the agreed terms. Whether your research is being conducted for an academic award or for consultancy purposes, many of the research processes are identical.

Level	Main degrees	Research report
Undergraduate	Bachelor of Arts (BA) Bachelor of Science (BSc)	Dissertation
Taught Master's	Master of Arts (MA) Master of Science (MSc) Master of Business Administration (MBA) Master of Research (MRes) Master of Management (MoM)	Dissertation
Master's by research	Master of Philosophy (MPhil)	Thesis
Taught doctorate	Doctor of Business Administration (DBA)	Thesis
Doctorate by research	Doctor of Philosophy (PhD)	Thesis

TABLE 2.1 Main degrees and associated research reports

2.3   GENERAL STANDARDS FOR RESEARCH AT DIFFERENT LEVELS

For all researchers, even those with a high level of experience, research is a process of enquiry and therefore a learning experience. In business research, as in other subject areas, a student project at undergraduate or postgraduate level affords a medium through which you can acquire the following skills and knowledge:

- skills for independent research, such as problem identification, problem definition, and the ability to plan and execute a research project appropriate to the problem under investigation; also, the ability to collect and analyse data, form conclusions and make practical recommendations
- skills for effective communication, such as verbal and presentational skills as well as written and organizational skills
- knowledge of research methodologies, methods and analytical techniques
- detailed knowledge of a particular topic, including the literature published in that area, its underlying concepts, theories and assumptions
- personal skills, such as resourcefulness, flexibility, creativity and clarity of thought, also the self-confidence that is gained as a result of managing an independent research project
- the ability to critically analyse a situation and to draw conclusions
- the knowledge to evaluate research carried out by others.

2.3.1   BACHELOR'S DEGREES

In many parts of the world, it is common for undergraduates studying for a *Bachelor's degree* (BA or BSc) to undertake a research project towards the end of their programme, which will result in a report usually known as a dissertation. This is not restricted to business and management degrees, but increasingly students of law, engineering and science must demonstrate an appreciation of business, and this is often achieved by means of a research project. You may find that you are required to have reached a prescribed standard in your course in order to proceed to this stage. In contrast to the assignments you have worked on for your other modules, where the lecturer determines the content and direction of the coursework, in a research project, you will be responsible for identifying a research question, deciding how the research will be designed and conducting it.

If you are on a degree programme that incorporates an industrial place-ment, your research project will normally be based on a business issue or problem that is relevant to your employment. This may give you the oppor-tunity to collect some *primary data*, which are original data collected by you at source (for example from your own experiments, questionnaire survey, interviews or focus groups). If you are on a full-time course with no place-ment, your research project is more likely to be based on *secondary data*, which are data that have been collected and published by someone else. Sources of secondary data include books, reports and government statistics, and the many sources of information available on the internet. We suggest you do not fall into the habit of referring to such a project as 'secondary research', as it is the data you are distinguishing as secondary while your analysis will produce original findings.

> ### KEY DEFINITIONS
> Primary data are data collected from an original source (for example your own experiments, surveys, interviews or focus groups).
>
> Secondary data are data collected from an exist-ing source (for example publications, databases and internal records).

The typical aims of an undergraduate research project are to:

- enable students to acquire analytical and problem-solving skills based on evaluation and synthesis within a work environment or a simulation of a practical situation
- provide active learning where the student identifies and defines the problem to be explored and the work to be completed, thus learning from the experience
- develop skills for independent research
- develop the ability to operationalize a business problem or issue (in other words, describe it in such a way that it can be measured)
- apply academic knowledge in the investigation of a problem or issue.

In general, you will be expected to demonstrate that you have an understanding of research methods appropriate to the chosen field and have investigated and evaluated an approved topic. Such research projects often fall into the category of applied research and are mainly descriptive in nature. This does not mean that you are not expected to adopt a critical and analytical approach. Indeed, students who can demonstrate these intellectual skills at the undergraduate level are likely to achieve high marks.

2.3.2   MASTER'S DEGREES

Master's degrees have various titles: the most common business and management degrees are the MA, MSc, MBA, MoM and MRes. The dissertation is an important element of these degrees and the requirements are similar to those for an undergraduate disser-tation. However, the standard of work demanded is higher with greater emphasis on the students demonstrating a critical and analytical approach. Degrees with titles such as Professional Master or Master by Course Work do not include a dissertation or contain only a small element of research. To undertake a taught Master's degree, other than an MBA, you normally need to have an undergraduate degree in a relevant discipline. Sometimes, professional qualifications or management experience can be substituted, as is often the case with entry to MBA programmes.

An MRes degree is a taught programme with a dissertation that prepares you for a doctorate (DBA or PhD), a career in commercial research or a career in one of the professions that requires advanced knowledge of research methodologies and methods.

A Master of Philosophy (MPhil) degree is a programme of supervised research. You will be required to demonstrate an understanding of research methods that are appropriate to the chosen field and that you have investigated and critically evaluated an approved topic. As this is a degree by research, there is considerable emphasis on the rigour with which the research has been conducted. As you will remember from our definition of research in Chapter 1, this means that your thesis must demonstrate that you have been systematic and methodical. Entry requirements for an MPhil are normally a good honours degree at Bachelor level, where you have achieved a specified high standard. In the UK, this is often an upper second or first class honours degree. Experience and relevant professional qualifications may be taken into consideration if your qualifications do not comply exactly with the entry criteria.

2.3.3   DOCTORATES

The two main *doctorates* are the DBA and PhD and may be studied on a part-time or full-time basis. These qualifications are at the highest level, but the DBA is usually regarded as a professional qualification and an extension of the MBA. Therefore, the research requirements are not as demanding as for a PhD, which is more of an academic qualification. However, you should bear in mind that there are variations between one country and another due to cultural differences. In the UK and many other European countries, a PhD is usually a programme of supervised research and students spend the greatest part of their time conducting individual research. The qualification is obtained by submission of a thesis and an oral defence of the thesis known as a *viva voce*. In North America, students spend the first two years taking a taught course with examinations, which must be passed before progressing to the dissertation stage.

The above distinctions are of a general nature and there are many variations between institutions within the same country. However, in all cases students must have critically investigated and evaluated an approved topic and also have made an independent and original contribution to knowledge. This contribution need not be revolutionary, but the research must result in a contribution to our understanding of the phenomenon that has been investigated.

Entry requirements for a DBA or PhD are likely to be a relevant Master's degree that has included research training. Therefore, you may be required to pass an MRes before you can proceed to your doctorate. If you are unable to register directly for a PhD, you may find it is possible to register for an MPhil and transfer to a PhD at a certain stage before completing the MPhil (when it is judged that your research project can be extended to meet the criteria of a PhD).

2.3.4   STANDARDS

Details of the *standards* you are expected to achieve will be specified by your institution. Table 2.2 provides a general guide to the typical maximum length of a dissertation or thesis at the different levels. The number of words in a document is easily calculated with the word count tool on your software. If you find this hard to visualize, you may prefer to estimate the length of your report in terms of number of pages. One A4 page contains approximately 500 words, but as research reports are traditionally presented in double or 1.5 spacing, 10,000 words would be about 40 pages. Tables, graphs, diagrams and other illustrations will extend your report, but appendices are normally excluded from the word count.

Level	Research report	Word count
Undergraduate	Dissertation	10,000 – 15,000
Taught Master's	Dissertation	20,000
Master's by research	Thesis	40,000
Taught doctorate	Thesis	50,000
Doctorate by research	Thesis	80,000

TABLE 2.2 Typical length of a dissertation or thesis

More important than the difference in length is the difference in substance between reports at various levels. Although all academic research should focus on one specific research problem, and in many cases its resolution, a dissertation is normally limited in terms of the extent of original inquiry; an MPhil thesis requires carrying out some original research, normally within the scope of existing theories; while a PhD thesis is expected to make a contribution to knowledge.

Howard and Sharp (1994) advise that it is important not to lose sight of the fact that the prime aim of writing up is to convince your examiners that you have satisfied the appropriate criteria laid down by your institution. Table 2.3 shows the main criteria to be satisfied by the different research reports resulting from each level of degree programme.

TABLE 2.3 Criteria to be satisfied by a dissertation or thesis

Level	Research report	Criteria
Undergraduate	Dissertation	A well-structured and convincing account of a study, the resolution of a problem or the outcome of an experiment Evidence of awareness of the literature
Taught Master's	Dissertation	An ordered, critical and reasoned exposition of knowledge gained through the student's efforts A comprehensive review of the literature
Master's by research	Thesis	Evidence of an original investigation or the testing of ideas Competence in independent work or experimentation An understanding of appropriate techniques Ability to make critical use of published work and source materials Appreciation of the relationship of the special theme to the wider field of knowledge Worthy, in part, of publication
Doctorate	Thesis	As for Master's degree by research, plus: Originality as shown by the topic researched or the methodology employed Distinct contribution to knowledge

Source: Adapted from Howard and Sharp (1994, p. 177).

2.4 CHOOSING AN INSTITUTION

A number of national and institutional factors need to be considered when *choosing the institution* that will award your degree. The country and the institution in which you study and/or work can have a major impact on your life. We often have little choice about this, as there may be family and financial issues that determine our choice or the fact that only one institution will accept you. Even if your choice is restricted, it is important to understand these factors, as they will help towards your success.

2.4.1 NATIONAL DIFFERENCES

In this discussion of *national differences* in academic research, we will focus on doctoral programmes, as these tend to reflect the general approach to research and what constitutes research. We will be referring to the conceptual issues and the associated terminology in Chapter 4; therefore, we will keep this preliminary review as jargon-free as possible. As explained above, there are two significantly different models of how doctoral research should be conducted and its role in academia. We will refer to these models as the North American model and the European model. Other countries have adopted one of these models or have adapted one of them to make it appropriate for their country's needs.

In the North American model, the full-time PhD has an emphasis on individually assessed taught courses, and part-time PhDs are uncommon. The programme would require you to complete a dissertation or thesis based on original research. The typical pattern is two years of taught courses with a comprehensive examination that you must pass. Successful candidates go on to spend the third year writing a research proposal, which is examined. The fourth year is when the research data are collected and analysed, and the student writes the thesis and submits it for examination.

The objective of the programme is not only to increase your knowledge and skills, but also to train you as a researcher. In some institutions, you will be required to take courses to develop your teaching skills and teach as part of the programme. During your research, you are normally expected to write and present a number of conference papers; you may also be expected to publish articles in academic journals. Your method of data analysis is likely to be statistical, as this has been the dominant approach for some years. In addition to your research, you will have other duties, such as helping your supervisor with his or her research and/or teaching. If you are seeking an academic career, these activities will help you to build up useful skills.

In the European model, taught doctorates are not widespread, although PhD students may be encouraged to attend short courses that are relevant to their topic. A full-time student can complete a PhD in three years, but this might be extended to four years or more if there are problems. There are opportunities for part-time PhDs, which usually take five or more years. Because of the low number of taught courses and the emphasis on individual research, the part-time model is successful but demanding. This is a difficult route and requires careful thought. If funding is a problem, the part-time route may be the only option.

2.4.2 INSTITUTIONAL DIFFERENCES

In addition to national differences in research models, there are also *institutional differences*. It is important to decide how important these are and how they affect you as a student or an employee.

In most countries, it takes at least one year to complete a full-time Master's degree and a full-time PhD will take three or more years. You may find an institution that offers a Master's degree in a matter of months or a PhD in two years or less. This may be possible, but you are advised to look very carefully at the credibility of the institution, the standards and success rates, and compare them to others in the same country. You should also be cautious of institutions that offer a large number of credits for previous study or work experience. Most respected institutions restrict the number of credits they grant and expect you to take the majority of your studies at their institution in order to receive an academic award.

2.4.3   REPUTATION OF THE INSTITUTION

Your choice of institution is likely to be influenced by its *reputation,* but the university or college with the highest reputation and the most expensive programme might not be the best one for you. What is more important is the knowledge and enthusiasm of the professors who will be teaching and/or supervising you. If possible, contact students who are currently studying in the institution you are considering and obtain their views. You will also find many publications give information about the different programmes offered by a wide range of universities and other academic institutions. You may be tempted to base your decision on the institution's ranking, but take care when interpreting these lists, as the criteria used to compile the ranking may not be the ones you would choose.

Another measure that can be used to assess universities and colleges is the quality of the programmes offered. National accreditation and quality assurance procedures form the basis for such an assessment, but some institutions have received accreditation from international bodies. The main international accreditations for business schools are:

- Association of Advanced Collegiate Schools of Business (AACSB)
- Association of MBAs (AMBA)
- European Quality Improvement System (EQUIS) awarded by the European Foundation for Management Development.

Academic institutions vary in terms of the specialist interests of their staff and the way in which subjects are taught. We look at the importance of having an experienced and interested supervisor in the next section, but in addition to the availability of a good supervisor, you need to consider other aspects when choosing an academic institution. Box 2.1 draws from research by Johnston (1995) and our own experience to provide a checklist for choosing an academic institution. Although some features may be of interest to undergraduate researchers, it is mainly aimed at postgraduate research students. It is unlikely that every institution you approach will be able to offer all these features, but the list provides an easy way of checking that you will have access to the maximum number of resources for enhancing your chances for a successful outcome.

BOX 2.1   Checklist for choosing an academic institution

- Are you provided with detailed information on the research programme at the outset and the rules and regulations that apply?
- Are you offered an interview with the programme director or a potential supervisor to explore the match between your research interests and the research activities and abilities of the supervisor?
- Is there a research training programme or, at the very least, a series of seminars on research methods, to provide you with knowledge and opportunities to meet other researchers?
- Is there a culture of conference attendance by supervisors and research students that will give you the opportunity to present papers and discuss your research with others?
- Are the library services, photocopying, printing, computer and other facilities adequate?
- Will you have access to common rooms where you can meet fellow researchers?
- Will you have access to facilities at evenings and weekends?
- If the institution is fairly large, is there a regular newsletter to help you keep in touch?

2.5   EMPLOYABILITY

It is important that you consider your future *employability* when choosing an academic institution and degree programme. The increasing levels of participation in higher education have resulted in the undergraduate degree no longer being a guaranteed route to a future career. Increasingly employers are assessing factors other than the degree when recruiting staff. A well conducted undergraduate research project can sometimes make the difference in obtaining the position you desire. This does mean that the project must be thorough and presented well. It must also be a topic that is of interest to the potential employer.

An alternative strategy to a career for some students is to take a Master's degree or a doctorate. We have already noted that a research project for a taught Master's degree will be expected to be at a higher level than for a Bachelor's degree and provides an opportunity to demonstrate your particular skills, knowledge and preferences. For example, if you have chosen a Master's in Marketing because you are seeking a career in that area, your research project should demonstrate your interest in a particular marketing issue and your research skills.

For those students going on to a doctorate, an academic career is the usual objective. To obtain a position as a full-time lecturer at a university in North America or the UK you will need a PhD and, preferably, publications in the form of conference papers and/or journal publications. Future promotions will be based on your publications in academic journals. In most of Europe, and throughout North America, all instructors are known as professors. In the USA and Canada, the ranks are assistant professor, associate professor and full professor. In the UK, instructors are known as lecturers and the title 'professor' is reserved for those whose research achievements have been recognized as being of particular worth by a committee of academic peers.

Distance learning and *on-line degrees* are becoming increasingly popular, but they vary in terms of quality. Therefore, you would be wise to reflect on why you want the qualification and what your own time and financial resources will allow you to do. If you are looking for an academic career in teaching and/or research, you may find that this type of qualification is not highly regard by appointment committees. The main reason for this is because the committee will want to ensure that the applicant has some experience of the pedagogic process in a university or college.

An academic post may be offered on a permanent contract (either full time or part time) or on a fixed period contract (either full time or part time). Fixed period contracts and part-time contracts may not require a PhD and publications record. This is because these contracts are rarely converted into permanent positions.

2.6   SUPERVISION

Supervision plays a vital role in both undergraduate and postgraduate degrees and is a formal requirement. In the UK, undergraduates and students on taught Master's degrees typically have one supervisor, whereas MPhil and doctoral students have two. In the latter cases, the supervisors will have specialist knowledge of the topic and at least one of them will have experience of successful supervision at that level.

The relationship between the student and the supervisors is very important and there should be frequent contact. Therefore, you need to have supervisors who will be interested in your research, supportive and with whom you can discuss your ideas and from whom you will receive timely feedback. In North America, doctoral research is more likely to be monitored and supervised by a committee. Therefore, the relationship with individual supervisors tends to be less important, but you may find some committee members are keen to become involved in your research.

> **KEY DEFINITIONS**
>
> A supervisor is the person responsible for overseeing and guiding a student's research.

2.6.1   CHOOSING A SUPERVISOR

Phillips and Pugh (1994) suggest that you obtain as much information as possible before *choosing a supervisor* by visiting prospective universities or colleges. Although this advice was aimed at PhD students, it is equally applicable to MPhil and other postgraduate students. This will allow you to meet potential supervisors and to assess the quality of the facilities and resources, and evaluate the relative importance of research in that institution. When talking to potential supervisors, you need to bear in mind that most academic staff are involved in four main activities:

- teaching
- writing teaching materials and/or text books
- managing departments, programmes or subject fields
- conducting research
- writing research papers, articles and reports.

If possible, talk to current research students or those who have been supervised in the past by the academic you have in mind. Box 2.2 provides a checklist for choosing a supervisor.

BOX 2.2   Checklist for choosing a supervisor

- Does the supervisor have knowledge and interest in your research topic?
- Is the supervisor sympathetic to your proposed methodology?
- Is the supervisor an experienced researcher?
- Has the supervisor got a record of successful supervisions?
- Has the supervisor got a good publication record?
- Has the supervisor got enough time to take on your supervision as well as managing his/her other work?

You need to bear in mind that selection is a two-way process in which the potential supervisor will also be assessing you and your research proposal. A supervisor may decline to take you on if your research topic holds no interest for him or her; if your research proposal is considered to have serious flaws or you do not appear to have a number of other characteristics that are likely to contribute to the successful completion of your research. The latter are particularly important if you are applying for an MPhil or doctorate, where you need to engage with your research at a deeper level and/ or maintain your momentum over a period of three or more years. Cryer (1997, p. 10) aptly describes these attributes as the non-paper entry qualifications for research students and her checklist is shown in Box 2.3.

BOX 2.3   Attributes supervisors look for in research students

- Ability to grasp concepts and reason analytically
- Motivation and perseverance in achieving objectives
- Capacity for independent thought
- Organizational skills
- Independence as a learner
- Self-confidence
- Enthusiasm for the research programme
- Nature and extent of any relevant work and life experience
- Nature and extent of any previously undertaken training in research
- Likelihood of establishing good working relationship
- Language skills, particularly for overseas candidates

Source: Cryer (1997, p. 10).

It is usually the responsibility of the head of the department or director of research to exercise as much care as possible in matching students to supervisors. He or she will take into account such factors as the research topic, the number of students already being supervised by that member of staff, and the student's academic ability and personality. Sometimes the student is accepted on condition that he or she undertakes to do a project in one of the ongoing areas of research in the department. Students who only have a general idea about their research topic may develop their ideas after discussions with their supervisors. However, a final decision should be made as soon as possible.

2.6.2   SUPERVISOR/SUPERVISEE RELATIONSHIP

Once you have agreed who your supervisor(s) will be, it is important to realize that the *supervisor/supervisee relationship* is a two-way relationship in which you play an active part. Howard and Sharp (1994) recommend that the student should:

- at the outset, attempt to find out the supervisor's views of the supervisor/student relationship; for example on impromptu versus formal meetings and punctuality
- agree with the supervisor the routine aspects of the relationship and take responsibility for their implementation; for example, agree the maximum interval between meetings and ensure it is not breached
- produce written lists of queries prior to meetings with the supervisor in order to define the agenda and structure the meeting
- keep written notes of meetings with the supervisor (even if the supervisor also does so) and submit copies to him/her
- agree with the supervisor the nature and timing of written material, such as progress reports and drafts chapters, to be submitted to him/her.

Although your supervisor(s) will play a very important role in guiding your research, 'it is the responsibility of the researcher to identify a [research] question' (Creedy, 2001, p. 116). Therefore, even if supervisors are willing to offer suggestions based on their research interests, you must take ownership of your research project and identify the specific research problem or issue and the research question(s) yourself.

Research into the supervision of postgraduate students (Phillips, 1984) shows that supervisory style is important. She found that the more supervisors left their students to get on with their work, intervening only when specifically asked for help, the shorter the length of time before the students became independent researchers. She argues that too much contact and cosseting delays the necessary weaning process.

From this, you can see that the ideal relationship is one where the researcher is initially tutored by the supervisor and eventually becomes a respected colleague. Thus, they start as master and pupil, and end up as equals. Therefore, it is important that you and your supervisor are well matched. This is not so difficult if you know the academic staff at the institution already. If you have chosen to continue your studies at the same university or college, you may have been stimulated by a particular subject and a particular lecturer, and wish to approach that person to be your supervisor. If you are registering for a degree at an institution that is new to you and you do not know the staff, you may have only a few days in which to talk to potential supervisors and other students.

The longer the period of research, the more important it is that the relationship between the supervisor and the supervisee is resilient enough to cope with every stage in the research process shown in Figure 2.1. The emotional commitment involved in conducting research should not be underestimated. Research involving independent inquiry requires considerable intellectual activity and often considerable stress. This is especially true of doctorates, where a major piece of research is conducted over several years. Your initial enthusiasm and interest may turn into frustration, boredom or writer's block, and you may begin seriously to question your ability to continue. However, with the help of your supervisor, you can minimize the likelihood of serious stress through careful planning and time management, and eventually reach the final phase when your main concern is to get the research finished.

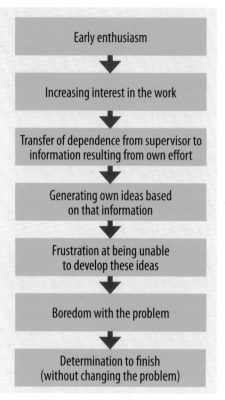

Early enthusiasm

↓

Increasing interest in the work

↓

Transfer of dependence from supervisor to information resulting from own effort

↓

Generating own ideas based on that information

↓

Frustration at being unable to develop these ideas

↓

Boredom with the problem

↓

Determination to finish (without changing the problem)

FIGURE 2.1 Changing attitudes shown by students during their research
Source: Adapted from Phillips (1984, p. 16).

2.6.3 SUPERVISION MODELS

There are a number of different *supervision models* and it would be a mistake to think exclusively in terms of one supervisor for each researcher. Although one supervisor per student is typically the model at the undergraduate level and on taught Master's courses, it is usual to have at least two supervisors for MPhil and doctoral research. As already mentioned, at some institutions there may be a committee. You may find that the administrative, pastoral and academic roles of supervision are delegated to different individuals, which reduces the risk of failure by allowing the student's progress to be monitored closely.

An alternative approach is *de facto supervision*. This model encourages the researcher to develop a number of different surrogate supervisors, possibly in other establishments, who can offer skills lacked by the main supervisor. This is particularly useful where company-based projects are concerned, where both academic and consultancy skills are required.

In the natural sciences, group and team projects are a widely used approach. Research students are often clustered round a major research issue and each student is part of the team. This allows specific areas of work within the same problem area to be the responsibility of individual researchers. Such approaches are research-skills based. On the other hand, business and management research in the social sciences is more likely to involve solitary, knowledge-based activities and include a relationship with one or more supervisors.

2.6.4 OTHER SOURCES OF SUPPORT

Apart from the support provided by your supervisor(s), other potential sources of support include *peer support* (fellow students), mentors, work colleagues, family and friends. You can find sources of peer support outside your institution by networking with other researchers at academic conferences and events for doctoral students. You should also attend any taught sessions offered, such as methodology courses.

The isolation that can sometimes be felt by students while conducting their research projects can be reduced by developing *support sets*. A set comprises approximately five students and a tutor and meets for a full day every one or two months. Each person is given an hour or so of the time available, during which the group focuses on a particular project or problem. This provides an opportunity to use the group as a sounding board, in addition to exchanging experiences and ideas. It also enables group members to support and encourage one another.

Set members need to be working in loosely related areas, in order to increase the chances of cross-fertilization of ideas without undue competition. The main requirement is that there are sufficient numbers of students attached to a department or faculty to produce viable group sizes. They may be supplemented by managers from companies who are not registered for a degree, but who wish to conduct their own in-company research. Support sets can be a feature of more traditional research activities in the social sciences and need not be founded exclusively on process. They should be seen as being additional to normal supervision arrangements and are particularly valuable in the early stages of a research project.

2.7   CONCLUSIONS

This chapter has given an overview of the general requirements and standards you can expect in relation to your dissertation or thesis. Views on what constitutes research around the world vary and there are no global rules that govern what universities and other institutions of higher education offer research students. Once you have determined the country in which you wish to study, you then need to identify the institutions that are well recognized and offer the type of programme you want. If you have the necessary entry qualifications, visit the institution and evaluate the quality of what they have to offer. You need to be wary of degree programmes that are very short or appear to offer a qualification without substantial work.

If you are a potential MPhil or doctoral candidate, you should arrange to meet potential supervisors. This also gives them the opportunity to assess your qualities and skills at the same time as discussing your proposed research. Part of your decision about where to study will rest on whether you can find an experienced supervisor who is interested in your research topic and willing to guide your endeavours. Some students will need to find more than one supervisor.

ACTIVITIES

1. If a research methods programme is available, obtain details of this. In addition, obtain a copy of the rules and regulations relating to your dissertation or thesis. Take particular note of the maximum word count and the length of time for doing the research/submission date.

2. Visit the library and examine past students' dissertations or theses. Look for those within your discipline to get a feel for the size and structure, and the amount of work required. Compare the contents pages and write notes on the similarities and differences in how they are structured and reflect on the reasons. While in the library, make notes on the resources available (for example access to on-line databases, the computer and printing facilities, arrangements for borrowing and photocopying, and the evening and weekend opening times).

3. Ask the programme director to put you in touch with a potential supervisor and arrange an informal meeting to explore the match between your research interests and those of the potential supervisor.

4. Ask the programme director or your potential supervisor to put you in touch with a student who is at a more advanced stage or who has successfully completed their research. Arrange a meeting with the student to obtain practical tips.

5. If you are a Master's or doctoral student, visit the common room and find out about evening and weekend access, and events where you can meet fellow researchers.

Learning objectives

When you have studied this chapter, you should be able to:

- identify any funding constraints

- determine the knowledge, skills and personal qualities researchers need

- use techniques for generating research topics

- negotiate access to data and consider ethical issues

- plan the management of the research process.

3.1   INTRODUCTION

A successful researcher establishes a firm base on which to develop his or her project. Projects fail, not because the researcher was lazy, incompetent or unmotivated, but because he or she did not recognize the importance of project management. You need to make certain that you have sufficient funds, a clear idea of what you are going to investigate, access to the relevant data, a realistic timetable and an efficient system for managing the process of the research. You also need to take account of any ethical guidelines or regulations when conducting your research. Time management is crucial, but 'there is no simple relationship between input of time and outputs of useful results' (Creedy, 2001, p. 117). Therefore, it is a combination of your practical and intellectual skills that will determine the quality of your research. This chapter examines the main practical issues you should take into account when planning your research.

3.2   FUNDING THE RESEARCH

Research is not a cost-free activity and, therefore, it is important to consider the funding implications when planning your research. Even if you were to conduct all your research in your college or university library, you would incur minor expenses, such as photocopying and printing. As soon as you start visiting other libraries and institutions, you will begin to incur expenses that are more substantial such as travelling and subsistence costs. You will also incur those types of expenses if you are conducting interviews as part of your research. If you are using a postal questionnaire, you will need to cover cost of printing, postage and stationery. Of course, this does not take account of your time, which in most cases is non-chargeable.

Unfortunately, research funds are difficult to obtain and you need to have a contingency plan if funding is essential to your project. There is a wide range of potential sources of funding and you should allow plenty of time for writing funding proposals: deadlines for applications are often tight and there is considerable competition for funds. You may wish to consider the following sources.

3.2.1   UNIVERSITY FUNDING

Some universities offer bursaries and grants to students from which you can fund any expenses you incur while conducting your research. Alternatively, you may be able to help on an existing large research project and in return receive a salary and/or have your expenses for your own project reimbursed. You may be able to use the part of the project you are working on as the basis for your dissertation or thesis. However, there are some drawbacks to this sort of arrangement, as you will have to demonstrate that the research you submit for your degree is your own work and not that of the group. In addition, you may find the demands of the work you are doing for the group supplant your own needs to complete your dissertation or thesis. Sometimes the arrangement also includes some teaching, but if you can agree suitable terms, you not only benefit from the financial rewards and access to data, but also from working with more experienced researchers.

Your university or college should also be able to direct you to potential sources of funding from national governments and the European Union. However, you should bear in mind that obtaining them is very competitive. Moreover, writing a successful proposal is difficult for an inexperienced researcher and you will need help from your supervisor(s).

3.2.2   COMMERCIAL SOURCES OF FUNDING

If you have a job or your degree programme includes an industrial placement, you have the opportunity to design a work-based study and your employer may be willing to reimburse any expenses you incur. Even at doctoral level, it may be possible to persuade a present or potential employer to cover your costs if you can demonstrate that your research will be useful to the business as well as contributing to your degree. Receiving funding from commercial sources has a number of disadvantages. Sponsors are more interested in solving their own problems than the academic requirements of your programme and you may find you are expected to conduct two parallel studies with a business report for your employer or commercial sponsor in addition to your dissertation or thesis. Therefore, you should weigh up very carefully the benefits of covering your research costs against the additional pressure this extra work will give you.

If you do not have the benefit of an interested employer, you may be able to find a business sponsor to help fund your research. You may be lucky to have contact with an individual who wants the research done because he or she is particularly interested in the topic (for example a relation or a family friend) or because he or she is conducting a larger project and is willing to meet the costs of your research if it feeds into the larger study (for example your supervisor). If you obtain funding from such a source, you must check the ownership of the data you generate and your independence.

3.2.3   FUNDING FROM PROFESSIONAL BODIES

Many of *the professional bodies* associated with business and management (for example the professional institutions that represent accountancy, banking, human resource management, marketing and purchasing) offer funding for research. Competition is keen and your proposed research needs to be carefully designed and relevant to the current research interests of the professional body to which you are applying. You may find it useful to include the name(s) of your supervisor(s) in the proposal, especially if that person is a member of the potential sponsoring body.

3.2.4   FUNDING FROM THE CHARITY SECTOR

Substantial funding is available from some charities and associations, although strict criteria often have to be met. Modest amounts to cover limited expenses such as travelling, postage and printing are less difficult to obtain.

3.3   KNOWLEDGE, SKILLS AND PERSONAL QUALITIES

Conducting research in business and management requires certain knowledge, skills and personal qualities and different attributes are needed at different stages in the research. Kervin (1992) summarizes the main stages in the research process as:

- research problem stages
- research design stages
- data gathering stages
- data analysis and interpretation stages.

The research problem stages include gathering preliminary data from the literature

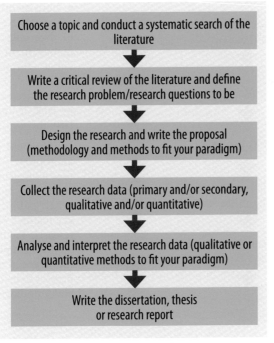

Choose a topic and conduct a systematic search of the
literature

Write a critical review of the literature and define
the research problem/research questions to be

Design the research and write the proposal
(methodology and methods to fit your paradigm)

Collect the research data (primary and/or secondary,
qualitative and/or quantitative)

Analyse and interpret the research data (qualitative or
quantitative methods to fit your paradigm)

Write the dissertation, thesis
or research report

FIGURE 3.1 Stages in the research process

and may also incorporate exploratory research (Kervin, 1992; Sekaran, 2003). This leads to the identification of the research problem and the development of the specific research questions to be addressed by the study. Before the main data gathering and analysis stages can commence, some studies require time for negotiating access and addressing ethical issues (Saunders, Lewis and Thornhill, 2007). Figure 3.1 shows a more detailed model of the stages in the research process than the one shown in Chapter 1.

Little has been written on the issues arising at each stage in the research process. Howard and Sharp (1994) identify 20 factors that have a beneficial, neutral or adverse effect on research projects, while Easterby- Smith, Thorpe and Lowe (1991) classify the qualities required of researchers under the headings of knowledge, skills and personal qualities. A study of eight successful researchers (Hussey, 2007) brought these factors together by examining the process of the research and the skills, knowledge and personal qualities needed at each stage. The main findings were as follows:

- *Knowledge* – Knowledge of research was particularly beneficial during the literature search, research design and writing stages. Business knowledge provided a context for negotiating access and enriched the analysis of data and illuminated the conclusions.
- *Skills* – Good administrative skills were particularly needed during the literature searching stage. Communication skills were most important when negotiating access and collecting data. Negotiating access and dealing with ethical issues tended to be regarded as challenges to be overcome and had little effect on the process of the research. Not surprisingly, communication skills were also of great benefit at the writing stage and when presenting conference papers. Researchers near the beginning of their careers regarded conferences as opportunities for networking, obtaining feedback and getting papers published in conference proceedings, while established academics tended to focus on writing articles for publication in academic journals rather than attending conferences. IT skills were beneficial during the data collection and data analysis stages.
- *Personal qualities* – Creativity was most important when identifying the research problem and research questions. Motivation was rated highly during the literature search, data analysis and writing stages. Perseverance was most needed at the data collection and writing stages. Participants referred to the discipline required in conducting interviews, administering questionnaires and maintaining

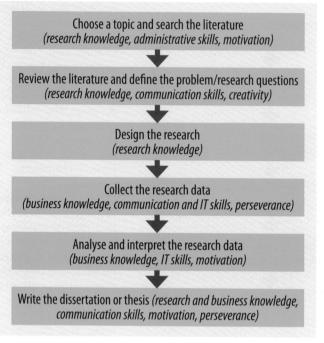

Choose a topic and search the literature
(research knowledge, administrative skills, motivation)

Review the literature and define the problem/research questions
(research knowledge, communication skills, creativity)

Design the research
(research knowledge)

Collect the research data
(business knowledge, communication and IT skills, perseverance)

Analyse and interpret the research data
(business knowledge, IT skills, motivation)

Write the dissertation or thesis *(research and business knowledge,
communication skills, motivation, perseverance)*

FIGURE 3.2 Attributes needed during the main stages in the research process

a consistently rigorous approach to every aspect of data collection. Time management was influential throughout the research, with every stage adversely affected by lack of time, particularly the writing stage.

It would appear that appropriate knowledge, time management and the ability to remain motivated and persevere are key features of successful research. Figure 3.2 develops our simple model of the stages in the research process to incorporate the above findings.

3.4 GENERATING A RESEARCH TOPIC

You may have already found a research topic because you have a particular interest in one of the subjects you have studied, or perhaps a topic has been allocated to you. However, some students delay starting their research because they have difficulty in generating a topic. If this applies to you, the best advice is to start by thinking of a general subject area that is relevant to your programme. Naturally, you are more likely to have a successful and enjoyable experience if you find this general subject area interesting! Then you could use a very simple technique known as *brainstorming*. You need at least one other interested person with whom to generate spontaneous ideas. Jot down a list of all the ideas that come up and then review them by deciding what you mean by each idea. For example, if you were interested in financial reporting, you could review the idea by asking yourself the following questions:

- What is financial reporting?
- Do I mean internal or external financial reporting?
- Which organizations produce financial reports?
- Is there a particular aspect of financial reporting I am interested in?
- Am I interested in the regulation of financial reporting?
- Am I interested in voluntary disclosure?
- Am I interested in the communication aspects?

Once you have begun to focus your ideas about financial reporting, you could turn your attention to such questions as:

- What is reported?
- When is it reported?
- To whom is it reported?
- What is the purpose of reporting?
- Are there any ethical issues?

Another way of approaching the problem might be to examine the various ways in which research can be designed or conducted. If you are still unable to generate a research topic the following techniques may be of help.

3.4.1   ANALOGY

KEY DEFINITIONS

Analogy is a means of designing a study in one subject by importing ideas and procedures from another area where there are similarities.

Analogy involves designing a research project in one subject by importing ideas and procedures from another area where you consider there are similarities. Thus, you are using the research developments in one area to illuminate how you could conduct your own study. It is also possible to develop a research topic if you are aware of methods of analysis that have been used in one study and that can be applied in your own work. The use of existing analytical techniques in a completely new and different area can result in a very interesting study that makes a contribution to our knowledge of the subject.

3.4.2   MORPHOLOGICAL ANALYSIS

Morphology is concerned with the study of form and *morphological analysis* involves drawing up a table and using it to analyse the general subject area that interests you. First, you define the key factors or dimensions of the subject, which you set out as the column headings. Then you list the various attributes of the factor or the ways in which it can occur under the headings. Finally, you define all feasible combinations of the attributes to generate a number of potential research projects. Obviously, your choice is influenced by your research paradigm.

In the example in Table 3.1, we have used the general subject area of research. We have defined our key dimensions as the type of research, the methodology and the unit of analysis.

TABLE 3.1 Morphological analysis for the topic: research

Types of research	Methodologies	Units of analysis
Exploratory	Cross-sectional study	An individual
Descriptive	Experimental study	An event
Analytical	Longitudinal study	An object
Predictive	Survey	A body of individuals
Quantitative	Action research	A relationship
Qualitative	Case study	An aggregate
Deductive	Collaborative research	
Inductive	Ethnography	
Applied	Grounded theory	
Basic		

The result of your analysis might indicate a descriptive research project that uses a survey for its methodology and focuses on a body of individuals as its unit of analysis; for example professional associations of accountants or lawyers. Another analysis might suggest an exploratory research project that uses a case study approach and is conducted in one division of a particular company. A third analysis might generate a predictive research project that uses experiments with individuals; perhaps a project where you test how alcohol abuse affects individual students' examination performance.

You should restrict yourself to defining only the key dimensions of your chosen subject, as you can see that morphological analysis can generate a huge number of potential projects!

> **KEY DEFINITIONS**
>
> Morphological analysis is a technique for generating research topics whereby the subject is analysed into its key attributes and a 'mix and match' approach is adopted.

3.4.3　MIND MAPS

Another way of generating a research topic is to use diagrams. There are a number of ways of constructing diagrams, depending on the purpose you have in mind. While diagrams show how things depend on one another, maps show relationships in space or time. A mind map is a highly creative and personal form of diagram. The process is not particularly systematic and focuses on key aspects, rather than detail. These key aspects are jotted down haphazardly, without any particular thought as to their position and are usually joined by lines to indicate connections and relationships.

Figure 3.3 shows an example of a mind map that focuses on the general subject of research. We started the map by writing the word 'research' and then as associated terms came to mind, we wrote them nearby and drew lines connecting them to the word 'research'. We then thought of additional terms and connected them, gradually working outwards. We only stopped because space was limited, but you can see that this process can be continued until you have identified the general subject for your project. Of course, this sort of activity does mean you need some prior knowledge of the topic.

> **KEY DEFINITIONS**
>
> A mind map is an infor-mal diagram of a person's idea of the key elements of a subject that shows connections and relationships.

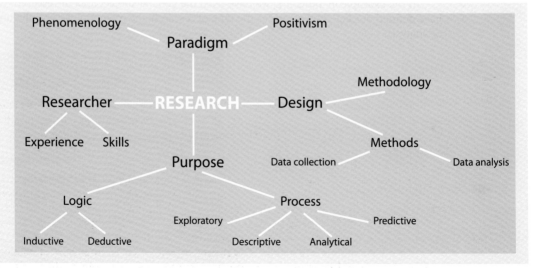

FIGURE 3.3 Mind map for the topic: academic research

3.4.4 RELEVANCE TREES

Another type of diagram that can be used as a device for generating a research topic is a *relevance tree*. The idea is to develop clusters of related ideas from a starting concept. To be most effective, the starting concept should be fairly broad. Figure 3.4 shows an example of a relevance tree which stems from the starting concept of 'communication'. Using our relevance tree, we identified a number of potential research topics; for example use of body language in formal meetings or, at a more general level, the different forms of two-way communication used in the workplace.

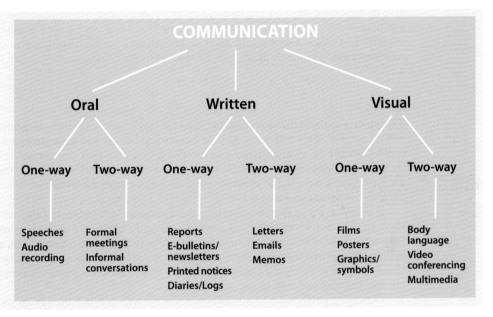

FIGURE 3.4 Relevance tree for the topic: business communication

3.5 NEGOTIATING ACCESS

If you are a part-time student or doing a placement project as part of a degree, your job may give you *access* to sources that will provide you with research data. Other students need to find their own sources and negotiate access to them. For example, if you have decided to collect your research data by designing a questionnaire and posting or emailing it to potential respondents, you will need to determine what types of people to send it to and obtain their names and contact details.

You may want to conduct a study that requires access to one or more organizations. The first step is to make use of any contacts you may already have. For example, your family and friends may be able to introduce you to an organization that might be interested in your research. Remember that they will only be able to supply an introduction and it will be up to you to negotiate the terms of access.

If the above fails, you may have to approach organizations without an introduction. Send a letter enclosing an outline of your research proposal, suitably modified for the organization. The letter must be addressed to an appropriate named person whose name you should be able to obtain from the firm's printed literature, its website or by ringing the firm and asking the switchboard operator. A well-composed letter addressed to the key person explaining why your project will be of interest to them is likely to be far more successful than 'cold-calling'. It is advisable to follow up with a telephone call to that person if you do not receive a reply to your letter within 10 days.

Your letter should present your project in the form of a brief research proposal, usually not more than two pages of A4. Your proposal should set out clearly the benefits to the organization and what access and information you will require. Remember that the organization will not want an academic document with citations, but a clear, concise, non-technical explanation of what the project is about in report form. If you can demonstrate that your research may provide answers to problems that their managers may be experiencing, you are more likely to be successful. Remember, the company will believe that it is doing you a favour, not vice versa, so be very sensitive in the requests you make. Once again, do your preliminary research so that you can focus your proposals on what is likely to be of interest to the company.

3.5.2 AGREEING TERMS

If the firm is interested, the manager or director you contact is likely to suggest an informal discussion. This will allow him or her to assess you and your project in greater depth than can be gleaned from your proposal. You may find that certain restrictions are placed on your research, such as how long you can spend in the organization, the documents you can see, the methods you can use, the personnel you can interview and the questions you can ask.

It is important to be sympathetic to the norms and procedures of the firm you are approaching. Some organizations may be willing to make verbal agreements on the telephone or at an informal meeting, while others require all the issues to be agreed in writing with formal terms of reference. Even if a verbal agreement is made, we recommend that you write a letter confirming exactly what has been agreed, with copies to the relevant members of staff in the organization.

Obtaining permission to publish from your research is not usually an issue at the undergraduate level as it is unlikely that you intend to publish your results externally. However, it is essential that research results are published if you are a postgraduate student wanting to pursue an academic career. You will need to explain that the research report will be used for your degree. If you wish to publish from the research at a later date, it is normal practice to seek prior permission from the organization. It is important to clarify who owns the data you have collected. At the end of your research you should provide the organization with a copy of your report, but beware of offering them a special or interim report, as this can be very time-consuming and expensive. However, if you have agreed to supply a report in exchange for access, you may have to write a special version, as your academic report is unlikely to be sufficiently user-friendly.

3.5.3 PERSONAL SAFETY

It is important to consider your personal safety when conducting research. You will be exposing yourself to new situations and meeting people of whom you have no previous knowledge. Fortunately, few problems arise, but it is important that you are aware of potential dangers and take the necessary steps to minimize them.

If you are negotiating access with a well-known organization, your safety is reasonably well assured, but with small, unknown organizations or individual interviews 'on site', caution is required. You should ensure that you have the full name, title and contact address of anyone you intend to visit. Attempt to establish their credibility beforehand by finding out if they are known to any of your colleagues and checking with your original source for the contact. If you have any doubts, ask your supervisor or a colleague to accompany you.

3.5.4   COURTESY

It is essential that you thank individuals and organizations for their assistance with your research, verbally at the time and afterwards by letter. If you have promised to provide copies of transcripts of interviews or a summary of your final report to participants, make sure that you do so promptly. If your work is published, you should send a copy to those in the participating organization(s) who have helped you and to individual participants where this is practical.

3.6   ETHICAL ISSUES

It is easy to think of *ethical issues* as being important only in the natural sciences, but in the social sciences is also 'difficult to conduct much research at all without running into ethical arguments' (Coolican, 1992 p. 249). The American Psychological Association has established its own ethical principles and many universities have their own research ethics policies, but in the absence of formal guidance, you should discuss and clarify the following main issues with your supervisor at an early stage.

3.6.1   VOLUNTARY PARTICIPATION

One of the most important ethical principles is that coercion should not be used to force people into taking part in the research. In academic research, it is also advisable to avoid offering financial or other material rewards to induce people to take part, as this will lead to biased results. People should be given information about what is required if they agree to take part and how much time it will take. Sometimes, consent is delayed because the potential participants have to ask permission from their line manager or your request has to be approved by a committee. This may take time and, if you are not successful, you will need sufficient time to identify others.

If the research has an experimental design, a balance must be struck between giving sufficient information to permit informed consent and avoiding jeopardizing the purpose of the research. Although it is not likely that participants in business and management research will be exposed to physical risks, it is important to avoid causing distress, stress or other psychological harm. Avoiding causing harm to participants is important for ethical reasons, but also because you could be sued if you harm someone.

3.6.2   ANONYMITY AND CONFIDENTIALITY

In principle, you should offer *anonymity* and *confidentiality* to all the participants in your research. Giving participants the opportunity to remain anonymous means assuring them that they will not be identified with any of the opinions they express. In questionnaire surveys, this may contribute to a higher response rate and increased honesty;

in interviews, it encourages greater freedom of expression and more open responses. However, in some studies it may be very important to state the name or position of participants because their opinions can only be appreciated in the context of their role. In such circumstances, it is imperative that the participant gives his or her consent. Another example of where permission must be sought is where you wish to name the author of an internal document.

> **KEY DEFINITIONS**
>
> Anonymity provides protection to participants by ensuring that their names are not identified with the information they give.
>
> Confidentiality provides protection to participants by ensuring that sensitive information is not disclosed and the research data cannot be traced to the individual or organization providing it.

Sometimes it is possible to resolve problems of anonymity by agreeing on confidentiality, which we discuss next, which focuses on the data collected rather than the identity of the participant. If confidentiality is a condition of giving you access to information, you will need to assure participants that the data you collect will be used in such a way that this information is not traceable to any particular individual. For example, your dissertation or thesis need not name the company or companies where you have negotiated access to data; it is sufficient to refer to the organization as an engineering company, a food retailer and so on (or company A, B, C and so on). Similarly, with individuals, they can simply be identified by their position (or interviewee A, B, C and so on), as they cannot be identified if the name of the company is not disclosed.

When writing to potential participants or at the top of any questionnaire you plan to distribute, you should include a sentence such as:

Neither your name nor the name of your company will be associated with your responses. Unless you have given permission otherwise, your contact details and all data you provide will be treated in the strictest confidence.

You should discuss the issues of anonymity and confidentiality with your supervisors and the organization(s) where you intend to collect your data as soon as possible to clarify these issues. If strict confidentiality is one of the conditions of access, you may be able to agree with the individuals and organization concerned that no one but your supervisor(s) and examiners will have access to your research and it will not be placed in the library or published in any way. Obviously, this would prevent you from writing or presenting any academic papers or articles on your research.

3.6.3 ETHICAL DILEMMAS

You may have spent some time negotiating access to an organization in order to conduct your research. Naturally, you will be grateful to them for their help and will spend some time developing a good relationship, but what would you do if during the course of your research you found out that the company was doing something illegal? For example, imagine that you are conducting research in a small factory which employs a hundred people in an economically depressed area. During your research you observe that proper safety guards are not fitted to the machines, but you know that fitting them would bankrupt the company and put people out of work. What action should you take?

- *Anonymity and confidentiality* – Although it is normal to offer anonymity and confidentiality to participants, you might receive information that you think should be passed on to someone else. For example, perhaps you are conducting research into the reasons for high wastage levels of materials in a production process and while interviewing employees, you discover that part of the wastage is due to one of them stealing goods.
- *Informed consent* – Although it is ethical to inform potential participants of the purpose of the research before they agree to participate, this could present problems in gaining

access and obtaining valid responses. For example, if you were to inform participants you were intending to observe that you are studying their working patterns, they might change their behaviour and this would distort your findings.

- *Dignity* – It would not be ethical to embarrass or ridicule participants, but unfortunately, this is easily done. The relationship between the researcher and the phenomenon under study is often complex and it is important to remember that participants may see you as someone with knowledge that they do not have or someone in authority. For this reason, it is important to be courteous and make sure they know they have a choice and will not be coerced into answering sensitive questions.

- *Publications* – The career of an academic is developed through publications and the success of a research student is achieved through the acceptance of their thesis or dissertation. History shows that there are some who are willing to invent data, falsify their results or plagiarize to get published, which is highly unethical. However, it is also unethical to exaggerate or omit results in order to present a more favourable picture. A more complex situation arises when your publication casts a bad light on an individual, group or organization. This can arise if you are conducting a comparative study, when you must discuss your results with great sensitivity.

As you can imagine, there are no easy answers to ethical dilemmas. Some commentators believe that ethical codes should be established for business research; others believe that rules are too rigid and leave loopholes for the unscrupulous; therefore, it is better to follow ethical principles. It has been argued that it is sometimes necessary to be vague about the purpose of the research, and even covert in collecting data, in order to achieve findings of value. It will be your responsibility to resolve these issues with your supervisor before you embark on your research. The checklist shown in Box 3.1 offers a useful starting point. Some of these questions expose a number of dilemmas, which we will explore when we look at the design of a research project and the methods for collecting data.

BOX 3.1 Checklist for ethical research

- Will the research process harm participants or those about whom information is gathered (indirect participants)?
- Are the findings of this research likely to cause harm to others not involved in the research?
- Are you violating accepted research practice in conducting the research and data analysis, and drawing conclusions?
- Are you violating community standards of conduct?

Source: Kervin (1992, p. 38).

3.7 PLANNING AND ADMINISTRATION

There is no doubt that time is a major enemy of all researchers and if you do not make realistic plans, you will run the risk of missing your deadlines. To plan your time you need to know how long your institution allows for the submission of your dissertation or thesis. You also need to know how to allocate your time across the different activities you will undertake.

SETTING A TIMETABLE

You need to agree a *timetable* with your supervisor and any individuals or organizations participating in your study. You may find that you need to negotiate access with more than one person in the organization and you should therefore plan to allow plenty of time for this stage. It is likely that the individuals concerned will be helping you with your research in addition to doing their normal jobs. Therefore, the time they are able to allocate to your research interests will be limited and must be arranged at their convenience.

A Bachelor's or taught Master's dissertation is normally completed within one academic year. Table 3.2 shows the approximate length of the registration period for postgraduate research degrees, but you should check the regulations in your institution, as times vary.

TABLE 3.2 Approximate length of research degrees

		Minimum	Maximum
MPhil thesis	Full time	18 months	36 months
	Part time	30 months	48 months
PhD thesis (transfer)	Full time	33 months	60 months
	Part time	45 months	72 months
PhD thesis (direct)	Full time	24 months	60 months
	Part time	36 months	72 months

TABLE 3.3 Approximate time for main stages of research

Stage	%
Choose a topic and search the literature	10
Review the literature and define the research problem/research questions	10
Design the research and write proposal	10
Collect research data	20
Analyse and interpret research data	20
Write dissertation or thesis	30
Total	100

Research is a time-consuming activity and the secret of completing on time is to draw up a timetable as soon as possible. You may find Table 3.3 a useful guide when apportioning your time to fit your deadline. Remember that the amount of time for completing your research depends on the qualification you are working towards and the regulations in your institution. Of course, these figures are only indicative and you will need to adjust this basic timetable to reflect your research design and allow additional time for resolving any problems.

A major weakness of Table 3.3 is that it implies that research takes place in orderly, discrete and sequential stages. Throughout this book you will find reminders that this is definitely not the case! Although we will be encouraging you to be methodical in your approach, you will find that all research contains stages that overlap. For example, you may need to go on collecting information about current research in your chosen field right up to the final draft, in order to be sure that you present an up-to-date picture.

Also, we must emphasize that although the writing-up stage is shown as a distinct activity at the end of the research process, you must get into the good habit of writing up your notes straight away. This means that you will start to write up your research, albeit in draft form, as soon as you start your project. When you have decided on the structure for your dissertation or thesis, you can amend and refine your notes, and place them in the appropriate chapters. It is important not to underestimate how long the writing-up stage takes, even when you have good notes and references on which to base your research report.

You may find it useful to look at some of the reasons for long completion times or, in the worst scenario, failure to complete. For a start, if you are inexperienced, you will find that everything takes longer than you expect. Therefore, it is important to plan your time carefully, with advice from your supervisor. If you are an undergraduate student you will only have a matter of months in which to complete your dissertation. You may have to balance your research activities against the demands of an industrial placement and/or your final year studies. If you are a graduate student without funding, you may have to juggle the demands of paid work with your research; indeed, you may be lecturing to students yourself. If you are a mature student, you may have both paid work and family life to fit in.

Many undergraduate students go on to study for a graduate degree straight after their finals. Because they know that they have several years in which to complete their research, they often overlook the importance of planning. The result is a slow start and this is a very common reason for late completion. A second common reason is perfectionism. Some students find it difficult to bring things to a conclusion. They are never satisfied with their results and are always thinking of ways in which to improve them, even before they have written them up. Thus, the writing-up stage is always postponed. Such students find it hard to see whether improvement really is necessary and whether it is desirable to spend so much time on that stage of the research to the detriment of later stages.

A third reason for late completion is that some students are distracted from the main research problem. Some students find the software programs for searching the literature, saving references, extracting data from databases, analysing qualitative or quantitative data, and designing tables, graphs and reports so absorbing that they do not give sufficient attention to the substance of the research. Other problems can occur if the student is not sufficiently focused and collects too much literature or too much research data and does not allow enough time for analysis. Sometimes there has been insufficient collation and analysis of the data and the student does not realize this deficiency until he or she begins to write up and has to break off to complete this earlier stage, often resulting in a delay of months rather than weeks.

An experienced supervisor will be aware of these and other problems. The best way to overcome them is to draw up a realistic timetable with your supervisor that shows the dates on which the various stages in the research process should be completed. It is important to do this at the earliest possible stage. Many students find it extremely helpful to know that they are expected to reach certain stages at certain times, as this removes some of the pressure of managing their time and organizing their research.

3.7.2 ORGANIZING MATERIALS

It will not take you too long to realize that a large part of research is concerned with *organizing materials*, which may range from articles copied from journals, questionnaires returned, newspaper cuttings, transcripts of interviews and notes you have made. Everyone devises their own system, but we find it useful to sort the materials into their different types and order them according to this classification.

Copies of articles and conference papers can be kept in a file alphabetically under the name of the author. There are several excellent software packages that allow you to collect your references and often enable you to download references and abstracts from libraries. For a PhD you may have several hundred articles; for an undergraduate project only a dozen or so. No matter how many you collect, it is important that they are stored systematically so that you can easily find them.

Primary materials, such as questionnaires and transcripts of interviews, should be numbered and dated and then filed in numerical order. You may find it useful to draw up an index for each set of files. In Chapter 8 we discuss the analysis of qualitative data and you will see that, to a large extent, the success of this rests on the efficient storing and referencing of primary materials. We give some examples in that chapter on how this can be achieved.

During your research you will probably collect a certain amount of miscellaneous materials, such as odd notes, quotations or cuttings, which may be important when you are writing your dissertation or thesis. Once you have decided on a draft structure, which you should do as early as possible, you can set up a file with dividers to separate each anticipated chapter and place these miscellaneous materials in the most appropriate chapter.

Keeping records is a very important component in the management of your research. In Chapter 6 we discuss an important aspect of your research known as the literature review and how to reference articles and books properly. It is essential that you keep a record of every article and book you read which might be useful in your own research. By this we mean a full reference. The references for articles and books can be kept either on a computer or on index cards; the latter are convenient to take with you to the library and can be completed there and then. Many students now use proprietary software that links into library systems and captures references that you can reprint in a variety of formats.

You will need to set up a filing system for your correspondence so that you can find the letter you wish to refer to. It is also important to maintain a record of contacts' names, addresses, telephone numbers and other details. A computerized record system is particularly useful if you are planning to send out a number of standard letters as the names and addresses can be merged with the standard letter at the time of printing (mail merge).

Finally, one further file you may wish to keep is one in which you can store instructions for using the library catalogue system, computerized databases and various software packages. This is also a good place to put leaflets on library opening times, safety requirements in laboratories and maps of various locations you may have to visit.

3.7.3 NETWORKING

In this context, *networking* simply means setting up and maintaining links with individuals in business and academic life during the course of your research. We have already discussed the importance of negotiating access and the courtesies required. Remember that all the contacts you make may be useful at some future date. Research is not a simple linear process of moving from one stage to the next, but often involves retracing your steps. The contacts you have made and maintained will assist you to do this.

There is nothing worse when you are writing up your research to find that you have not collected an essential statistic from a company or one of your interviews is incomplete. If you wrote to the individuals who have helped you along the way, thanking them for their assistance, it is easier to go back to them for the missing data. Similarly, if you have sent them any reports or articles resulting from your research, you are more likely to be successful if you approach them at a later date with a request to conduct further research.

It is also important to establish and maintain links with academic colleagues in your own and other institutions. These may be people interested in the same or a similar area of research you meet in the common room, on courses or at academic conferences, with whom you can exchange articles and talk over ideas and problems. You may also be able to exchange early drafts of your dissertation or thesis for mutual comment and criticism.

3.8   CONCLUSIONS

This chapter has been about preparing yourself to do research. We have given advice on critical issues, such as sources of finance, and also explained more academic issues such as generating a research topic and the skills and experiences you require at different stages of a project. It is important that you appreciate that research is more than an investigation; it is also an activity that calls for efficient project management if it is to be successful.

We have also emphasized the importance of setting a timetable. Once you commence your investigations you do not want to be slowed down because you have not been able to organize yourself properly. Efficient organization also means that you are more likely to stick to the schedule you have set. In research you are frequently working to deadlines. If you miss the critical deadlines you may not get a second chance.

Unfortunately, many students ignore questions of ethics, anonymity and confidentiality until they are confronted with them. These considerations are becoming increasingly important and you may find that your research proposal has to be approved by a university ethics committee before you can proceed. The success of the project will be determined by how well you establish the foundations that we have described in this chapter.

ACTIVITIES

1. Generate a mind map that explores the funding implications of your research and how you can overcome any problems. Discuss your mind map with other students, your lecturers or potential supervisor to evaluate how realistic your assumptions are and to share solutions.

2. Use any two of the techniques described in this chapter to generate a research topic. Discuss the nature of the topic you have generated with other students and whether it would make a feasible research project.

3. In pairs, act out a situation where one of you takes the role of someone seeking access to an organization to conduct research and the other is the senior manager who has the power to grant your request. If possible, record or video the interview and analyse the process.

4. You are conducting research in a charity that saves the lives of many children. The organization has an excellent reputation and receives substantial government funding. During the course of your research you discover that irregular payments have been made to people outside the organization. The financial controller explains that if the charity did not make these payments, their workers would not get access to certain parts of the world where law and order has broken down. Moreover, if the charity workers did not get this access, children would die. How do you deal with this ethical problem?

5. Draft a section for your CV that describes the ways in which your research will provide transferrable skills and knowledge that will enhance your employability.

PROGRESS TEST

Complete the following sentences:

1. Designing a research project in one subject by importing ideas and procedures from another area where there are similarities involves the use of _____.

2. A technique for generating a research topic whereby the subject is analysed into its key attributes and a 'mix and match' approach is adopted is known as _____.

3. An individual's idea of the key aspects of a subject illustrated in an informal diagram that shows connections and relationships is called a _____.

4. A diagram that can be used as a device for generating research topics whereby clusters of ideas are developed from a fairly broad starting concept is known as a _____.

5. Principles that guide people's behaviour are known as _____.

Are the following statements true or false?

6. After you have conducted your research, your university will reimburse any costs.

7. Before you conduct your research, you need to be sure you can collect the research data.

8. Before you conduct your research, you need to know it will not cause harm to others.

9. Coercion is part of accepted research practice.

10. Plagiarism is part of accepted research practice.

Multiple choice questions:

11. Funding for a student's research is called a:
    a) bursary
    b) grant
    c) scholarship
    d) any of the above

12. The most important personal quality for a researcher is:
    a) inspiration
    b) motivation
    c) perseverance
    d) any of the above

13. If you offer anonymity to participants in your research, you will:
    a) not ask their names
    b) not disclose their names
    c) refer to them using a secret code
    d) any of the above

14. If you offer confidentiality to participants in your research, you will:
    a) not link their views with their names
    b) not disclose sensitive information
    c) refer to them using a secret code
    d) any of the above

15. Informed consent means you have told the participants:
    a) they have been chosen to take part in the research
    b) what the research is about before inviting them to take part
    c) what the research is about and they have agreed to take part
    d) your supervisor has been informed that you have access to data

4

Identifying your research paradigm

Learning objectives

When you have studied this chapter, you should be able to:

- describe the main features of positivism

- describe the main features of interpretivism

- compare the assumptions of the two main paradigms

- discuss the strengths and weaknesses of pragmatism

- identify your research paradigm.

4.1   INTRODUCTION

Now you have begun to understand the nature of research and we have dealt with some of the practical issues, it is time to look at the philosophical issues that underpin research. This chapter introduces a number of new terms that will help you to extend your knowledge of how research is conducted. We introduce the ideas in a way that allows you to develop your knowledge incrementally and you will soon be using your extended vocabulary with confidence. Your new understanding will provide a valuable framework for expressing your ideas about your proposed research when you talk to your supervisor and other researchers, and will also help you absorb information from any preliminary reading you are doing.

If you are an undergraduate or on a taught Master's degree, you will probably face two major constraints when doing your research. The first is the relatively short period of time you will have to conduct your research, and the second is the relatively short length of your dissertation. Therefore, you may not find it possible or necessary to explore the philosophical issues in this chapter in any great depth. However, other Master's students and all doctoral students need greater understanding of research philosophies and should use the references in this chapter as a guide to further reading.

4.2   THE TWO MAIN PARADIGMS

A *research paradigm* is a philosophical framework that guides how scientific research should be conducted. Philosophy is 'the use of reason and argument in seeking truth and knowledge, especially of ultimate reality or of general causes and principles' (*Oxford Compact Dictionary and Thesaurus*, 1997, p. 557). People's ideas about reality and the nature of knowledge have changed over time and, therefore, new research paradigms emerge in response to the perceived inadequacies of earlier paradigms. This is captured in Kuhn's definition: 'Paradigms are universally recognized scientific achievements that for a time provide model problems and solutions to a community of practitioners' (Kuhn, 1962, p. viii).

> **KEY DEFINITIONS**
>
> A research paradigm is a framework that guides how research should be conducted, based on people's philosophies and their assumptions about the world and the nature of knowledge.

For many hundreds of years there was only one research paradigm because the 'scientific achievements' referred to by Kuhn (1962) stemmed from one source. Today we refer to that source as the *natural sciences* to distinguish them from the *social sciences*. The emergence of the social sciences led to the development of a second research paradigm.

According to Smith (1983), until the late nineteenth century, research had focused on inanimate objects in the physical world, such as physics, which focuses on the properties matter and energy and the interaction between them. The systematic methods used by these scientists, involved observation and experiment, and they applied inductive logic to discover explanatory theories that could be used for prediction. Their beliefs about the world and the nature of knowledge were based on *positivism*, which has its roots in the philosophy known as realism. Positivism was developed by theorists such as Comte (1798–1857), Mill (1806–1873) and Durkheim (1859–1917).

With the advent of industrialization and capitalism, researchers began to turn their attention to social phenomena. A phenomenon (plural phenomena) is 'an observed or apparent object, fact or occurrence, especially one where the cause is uncertain' (*Oxford Compact Dictionary & Thesaurus*, 1997). Initially, the new social scientists used the methods established by the natural scientists, but the suitability of the traditional scientific methods was challenged by a number of theorists, which led to a debate that lasted

*Some authors refer to phenomenology (as we did in previous editions of this book), but we have now decided to use interpretivism as it suggests a broader philosophical perspective.

many decades (Smith, 1983). The alternative to positivism can be loosely labelled as *interpretivism*,* which is based on the principles of idealism, a philosophy associated with Kant (1724–1804) and subsequently developed by Dilthey (1833–1911), Rickert (1863–1936) and Weber (1864–1920).

4.2.1   POSITIVISM

As you can see from the historical developments outlined above, *positivism* provided the framework for the way research was conducted in the natural sciences and the scientific methods are still widely used in social science research today. Positivism is underpinned by the belief that reality is independent of us and the goal is the discovery of theories, based on empirical research (observation and experiment). Knowledge is derived from 'positive information' because 'every rationally justifiable assertion can be scientifically verified or is capable of logical or mathematical proof' (Walliman, 2001, p. 15). Today, researchers conducting business research under a paradigm that stems from positivism still focus on theories to explain and/or predict social phenomena. They still apply logical reasoning so that precision, objectivity and rigour underpin their approach, rather than subjectivity and intuitive interpretation. Because positivists believe reality is independent of us, they assume the act of investigating social reality has no effect on that reality (Creswell, 1994).

> **KEY DEFINITIONS**
>
> Positivism is a paradigm that originated in the natural sciences. It rests on the assumption that social reality is singular and objective, and is not affected by the act of investigating it. The research involves a deductive process with a view to providing explanatory theories to understand social phenomena.

Under positivism, theories provide the basis of explanation, permit the anticipation of phenomena, predict their occurrence and therefore allow them to be controlled. Explanation consists of establishing causal relationships between the variables by establishing causal laws and linking them to a deductive or integrated theory. Thus, social and natural worlds are both regarded as being bound by certain fixed laws in a sequence of cause and effect. You will remember from Chapter 1 that a variable is an attribute of a phenomenon that can change and take different values, which are capable of being observed and/or measured; and a theory is a set of interrelated variables, definitions and propositions that specifies relationships among the variables. Since it is assumed that social phenomena can be measured, positivism is associated with quantitative methods of analysis.

4.2.2   INTERPRETIVISM

Since *interpretivism* developed as a result of the perceived inadequacy of positivism to meet the needs of social scientists, it is important to understand the main criticisms of positivism. Box 4.1 sets out the main arguments.

BOX 4.1   Main criticisms of positivism

- It is impossible to separate people from the social contexts in which they exist.
- People cannot be understood without examining the perceptions they have of their own activities.
- A highly structured research design imposes constraints on the results and may ignore other relevant findings.
- Researchers are not objective, but part of what they observe. They bring their own interests and values to the research.
- Capturing complex phenomena in a single measure is misleading (for example it is not possible to capture a person's intelligence by assigning numerical values).

KEY DEFINITIONS

Interpretivism is a para-
digm that emerged in
response to criticisms
of positivism. It rests
on the assumption that
social reality is in our
minds, and is subjec-
tive and multiple.
Therefore, social
reality is affected by
the act of investigating
it. The research
involves an inductive
process with a view to
providing interpretive
understanding of social
phenomena within a
particular context.

Interpretivism is underpinned by the belief that social reality is not objective but highly subjective because it is shaped by our perceptions. The
researcher interacts with that being researched because it is impossible to
separate what exists in the social world from what is in the researcher's mind
(Smith, 1983; Creswell, 1994). Therefore, the act of investigating social
reality has an effect on it. Whereas positivism focuses on measuring social
phenomena, interpretivism focuses on exploring the complexity of social
phenomena with a view to gaining interpretive understanding. Therefore,
rather than adopt the quantitative methods used by positivists, interpretivists
adopt a range of methods that 'seek to describe, translate and otherwise come
to terms with the meaning, not the frequency of certain more or less naturally occurring phenomena in the social world' (Van Maanen, 1983, p. 9).
These important differences lead to a very broad conclusion that interpretive
research is any type of research where the findings are not derived from the
statistical analysis of quantitative data (Strauss and Corbin, 1990).

4.2.3 APPROACHES WITHIN THE TWO MAIN PARADIGMS

Just as realism gave way to positivism and idealism gave way to what we are loosely
referring to as interpretivism, many new paradigms have emerged over the years and
few researchers now adopt the pure forms of the main paradigms. New paradigms are
distinguished by differences in the philosophical assumptions on which they rest. You
may find it helpful to think of positivism and interpretivism as the extremities of a
continuous line of paradigms that can exist simultaneously, as illustrated in Figure 4.1.
As you move along the continuum, the features and assumptions of one paradigm are
gradually relaxed and replaced by those of the next (Morgan and Smircich, 1980).

Positivism ⟵⟶ Interpretivism

FIGURE 4.1 A continuum of paradigms

In addition to reading about different paradigms that were developed towards the
end of the nineteenth century and beyond (for example hermeneutics, phenomenology, existentialism, critical rationalism, linguistics, conventionalism), you may also
come across a number of terms that describe different approaches with the main paradigms. You will find the term 'paradigm' is used somewhat inconsistently in the literature because it has different meanings for different people in different disciplines, in
different parts of the world and over different periods of time. For example, Mingers
(2001) points out that the version of paradigms described by Kuhn (1970) is less
restrictive than that described by Burrell and Morgan (1979). To help clarify the uncer-
tainties, Morgan (1979) suggests paradigm can be used at three different levels:

- at the philosophical level, where the term is used to reflect basic beliefs about the
  world
- at the social level, where the term is used to provide guidelines about how the
  researcher should conduct his or her endeavours
- at the technical level, where the term is used to specify the methods and techniques,
  which ideally should be adopted when conducting research.

Table 4.1 shows some of the more common terms used to describe approaches within the two main paradigms. You should be aware that the terms under a particular category are not necessarily interchangeable, as they were coined by researchers wishing to distinguish their approach from others. In some cases, the term is being used at the social level (for example a subjectivist approach) or at the technical level where it refers to a particular method for collecting and/or analysing data (for example a qualitative approach). At the undergraduate level, these nuances may not be important, but a post-graduate researcher may be required to argue the appropriateness of the paradigm and the terms he or she is using.

TABLE 4.1 Approaches within the two main paradigms

Positivism	Interpretivism
Quantitative	Qualitative
Objective	Subjective
Scientific	Humanist
Traditionalist	Phenomenological

4.3   ASSUMPTIONS OF THE MAIN PARADIGMS

Drawing on a number of other authors, Creswell (1994 and 1998) provides a summary of the philosophical assumptions that underpin the two main paradigms, which he refers to as the quantitative and the qualitative paradigms. Table 4.2 is adapted from his work.

TABLE 4.2 Assumptions of the main paradigms

Philosophical assumption	Positivism	Interpretivism
Ontological assumption (the nature of reality)	Reality is objective and singular, separate from the researcher	Reality is subjective and multiple, as seen by the participants
Epistemological assumption (what constitutes valid knowledge)	Researcher is independent of that being researched	Researcher interacts with that being researched
Axiological assumption (the role of values)	Research is value-free and unbiased	Researcher acknowledges that research is value-laden and biases are present
Rhetorical assumption (the language of research)	Researcher writes in a formal style and uses the passive voice, accepted quantitative words and set definitions	Researcher writes in an informal style and uses the personal voice, accepted qualitative terms and limited definitions
Methodological assumption (the process of research)	Process is deductive. Study of cause and effect with a static design (categories are isolated beforehand) Research is context free Generalizations lead to prediction, explanation and understanding Results are accurate and reliable through validity and reliability	Process is inductive. Study of mutual simultaneous shaping of factors with an emerging design (categories are identified during the process) Research is context bound Patterns and/or theories are developed for understanding Findings are accurate and reliable through verification

Source: Adapted from Creswell (1994, p. 5 and 1998, p. 75).

Before you can design your research project, you must consider the above questions. If you are still developing your understanding of research, you will probably find some of the questions difficult. Your answers will give you some indication of your orientation at this stage by indicating whether your paradigm is broadly positivist (most answers in the quantitative column) or interpretivist (most answers in the qualitative column). However, this may change as you progress with your studies. To help you with your analysis, we will provide some explanations of the terms used in the table. Remember that we are describing the assumptions that underpin the pure forms of the main paradigms. The first three assumptions are interrelated and if you accept one of them within a particular paradigm, you will find the other two assumptions for that paradigm are complementary.

4.3.1   ONTOLOGICAL ASSUMPTION

The *ontological assumption* is concerned with the nature of reality:

- Positivists believe social reality is objective and external to the researcher. Therefore, there is only one reality.
- Interpretivists believe that social reality is subjective because it is socially constructed. Therefore, each person has his or her own sense of reality and there are multiple realities.

4.3.2   EPISTEMOLOGICAL ASSUMPTION

The *epistemological assumption* is concerned with what we accept as valid knowledge. This involves an examination of the relationship between the researcher and that which is researched:

- Positivists believe that only phenomena that are observable and measurable can be validly regarded as knowledge. They try to maintain an independent and objective stance.
- On the other hand, interpretivists attempt to minimize the distance between the researcher and that which is researched. They may be involved in different forms of participative enquiry. This polarity between the two approaches has been captured by Smith (1983, pp. 10–11) who argues, 'In quantitative research facts act to constrain our beliefs; while in interpretive research beliefs determine what should count as facts.'

4.3.3   AXIOLOGICAL ASSUMPTION

The *axiological assumption* is concerned with the role of values:

- Positivists believe that the process of research is value-free. Therefore, positivists consider that they are detached and independent from what they are researching and regard the phenomena under investigation as objects. Positivists are interested in the interrelationship of the objects they are studying and believe that these objects were present before they took an interest in them. Furthermore, positivists believe that the objects they are studying are unaffected by their research activities and will still be present after the study has been completed. These assumptions are commonly found in research studies in the natural sciences, but they are less convincing in the social sciences, which are concerned with the activities and behaviour of people. Various studies have shown that the process of inquiry can influence both researchers and those participating in the research.

- In contrast, interpretivists consider that researchers have values, even if they have not been made explicit. These values help to determine what are recognized as facts and the interpretations drawn from them. Most interpretivists believe that the researcher is involved with that which is being researched.

4.3.4   RHETORICAL ASSUMPTION

We now move on to the *rhetorical assumption*, which is concerned with the language of research. This is particularly important when you write your research proposal and your final dissertation or thesis. These documents should be complementary to your paradigm, but they must also be written in a style that is acceptable to your supervisors and examiners.

- In a positivist study, it is usual to write in a formal style using the passive voice. For example, instead of writing, 'As part of my research, I observed a group of employees ...' in your dissertation or thesis you will write, 'As part of the research, observations were made of a group of employees ...' This is because you should try to convey the impression that your research was objective, that rigorous procedures were adopted and any personal opinions and values you possess were not allowed to distort the results. You will use the future tense in your proposal. For example, 'Observations of a group of employees will be made'.
- The position is less clear in an interpretive study. In many disciplines, the preferred style will reflect the immediacy of the research and researcher's involvement. Therefore, you would write in the first person using the future tense in the project proposal and the present tense in your dissertation or thesis. However, we advise that you review the literature in your discipline and find out what is acceptable to your supervisor.

4.3.5   METHODOLOGICAL ASSUMPTION

The *methodological assumption* is concerned with the process of the research:

- If you are a positivist, you are likely to be concerned with ensuring that any concepts you use can be operationalized; that is, described in such a way that they can be measured. Perhaps you are investigating a topic that includes the concept of intelligence, and you want to find a way of measuring a particular aspect of intelligence. You will probably use a large sample and reduce the phenomena you are examining to their simplest parts. You will focus on what you regard are objective facts and formulate hypotheses. Your analysis will look for association between variables and/or causality (one variable affecting another).
- If you are an interpretivist, you will be examining a small sample, possibly over a period of time. You will use a number of research methods to obtain different perceptions of the phenomena and in your analysis you will be seeking to understand what is happening in a situation and looking for patterns which may be repeated in other similar situations.

4.3.6   A CONTINUUM OF PARADIGMS

Morgan and Smircich (1980, p. 492) offer 'a rough typology for thinking about the various views that different social scientists hold'. Table 4.3 illustrates two of the core assumptions and the associated research methods for the six categories they identify.

TABLE 4.3 Typology of assumptions on a continuum of paradigms

Positivism					Interpretivism

Ontological assumption	Reality as a concrete structure	Reality as a concrete process	Reality as a contextual field of information	Reality as a realm of symbolic discourse	Reality as a social construction	Reality as a projection of human imagination
Epistemological stance	To construct a positivist science	To construct systems, process, change	To map contexts	To understand patterns of symbolic discourse	To understand how social reality is created	To obtain phenomeno-logical insight, revelation
Research methods	Experiments, surveys	Historical analysis	Interpretive contextual analysis	Symbolic analysis	Hermeneutics	Exploration of pure subjectivity

Source: Adapted from Morgan and Smircich (1980, p. 492).

Starting at the extreme positivist end of the continuum (which Morgan and Smircich refer to as the objectivist end), there are those who assume that the social world is the same as the physical world. Their ontological assumption is that reality is an external, concrete structure which affects everyone. As the social world is external and real, the researcher can attempt to measure and analyse it using research methods such as laboratory experiments and surveys.

At the second stage of the continuum, reality is regarded as a concrete process where 'the world is in part what one makes of it' (Morgan and Smircich, 1980, p. 492). The third stage is where reality is derived from the transmission of information which leads to an ever-changing form and activity. At the fourth stage, 'the social world is a pattern of symbolic relationships and meanings sustained through a process of human action and interaction' (Morgan and Smircich, 1980, p. 494). At the fifth stage individuals through language, actions and routines create the social world. At the sixth, and extreme interpretivist end of the continuum (which Morgan and Smircich refer to as the subjectivist end), reality is seen as a projection of human imagination. Under this assumption, there may be no social world apart from that which is inside the individual's mind.

4.4   COMPARING THE TWO MAIN PARADIGMS

The particular paradigm you adopt for your research will be partly determined by your assumptions, but it will be influenced by the dominant paradigm in your research area and the nature of the research problem you are investigating. It is important to remember that one paradigm is not 'right' and the other 'wrong', but you may find that a particular paradigm is more acceptable to your supervisors, examiners or the editors of journals in which you wish to publish your research. It may not be clear as to why they favour a particular paradigm, as in some cases they are merely following a tradition in the discipline.

To help you discuss your decision with your supervisor, Table 4.4 compares the main features of the two paradigms, which we have polarized in order to contrast them.

TABLE 4.4 Features of the two main paradigms

Positivism tends to:	Interpretivism tends to:
Use large samples	Use small samples
Have an artificial location	Have a natural location
Be concerned with hypothesis testing	Be concerned with generating theories
Produce precise, objective, quantitative data	Produce 'rich', subjective, qualitative data
Produce results with high reliability but low validity	Produce findings with low reliability but high validity
Allow results to be generalized from the sample to the population	Allow findings to be generalized from one setting to another similar setting

As we have already suggested, it is helpful to think of the two main paradigms as being at opposite ends of a continuum. Regardless of which paradigm you employ, it is important to pay attention to all its features and ensure there are no contradictions or deficiencies in the way you design your research. The table introduces some new terms and concepts, which we will now discuss.

4.4.1   SAMPLE SIZE

A sample is a subset of a population. In a positivist study, the sample is chosen to be representative of the population from which it is drawn. Therefore, care is taken to ensure that the sample is unbiased in the way it represents the phenomena under study (a random sample, for instance). A population is any precisely defined body of people or objects under consideration for statistical purposes. Examples of a set of people in a business research project might be the working population of a particular country; all skilled people in a particular industry; all workers of a certain grade in a particular business, or all trainees in a particular department of that business. A collection of items might be all green saloon cars registered in a particular year in a particular region, or one day's production of medium-sliced wholemeal bread at a particular factory.

Sample size is related to the size of the population under consideration. There is no need to select a sample if it is feasible to study the entire population. In Chapter 10, we describe the methods for selecting a representative sample and the minimum size that allows positivist researchers to generalize the results from the sample to the population. This is not an issue for interpretivists because their goal is to gain rich and detailed insights of the complexity of social phenomena. Therefore, they can conduct their research with a sample of one.

> **KEY DEFINITIONS**
>
> A population is a precisely defined body of people or objects under consideration for statistical purposes.
>
> A sample is a subset of a population. In a positivist study, the sample is chosen to represent an unbiased subset of the population.

4.4.2   LOCATION

Location refers to the setting in which the research is conducted. For example, a positivist might design an experiment in a laboratory where it is possible to isolate and control the variables being investigated. It would be important to investigate the research problems in an artificial setting if you were investigating the effect of lack of sleep on drivers or the effect of alcohol on drivers or shift workers, as it would not be safe to do it in the workplace. However, most positivist research in the social sciences today is based on secondary data (published data) or in natural locations (for example the workplace). Some researchers refer to this as *field research*, a term that illustrates the longevity of the link with the methods of the natural scientists. An example of field research is a study that evaluates the impact of a new training scheme on the productivity levels in a factory. One of the challenges if you are conducting research in a natural setting is how to control for the influence of other variables, such as noise and temperature levels or the activities of other employees.

Studies designed under an interpretive paradigm are likely to be conducted in a natural setting rather than an artificial location. As the researcher is interested in exploring the complexity of phenomena, he or she will not attempt to control any characteristics of the phenomenon under study.

4.4.3   THEORIES AND HYPOTHESES

The normal process under a positivist paradigm is to study the literature to identify an appropriate *theory* (sometimes referred to as a theoretical model) and then construct a *hypothesis*. A hypothesis is an idea or proposition that is developed from the theory, which you can test using statistics. For example, contingency theory (Fiedler, 1964) contends that that there is no 'best' way to manage an organization because effective management is contingent on the fit between the organization and its environment, and the fit between the organization's subsystems. It is also contingent on the appropriateness of the management style to the nature of the work group and their tasks. Just taking one of these factors, you might decide to test the hypothesis that there is a relationship between effective management (the dependent variable) and the amount of information the manager has about the tasks undertaken by subordinates (the independent variable). You would have to decide how to measure the two variables first and then collect the data and use a statistical test for association.

Under an interpretive paradigm, you may not wish to be restricted by existing theories or there may be no existing theory. Therefore, you may carry out your investigation to describe different patterns that you perceive in the data or to construct a new theory to explain the phenomenon. If the research was an exploratory study, the findings could be used to develop hypotheses that are tested in a subsequent main study.

> **KEY DEFINITIONS**
>
> Empirical evidence is data based on observation or experience.
>
> A hypothesis is a proposition that can be tested for association or causality against empirical evidence.
>
> A theory is a set of interrelated variables, definitions and propositions that specifies relationships among the variables.
>
> A variable is a characteristic of a phenomenon that can be observed or measured.

4.4.4   QUANTITATIVE AND QUALITATIVE DATA

In contrast to a number of researchers, we prefer to reserve the use of the terms *quantitative* and *qualitative* to describe data rather than paradigms. This because the data collected in a positivist study can be quantitative (that is, data in a numerical form) and/or qualitative (that is, data in a nominal form such as words, images and so on).

In a positivist study, it is likely that the purpose of collecting qualitative data is to ensure that all key variables have been identified or to collect information that will be quantified prior to statistical analysis. This contrasts with a study designed under an interpretive paradigm, where there is no intention of analysing data statistically and therefore no desire to quantify qualitative research data. Some researchers blend the qualitative and quantitative data to such an extent that it is difficult to determine which paradigm is being used. We advise students to be wary of doing this, as it may not be acceptable to your supervisors and examiners.

If you adopt a positivist paradigm, it is essential that your research data

> **KEY DEFINITIONS**
>
> Qualitative data are data in a nominal form.
>
> Quantitative data are data in a numerical form.

are highly specific and precise. Because measurement is an essential element of the research process under this paradigm, you must apply considerable rigour to ensure the accuracy of the measurement. Under an interpretive paradigm, the emphasis is on the quality and depth of the data collected about a phenomenon. Therefore, the qualitative data collected by interpretivists tend to be rich in detail and nuance (that is, levels of meaning).

Bonoma (1985) argues that all researchers desire high levels of *data integrity* and *results currency*. Data integrity describes characteristics of research that affect error and bias in the results, whilst results currency refers to the generalizability of results. Bonoma claims that positivist methods, such as laboratory experiments, are higher in data integrity than the methods used by interpretivists. However, methodologies used by interpretivists, such as case studies, tend to be high in results currency because they have contextual relevance across measures, methods, paradigms, settings and time. In any research project, there is likely to be a trade-off between data integrity and results currency. In other words, data integrity can only be achieved by sacrificing results currency.

4.4.5   RELIABILITY

Reliability is concerned with the findings of the research and is one aspect of the credibility of the findings; the other is validity. You need to ask yourself whether the evidence and your conclusions will stand up to close scrutiny (Raimond, 1993, p. 55). For a research result to be reliable, a repeat study should produce the same result. For example, if you found that a group of workers who had attended a training course doubled their previous productivity levels, your result would be reliable if another researcher replicated your study and obtained the same results. Replication is very important in positivist studies.

Whereas reliability tends to be high in positivist studies, under an interpretive paradigm, reliability is often of little importance or may be interpreted in a different way. The qualitative measures do not need to be reliable in the positivist sense. However, importance is placed on whether observations and interpretations made on different occasions and/or by different observers can be explained and understood. As interpretivists believe that the activities of the researcher influence the research, the replication in the positivist sense, would be difficult to achieve. Therefore, the emphasis is on establishing protocols and procedures that establish the authenticity of the findings.

> **KEY DEFINITIONS**
>
> Reliability refers to the absence of differences in the results if the research were repeated.

It is often possible to design a research study where reliability is high, but validity, which we discuss in the next section, is low. For example, perhaps you are attempting to establish the criteria on which bank managers decide to grant overdrafts to customers. There are some very rational criteria, such as income levels, security of employment, past evidence of repayment and home ownership, and it is possible that repeated questionnaire surveys of bank managers would demonstrate that these are the important criteria. However, observation or in-depth interviews might establish other criteria that are equally important. These could be apparently less rational criteria, such as the bank manager not liking the look of the applicant or how he or she speaks.

4.4.6   VALIDITY

Validity is the extent to which the research findings accurately reflect the phenomena under study. 'An effect or test is valid if it demonstrates or measures what the researcher thinks or claims it does' (Coolican, 1992, p. 35). Research errors, such as faulty research procedures, poor samples and inaccurate or misleading measurement, can undermine validity. For example, you may be interested in whether employees in a particular company understand their company's pension scheme. Therefore, you ask them to calculate their pension entitlements. However, you do not know whether their answers reflect their understanding of the scheme, whether they have read the scheme, how good they are at remembering the details of the scheme, or their ability to make calculations.

Because positivism focuses on the precision of measurement and the ability to be able to repeat the experiment reliably, there is always a danger that validity will be very low. In other words, the measure does not reflect the phenomena the researcher claims to be investigating. On the other hand, interpretivism focuses on capturing the essence of the phenomena and extracting data that provide rich, detailed explanations. The interpretivist's aim is to gain full access to the knowledge and meaning of those involved in the phenomenon and consequently validity is high under such a paradigm.

There are a number of different ways in which the validity of research can be assessed. The most common is face validity, which simply involves ensuring that the tests or measures used by the researcher do actually measure or represent what they are supposed to measure or represent. Another form of validity that is important in business research is *construct validity*. This relates to the problem that there are a number of phenomena which are not directly observable, such as motivation, satisfaction, ambition and anxiety. These are known as hypothetical constructs which are assumed to exist as factors that explain observable phenomena. For example, you may be able to observe someone shaking and sweating before an interview. However, you are not actually observing anxiety, but a manifestation of anxiety.

With hypothetical constructs, you must be able to demonstrate that your observations and research findings can be explained by the construct. It would be easy to fall into the trap of claiming that employees achieve high levels of productivity because they love their work, when in fact they are working hard because they are anxious about the security of their jobs during a period of economic recession.

4.4.7   GENERALIZABILITY

Generalization is concerned with the application of research results to cases or situations beyond those examined in the study. Generalizability is 'the extent to which you can come to conclusions about one thing (often a population) based on information about another (often a sample)' (Vogt, 1993, p. 99). If you are following a positivist paradigm, you will have selected a sample and you will be interested in determining how confident you are in stating that the characteristics found in the sample will be present in the population from which you have drawn your sample.

However, Gummesson (1991) argues that using statistics to generalize from a sample to a population is just one type of generalization; interpretivists may be able to generalize their findings from one setting to a similar setting. He supports the view of Normann (1970) who contends that it is possible to generalize from a very few cases, or even a single case, if your analysis has captured the interactions and characteristics of the phenomena you are studying. Thus, you will be concerned with whether the patterns, concepts and theories that have been generated in a particular environment can be applied in other environments. To do this, you must have a comprehensive and deep understanding of the activities and behaviour you have been studying.

4.5   PRAGMATISM

We have emphasized that the two main paradigms represent two extremes of what can be described as a continuum of paradigms and that paradigms are based on mutually exclusive philosophical assumptions about the world and the nature of knowledge. Most students will find their paradigm falls broadly within one of the two main paradigms. This is also true for experienced researchers, who over time may modify their philosophical assumptions and move to a new position on the continuum. Thus, the philosophical assumptions of the researcher's paradigm provide the theoretical framework that underpins the methodology in the majority of research studies in business and management.

In the past few decades, however, some researchers have begun to argue that *pragmatism* should be the key factor in determining the methodology. Rather than be 'constrained' by a single paradigm, pragmatists advocate that researchers should be 'free' to mix methods from different paradigms, choosing them on the basis of usefulness for answering the research question(s). Pragmatists suggest that by ignoring the philosophical debate about reality and the nature of knowledge, the weaknesses of one paradigm can be offset with the strengths of the other. This pluralist approach is an attempt to 'cross the divide between the quantitative and the qualitative and the positivist and the non-positivist' (Curran and Blackburn, 2001, p. 123).

Drawing on his interpretation of other writers, Creswell (2003) sets out seven strictures of pragmatism and compares them with his views of mixed methods research. We discuss three of the knowledge claims he extracts below.

- *Pragmatism is not committed to any one system of philosophy and reality.* This is certainly one of the main claims by pragmatists, but your supervisor and examiners may not be sympathetic to this view if they believe that without a commitment to one paradigm, there is no theoretical framework to support your methodology. Our advice is to consider the views of your supervisor (and your eventual examiners) very carefully before declaring yourself a pragmatist in your proposal. You may find that what you are trying to do is to mix methods from the same paradigm, rather than abandon your assumptions completely. This is known as triangulation and is discussed in Chapter 5.
- *Individual researchers have freedom of choice.* Although one is always sympathetic to claims of academic freedom, having a choice should not lead to an absence of rationality in your choice of research design and rigour in the application of your methods. If you are seeking a higher qualification or research publications, you will find that those who will evaluate your research may have strong opinions on what is good research. Certainly, you have a choice but you should know why you make a particular choice.
- *Pragmatists believe we need to stop asking questions about reality and the laws of nature.* A quick search of the literature will produce numerous articles that ask questions about reality, but few of them come up with satisfactory answers. Most students will need to demonstrate their understanding of the debate and be able to defend the position that they adopt.

KEY DEFINITIONS

A *method* is a technique for collecting and/or analysing data.

A *methodology* is an approach to the process of the research, encompassing a body of methods.

Our advice to students who are thinking of adopting a pragmatic approach is to discuss it with your supervisor as soon as possible. You must be able to justify your stance if you seeking a higher degree or considering publishing an article based on your research in an academic journal. At the undergraduate level, it is unlikely that you will be required to discuss your paradigm, as most supervisors will be focusing on your methodology and your ability to apply your methods and draw conclusions. They may expect you to analyse both qualitative and quantitative data; not because you have adopted any particular paradigm, but because they want to be certain you know how to handle both.

In several parts of this chapter, we have used the terms *method* and *methodology* and this is a good point at which to distinguish between them. A *method* is a technique for collecting and/or analysing data. As a general term, methodology refers to the study of methods (for example, a student on a taught course might study research methodology). However, in the context of a specific study, it refers to the approach to the process of the research, encompassing a body of methods (for example the methodology chapter in a proposal, dissertation or thesis that describes and justifies the overall research strategy and methods). In some cases, a research strategy embodying a particular set of methods has become established through widespread use in particular disciplines (for example grounded theory, which we discuss in Chapter 9.)

4.6　CONCLUSIONS

We have introduced a number of concepts in this chapter that may be new to you. It is essential for you to understand your research paradigm, as this provides a framework for designing your study. The two main paradigms are positivism and what can be loosely referred to as interpretivism. In this chapter, we have examined how the core ontological, epistemological, axiological, rhetorical and methodological assumptions of the two main paradigms differ. Positivism and interpretivism lie at opposite ends of a continuum of paradigms with a range of other paradigms between them. Two key features that characterize research findings are reliability and validity. Reliability refers to being able to obtain the same results if the study were replicated. Reliability is likely to be higher in a positivist study than in a study designed under an interpretive paradigm. Validity refers to the research findings accurately representing what is happening in the situation. Validity is likely to be higher in an interpretivist study than a positivist study.

If you are doing research at Master's or doctoral level, you will need to explain your paradigm and justify your methodology and methods. Methodological triangulation is where the research design includes complementary methods from within the same paradigm. It is essential that triangulation is an integral part of the design and not an attempt to rectify a poorly designed study and you are not advised to mix methods from opposing paradigms.

Once you have identified your paradigm, you can determine which methodology and methods will be appropriate. This will mean you have reached the research design stage and you will be in a position to develop your research proposal. If you are doing research at the undergraduate level, it is likely that you will not have to concern yourself too much with paradigms and will concentrate instead on managing the research process, collecting the data and analysing them. This is covered in subsequent chapters.

ACTIVITIES

1. You have a set of weighing scales that always register 5 kilos above your actual weight. Your friend has a set of scales that measures his or her weight accurately, but sometimes shows it as 7 kilos above or below her true weight. Explain how these occurrences can be regarded as issues of reliability and/or validity or reliability.

2. You are planning a research study that will investigate the feelings of the devoted fans of a local sports team in situations when it wins and when it loses. Compare the advantages and disadvantages of the two main paradigms for this purpose and decide which approach would give you the best understanding.

3. The marketing director of a company promoting health clubs asks you to assess the effectiveness of a recent advertising campaign they ran in a magazine. Compare the advantages and disadvantages of the two main paradigms for this purpose. Then decide whether the marketing director will expect a qualitative or quantitative analysis and which would be the easiest paradigm for you to adopt.

4. Thousands of years ago a Buddhist monk called Chuang Tzu wrote: 'I dreamt I was a butterfly, flitting around in the sky; then I awoke. Now I wonder, am I a man who dreamt he was a butterfly, or am I a butterfly dreaming I am a man?' Decide which of the five core assumptions associated with the main paradigm this addresses and how you would you answer Chuang Tzu's dilemma.

5. Paradigm quiz
    Indicate whether you agree (tick the box) or disagree (put a cross in the box) with the following statements. There are no right or wrong answers and the exercise should not be taken too seriously!

    a) Quantitative data are more scientific than qualitative data. ☐
    b) It is important to state the hypotheses before collecting data. ☐
    c) Surveys are probably the best way to investigate business issues. ☐
    d) Unless a phenomenon can be measured reliably it cannot be investigated. ☐
    e) A good knowledge of statistics is essential for all approaches to business research. ☐
    f) Case studies should only be used for exploratory research. ☐
    g) Using participant observation to collect data is of little value in business research. ☐
    h) Laboratory experiments should be used more widely in business research. ☐
    i) It is impossible to generate theories from research into business issues. ☐
    j) Researchers must remain objective and independent from the phenomena they study. ☐

    Interpretation:
    More ticks than crosses = positivist
    More crosses than ticks = interpretivist
    Equal number of each = undecided

    Once you have finished, critically reflect on why this quiz might not be very effective in diagnosing your paradigm.

PROGRESS TEST

Complete the following sentences:

1. A philosophical framework that guides how scientific research should be conducted is known as a research _____.

2. The two main paradigms can be loosely described as _____ and interpretivism.

3. The extent to which the research findings can be extended to other cases or to other settings is known as _____.

4. A technique for collecting research data is known as a research _____.

5. A technique for analysing research data is known as a research _____.

Are the following statements true or false?

6. Empirical evidence is data collected from an interview or a survey.

7. Only interpretivists conduct exploratory or descriptive studies.

8. Only positivists conduct analytical studies.

9. Only quantitative data are collected in a study based on a positivist paradigm.

10. A study designed to test a hypothesis is based on a positivist paradigm.

Multiple choice questions:

11. The belief that the researcher is independent from that being researched is based on his or her:
    a) ontological assumption
    b) epistemological assumption
    c) axiological assumption
    d) methodological assumption

12. The belief that the process of research is deductive and context-free is based on the researcher's:
    a) ontological assumption
    b) axiological assumption
    c) rhetorical assumption
    d) methodological assumption

13. The belief that research is value-free and biased is based on the researcher's:
    a) ontological assumption
    b) epistemological assumption
    c) axiological assumption
    d) rhetorical assumption

14. The belief that reality is objective, singular and external is based on the researcher's:
    a) ontological assumption
    b) epistemological assumption
    c) rhetorical assumption
    d) methodological assumption

15. The belief that the research should be written in an impersonal, formal style is based on the researcher's:
    a) ontological assumption
    b) axiological assumption
    c) rhetorical assumption
    d) methodological assumption

5

Choosing a methodology

Learning objectives

When you have studied this chapter, you should be able to:

- describe the main methodologies associated with positivism

- describe the main methodologies associated with interpretivism

- compare the strengths and weaknesses of methodologies

- discuss the strengths and weaknesses of triangulation

- choose a methodology that reflects your paradigm.

5.1   INTRODUCTION

You will remember from Chapter 4 that a paradigm is more than just a philosophical framework; it also guides how research should be conducted. Therefore, once you have identified your research paradigm, you can start thinking about your research strategy. This means choosing a *methodology* that reflects the philosophical assumptions of your paradigm. If you are a student, you may decide that considerable weighting should be placed on the feasibility of your research strategy and any expectations your supervisor may have, as gaining an academic qualification will be one of your main aims.

This chapter offers a guide to some of the most widely used methodologies. We discuss them under the two main paradigms, but you should remember that some can be adapted for use under either paradigm. We start with an overview and then describe the methodologies traditionally associated with positivism. These have been developed to support a deductive process, where generalizations lead to prediction, explanation and understanding. We then examine the methodologies associated with interpretivism, which support an inductive process, where patterns and/or theories are developed to understand phenomena (Creswell, 1998). In some studies, there may be scope to employ multiple methods and, therefore, we also discuss the advantages and disadvantages of *triangulation*.

5.2   LINK BETWEEN PARADIGM AND METHODOLOGY

In the last chapter, we emphasized that positivism and interpretivism are the two main paradigms that lie at the extremities of what Morgan and Smircich (1980) describe as a continuum of paradigms. In Chapter 4, we explained that your research paradigm is a philosophical framework that guides how research should be conducted. You will find there is a wide range of methodologies and methods for collecting and analysing your research data, and it is important that you choose those that meet the philosophical assumptions of your paradigm. Research data can be *primary* or *secondary* data. Primary data are data generated from an original source, such as your own experiments, questionnaire survey, interviews or focus groups, whereas secondary data are data that have been collected from an existing source, such as publications, databases and internal records, and may be available in hard copy form or on the internet.

> ### KEY DEFINITIONS
>
> A method is a technique for collecting and/or analysing data.
>
> A methodology is an approach to the process of the research, encompassing a body of methods.
>
> Primary data are data generated from an original source, such as your own experiments, surveys, interviews or focus groups.
>
> Secondary data are data collected from an existing source, such as publications, databases and internal records.

If you are designing a study under a positivist paradigm, in most disciplines you may not have to expend much energy in justifying your methodology and methods. This is because positivism still tends to dominate in many areas of business research, although the number of studies designed under an interpretive paradigm is increasing. If you are designing such a study, in some disciplines you may find it necessary to provide a stronger rationale for your methodology and give a more detailed explanation of your methods to convince your supervisor and/or research committee that your study will be rigorous and methodical.

It is important to remember that the two main paradigms represent the two extremities on the continuum and that your paradigm and associated methodology and methods may represent a blending of some of the philosophical assumptions. Nevertheless, a coherent research strategy will ensure that the choices broadly reflect the core assumptions of one of the two main paradigms. If you are having trouble identifying your paradigm, you can take comfort from Creswell

(2003), who suggests that the knowledge claims, strategies and methods used by the researcher determine the tendency of the research approach. He suggests:

- The issue or concern to be addressed needs to be considered fully and the research needs to be designed that best matches the problem.
- The researcher needs to consider his or her skills and experience, and assess which approach best complements these.
- The researcher needs to consider the audience to whom the findings from the research will be addressed.

Table 5.1 lists some of the main methodologies used in the social sciences, some of which are adaptable for use under either paradigm. This is not an exhaustive list and we advise you to examine others you come across when studying previous research on your chosen topic.

TABLE 5.1 Methodologies associated with the main paradigms	
Positivism	Interpretivism
Experimental studies	Hermeneutics
Surveys (using primary or secondary data)	Ethnography
Cross-sectional studies	Participative enquiry
Longitudinal studies	Action research
	Case studies
	Grounded theory
	Feminist, gender and ethnicity studies

5.3 METHODOLOGIES ASSOCIATED WITH POSITIVISM

5.3.1 EXPERIMENTAL STUDIES

An *experimental study* is used to investigate the relationship between variables, where the independent variable is deliberately manipulated to observe the effect on the dependent variable. Experimental studies permit causal relationships to be identified. The aim is to manipulate the *independent variable* (for example noise levels) in order to observe the effect on the *dependent variable* (for example the productivity of factory workers). The experiment is conducted in a systematic way in a laboratory or a natural setting.

One of the advantages of conducting experiments in an artificial setting is that the researcher is better able to eliminate certain variables or keep some variables constant. This is necessary because one of the main challenges is to control *confounding variables*. These are variables that obscure the effect of another variable. For example, a subject's behaviour may alter merely as a result of being watched or because he or she is in an unfamiliar environment. An artificial setting also helps control *extraneous variables*. These are other variables apart from the independent variables that might have an effect on the dependent variable. Although field experiments offer the advantage that

> **KEY DEFINITIONS**
>
> An experimental study is a methodology used to investigate the relationship between variables, where the independent variable is deliberately manipulated to observe the effect on the dependent variable.

they are conducted in a natural setting, you may not have such strong control over confounding and extraneous variables. For example, if your study involves an investigation of the relationship between productivity and motivation, you may find it difficult to exclude the effect on productivity of other factors such as a heatwave, a work-to-rule, a takeover or problems the worker may be experiencing at home.

If you choose to conduct an experimental study, the nature of the research problem and the access you have managed to negotiate are likely to play a significant role in determining the specific design. The main choices are as follows:

- In a *repeated-measures design*, the experiment is repeated under different conditions. For example, perhaps you are interested in assessing employees' performance in operating complicated machinery under noisy conditions. You could ask the employees (the subjects of the experiment) to operate the machinery when it was noisy and measure the time taken to perform a particular task and the number of errors. You might ask the same employees to conduct the same task under quiet conditions. If the results are not the same, and all other variables have been controlled, it would be reasonable to assume that the change in performance is due to the level of noise. One problem with this approach is that an employee's performance may be better on the second occasion because they have rehearsed the task by doing it the first time. On the other hand, they may perform less well the second time because they have become bored. These are examples of the *order effect* and the easiest of several solutions to this problem is to ensure there is sufficient time between experiments to remove any ordering effects.

- In an *independent-samples design*, two groups are selected. For example, one group of employees operates the machinery under noisy conditions and the other operates the same machinery under quiet conditions. This provides data from two independent samples, which can be compared. The major problem with this approach is that there may be other differences between the two samples, such as the age, experience and training of the employees. To avoid such inequalities, the employees can be allocated randomly to each group.

- A *matched-pairs design* is a more rigorous approach, which attempts to eliminate other differences between the two groups, by matching pairs of employees and allocating one to each group. Of course, there may be some difficulty in identifying which characteristics should be matched and ensuring that there are enough employees to obtain a sufficient number of matched pairs.

- A *single-subject design* is useful when only a few subjects are available, but this makes it difficult to make generalizations. However, despite this drawback, findings from such a study can be useful in providing knowledge about the phenomena under study in that particular context.

To select the most appropriate design, Kervin (1992) suggests you need to consider three main factors:

- The number of groups: You will compare two or more groups of cases, or look for variations within one group.
- The nature of the groups: It will be important to know how the group is formed, for example by using random allocation or matched cases.
- The timing of the experiments: In our earlier example of a repeated-measures design to measure the effect of noise levels on performance, the experiment was conducted twice only, but it could have been repeated several times on different occasions. However, this is not always possible and you may be limited to collecting evidence from the same groups at one point in time only.

Once you have decided on the type of experimental design, you need to determine the size of your sample. One criterion to use is what you intend to do with the data. Coolican (1992) argues that when the experimental independent variable can be assumed to have a similar effect on most people, the optimum sample size is about 25 to 30. Experimental studies in a laboratory or in a natural setting (often referred to as field experiments) present specific challenges to the researcher. If you choose to conduct an experimental study, you will need to recognize the limitations of the methodology.

You need to bear in mind that it can be very difficult to arrange experiments in business research due to the difficulty in finding suitable subjects with the time to participate. Many laboratory experiments have been criticized because they use students as surrogates in an attempt to overcome this problem. Experiments also suffer from the criticism that they focus very narrowly on particular variables and are conducted in an artificial setting, thus failing on both counts to reflect the real world. Barber (1976) identifies a number of other problems relating to the investigator (the researcher in overall control of the study) and the experimenter (the person carrying out the experiment). These range from poor research design and inaccurate recording, to fudging the results.

Despite these drawbacks, Dobbins, Lane and Steiner (1988) argue that laboratory experiments are valuable and that even studies using students as subjects have validity. They recommend that the choice of research method should be based on the purpose of the research and the researcher's paradigm. In their view, laboratory experiments are useful for examining work behaviour at the individual level. It is also evident that some activities are best controlled in a laboratory (for example it would not be a good idea to test the influence of alcohol by asking participants to drive on a public highway).

Others, such as Blumer (1980), argue that laboratory procedures are artificial and inconsistent with the epistemology implied by the interaction theory. Nevertheless, they can be used in an interpretivist study, but the relationship between the researcher and the participants will have a certain level of authoritarianism and the experiments do not give a faithful representation of social action in everyday life. Couch (1987) rejects many of these criticisms and claims that laboratory experiments can be used fruitfully in an interpretivist study, but that care must be taken with the research design. He recommends that the situation should be structured so that participants pay only minimal attention to the researcher. If possible, a mini-social world of short duration, but with a high level of authenticity, should be created in the laboratory. This may require an elaborate layout and the researcher to be involved in a particular role within the phenomenon being studied. The analysis of the data will be based on video recordings and transcriptions. 'The use of the laboratory and recording devices … [does not] require acceptance of the ontology' (Couch, 1987, p. 166). The results of the field studies can then be compared with the results of laboratory studies so that 'grounded theories of social construct that have universal application can be constructed' (Couch, 1987, p. 175).

5.3.2   SURVEYS

In a positivist study, a *survey* methodology is designed to collect primary or secondary data from a sample, with a view to analysing them statistically and generalizing the results to a population. If you are planning to collect secondary research data, we suggest you avoid using the term 'secondary research', as it is the data you are distinguishing as secondary while your analysis will produce original findings.

If the population is small, it is possible to collect data about every member of the

We will be looking at the various sampling methods in Chapter 10.

KEY DEFINITIONS

A **population** is a precisely defined body of people or objects under consideration for statistical purposes.

A **sample** is a subset of a population. In a positivist study, a random sample is chosen to provide an unbiased subset of the population.

A **survey** is a methodology designed to collect primary or secondary data from a sample, with a view to generalizing the results to a population.

population, but this is too expensive and time-consuming for a large population. Therefore, a random sample is chosen to represent an unbiased subset of the population and statistical methods are used to test the likelihood that the characteristics of the sample are also found in the population. We will be looking at the various sampling methods in Chapter 10.

Surveys can be divided into two types, according to their purpose:

* The purpose of a *descriptive survey* is to provide an accurate representation of phenomena at one point in time or at various times (for example a consumer survey to investigate customers' views on new products or services being developed by the business; an attitude survey to investigate the views of employees on a new productivity scheme).
* An *analytical survey* is conducted to determine whether there is a relationship between pairs of variables or multiple variables. If you wish to carry out this type of survey, you will need to develop a theoretical framework from the literature so that you can identify the dependent and independent variables in the relationship. This may sound a bit technical now, but we will be explaining this in subsequent chapters.

There are several methods for collecting survey data in a positivist study, including postal questionnaires, internet questionnaires, telephone interviews and face-to-face interviews. A structured questionnaire will be used so that all participants are asked the same questions in the same order. We will compare these methods in Chapter 10.

A survey methodology can also be used in an interpretivist study. In this case, selecting a sufficiently large and unbiased sample for the survey is not crucial, because the aim of the research is not to generalize to the population, but to gain insights from the cases in the sample. Therefore, you could ask for volunteers to participate in the research, which would not be suitable under a positivist paradigm.

5.3.3   CROSS-SECTIONAL STUDIES

Cross-sectional studies are designed to obtain research data in different contexts, but over the same period of time. They are often used to investigate economic characteristics in surveys of large numbers of organizations or people. Typically, the organizations would represent a range of industries, and the research would look for similarities and differences between industries. In studies focusing on people, employees working in different parts of an organization might be selected to ascertain similarities and differences between groups. For example, if you are investigating the association between labour turnover and productivity, you could select a sample of work groups where you know that labour turnover or productivity differ. You could then collect data relating to a group of workers from factory A and a group of workers doing the same jobs in factory B and conduct statistical tests to examine the correlation between the variables under study.

KEY DEFINITIONS

A **cross-sectional study** is a methodology used to investigate variables or a group of subjects in different contexts over the same period of time.

Cross-sectional studies are conducted when there are time constraints or limited resources. The data are collected once, over a short period of time, before they are analysed and reported. Thus, cross-sectional studies provide a snapshot of research phenomena. One of the problems with this research strategy is how to select a sample that is large enough to be representative of the population. A second problem is how to isolate the phenomena under study from all the other factors that could influence the correlation. Finally, cross-sectional studies do not explain why a correlation exists; only that it does or does not exist. On the other hand, cross-sectional studies are inexpensive and are conducted simultaneously, so that there is no problem of change taking place due to the passage of time.

5.3.4   LONGITUDINAL STUDIES

A *longitudinal study* is often associated with a positivist methodology, but can also be used under an interpretive paradigm. It is the study of variables or a group of subjects over a long period of time. The aim is to examine the dynamics of a research problem by investigating the same variables or group of people several times (or continuously) over the period in which the problem runs its course. This can be a period of several years. Repeated observations are taken with a view to revealing the relative stability of the phenomena under study; some will have changed considerably, others will show little sign of change. Such studies allow the researcher to examine change processes within a social, economic and political context. Therefore, it should be possible to suggest likely explanations from an examination of the process of change and the patterns that emerge from the data. Adams and Schvaneveldt (1991) suggest that by observing people or events over time, the researcher has the opportunity to exercise some control over the variables being studied.

> **KEY DEFINITIONS**
>
> A longitudinal study is a methodology used to investigate variables or a group of subjects over a long period of time.

Because of the smaller sample size, it is easier to negotiate access and produce significant results for a longitudinal study of an organization than for a cross-sectional study. However, once started, the study must be continued and there is the problem of losing subjects during the course of the study. Moreover, this methodology is very time-consuming and expensive to conduct. It is unlikely to be appropriate for research students on taught courses as it requires the researcher to be involved for a number of years for the advantages to be enjoyed. However, it may be possible to conduct a longitudinal study using secondary data. The government and other bodies publish a considerable amount of data on various social and economic factors, such as employment, home ownership, household expenditure and income. By concentrating on a specific area, you could investigate whether there have been significant changes over a period of time and how these changes might be explained. In Chapter 12, we explain a technique known as *time series analysis*, which is a useful method for analysing quantitative data from a longitudinal study.

A longitudinal study under an interpretivist paradigm would focus on qualitative data. Stebbins (1992) describes a chain of studies and what he refers to as concatenated exploration. Each link in the chain is an examination or re-examination of a related group or social process, or an aspect of a broader category of groups or social processes. The early studies in the chain are mainly exploratory, but as the chain of studies progresses, *grounded theory* is generated (discussed later in this chapter). He argues that the chain of qualitative case studies improves the applicability and validity of the findings. In addition, the researcher gains in knowledge and understanding of the subject as the research develops, and can take account of social processes instead of concentrating only on individuals.

5.4   METHODOLOGIES ASSOCIATED WITH INTERPRETIVISM

5.4.1   HERMENEUTICS

Hermeneutics is a *methodology* that focuses on the interpretation and understanding of text in the context of the underlying historical and social forces. It assumes that a relationship exists between the direct conscious description of experience and the underlying dynamics or structures. Hermeneutics was originally concerned with interpreting ancient scriptures, but the approach was formalized and its scope broadened by Dilthey (1976) and others. Although it is still associated with the interpretation of historical texts, hermeneutics has been applied to research in law, where the reasons behind judgements or statutes are sought. According to Lindlof (1995, p. 31), 'The method can be applied to any situation in which one wants to "recover" historical meaning' and the process involves continual reference to the context (Ricoeur, 1977) when interpreting the meaning of contemporary or historic text.

> **KEY DEFINITIONS**
>
> Hermeneutics is a methodology that focuses on the interpretation and understanding of text in the context of the underlying historical and social forces.

Taylor (1990) links hermeneutics with *repertory grid technique*, which is a method used to provide mathematical representation of the perceptions and constructs an individual uses to understand and manage his or her world. We discuss this method in more detail in Chapters 8 and 9. Taylor's rationale is that the five criteria for text established by Ricoeur (1981) can be rewritten for the data generated by repertory grid technique:

- Words and numbers convey meaning.
- Numbers are chosen according to a structured rationale.
- There is a relationship between this structured rationale and the intended meaning.
- The work of this intended meaning is a projection of a world.
- The uncovering of this meaning is through the mediation of self-understanding.

Taylor stresses the importance of the researcher as an interpreter and a reiterative process of relabelling and reanalysing the data in a hermeneutic circle, since the meaning of any part of the text cannot be understood without reference to other parts, the complete text and the historical and social context. Although hermeneutics is not a widely used methodology in business research, Taylor's unusual approach illustrates the importance of being flexible in classifying methodologies and methods and the value of creativity.

5.4.2 ETHNOGRAPHY

Ethnography is a methodology derived from anthropology (the study of people, their societies and their customs) in which the researcher uses socially acquired and shared knowledge to understand the observed patterns of human activity. Ethnography* 'provides insights about a group of people and offers us an opportunity to see and understand their world' (Boyle, 1994, p. 183). Werner and Schoepfle (1987) claim that ethnography is any full or partial description of a group.

*Ethono- means folk and *-graphy* means description.

The aim of ethnography is to interpret the social world in the same way as the members of that particular world do. The main method of data collection is *participant observation*, where the researcher becomes a full member of the group being studied. The research normally takes place over a long period of time (often many months), which makes it difficult for students on taught courses. The research takes place in a clearly defined natural setting, such as a factory, and involves direct participation in the activities taking place.

> **KEY DEFINITIONS**
>
> Ethnography is a methodology in which the researcher uses socially acquired and shared knowledge to understand the observed patterns of human activity.

Bogdan and Taylor (1975) and Patton (1990) offer a number of suggestions for researchers conducting ethnographic studies, which can be summarized into the following stages:

- Build trust as early as possible.
- Become as involved as you can with the phenomena, but maintain an analytical perspective.

- Develop strong contacts with a few key informants.
- Gather data from as many different sources as possible, using multiple methods.
- Capture participants' views of their experiences in their own words, but remember the limitations of their perspectives.
- Write up field notes as soon as possible after leaving the setting and do not talk to anyone until you have done so.
- Be descriptive when taking your field notes and draw diagrams of physical layouts.
- Include your own experiences, thoughts and feelings as part of your field notes.
- As fieldwork draws to a close, concentrate on making a synthesis of your notes.

A considerable number of disciplines have used ethnography, and business is no exception. Some of them are reviewed by Gill and Johnson (1991). However, there are a great many schisms and 'ethnography is perhaps the most hotly contested site in qualitative research today' (Denzin and Lincoln, 1994, p. 203). These divisions have led to a number of different styles of ethnography, which depend on the skills and training of the researcher, and the nature of the group with which the ethnographer is working.

Students conducting ethnographical studies face a number of problems. First, you have to select an organization in which your particular research interests are present and negotiate access. Second, you have to develop a high degree of trust in those you work with to ensure that you collect the data. Third, if you are using full participation to do your research, you must cope with being a full-time member of a work group as well as doing the research. Finally, there is the issue of whether the particular setting or group best reflects the research interests and whether it will be possible to generalize from the findings. Despite these difficulties, there are a number of advantages. You obtain first-hand experience of the context being studied. Direct observation aids your understanding and interpretation of the phenomena under study, and participation in events may lead those being observed to reveal matters to you or in front of you that might not be known otherwise. When writing up your research it is important to capture the experiences that the group have gone through by quoting the participants' own words and describing the context in which they were uttered.

5.4.3   PARTICIPATIVE ENQUIRY

> **KEY DEFINITIONS**
>
> Participant enquiry is a methodology that involves the participants as fully as possible in the study, which is conducted in their own group or organization.

Participative enquiry is a methodology that involves the participants as fully as possible in the study, which is conducted in their own group or organization. The research may even be initiated by a member of the group and the participants are involved in the data collection and analysis. The participants also determine the progress and direction of the research, thus enabling the researcher to develop questions and answers as a shared experience with a group as co-researchers (Traylen, 1994). Therefore, this type of methodology is 'about research with people rather than research on people' (Reason, 1994a, p. 1).

Concerns about the traditional model of research, which implies an authority imbalance in the relationship between the researcher and the researched, and the associated ethical issues, have led to the development of a strategy that increases the involvement of participants. The objective is to produce higher quality data, but also to address the philosophical arguments and the democratic right of individuals to participate in a study. As one commentator puts it, 'I believe and hope that there is an emerging world view, more holistic, pluralist and egalitarian, that is essentially participative' (Reason, 1994b, p. 324). De Venney-Tiernan, Goldband, Rackham and Reilly (1994) contend that the methodology can be employed successfully by novices and those who do not consider themselves to be academics.

Reason (1994b) identifies three types of approach:

- In a study based on *co-operative enquiry*, all those involved in the research are co-researchers, whose thinking and decision-making contribute to generating ideas, designing and managing the project, and drawing conclusions from the experience; they are also co-subjects who participate in the activity being researched.
- In *participatory action research*, the aim is to challenge the power relationship in society. Such studies are often concerned with capturing the knowledge and experiences of oppressed groups.
- The third approach is *action research* (or *action science*), which we describe next.

The basis for all these approaches is that they see 'human beings as co-creating their reality through participation, experience and action' (Denzin and Lincoln, 1994, p. 206).

5.4.4 ACTION RESEARCH

Action research is a methodology used in applied research to find an effective way of bringing about a conscious change in a partly controlled environment. Thus, the main aim of action research is to enter into a situation, attempt to bring about change and to monitor the results. For example, you might use it in a study aimed at improving communications between management and staff in a particular organization. The philosophical assumptions that underpin action research are that the social world is constantly changing, and the researcher and the research are part of this change. The term was coined by Lewin (1946) who saw the process of enquiry as forming a cycle of planning, acting, observing and reflecting.

> **KEY DEFINITIONS**
>
> **Action research** is a methodology used in applied research to find an effective way of bringing about a conscious change in a partly controlled environment.

It is usual to conduct action research within a single organization and it is therefore similar to a case study approach in many of its procedures. The planning stage is concerned with identifying the objective it is intended to achieve, and how this may be done. The first phase of action is implemented and its effects observed and reflected on before modifying the overall plan, if appropriate. The close collaboration that is required between the researcher and the client organization poses a number of problems. Some action research may not be very far removed from a problem-solving, consultancy project.

From the beginning, the researcher and the client must be agreed on the aims of the study. There will be mutual control of the research and analysis of the results. The final action plan to be implemented is usually the client's responsibility, supported by the researcher. The research report is often published jointly.

There is considerable debate among academics as to the nature of this methodology, although 'improvement and involvement seem central to all users of the term' (Robson, 1993, p. 439). Furthermore, there is collaboration between researchers and practitioners, with the latter participating in the research process. However, it is argued that these features alone do not make for good research and some projects labelled action research 'have been closer to consultancy or journalism' (Gummesson, 1991, p. 102). To avoid such criticisms, some researchers prefer the term *action science*, the main characteristics of which are described by Gummesson as follows:

- Action science always involves two goals: solve a problem for the client and contribute to science.
- The researcher and the client should learn from each other and develop their competencies.

- The researcher must investigate the whole, complex problem, but make it simple enough to be understood by everyone.
- There must be co-operation between the researcher and the client, feedback to the parties involved and continuous adjustment to new information and new events.
- Action science is primarily applicable to the understanding and planning of change in social systems and thus is a suitable research and consulting strategy for business organizations.
- The corporate environment and the conditions of business must be understood before the research starts.
- The methodology should not be judged solely by the criteria used for the paradigm, but by criteria more appropriate for this particular methodology.

5.4.5　CASE STUDIES

A *case study* is a methodology that is used to explore a single phenomenon (the case) in a natural setting using a variety of methods to obtain in-depth knowledge. The importance of the context is essential. Eisenhardt (1989, p. 534) refers to the focus on 'understanding the dynamics present within single setting', while Bonoma (1985, p. 204) notes that it must be 'constructed to be sensitive to the context in which management behaviour takes place'. The case may be a particular business, group of workers, event, process, person, or other phenomenon. Detailed information is collected about the chosen case, often over a very long period of time. One or more cases can be selected.

> **KEY DEFINITIONS**
>
> A case study is methodology that is used to explore a single phenomenon (the case) in a natural setting using a variety of methods to obtain in-depth knowledge.

Yin (2003) identifies the characteristics of case studies as follows:

- The research aims not only to explore certain phenomena, but also to understand them within a particular context.
- The research does not commence with a set of questions and notions about the limits within which the study will take place.
- The research uses multiple methods for collecting data, which may be both qualitative and quantitative.

These characteristics are set in an interpretivist paradigm and if you were taking a more positivist approach, you might develop a theoretical framework and specific research questions.

The different types of case study are not well delineated and one type may be combined with another. *Exploratory case studies* are used where there are few theories or a deficient body of knowledge. Scapens (1990) adds four other types:

- *descriptive case studies,* where the objective is restricted to describing current practice
- *illustrative case studies,* where the research attempts to illustrate new and possibly innovative practices adopted by particular companies
- *experimental case studies,* where the research examines the difficulties in implementing new procedures and techniques in an organization and evaluating the benefits
- *explanatory case studies,* where existing theory is used to understand and explain what is happening.

Opportunist case studies are where the opportunity to examine a phenomenon arises because the researcher has access to a particular business, person or other case (Otley and Berry, 1994). Although such a study may be limited to just a few aspects of organizational life, the results can be extremely stimulating and original.

The main stages in a case study are as follows:

1. Selecting the case – It is not usually necessary to find a representative case or set of cases because you will not be attempting statistical generalizations to show that you can generalize from your sample to a larger population. However, you may be attempting theoretical generalizations where you propose that the theory applied in one set of circumstances can be generalized to another. You may wish to select a critical case that encompasses the issues in which you are most interested. You may also decide that you require more than one case. Similar cases will help to show whether your theory can be generalized and dissimilar cases will help to extend or modify any theory.

2. Preliminary investigations – Bonoma (1985) refers to this as drift and it is the process of becoming familiar with the context in which you are going to conduct your research. Some researchers believe that it is best to keep your mind free of any prior beliefs and to learn from the naturalistic evidence at this stage. Others disagree with this approach and consider that the researcher approaches the project with either explicit or implicit theories. To determine your approach, it may be helpful to reflect on your paradigm and also to consider the purpose you attribute to your research.

3. Data collection – You will need to determine how, where and when to collect data. The methods used to collect data in a case study include documentary analysis, interviews and observation. Eisenhardt (1989, p. 534) advises that it is usually best to 'combine data collection methods such as archive searching, interviews, questionnaires and observations. The evidence may be qualitative (e.g. words), quantitative (e.g. numbers) or both'.

4. Data analysis – You have a choice of within-case analysis or cross-case analysis. If you use the former, it is essential that you become totally familiar with the material. This should enable you to build up separate descriptions of events, opinions and phenomena, which can be used to identify patterns. If you use cross-case analysis, you may choose to draw out any similarities and differences to help you identify common patterns.

5. Writing the report – Writing up case study material can be challenging in terms of determining an appropriate structure and demonstrating that your analysis and conclusions can be linked to the masses of data you will have collected. Students often find a chronological structure is the easiest to adopt, as this means they can relate the unfolding of events as they occur. In an interpretivist study, it is essential that you quote extensively from the data you have collected. Diagrams are often helpful for explaining the patterns you see emerging.

Although a case study methodology has many advantages, access to a suitable case can be difficult to negotiate and the research is very time-consuming. It is also difficult to decide on the scope of your study. Although you may be focusing on a particular organization or group of individuals, they do not exist in a vacuum, but interact with the rest of society. Moreover, your case will have a history and a future, and you will find it difficult to understand the events in a particular period of time without knowledge of what went before and what may follow.

5.4.6   GROUNDED THEORY

Grounded theory is a methodology in which a systematic set of procedures is used to develop an inductively derived theory about phenomena. It was conceived by Glaser and Strauss (1967) as a reaction to positivist studies that start with a theoretical framework, establish hypotheses and collect data that can be used to test the hypotheses. Glaser and Strauss considered that such an approach could lead to early closure where

the researchers only collect data relevant to their theories and ignore data
that could be useful for explaining what was happening. The methodology
does not depend on a priori theories, but uses the data generated by the
phenomena being studied to generate a theory. Grounded theory is 'one of
the interpretive methods that share the common philosophy of phenomenology – that is, methods that are used to describe the world of the person or
persons under study' (Stern, 1994, p. 273).

The overall features of grounded theory have been summarized by
Silverman (1993, p. 46) into the following three stages:

- an initial attempt to develop categories that illuminate the data
- an attempt to 'saturate' these categories with many appropriate cases in order to
  demonstrate their importance
- developing these categories into more general analytic frameworks with relevance
  outside the setting.

Developed for behavioural research in nursing, grounded theory is a methodology
that has been developed and used in many other disciplines. We look at the procedures
involved in grounded theory in Chapter 8.

5.4.7   FEMINIST, GENDER AND ETHNICITY STUDIES

There are a number of different perspectives on social stratification. *Feminist studies* are
used to investigate and seek understanding of phenomena from the perspective of the
role of women in society vis à vis men, while *gender studies* are concerned with the experiences of both men and women. On the other hand, *ethnicity studies* focus on the experiences of different ethnic groups in society (often on particular ethnic minority
groups). Some studies examine both sexual and racial equality.

At a methodological level, a feminist perspective is concerned with challenging 'the
traditional research paradigm from the point of view of the politics and ideol-
ogy of the women's movement' (Coolican, 1992, p. 27). Thus, it challenges
the traditional methods by which knowledge is generated and the source of
the views of the world such knowledge reflects. Advocating a feminist methodology does not mean that the full range of methodologies is not open and
useful to everyone. 'It would fall back onto old stereotypes to suggest that
women didn't tend to use quantification or feel happy testing hypotheses
statistically' (Coolican, 1992, p. 127). It is also possible to combine a feminist
perspective with another methodology, such as Treleaven's (1994) collaborative enquiry with women as staff development.

Hyde (1994) captures her initial understanding of using a feminist perspective in
the following three principles:

- knowledge is grounded in the experiences of women
- the research benefits women
- the researcher immerses herself or himself in or exhibits empathy for the world
  being studied.

Adopting a feminist methodology can present both theoretical and practical problems. Gregg (1994) describes difficulties when she interviewed women who held contrast-
ing opinions to her own. Sometimes there was 'a tension between accepting what the
women said … and wanting to hold onto a particular feminist view, a vision of a feminist
future as part of a commitment to social change' (Gregg, 1994, p. 53). It has been argued

that the language of research can be a barrier. 'It is quite difficult for women to be speaking subjects – harder than for men – and that is true both for women as our research subjects and for us as researchers when we write and talk about our research' (DeVault, 1990, p. 112). Despite these difficulties, feminism brings a new perspective to research and offers insights and understanding of problems that might otherwise be unavailable.

5.5   TRIANGULATION

Triangulation is the use of multiple sources of data, different research methods and/or more than one researcher to investigate the same phenomenon in a study.* This can reduce bias in data sources, methods and investigators (Jick, 1979). In addition, the use of different methods by a number of researchers studying the same phenomenon should lead to greater validity and reliability than a single method approach, providing they all reach the same conclusions (Denzin, 1978).

> * The term 'triangulation' is used in surveying and navigation, where an area is divided into triangles and each triangle provides three reference points. This allows an object within a particular triangle to be located.

A simple example of using multiple sources of data might be to ask a number of people to describe a red rose being grown for the Valentine's Day market. You could get a perfectly adequate description by asking one person to describe the colour of the flower, but you would get a much broader picture if you asked a several people to consider a different aspect of the rose, such as the fragrance, the shape of the flower, the texture of the petals, the glossiness of the leaves, the characteristics of the stem, and so on. By collating all these separate impressions, you could get a much richer picture of the way the participants experience the physical aspects of the rose.

Easterby-Smith, Thorpe and Lowe (1991) analyse the potential elements of triangulation in research studies into four main types:

> **KEY DEFINITIONS**
>
> **Triangulation** is the use of multiple sources of data, different research methods and/or more than one researcher to investigate the same phenomenon in a study.

- Triangulation of theories – A theory is taken from one discipline (for example psychology) and used to explain a phenomenon in another discipline (for example accounting).
- Data triangulation – Data are collected at different times or from different sources in the study of a phenomenon.
- Investigator triangulation – Different researchers independently collect data on the same phenomenon and compare the results.
- Methodological triangulation – More than one method is used to collect and/or analyse the data, but it is important to choose them from the same paradigm (for example exploratory interviews to identify key issues and provide insights into the issues before conducting a questionnaire survey).

Most students can consider using triangulation, but unless you are part of a research team, it is unlikely you will be able to use investigator triangulation. Some of the limitations of methodological triangulation are that replication is more difficult (particularly if qualitative data are generated) and data collection and analysis become more time-consuming and expensive.

5.6   CONCLUSIONS

This chapter and Chapter 4 should have given you a valuable framework for your study. You will need to make a choice about the paradigm you will adopt at an early stage in your research. Clarity about your paradigm is essential for the progress of your research as it determines your choice of research strategy (your methodology). This, in turn, will lead you to a range of associated methods for collecting and analysing your research data.

It is not uncommon in business research to use triangulation, particularly in terms of data triangulation and methodological triangulation. This allows you to take a broader, complementary view of the research problem or issue. However, triangulation must be an integral part of your research strategy; it cannot be used to rectify a poorly designed study. We will be examining this in Chapter 7. Before you can progress to this important milestone, you need to choose a research topic and start reading the literature so that you review the existing body of knowledge and find out how previous research was conducted. We explain this stage in Chapter 6.

ACTIVITIES

1. Select three different academic journals that publish research in your field of study. In each case, read the abstracts and list the different types of methodology used. Decide whether the editor of each journal favours positivist or interpretive approaches.

2. The manager of a large business in your neighbourhood believes that the morale of employees is low. Select one positivist methodology and one interpretive methodology that you could use to investigate the problem. List the advantages and disadvantages of each.

3. Imagine you are a member of a research committee about to interview students about their proposed research. One proposal uses triangulation. Prepare five questions you would ask to ensure that the student is aware of some of the dangers of this approach and the advantages.

4. You want to find out what brand of toothpaste people normally buy and why they use that brand. You have just conducted your first interview as part of an interpretive study. List the information you can extract from the following transcript.

    INTERVIEWER: Why did you buy the brand of toothpaste you are using at present?

    RESPONDENT: Well, my wife and I usually get the one that's on special offer. It's not that money is tight – that's what she chooses to do. So we tend to get the one where there's money off, 25% extra free, two for the price of one and so on. But last week the brand on special offer was a new one – we hadn't seen it before. It's really good because it has a strong minty taste. I don't like the ones with fancy fruit flavours. This new one's good – I like it a lot. [Pause] What's it called, now? I can't remember the name of it at the moment. [Pause] That's funny because I clean my teeth at least twice a day, so I see the tube often enough! Anyway, my wife likes it too and I think we'll buy it again, even if it's not discounted when we need to buy the next tube. When you get to my age it is important to look after your teeth, you know!

5. Now consider a positivist approach to the same issue. You have decided to use a self-completion questionnaire to survey households in your area. Design a one-page questionnaire to find out what brand of toothpaste people normally buy and their reasons. Your first question will list various brands of toothpaste and ask the respondent to indicate the one he or she normally uses. You should base your subsequent questions on the information you can extract from the above interview transcript. Then compare the advantages and disadvantages of the two approaches you have taken in questions 4 and 5.

PROGRESS TEST

Complete the following sentences:

1. The choice of methodology must complement the assumptions of the researcher's _____.

2. A methodology where the independent variable is manipulated to observe the effect on the dependent variable is known as an _____ study.

3. A methodology used to collect research data from a sample with a view to generalizing the results to a population is known as a _____.

4. A methodology that focuses on the understanding of text in the context of the underlying history and social forces is known as _____.

5. A methodology in which the researcher uses socially acquired and shared knowledge to understand the observed patterns of human activity is known as _____.

Are the following statements true or false?

6. In a longitudinal study, data are collected in different contexts over the same period of time.

7. In a case study, multiple methods are used to collect data in a natural setting.

8. In grounded theory, a systematic set of procedures is used to test theory.

9. In data triangulation, theory from one discipline is used to explain a phenomenon in another.

10. In methodological triangulation, more than one method from the same paradigm is used to collect and/or analyse the data.

Multiple choice questions:

11. The approach to the process of the research, encompassing a set of techniques is known as the:
    a) methodology
    b) morphology
    c) mythology
    d) technology

12. A technique for collecting and/or analysing research data is known as a:
    a) method
    b) methodology
    c) paradigm
    d) technology

13. Primary research data are collected from:
    a) the most important source
    b) a perfect source
    c) an original source
    d) a published source

14. A methodology used to investigate variables or a group of subjects over a number of years is known as:
    a) a cross-sectional study
    b) a dissectional study
    c) a latitudinal study
    d) a longitudinal study

15. Participant enquiry is a methodology in which:
    a) all participants co-operate as both subjects and researchers
    b) the experiences of oppressed groups in society are investigated
    c) an effective way of bringing about change in a partly controlled environment is sought.
    d) any of the above

6

Searching and reviewing the literature

Learning objectives

When you have studied this chapter, you should be able to:

- identify potential sources of secondary data

- search the literature

- record your references

- review the literature, citing your sources

- identify your main research question.

6.1   INTRODUCTION

Before you can start the process of searching and reviewing the literature, you need to have identified a *research topic*. Most students have no difficulty in doing this because they have a particular interest in an aspect of one of the subjects they have studied. In some cases, the topic may be allocated. If you are having difficulty in identifying a research topic, try one of the techniques we explained in Chapter 3 to help you generate ideas.

The task of searching and reviewing the literature represents a significant proportion of the total time you will spend on your research and you need to start both activities as soon as possible. In this chapter, we will explain how to conduct a systematic *literature search* and a critical *review* of the literature that is relevant to your study. Many researchers do much of their searching on the internet, using websites that give access to databases containing academic journal articles and other scholarly papers. We recommend that you are selective about the websites you search, to ensure that you only collect information from authoritative sources.

It is essential to keep accurate records so that you can acknowledge the sources of the information that provides the basis of your research. You will need to apply the rules of the bibliographic referencing system that is appropriate to your discipline and acceptable to your supervisor. Once you have collected the literature that is relevant to your study, you will need to write a literature review that evaluates this body of knowledge. In this chapter we will explain what this entails.

6.2   SEARCHING THE LITERATURE

Your *literature search* can start as soon as you have your first thoughts on a potential topic and it will continue until you submit your dissertation or thesis. In this context, the *literature* refers to the existing body of knowledge. Therefore, a literature search can be defined as a systematic process with a view to identifying the existing body of knowledge on a particular topic. Knowledge is disseminated through various types of publication, which can be in hard copy or digital form, and the data can be qualitative (such as text or illustrations) or quantitative (such as tables or statistics).

The underlying purpose of the literature search is to collect as many relevant items of literature as possible and read them. In the process, you will learn more about the subject and the methodologies used in previous research, which is necessary before you can write a critical review of the literature. This will provide an analysis of what is already known about the phenomena you are going to study and also identify gaps and deficiencies in our knowledge, some aspect of which your study will address.

> **KEY DEFINITIONS**
>
> The literature is all sources of published data on a particular topic.
>
> A literature search is a systematic process with a view to identifying the existing body of knowledge on a particular topic.

6.2.1   THE LITERATURE

The *literature* refers to all sources of secondary data that are relevant to your study. Secondary data are data collected from an existing source, such as:

- books on the topic and on methodology
- research reported in books, articles, conference papers and reports
- coverage of business topics in professional journals, newspapers and broadcast media
- government and commercially produced statistics and industry data

- archives
- statutory and voluntary corporate reports
- internal documents and records of organizations
- e-resources, such as on-line databases and the internet.

At undergraduate level, it may be acceptable to refer to textbooks, but at Master's and doctoral level, you must locate original sources of knowledge. By exploring what others have contributed to your area of interest, you will be in a better position to iden-

<table>
<tr><td>

KEY DEFINITIONS

A theoretical framework is a collection of theories and models from the literature which underpins a positivist study. Theory can be generated from some interpretivist studies.

</td><td>

tify a particular research problem or issue to investigate. Your reading should help you understand the main issues within the topic and also the method-ologies used in previous studies. If you are a positivist, you will be looking for theories and models so that you can develop a theoretical framework and hypotheses for your study. You can see how your ideas compare with what has gone before, and develop existing ideas or create new ones. Your litera-ture search will continue throughout your study, so that your literature review will reflect the current state of knowledge.

</td></tr>
</table>

6.2.2   PROCEDURE FOR A SYSTEMATIC LITERATURE SEARCH

In Chapter 1, we defined research as being systematic and methodical and you can demonstrate this in your methodology chapter when describing how you conducted your literature search. Initially, the subject of your research is likely to be fairly broad, which means your search will be in general terms only. Box 6.1 shows a general proce-dure for conducting a systematic literature search.

BOX 6.1   Procedure for a systematic literature search

- Draw up a list of sources (journal databases, subject-related websites, bibliographic catalogues and other lists your business librarian suggests).

- Define the scope of the research.

- Determine key words you can use for searching, including alternative spellings and synonyms.

- Search each source, keeping a record of your progress (for example: *Journal of Drinking Habits*: Searched 1990–2009 using keywords ...) and full details of relevant publications so that you can read them later and, if relevant, reference them in your work.

- Only collect literature that is relevant to your research in terms of the topic, theory and methodology. In the academic literature, select articles from high-quality journals that review the literature, describe the methods used, discuss the results and draw conclusions.

- Start with the most recent publications and work back in time, using the references at the end of relevant publications to lead you to previous studies.

- When you start to recognize the references cited in other works, you are nearing the end of your first search.

- To keep up to date with the literature, continue searching the literature throughout the project.

6.2.3   DEFINING THE SCOPE

The first step is to define the *scope* and context for your search, which will help limit the material you collect to that which is relevant. Limitations include:

- *Time* – for example, it may not be worth searching more than five years back if the phenomenon you are interested in is some kind of new technology. Find an appropriate cut-off date; it can be adjusted if necessary.

- *Geography* – for example a city, region, country or a comparison of two or more of these.
- *Single or multidisciplinary approach* – for example the development of new software programmes in accountancy.
- *Single discipline, but multi-concept approach* – for example the role of employee appraisals in staff development.

The next step is to decide what sort of information you require. Very recent topics are not likely to be covered by books; journals and newspapers will be the most relevant places to look for information relating to recent events. You may find that some information, for example about a company's corporate strategy or organizational structure, may only be available in internal documents. These may be confidential or difficult to obtain. However, by considering carefully what type of information you expect to find, you can restrict your search to those types only, thus saving yourself valuable time.

You may be able to find much of the information you need from your own institution's library and subscriptions to databases. You need to read abstracts of articles and peruse the information from other sources; if the article or other item of literature is relevant to your research, you will need to print or photocopy a full copy. This may mean visiting another library, or requesting an inter-library loan, for which there may be a charge. You need to allow plenty of time to allow for such delays.

6.2.4   DETERMINING KEY WORDS

Once you have decided where to start searching, you must identify the key words associated with your research topic that you will use to start off your first search. Although you will later develop some more words from reading the literature you find, you may need some lateral thinking to get you started, such as alternative English spellings and synonyms. For example, if your research is going to focus on the marketing of lager and beer in the UK, you might start your search using key words such as 'marketing' 'advertising', 'lager', 'beer' and 'UK'. As you develop your literature search you may want to widen your search by including 'alcoholic beverages' or narrow it to 'mild', 'bitter', 'real ale' or 'stout'.

When searching, you need to bear in mind that you are seeking authoritative sources. Although you might find it helpful, your supervisors and examiners are not likely to consider sources such as lecture notes (from your institution or another) and open resources such as Wikipedia as authoritative; you will need to seek out the original sources, to which their authors refer. You need to adopt a systematic approach and general surfing of the internet is not advised. We recommend that you take advantage of any tutorials run by your library on how to access and search the e-resources to which your institution subscribes. You can also try academic search engines such as *Google Scholar,* the websites of national and international professional bodies, government departments and other organizations with activities that are relevant to your research topic.

In a simple search, you enter all your key words together in the search box. However, you may be overwhelmed by the thousands of 'hits'. We advise you to investigate the advanced search options that may be available. In many cases, this permits the use of Boolean proximity and adjacency operators to narrow the search or, in the case of too few 'hits', to broaden it. Table 6.1 gives examples of Boolean operators used in ProQuest, an e-resource that contains millions of articles from academic journals and other publications.

6.3   REFERENCING

Whether you are an undergraduate, postgraduate or doctoral student, you must ensure that you follow one of the standard systems for *referencing*. All systems provide rules for making citations and references.

6.3.1   CITATIONS AND REFERENCES

A citation is an acknowledgement in your text of the original source of information or ideas, whether reproduced exactly, paraphrased or summarized. This means the originator of theories, models and arguments, illustrations, diagrams, tables, statistics and any other information that you are using in your work must be acknowledged. Citations are important because they:

- provide evidence of your literature searching and the range of your reading
- help you support your arguments using the authority of the source you have cited
- help the reader to distinguish between your work and the existing body of knowledge, thus avoiding accusations of plagiarism.

References are a list containing the bibliographic details of the sources cited in the text. They are important because they:

- provide full bibliographic details that support the citations
- allow supervisors, examiners and other researchers to locate the source of the works you have cited.

We distinguish between a *bibliography* and a *list of references* because a bibliography can be a catalogue of publications, not a specific list of those that have been used and, therefore, cited. Some researchers use the terms interchangeably and you should check what the preferred terminology is in your institution.

There are two main groups of referencing systems: author–date systems, such as the *Harvard system* or the *American Psychological Association (APA) system*, and number-based systems, such as the *Vancouver system*. You will need to find out what is appropriate in your discipline and acceptable to your supervisor before deciding which method to adopt. The important thing to remember is to apply the rules consistently. This means you must first study the rules. Do not be tempted to copy someone else's style, as publishers often use adaptations to create their own house style. Of course, if you are submitting your work for publication, follow the journal's house style. The examples of the Harvard system we show in the next section are based on British Standards, BS 5605:1990.

> **KEY DEFINITIONS**
>
> A citation is an acknowledgement in the text of the original source from which information was obtained.
>
> References are a list containing bibliographic details of the sources cited in the text.

6.3.2   THE HARVARD SYSTEM

The Harvard system is widely used in most business and management research, and other social sciences. It is also used in anthropology and some of the life sciences. The APA system is more commonly used in North America. It is very similar to the Harvard system and both use the author–date system to acknowledge the source of information. Thus, citations in the text are shown as the surname of the author(s) and the date of publication, plus the page number if a quotation is used (or any other exact reproduction of data, such as a table, diagram or illustration). If a printed document or on-line material is not paginated or not dated, use n.p. or n.d. as appropriate.

When citing more than one source, you should place the author–date information in chronological order with the oldest first. If there are two authors, both should be named in all citations. If there are three or more authors, all their names should appear the first time you refer to the publication and thereafter you need only use the name of the first author followed by *et al.* This is the abbreviation of the Latin phrase *et alia*, which means 'and the others' (hence the abbreviation is in italic followed by a full stop). If you are citing more than one author with the same surname, you should include their initials in the text to avoid confusion. Box 6.2 shows a range of examples of how to make citations under the Harvard system.

BOX 6.2   Citations under the Harvard system

Authors' words are paraphrased

The availability of data is a key factor in determining the successful outcome of a research project (Collis and Hussey, 2003)

or

Collis and Hussey (2003) argue that the availability of data is a key factor in determining the successful outcome of a research project

or authors' words are quoted to emphasize authority of source

'The availability of data is crucial to the successful outcome of your research' (Collis and Hussey, 2003, p. 116).

First citation for three or more authors

Exploratory research by Collis, Dugdale and Jarvis (2001) identified . . .

Thereafter

Building on Collis *et al.* (2001), Collis and Jarvis (2002) and Collis, Jarvis and Skerratt (2004) studied . . .

More than one source

A number of studies (Carsberg, Page, Sindall and Waring, 1985; Barker and Noonan, 1996; Pratten, 1998) have investigated . . .

Author with more than one publication in the same year

Quarterly surveys by Business Monitor (2005a, 2005b, 2005c and 2005d) indicated that . . .

Secondary citation

Findings from a case study by Bloomfield (cited in Melrose, 2009) suggest that . . .

Distinguishing authors with the same name

R. Hussey (2006) and A. Hussey (2006) examined the effect of . . .

Under the Harvard system, the bibliographic details of the sources cited in the text are presented in the list of references in alphabetical order by author's name. This list is shown at the end of the document, which means you can still use numbered footnotes or endnotes. The list of references is not included in your word count.

Box 6.3 shows examples of references (and their punctuation) under the Harvard system and Box 6.4 illustrates how they are presented in alphabetical order in the list of references at the end of the document. With e-resources, you need to add the URL for the item (the web link) and date you accessed the item. The latter is shown in square brackets. You are advised to copy and paste the URL, as a full stop, comma or slash in the wrong place can lead to problems for you or anyone else wanting to locate the item.

We also advise that you test the URL to ensure that it does not need updating, before submitting your work.

BOX 6.3   Examples of references

Article in an on-line journal

Collis, J. and Jarvis, R. (2002) 'Financial information and the management of small private companies', *Journal of Small Business and Enterprise Development*, 9 (2), pp. 100–10. http://www.emeraldinsight.com/10.1108/14626000210427357 [Accessed 25 August 2008].

Article in a printed journal

Collis, J., Jarvis, R. and Skerratt, L. (2004) 'The demand for the audit in small companies in the UK', *Accounting and Business Research*, 34 (2), pp. 87–100.

On-line report

Collis, J. (2003) *Directors' Views on Exemption from Statutory Audit*, URN 03/1342, October, London: DTI. http://www.berr.gov.uk/files/file25971.pdf [Accessed 30 June 2008].

Book

Collis, J. and Hussey, R. (2003) *Business Research*, 2nd edition, Basingstoke: Palgrave Macmillan.

Chapter in a book

Collis, J., Dugdale, D. and Jarvis, R. (2001) 'Deregulation of Small Company Reporting in the UK', in McLeay, S. and Riccaboni, A. (eds) *Contemporary Issues in Accounting Regulation*, Boston: Kluwer, pp. 167–85.

BOX 6.4   List of references under the Harvard system

References

Collis, J. (2003) *Directors' Views on Exemption from Statutory Audit*, URN 03/1342, October, London: DTI. http://www.berr.gov.uk/files/file25971.pdf [Accessed 30 June 2008].

Collis, J., Dugdale, D. and Jarvis, R. (2001) 'Deregulation of Small Company Reporting in the UK', in McLeay, S. and Riccaboni, A. (eds) *Contemporary Issues in Accounting Regulation*, Boston: Kluwer, pp. 167–85.

Collis, J. and Hussey, R. (2003) *Business Research*, 2nd edition, Basingstoke: Palgrave Macmillan.

Collis, J. and Jarvis, R. (2002) 'Financial information and the management of small private companies', *Journal of Small Business and Enterprise Development*, 9 (2), pp. 100–10. http://www.emeraldinsight.com/10.1108/14626000210427357 [Accessed 25 August 2008].

Collis, J., Jarvis, R. and Skerratt, L. (2004) 'The demand for the audit in small companies in the UK', *Accounting and Business Research*, 34 (2), pp. 87–100.

6.3.3   THE VANCOUVER SYSTEM

We will explain the *Vancouver system* because it is used in some business disciplines, such as computer sciences. It is also used in mathematics, biochemistry, physics and other natural sciences. In the Vancouver system, citations are acknowledged using sequential superscript numbers throughout the text (instead of author–date) and the references are shown as footnotes or as end notes in numerical order (instead of alphabetical order). Numbered footnotes or endnotes are easy to insert in *Word* and other software programs. However, one of the drawbacks of the Vancouver system is that it prevents you from using numbered footnotes or endnotes for other purposes. Box 6.5 shows how the Vancouver system works in the text and Box 6.6 shows the list of references in numerical order.

BOX 6.5   Citations under the Vancouver system

Authors' words are paraphrased

The availability of data is a key factor in determining the successful outcome of a research project.[1]

or

Collis and Hussey[1] argue that the availability of data is a key factor in determining the successful outcome of a research project.

or authors' words are quoted to emphasize authority of source

'The availability of data is crucial to the successful outcome of your research.'[1]

First citation for three or more authors

Exploratory research by Collis, Dugdale and Jarvis[2] identified . . .

Thereafter

Building on Collis et al.,[3] Collis and Jarvis[4] and Collis et al.,[5] examined . . .

More than one source

Several studies[6–8] have investigated . . .

BOX 6.6   List of references under the Vancouver system

References

[1] Collis, J. and Hussey, R. (2003) *Business Research*, 2nd edition, Basingstoke: Palgrave Macmillan.

[2] Collis, J., Dugdale, D. and Jarvis, R. (2001) 'Deregulation of Small Company Reporting in the UK', in McLeay, S. and Riccaboni, A. (eds) *Contemporary Issues in Accounting Regulation*, Boston: Kluwer, pp. 167–85.

[3] ibid. (the Latin abbreviation of *ibidem*, meaning from the same source as previously cited).

[4] Collis, J. and Jarvis, R. (2002) 'Financial information and the management of small private companies', *Journal of Small Business and Enterprise Development*, 9 (2), pp. 100–10. http://www.emeraldinsight.com/10.1108/14626000210427357 [Accessed 25 August 2008].

[5] Collis, J., Jarvis, R. and Skerratt, L. (2004) 'The demand for the audit in small companies in the UK', *Accounting and Business Research*, 34 (2), pp. 87–100.

[6] Carsberg, B. V., Page, M. J., Sindall, A. J. and Waring, I. D. (1985) *Small Company Financial Reporting*, London: Prentice Hall.

[7] Barker, P. C. and Noonan, C. (1996) *Small Company Compliance with Accounting Standards*, Dublin: Dublin City University.

[8] Pratten, C. (1998) *The Uses of the Accounts of Small and Medium-sized Companies and the Effects of the Audit Exemption Regime*, London: ICAEW.

In this section we have concentrated on the most common needs of students when using citations and references. However, Winkler and McCuen-Metherell (2007) are an excellent source of further information.

6.4   REVIEWING THE LITERATURE

Once you have collected the literature that is relevant to your study, you will need to write a *literature review*. A literature review is a critical evaluation of the existing body of knowledge on a topic, which guides the research and demonstrates that relevant literature has been located and analysed. Therefore, it should provide 'a statement of the state of the art and major questions and issues in the field under consideration' (Gill and Johnson, 1991, p. 21).

At the proposal stage, a preliminary review of the literature helps develop your subject knowledge and provide a context for your research questions. A preliminary review is relatively brief and usually focuses on the seminal studies (the most influential previous research) and the main theories (if appropriate to your paradigm). Most researchers highlight the limitations of their work and suggest avenues for future research. This is useful, because you are looking for gaps and deficiencies in the literature that suggest a business problem or issue to investigate.

When you write a full review of literature for your dissertation or thesis, you will also need to demonstrate an appropriate level of intellectual ability and scholarship. At that stage, your literature review will be large enough to occupy at least one chapter (more than one if the literature is large or your study has been designed as an exhaustive review of the literature).

> **KEY DEFINITIONS**
>
> A literature review is a critical evaluation of the existing body of knowledge on a topic, which guides the research and demonstrates that the relevant literature has been located and analysed.

6.4.1   NATURE AND PURPOSE OF A LITERATURE REVIEW

It may be very satisfying to know that you have a fine collection of literature neatly filed away (or piling up impressively in the corner), but you need to start reading and analysing it in order to develop your research proposal and design your study. As you read, you will learn more about the subject and the methodologies used in previous research. You may find the questions shown in Box 6.7 useful as a checklist when you first start reading the literature.

BOX 6.7   Checklist for reading the literature

- What was the purpose of the study and how does it differ from other studies and my own research?
- How was the research conducted and how does that differ from other studies and my own research?
- What were the findings and how do they differ from other studies and my own research?
- What were the limitations and weaknesses of the study?

6.4.2   GENERAL ANALYTICAL APPROACH

You need to adopt a systematic approach when analysing your collection of articles and other items from the literature. Many researchers adopt a thematic approach, which involves categorizing the themes in the relevant literature. Both subject-related categories and methodology-related categories are likely to be broken down into various subgroups, which will emerge from your reading of the article. Without formally recognizing it, you will begin this process when you generate your key words for searching the literature. Your thematic analysis of the literature can be facilitated if you record key details of the previous studies in a spreadsheet. This allows you to sort the data into different groups to help you structure your literature review (one article is likely to be included in many subgroups). Table 6.3 suggests a basic format, which you can adapt to suit your needs. We have included the standard author–date information to identify the publication, but also the date when the study was conducted, as many articles are not published for a year or more after the research has been completed.

TABLE 6.3 Recording and categorizing previous studies						
Author and date	Subject categories	Methodology categories	Sample size	Response rate (if applicable)	Date of study	Location/ country

6.4.3 NETWORK ANALYSIS OF PRIMARY CITATIONS

Ryan, Scapens and Theobald (2002) offer a structured approach to analysing the literature, using a network diagram to illustrate relationships between primary citations. This approach is based on the assumption that articles in the literature are 'a series of nodes in an interlinked network of theoretical and empirical developments' (Ryan *et al.*, 2002, pp. 186–7). Box 6.8 shows the main steps in constructing a network diagram for this purpose.

BOX 6.8 Procedure for generating a network of primary citations

1. From the literature you have collected, select all the articles that are published in what you consider are the top two or three journals among those represented. From these articles, select those that have been published in the most recent year. These are the ones you will analyse first.

2. Examine each article to identify which item from the literature is the most important to the author's study. This is the primary citation for that article. Do the same for the other articles published that year.

3. Place all the primary citations for the most recent year as nodes in an oval text box at the bottom of your diagram and use Author (Date) to label them.

4. Repeat this process at five-yearly intervals to add new nodes to the diagram that reflect the year of publication. Draw links between nodes to identify the literary antecedents (similar to a family tree). Identify the node that lies at the core of the literature (the one with the most 'descendants') by putting it in a rectangular text box. This allows you to illustrate the theoretical framework that unites the literature.

5. The final step is to determine the motivation for each article, and the methodological rationale that links them.

Source: Adapted from Ryan *et al.* (2002).

6.4.4 WRITING THE LITERATURE REVIEW

Once you have reflected on your analysis, you are ready to start structuring and writing your review of the literature. Box 6.9 provides a general guide to writing a literature review.

BOX 6.9   Guide to writing a literature review

- Select only material that is relevant to the topic, industry, methodology and so on
- Identify themes and group the material
- Define key terms and draw out the important features
- Compare results and methods of previous studies
- Be critical and demonstrate relevance to your research
- Set the context for your study (a deductive approach suggests you will identify a theoretical framework and hypotheses)
- Identify gaps or deficiencies in the literature that your study will address
- Conclude with your research question(s)
- Acknowledge other people's contribution to knowledge using the Harvard system of referencing.

You need to ensure that you have included all the major studies that are relevant to your study. You may also consider it diplomatic to refer to any relevant publication by your supervisor(s) and external examiners! A previous study may be relevant because it focuses on the same or a similar research problem or issue to the one you have in mind. Sometimes students become disillusioned because they think there is no literature on the issue they want to investigate. For example, if you are investigating labour turnover in hotels in Poland, perhaps you will not be able to find any other similar studies. However, you may find research has been done on this topic in other countries or there are studies of other HRM issues in Poland that illuminate your research. A second way in which previous research can be relevant is the methodology used. References to studies that have used the research methodology you propose using, or a different research methodology in a similar subject area, are essential. If you decide the item is not relevant, put it in a safe place in case you change your mind later.

A critical analysis of the literature identifies and appraises the contribution to knowledge made by others and comments on any weaknesses. Such comments may focus on such matters as the reliability, validity and generalizability of the findings, which we discussed in Chapter 4. The gaps and deficiencies in the literature are relevant because they suggest the specific areas where further research is needed. Most researchers highlight the limitations of their work and suggest avenues for future research. If you have difficulty in identifying a specific research problem or issue, consider:

- testing a theory in a different setting
- making a new analysis of existing data
- replicating a previous study to provide up-to-date knowledge.

Reviewing the literature involves 'locating, reading and evaluating reports of research as well as reports of casual observation and opinion' (Borg and Gall, 1989, p. 114). Therefore, a literature review is not merely a description of previous studies and other material you collected during your literature search but requires a critical analysis. Unfortunately, some students do not recognize this, as Bruce (1994) found out. She analysed the views of 41 students at an early stage in their studies and identified six ways in which they viewed the literature review. It may be useful to think of these categories as being successive layers in a student's understanding of the nature of and purpose of a literature review, with the deeper level of understanding captured by the last three descriptions:

- a list, with the primary focus on listing what was read, rather than extracting and using the knowledge in the literature
- a search, with the emphasis on finding the existing literature
- a survey, where the researcher is interested in the knowledge in the literature, but does not relate it to his or her own activities
- a vehicle for learning, where the researcher considers he or she is improving his or her personal knowledge on the subject
- a research facilitator, where the researcher improves not only his or her own knowledge, but the literature has an impact on the research project itself
- a report, which is a synthesis of the literature and the earlier experiences the researcher has engaged in.

Box 6.10 shows a simple example of how to avoid summarizing one article after another and turning your review into the equivalent of a shopping list.

BOX 6.10 Avoiding a shopping list approach

Shopping list approach

Davis (2005) found that white rabbits bred more prolifically than those with dark coloured fur.

Smith (2006) argued that Davis had not defined 'dark' fur.

Jones (2007) used five well-defined colours of rabbit in his study and found white rabbits were the most prolific breeders.

Attempt at synthesis

The identification of the colour of a rabbit's fur as a predictor of fertility is controversial. Although it has been claimed that white rabbits are more prolific breeders than other colours (Davis, 2005), the reliability of this conclusion has been questioned on the grounds that non-white colours have not been clearly defined (Smith, 2006). Evidence from a recent study by Jones (2007) suggests that white rabbits are indeed more prolific breeders than four other well-defined colours of rabbit.

6.5 AVOIDING PLAGIARISM

Plagiarism is the act of taking someone's words, ideas or other information and passing them off as your own because you fail to acknowledge the original source. It is a form of academic misconduct that is taken very seriously, as it is the equivalent of stealing intellectual property.

Plagiarism is easily avoided if you follow the rules of one of the standard referencing systems, such as the Harvard or Vancouver systems we have described in this chapter. In this chapter, we have emphasized the absolute necessity of applying the rules of the referencing system you are using when writing your literature review, but we would now like to emphasize that this is necessary throughout your work, whether you are writing your research proposal, the final dissertation or thesis, or an academic paper after you have completed your research.

The reason why it is imperative you avoid plagiarism is that your supervisors, examiners and others evaluating your research need to distinguish between the contribution to knowledge made by others and the contribution made by your study. It is your responsibility to ensure that your work is meticulously referenced, that every quotation is enclosed in quotation marks and, whether it is text, a table, a diagram or other item that is reproduced, you show it exactly as it is in the original. This includes the punctuation, any emphasis (such as capital letters, italics or bold) and layout. This does not apply if you are using your own words or developing someone else's table, diagram or other item, where you still acknowledge the source but can present the data as you choose.

We now want to explain a different example of plagiarism, which concerns submitting a piece of your own work for assessment if you have already received credits for it on another course. You cannot use the same research report you had assessed as part of a previous course or degree programme as your dissertation or thesis for a subsequent award.

It is not a defence to say you were not aware that you had committed plagiarism. Therefore, you need to familiarize yourself with the regulations (and penalties) that apply in your institution. If you are still in any doubt about what constitutes plagiarism, seek advice from your supervisor. To help you avoid the pitfalls, Box 6.11 provides a checklist for referencing.

BOX 6.11 Checklist for referencing under the Harvard system

- Have I acknowledged other people's work, ideas and all sources of secondary data?
- Have I enclosed quotations in quotation marks and cited the author(s), date and page number in the original source?
- Have I acknowledged the source of all tables, diagrams and other items reproduced, including the number of the page in the original source?
- Have I applied the rules consistently?
- Have I included full bibliographic details for every source cited in my list of references?

6.6 CONCLUSIONS

Searching and reviewing the literature is a major part of your research and, although an intensive phase at the start of the project, will continue on a smaller scale until you submit your dissertation or thesis. Therefore, it is essential to start as soon as possible. This will be when you have chosen a general topic that is relevant to your course; it does not matter that you have not yet identified a particular research problem or issue to investigate, because you will identify this from studying the literature and identifying the need for your study. Most students will be required to incorporate a preliminary literature review in their research proposal, and this will be essential if you are applying for funding. All students will need to write a comprehensive critical literature review for their dissertation or thesis.

Searching the literature is time-consuming. It is rarely a problem locating literature but often a matter of not becoming overwhelmed by the number of items found. In this chapter we have given you guidance on how to define the scope of your research and narrow your search so that you focus as closely as possible on the relevant literature. You will then need to become familiar with the literature, which means setting aside plenty of time to read it, select what is relevant to your study and analyse it using a systematic method. You will write about the methods you used to search the literature (and what sources you searched) and how you analysed the material in your methodology chapter in your dissertation or thesis. In your proposal, you only need to indicate the main sources you will use, such as the journals and databases to which your institution subscribes.

In your literature review, and throughout your research, you must cite your sources correctly and provide full bibliographic details in your list of references. We have explained the principal rules of the Harvard and Vancouver systems, but you must check which system you are expected to use. If your institution uses the APA system, you will find it is very similar to the Harvard system. More information on referencing will be available from your lecturers, supervisors and librarians. It is your responsibility to ensure that you have not committed plagiarism. Many institutions use detection software to check for this and your supervisor will also be alert to this form of cheating. We have warned you about the dangers of plagiarism because it is taken very seriously and the penalties are harsh.

Remember that your literature review is not a shopping list and you must write a critical analysis that provides the context for your research, and concludes by identifying the need for your study and the main research question(s) it addresses. If you are a positivist, an important function of the literature review is to identify your theoretical framework and hypotheses. Box 6.12 shows a checklist for a literature review that draws together some of the key issues.

BOX 6.12 Checklist for the literature review

- Have you cited the most important experts in your field?
- Have you referred to major research studies which have made a contribution to our knowledge?
- Have you referred to articles in the most important academic journals in your area?
- Have you identified any major government or other institutional study in your research field?
- Have you identified studies that use the same paradigms and methodologies you propose?
- Have you identified serious criticisms of any of the studies conducted?
- Have you avoided plagiarism?

ACTIVITIES

1. Take four different journals from different disciplines in your library and identify which system of referencing each journal uses.

2. Using an appropriate bibliographic database, search for information on a well-known company in your own country. Limit your results by date, country or any other variable available on the database. Repeat this with another database and compare the number of 'hits' you get and the features of the search facilities and presentation of the results.

3. Identify a major author in your field of research and conduct a search for all articles he or she has written. If any are co-authored, search for articles published by each author individually.

4. List the main findings of six key articles on your field of research. Then write a synthesis of the findings in no more than two paragraphs.

5. Literature review exercise

The following reviews have been written by two students who have read the same articles. Which do you think is the better review and why?

Review 1

The popularity of roller-blading in the UK has its roots in the 1990s. Jane Iceslider (1990) describes roller-blading as a means of keeping fit for ice skating during the summer months. In a later article she reinforces this view, as evidenced by her comment, 'All my ice-skating friends use roller-blading as part of their fitness training' (Iceslider, 1992, p. 56).

Greg Sniffer, a reformed drug dealer, argues that roller-blades provide 'quick escape from any nosy cops' (Sniffer, 1998, p. 122).

Social worker, John Goodchild, describes roller-blading as 'a non-contact dance replacement activity for young people' (Goodchild, 1996, p. 29). He cites the growing popularity of children's roller discos in support of his claim. In a later article he notes that 'rollerblading is becoming an environmentally friendly means of transportation in urban locations' (Goodchild, 1999, p. 30).

In his school magazine, Jason Scruff, describes roller-blading as being great fun, adding that all his mates go roller-blading (Scruff, J., 1996). In the same article he mentions how using roller-blades allows him to finish his paper round much faster than when walking. In an accompanying article, Melanie Scruff (Jason's sister), contends that 'roller discos are a great place to meet boys' (Scruff, M., 1996, p. 3) and that she would rather roller-blade into town to meet friends on a Saturday than walk or catch the bus.

Review 2

There is little agreement between authors for the reasons why people roller-blade in the UK. Initially it appears to have been a keep-fit activity (Iceslider, 1990 and 1992), but over time roller-blading appears to have become a fashionable activity (Goodchild, 1996), a social activity (Scruff, M., 1996) and a means of transport for work (Sniffer, 1998; Goodchild, 1999) and leisure (Scruff, M. 1996).

There is some evidence that young people have multiple reasons for roller-blading. For example, one teenager's motivation for roller-blading was in part due to following trends, but also to the speed of transportation compared with walking (Scruff, J., 1996).

Although it is possible that Goodchild (1996 and 1999) has based his conclusions on observation of particular cases of children's behaviour, there appears to have been no formal research into the reasons for the popularity of roller-blading in the UK. Therefore, there is scope for an exploratory study to identify the main motivations for the popularity of this activity.

References

Goodchild, J. D. (1996) 'The sociology of rollerblading', Journal of Street Credibility, 1 (1), pp. 29–33.

Goodchild, J. D. (1999) 'Rollerblading to save the planet', Journal of Street Credibility, 3 (3), pp. 8–9.

Iceslider, J. (1990) 'Why I rollerblade', Journal of Fitness, 3 (2), pp. 21–2.

Iceslider, J. (1992) 'Rollerblade your way to fitness', Journal of Fitness, 5 (1), pp. 53–6.

Scruff, J. (1996) 'Roller discos and boys', Kingston School Magazine, Summer term, p. 4.

Scruff, M. (1996) 'Rollerblading is cool', Kingston School Magazine, Summer term, p. 3.

Sniffer, G. (1998) 'How I kicked the habit', Rehabilitation Quarterly, Winter, pp. 122–5.

Adapted from 'A Mock Literature Review' (Anon.)

PROGRESS TEST

Complete the following sentences:

1. In research, the existing body of _____ is known as the literature.

2. A literature search involves collecting secondary _____.

3. Before you can search the literature, you need to identify a number of ____ _____ so that you can search for items that are relevant to your study.

4. The bibliographic list of all the sources of information cited in a document is known as a list of _____.

5. The systematic way in which you search and review the literature is described in your _____ chapter.

Are the following statements true or false?

6. A literature search is not needed if a literature review has already been published on your research topic.

7. A literature review only covers previous research and other sources of relevant published material on the research topic.

8. A literature review is a way of learning about the research topic.

9. A literature review is a systematic survey of relevant publications.

10. A literature review identifies the research questions the researcher will address.

Multiple choice questions:

11. The literature is a source of:
    a) perfect data
    b) primary data
    c) historical data
    d) unpublished data

12. The purpose of a critical literature review is to be:
    a) analytical
    b) complimentary
    c) derogatory
    d) descriptive

13. The result of criticizing constructively or setting out a reasoned argument in steps is known as:
    a) a debate
    b) a devolution
    c) an evaluation
    d) an evolution

14. Using analogy to identify a research topic or methodology involves:
    a) using physical variables to represent numbers
    b) determining the constituent parts of variables
    c) reasoning based on parallel cases
    d) conducting an exploratory study

15. The rationale for using a referencing system is that:
    a) references can be pasted from digital sources
    b) software can be used to organize references
    c) previous studies are identified
    d) the source of existing knowledge is identified

7

Writing your research proposal

Learning objectives

When you have studied this chapter, you should be able to:

- identify a research problem or issue

- determine the purpose of the research

- identify the main research question(s)

- choose the research strategy and methods

- write a research proposal.

7.1   INTRODUCTION

Having identified your research paradigm, selected a research topic and begun to investigate the relevant literature, you are now ready to design your study and write your *research proposal*. If you are a student, the intellectual sophistication and length of your proposal will depend on the level and requirements of your programme, but once accepted by your supervisor(s), this critical document provides you with a detailed plan for your study. If you are bidding for research funds, your proposal will also play an important role.

This chapter draws together much of the information and guidance given in earlier chapters. For most students, writing their research proposal is the first formal milestone in their studies and paves the way for their dissertation or thesis. If you are studying for a Master's degree or a doctorate, it is likely that your research proposal will need to be more substantial than that required at the undergraduate level. This means you will have to spend some time working on it to obtain the approval of your supervisor(s) and/or research committee.

We start by guiding you through the process of designing your research and then go on to explain how to communicate the main features of your proposed study in your research proposal. It is important to remember that we are only able to give general advice, and you will need to follow the specific requirements of your institution.

7.2   OVERVIEW OF RESEARCH DESIGN

Before you can write your research proposal, you must spend some time designing your proposed study. *Research design* is the 'science (and art) of planning procedures for conducting studies so as to get the most valid findings' (Vogt, 1993, p. 196). Determining your research design will give you a detailed plan which you will use to guide and focus your research. Whether you are on an undergraduate course or are a postgraduate student, you will be expected to set out your research design in a document known as a 'research proposal'. This is an important step because it is on the basis of your proposal that your research study will be accepted or rejected.

Before you can begin designing your project, you need to have identified your research paradigm and have chosen a research topic. You will remember that your choice of paradigm has important implications for your choice of research strategy and methods for collecting and analysing data. It also influences your choice of research problem and research questions. Figure 7.1 shows the main steps in research design. This simple model suggests the process is linear and moves smoothly from the research problem to the expected outcome. In practice, however, the process is often circular, reiterative and time-consuming, so do not be surprised if you find yourself constantly reviewing previous stages as you progress.

The first step in designing your research is to identify a *research problem* or issue to investigate. However, you must remember that this does not take place in a vacuum, but in a particular context. Although you may have already determined your research paradigm, you might find that you have selected a research problem where you consider it is necessary to change some of your basic assumptions. Therefore, you may have to review your choice of paradigm and reflect on how appropriate it is to the problem you have identified. Another possibility is that you have picked a problem which is not acceptable to your supervisor or which for practical reasons cannot be investigated.

You will need to refine your research problem by providing a succinct *purpose statement* and developing *research question(s)*. In a positivist study, you will develop a *theoretical*

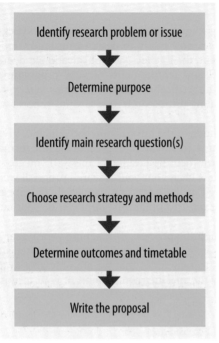

FIGURE 7.1 Main steps in research design

framework which will lead to *hypotheses*. In an interpretivist study, you are more likely to determine the purpose of your research and construct only one or two questions that you will refine and modify, and set within a theoretical context during the course of the research itself. The final stages of your research design will be defining terms, establishing your methodology and giving an indication of the expected outcome. It is important to remember that 'the more sophisticated and rigorous the research design is, the greater the time, costs, and other resources expended on it will be' (Sekaran, 2003, p. 118).

In the following sections we consider each of these activities separately. However, it is important to remember that although we have shown them in a linked sequence, in practice, research is seldom quite so straightforward and orderly. It is highly likely that you will have to retrace your steps and review some of the earlier stages as more information and more problems come to light in the later stages of constructing your research design. We will now examine each of the stages of research design shown in Figure 7.1 in detail.

7.3   THE RESEARCH PROBLEM

7.3.1   IDENTIFYING A RESEARCH PROBLEM

You will remember from previous chapters that a research project must focus on a specific *problem* or issue. If you are a student, this topic must be relevant to your degree programme and, if you are receiving funding, it must be relevant to your sponsor. Of course, it must also be a topic that is of interest to you!

When you have chosen your research problem, you will find it useful to write a simple statement describing it to help you to remain focused while planning the design of your research. Table 7.1 gives some examples of business research problems other students have identified.

Identifying a research problem or issue is always an exploratory and reiterative phase in your research. There are a number of ways in which you can develop your ideas within a general topic of interest. These include reading the relevant literature, discussions with your lecturers and other students, and looking at previous students' dissertations and theses. When choosing a research problem, you need to bear in mind that your study must be achievable in terms of the resources available, your skills and the time constraints imposed by the submission date. It must also be sufficiently challenging to meet the academic standards expected at your level of study.

> **KEY DEFINITIONS**
>
> The research problem is the specific problem or issue that is the focus of the research.

TABLE 7.1 Examples of research problems

Research topic	Research problem
Accounting regulations	Whether accounting practices should be regulated by the government or by the accounting profession
Corporate governance	How corporate governance can be extended to employee communications
Financial accounting in the NHS	The use of financial accounting by doctors in general practice
Financial reporting	The most effective ways for communicating financial information to stakeholders
Environmental issues in accounting ethics	The criteria by which shareholders measure 'green' companies
Environmental issues in manufacturing	The influence of 'green' factors on supplier selection in the manufacturing sector
Gender issues in employment	The effect of career-break schemes on the recruitment and retention of skilled staff
Public service announcements as a method of communication	The effectiveness of public service announcements for communicating with students

The classic way in academic research is to read the literature on the topic of interest to you and identify any gaps and deficiencies in previous studies, since these will indicate opportunities for further research. Figure 7.2 shows a useful procedure for doing this. Identifying a research problem or issue can be a lengthy business since you have to keep revising your initial ideas and referring to the literature until you arrive at a business problem or issue you think will lead to a researchable project. You know that you are arriving at this stage when you can start generating suitable research questions.

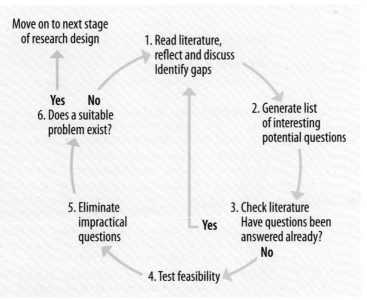

FIGURE 7.2 Identifying a research problem

Your initial search will probably result in three or four projects within your broad area of interest. You now need to compare them so that you can select one. At this stage it is helpful to eliminate any research problem which you consider is less likely to lead to a successful outcome. Although you may select a topic that is of great interest to you (and your supervisor), at the end of the day you will want to submit a research report which receives a high mark from the examiner or is accepted by the research/doctoral committee. Therefore, you need to examine your list of potential research problems critically and make certain that you select the one which is likely to give you the highest chance of success. We next discuss the specific issues that give some indication of which of the research problems or points you identify are likely to be the most researchable.

7.3.2   ACCESS TO DATA

KEY DEFINITIONS

Data are known facts or things used as a basis for inference or reckoning.

The availability of data is crucial to the successful outcome of your research. The term data refers to known facts or things used as a basis for inference or analysis. You will need to find out whether you will be able to have access to all the secondary and/or primary data you need for your study. Although you may be able to think of a number of interesting problems, your final choice may be constrained because the necessary data is either not available or is very difficult to collect.

Many students fail to appreciate the barriers to collecting data. For example, postal questionnaire response rates are often very low; 20% is typical. Companies will rarely give commercially sensitive information and in many cases may not have suitable records to allow them to give the required data. Therefore, before deciding on your research project, you must be sure that you will be able to get the data and other information you will need to conduct your research. Table 7.2 provides a checklist which you may find useful for assessing the availability of data.

TABLE 7.2 Assessing the availability of data

Type of data	Source
The literature	Check databases containing academic articles, the library catalogue, and internet resources.
Official statistics	National jurisdictions, the European Commission and international organizations such as the World Bank publish statistics on their websites. Some may be available in your library.
Industry data	You may need background information about a particular industry. Check your library catalogue, databases and the internet.
Company data	Information is available on the company's website and the company's annual report and accounts (which contains extensive narrative information in the case of listed companies). Check your library catalogue for other publications.
Internal data	List the information you will require and get permission/confirmation of access in writing. Do not use unethical methods, such as asking a friend who happens to work in the accounts department!
People	How many will you need to see? Do you know them already? Have you got the necessary communication skills and recording equipment? Do you have sufficient funds and time?
Surveys	Where will you find a list of relevant organizations and contact details? How many interviews or questionnaires will you need for your analysis? What response rate to do you anticipate? Do you have sufficient funds and time?

7.3.3 YOUR SKILLS AND RESOURCES

When planning your research, you need to consider what you will need to know and do to complete your research. You should be able to gain a reasonable understanding of your subject area by reading the relevant literature search, but you will also need other skills, such as:

- IT skills for searching the literature and analysing data
- creative skills for designing questions and communicating concepts
- verbal communication skills for interviewing
- knowledge of statistics if you are planning a quantitative analysis
- general analytical skills if you are planning to interpret qualitative data
- verbal and written communication skills for presenting your research.

If you know that you have certain weaknesses, you need to assess whether you can overcome them in the time available. Your project is a period of development and you should welcome any opportunity to improve your skills and exploit your existing strengths.

When considering different research problems, it is useful to look at the implications of your choice. Creswell (1994) offers the criteria shown in Box 7.1 which can be used in assessing a research topic.

BOX 7.1   Criteria for assessing a research topic

- Is the topic researchable, given time, resources, and availability of data?
- Is there a personal interest in the topic in order to sustain attention?
- Will the results from the study be of interest to others [...]?
- Is the topic likely to be publishable in a scholarly journal (or attractive to a [research] ... committee?
- Does the study (a) fill a void, (b) replicate, (c) extend, or (d) develop new ideas in the scholarly literature?
- Will the project contribute to career goals?

Source: Creswell (1994, p. 3).

7.4 PURPOSE OF THE RESEARCH

7.4.1 DETERMINING THE UNIT OF ANALYSIS

Once you have chosen a suitable research problem or issue, your next task is to identify the overall *purpose* of the research and determine the *unit of analysis*. The unit of analysis is the phenomenon under study, about which data are collected and analysed, and is closely linked to the research problem and research questions. In business research, a unit of analysis might be a particular organization, division or department within an organization, or a more general group, such as business owners, managers, advisers or regulators. It could also be an inanimate object such as a particular type of event, decision, procedure, contract or communication (Blumberg, Cooper and Schindler, 2005).

KEY DEFINITIONS

The unit of analysis is the phenomenon under study, about which data are collected and analysed.

Kervin (1992) suggests that it is generally best to select a unit of analysis at as low a level as possible. This should be at the level where decisions are made. Table 7.3 shows the different units of analysis, starting at the lowest and simplest level.

TABLE 7.3   Units of analysis

Unit of analysis	Example
An individual	A manager, union member, lender, supplier or customer
An event	A merger, strike, relocation, acquisition, change of leadership, decision to diversify or expand
An object	A machine, a product, service, or document
An organization or group of people	A type of business, division, department, committee or level of employee
A relationship	A customer/supplier relationship, manager/subordinate relationship, management/union relationship or head office/branch relationship
An aggregate	A collection of undifferentiated individuals or bodies with no internal structure, such as companies in a certain industry, businesses of a certain size or in a particular location

Source: Adapted from Kervin (1992, pp. 87–9).

Once you have determined your unit of analysis, you can state the purpose of your study clearly and succinctly. This can be achieved by writing a *purpose statement*. The purpose statement is usually only two or three sentences long and is normally provided in a separate section in the research proposal (and subsequently in the final research report). The content of the purpose statement depends on whether you are designing your research under a positivist or an interpretivist paradigm.

7.4.2   PURPOSE STATEMENT IN A POSITIVIST STUDY

In a positivist study, a purpose statement identifies the variables to be studied, the relevant theory and the methods to be employed. It should also refer to the sample and the unit of analysis.

When writing your purpose statement for your proposal, you will use the future tense, but in your research report, dissertation or thesis you will use the past tense because the study will have been completed. Your writing style will reflect your rhetorical assumptions. You will write in a formal style using the passive voice, accepted quantitative words and set definitions. For example, instead of writing 'I will hold interviews with …' or 'I held interviews with …' you will write 'Interviews will be held with …' or 'Interviews were held with …'. You are trying to convey the philosophical assumptions (see Chapter 4) that are appropriate to your paradigm, emphasizing your independence from what you propose to study and your objectivity in measuring reality.

Creswell (1994) suggests that scripting can be useful when preparing a purpose statement, which involves filling in blanks in text based on cues in the sentence. Box 7.2 shows a simple model for a positivist study that can be used as the basis for constructing your purpose statement (the alternatives in brackets are the prompts).

> **KEY DEFINITIONS**
>
> A purpose statement is a statement (usually two or three sentences long) that describes the overall purpose of the research study.

7.4.3   PURPOSE STATEMENT IN AN INTERPRETIVIST STUDY

There is more variation among purpose statements relating to interpretivist studies. It is normal to emphasize the methodology employed and to imply the inductive nature of the research. The central phenomenon being explored should be described as well as the location for the study. To reflect the rhetorical assumption of this paradigm, you should write in an informal style and use the personal voice, accepted qualitative terms and limited definitions. For example, instead of writing 'Interviews will be held with …' or 'Interviews were held with …', you will write 'I will hold interviews with …' or 'I held interviews with …'. Throughout the purpose statement, you are trying to convey the philosophical assumptions that are appropriate to your paradigm, emphasizing your interaction with what you propose to study and your subjectivity in interpreting reality.

BOX 7.2   Simple model of a purpose statement for a positivist study

The purpose of this _____ (experimental? survey?) study _____ (is? was? will be?) to test the theory of _____ that _____ (compares? relates?) the _____ (independent variable) to _____ (dependent variable) for _____ (subjects? sample?) at _____ (research site). The independent variable(s) _____ will be defined generally as _____ (provide general definition). The dependent variable(s) will be defined generally as _____ (provide general definitions), and the intervening variable(s), _____ (identify the intervening variables) will be statistically controlled in the study.

Source: Creswell (1994, p. 64).

Box 7.3 illustrates a simple model that can be used as the basis of a purpose statement for an interpretivist study.

BOX 7.3   Simple model of a purpose statement for an interpretivist study

The purpose of this study _____ (is? was? will be?) to _____ (understand? describe? develop? discover?) the _____ (central concept being studied) for _____ (the unit of analysis: a person? processes? groups? site?) using a _____ (method of inquiry: ethnographical design? grounded theory design? case study design? phenomenological design?) resulting in a _____ (cultural picture? grounded theory? case study? phenomenological description of themes or patterns?). At this stage in the research the _____ (central concept being studied) will be defined generally as _____ (provide a general definition of the central concept).

Source: Creswell (1994, p. 59).

7.5   THE RESEARCH QUESTIONS

7.5.1   IDENTIFYING RESEARCH QUESTION(S)

Whereas the purpose statement gives details of the general direction of the study, a *research question* states the specific line of enquiry the research will investigate and attempt to answer. Therefore, your research questions provide a focus for your endeavours and are not the actual questions you might use in a questionnaire or interview. Identifying the research question(s) is a crucial stage in your research because it lies at the heart of your research design.

Figure 7.3 shows a simple model of how you can develop research questions. At each stage in the process you need to read, reflect and discuss what you are doing with others. The people you discuss your research with may be fellow students as well as your supervisor. We have already identified research as a process of enquiry, so the outcome of your investigation will be answers.

KEY DEFINITIONS

A research question is a specific question the research is designed to investigate and attempt to answer.

However, you must ensure that the answers will be of interest or importance, otherwise your research will not receive much attention.

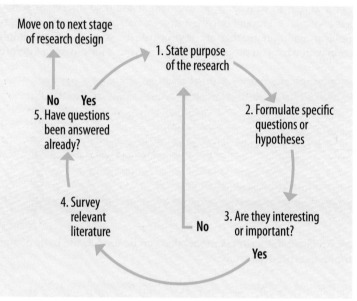

FIGURE 7.3 Identifying research questions

Before launching your investigations, you must search the relevant literature to see if anyone else has already answered your particular questions. If not, you can commence your research. However, if work has already been done in your chosen area, you may have to find ways of amending your proposed research so that it will produce new findings by extending or updating the existing body of knowledge.

7.5.2 ROLE OF THEORY

A *theoretical framework* is a collection of *theories* and models from the literature. It is a fundamental part of most research studies and underpins the research questions. However, these can also be suggested by empirical evidence (from an exploratory study, for example), from which you subsequently develop a theory and construct propositions to test. A *theory* is 'a set of interrelated constructs (variables), definitions and propositions that presents a systematic view of phenomena by specifying relationships among variables with the purpose of explaining natural phenomena' (Kerlinger, 1979, p. 64). On a more simple level, theories are 'explanations of how things function or why events occur' (Black, 1993, p. 25).

Although some applied research has no theoretical background, if theory exists, you can develop a testable *hypothesis*. A hypothesis is a proposition that can be tested for association or causality against empirical evidence using statistics. Thus, hypotheses are associated with the positivist paradigm where the logic of the research is deductive and quantitative methods of analysis are used. However, Blaikie (2000, p. 10) argues that in some studies 'the testing is more in terms of a discursive argument from evidence' rather than the results of statistical tests.

According to Merriam (1988), theories can be classified into three types:

- grand theories, which are most often found in the natural sciences
- middle-range theories, which are placed higher than mere working hypotheses, but do not have the status of a grand theory
- substantive theories, which are developed within a certain context.

Laughlin (1995) argues that in the social sciences it is not possible to have a grand theory, only skeletal theory, where 'empirical data will always be of importance to make the skeleton complete in particular contexts' (Laughlin, 1995, p. 81). This does not mean that the theory will be changed or permanently completed, but will remain as a general framework within which a study can be conducted. Glaser and Strauss (1967) emphasize the importance of substantive theories, where theory is derived from the data (which they describe as *grounded theory*).

Given these differences of opinion, you may find it confusing trying to develop a theoretical framework. However, there are a number of theories, concepts and models from which you can draw, and you will discover them when you study the literature on your chosen topic. They are important in many studies because they provide possible explanations for what is observed.

7.5.3 RESEARCH QUESTIONS IN A POSITIVIST STUDY

For a study designed under a positivist paradigm, Black (1993) recommends a specific research question, followed by a number of *hypotheses*. Kerlinger (1986)]suggests that good research questions for a positivist study should:

- express a relationship between variables
- be stated in unambiguous terms in question form
- imply the possibility of empirical testing.

Your hypotheses will be based on theory. Each hypothesis is a proposition about the relationship between two variables that can be tested for association or causality against the empirical evidence you collect for your study.

Your hypothesis will identify the independent variable and the dependent variable. The null hypothesis (H_0) states that the two variables are independent of one another and the alternate hypothesis (H_1) states that they are associated with one another. The null hypothesis is always stated first. For example, if you thought that older employees might work more slowly than young employees, your null hypothesis would be:

H_0 There is no relationship between an employee's age and productivity.
H_1 There is a relationship between an employee's age and productivity.

In this example, age is the independent variable and productivity is the dependent variable. The purpose of your research will be to test specific aspects of any theory you may have found in the literature which suggests that there is a relationship between age and productivity level. Using the null hypothesis ensures that you adopt a cautious and critical approach when you are conducting statistical tests on your data.

Sometimes theory suggests that there is a possible direction for the relationship. In this case, you may decide to use a directional hypothesis. For example:

H_0 Productivity does not decrease as an employee increases in age.
H_1 Productivity decreases as an employee increases in age.

As you will have a number of hypotheses, it is important to use a formal, rhetorical style by repeating the same key phrases in the same order. For example:

There is no relationship between an employee's age and the level of productivity.
There is no relationship between an employee's age and the level of absenteeism.
There is no relationship between an employee's age and degree of skill.

7.5.4   RESEARCH QUESTIONS IN AN INTERPRETIVIST STUDY

In an interpretivist study, a theoretical framework may be less important or less clear in its structure. Some researchers attempt to approach their analysis with no prior theories, as they consider doing so would constrain and blinker them. Instead, they focus on trying to develop a theoretical framework, which is sometimes referred to as a model or substantive theory. It has been argued that 'even in wanting to escape theory, to be open-minded or wanting to believe that theorizing was unimportant to science, we would be practising a theory' (Slife and Williams, 1995, p. 9).

In some interpretivist studies, the research question takes the form of a grand tour question (Werner and Schoepfle, 1987), which is a single research question posed in its most general form. For example, 'How do employees cope with redundancy in an area of high unemployment?' By doing this, the researcher does not block off any other potential lines of enquiry. This is necessary where an emerging methodology, such as grounded theory, is used and one stage of the research guides the next stage. Nevertheless, the aim of a grand tour question is to focus the study on certain phenomena or a particular direction. It may need to be refined during the course of the research and this may mean you need to change the title of your project to reflect the final research question(s). Creswell (1994) advises one or two grand tour questions, followed by no more than five to seven subsidiary questions.

The criteria for a good research question are less clear in interpretivist studies than in positivist studies. This is due to the importance of the interaction between the researcher and the subject of the study in the former. If you are planning to conduct an interpretivist study, you will find that your research questions often evolve during the process of research and may need to be refined or modified as the study progresses. You will find that there are different customs in different interpretivist methodologies, which will be apparent from the literature you read on your topic. The best advice is to concentrate on the language of the question. It is usual to begin the research questions with 'what' or 'how' and to avoid terms associated with positivism, such as 'cause', 'relationship' or 'association'. Creswell (1994) suggests that you should:

- avoid wording that suggests a relationship between variables, such as 'effect', 'influence', 'impact' or 'determine'
- use open-ended questions without reference to the literature or theory, unless otherwise dictated by the research design
- use a single focus and specify the research site.

Finally, you should not underestimate the influence of your paradigm on your research design. Box 7.4 illustrates this with two examples based on the same research problem and research questions.

BOX 7.4   Example of the influence of paradigm on research design

Topic: Gender issues in employment

Research problem: The effect of the new career-break scheme in Firm A on the recruitment and retention of skilled staff

Research question: How has the new career-break scheme contributed to employment in Firm A?

- What is the nature of the scheme? (descriptive)
- What effect has it had on recruitment of male and female skilled staff? (analytical)
- What effect has it had on the retention of male and female skilled staff? (analytical)

Methodology for a positivist study:

- Research strategy: Case study
- Methods: Statistical analysis of (a) secondary data from staff employment records and (b) primary data from a self-completion questionnaire survey of staff

Methodology for an interpretive study:

- Research strategy: Case study
- Methods: Thematic analysis of data from semi-structured interviews with staff (primary data)

7.6   WRITING THE RESEARCH PROPOSAL

7.6.1   OVERVIEW

A research proposal is a document that sets out the research design for a proposed study. It explains what is already known about the research topic, the purpose of the research and the main research question(s). It also describes the proposed methodology (including justification for the methods used to select a sample, collect and analyse the research data), the scope of the research and any limitations. It should incorporate a timetable and often concludes with comments on the contribution of the proposed research (the expected outcomes).

> **KEY DEFINITIONS**
>
> A research proposal is a document that sets out the research design for a proposed study.

Most institutions have a formal process for submitting a research proposal and instructions concerning the contents and the maximum word count. Your supervisor and/or research committee will be looking at academic issues as well as the feasibility of the proposed study.

The main academic issues being assessed are:

- The proposed study is based on the literature and is academically robust. You do this by demonstrating that you are familiar with the literature and have identified a main research question.
- The methodology clearly states the source(s) from which you will collect the research data, why you are collecting the data, when you are going to collect the data, and how you are going to collect and analyse the data. Be careful not to overlook the importance of explaining your method for selecting a sample or cases and your method(s) of analysis.
- Postgraduate students may need to state how the proposed study will make a contribution to knowledge and doctoral students may have to identify conferences and academic journals where they plan to disseminate their research.

The main practical issues being assessed are:

- You have access to the research data (primary, secondary or both). If your research requires access to confidential data, you must provide documentary evidence from the organization(s) and/or individual(s) confirming that access has been granted.
- You have access to any finance needed to conduct the research and there are no major time constraints that would prevent the completion of the project. Therefore, if you are struggling on a student grant, do not design a study that requires extensive travelling to obtain your data that would be both time-consuming and expensive.
- The outcome is achievable.

Although it is best to use the standard format if your institution provides one, there is still plenty of flexibility to allow you to put your research proposal in its best light. Table 7.4 shows a typical structure of a research proposal, together with some guidance on the proportion of space you should consider devoting to each section.

TABLE 7.4 Indicative structure of a research proposal

	% of proposal
1. Introduction - The research problem or issue and the purpose of the study - Background to the study and why it is important or of interest - Structure of the remainder of the proposal	15
2. Preliminary review of the literature - Evaluation of key items in the literature - Theoretical framework (if applicable) - Where your research fits in and the main research question(s)	40
3. Methodology - Identification of paradigm - Justification for choice of methodology and methods - Scope of the research and the limitations of the research design	40
4. Outcomes and timetable	5
References (do not number this section)	100

The detailed content of your proposal will depend on the nature of your research project and how you intend to conduct it, but we are now ready to look at the main items.

7.6.2 TITLE

The title of your proposed study should be as brief as possible. Creswell (1994) advises that you should not use more than 12 words and that you should consider eliminating most articles and prepositions, and make sure that it includes the focus or topic of the study. Wilkinson (1991) suggests that you eliminate superfluous words, such as 'Approach to …' or 'A study of …'. If you are carrying out research in one particular company or industry, make this clear.

7.6.3   INTRODUCTION

The research problem or issue that is the focus of the study should be stated clearly in your introduction. It can usually be expressed in one or two sentences. Resist the temptation to write in sentences that are so long that no one can understand them! Try showing your explanation of the research problem to fellow students, family and friends; if they understand it, it is likely you will impress your supervisor with your clarity.

You may find it helpful to follow this with a little background explaining why this issue is important or of interest, and to whom. This would be an appropriate place to define key terms as they arise in your narrative. You could conclude the introduction by explaining the purpose of the proposed study (using one of the model purpose statements we illustrated earlier, if you find this helpful).

You should define key terms (and any common terms you are using in a novel way) on the first occasion that you use them. You should use a definition from an authoritative academic source, such as a specialist dictionary in your discipline. We do not advise you to use Wikipedia or on-line sources from websites that can be posted or edited by the public. Remember that the definition should be in quotation marks and you should cite the name of the author(s), the year of publication and page number(s) in brackets next to the quotation. In a positivist study, this is essential and enhances the precision and rigour of your research.

7.6.4   PRELIMINARY LITERATURE REVIEW

Your preliminary review of the literature should be a critical analysis of the main studies published that are relevant to your chosen research problem or issue you intend to investigate. Do not fall into the trap of taking a 'shopping list' approach to writing about the previous research you have identified in academic journals, books and other sources and remember that your lecturer's slides are not publications! At this stage, you are not expected to review the entire body of existing knowledge on the topic. Your supervisor will be familiar with the literature, so it is imperative that you cite the key authors and refer to the main theories and models. If you are using grounded theory in an interpretivist study, you will still write a preliminary review of the literature, but you will not need to identify a theoretical framework. If you are adopting a grounded theory methodology, you will need to provide a convincing argument for this choice in your methodology section.

Your preliminary literature review should conclude with an explanation of where your research fits into the gaps in the literature (for example where no knowledge exists about a particular phenomenon in a particular context) or deficiencies in the literature (for example where existing knowledge is out of date). This will include stating your main research question(s) and hypotheses (if applicable). Of course, your research question(s) must relate to the research problem you identified in your introduction, and they must be feasible. It is better to omit a question if you know it will be very difficult to address, rather than include it because it looks impressive.

7.6.5   METHODOLOGY

The methodology section in your proposal is where you explain and justify your proposed research strategy and methods for selecting a sample or cases, and for collecting and analysing the data. This section is important because it shows how you intend to investigate your research questions. You should be aware by now that your choice is dictated by your research paradigm. Therefore, it is essential to recognize the paradigm you have adopted, but you do not need to justify it. You can provide a rationale for your choice of methodology by weighing up the advantages and disadvantages of alternatives.

Whatever the size of your proposed study, you will have to constrain your enquiries in a number of ways. Therefore, you will need to state the *delimitations* that establish the scope of your research. For example, you may confine your interviews to employees in Firm A or you may restrict your postal questionnaire to particular businesses in a particular geographical area. It can be more difficult to define the scope in an interpretivist study because the nature of the research is one of exploration and discovery.

An approach that can be used under either paradigm is to deconstruct your research question or hypothesis. Parker (1994) illustrates this with a hypothesis from a positivist study, which is shown in Figure 7.4. The process enables you to explain every term in considerable detail within the context of your proposed research. Not only does this give you considerable insight into your research, but you are in a better position to communicate it in your proposal (and dissertation, thesis or research report).

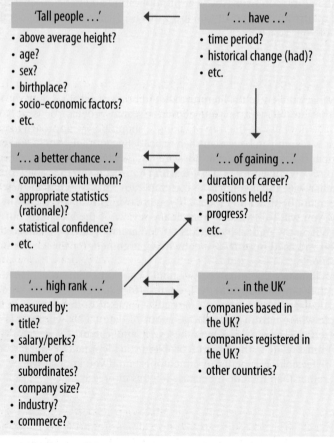

FIGURE 7.4 Example of deconstruction
'Tall people have a better chance of gaining high rank in the UK'
Source: Adapted from Parker (1994, p. 24).

Most students will need to discuss issues such as reliability, validity and generalizability, and all students should state the *limitations* of their study. A limitation describes a weakness or deficiency in the research. For example, you may be planning a small exploratory study, from which only tentative conclusions can be drawn. This might be because you are planning a positivist study using a convenience sample rather than a random sample, or you are planning an interpretivist study but do not have the resources to conduct an in-depth case study. Sometimes additional limitations become apparent after the proposal stage and you will need to comment on these when you write your dissertation or thesis.

> **KEY DEFINITIONS**
>
> A delimitation establishes the scope of the research.
>
> A limitation is a weakness or deficiency in the research.

Students are often reluctant to mention problems with their research. There is no need to emphasize them at the proposal stage, and a comment is usually sufficient. However, you should not ignore them, as they serve two useful purposes:

- to identify potential difficulties, which can be discussed with your supervisor to ascertain whether they need to be resolved or whether they are acceptable in the context of your research design
- to signal at an early stage some of the issues you will need to address during the course of the research and when writing up the research.

7.6.6 OUTCOMES AND TIMETABLE

At the proposal stage, you cannot describe the outcome of your research in terms of your findings. Therefore, the final section in your proposal is brief and will focus on the expected contribution of the research. One way to express this is to refer to the purpose of the research. For example, if the purpose of your research is to investigate the impact of a new career-break scheme in Firm A, your expected outcomes are a description of the new scheme and an analysis of the impact of the scheme on the recruitment and retention of staff in Firm A. At all levels of research, but particularly at the doctoral level, it is important to emphasize that one outcome of the research is expected to be a contribution to knowledge. In your proposal, this can be stated in terms of the gaps and deficiencies you have identified in the literature.

Your proposed study must take account of the time constraints placed on the project by the submission date. You can use a Gantt chart with horizontal lines showing the timing of each stage to summarize your timetable. We advise you to discuss your draft timetable with your supervisor. Even experienced researchers find that research always takes up more time than you think it will, so do allow a contingency for delays due to exams, job interviews, holidays, illness and so on. Jankowicz (1991) gives estimates of standard times for some project activities. These include one day for preparing a ten-question interview schedule and four weeks for piloting a large questionnaire. You must be realistic about the amount of time you have available and what you can achieve in that time.

7.6.7 ADDITIONAL INFORMATION

In some cases, you may need to include a statement of special resources required in your proposal (for example specialist software or access to particular libraries or organizations). If you are applying for funding, you will need to supply a budget for travelling to interviews, printing questionnaires, postage, purchasing reports and papers that are not available on loan and so on. Table 7.5 shows an example of how you might set out your budget (the figures are illustrative and the cost of the researcher's time is not included).

TABLE 7.5 Research budget

Nature of expense	Basis of calculation	Cost €	Comment
Travelling expenses	30 interviews at €30 each	900	Car mileage from the university
Research reports	10 reports at €15 each	150	Not available from library
Research assistant	100 hours at €15 per hour	1,500	Data input and analysis
Conference	Fees, travel and hotel	1,020	Dissemination of results
Submission of article	Submission fee	30	*World Journal of Management*
	Total	3,600	

If you are applying for funding, you may also be asked to provide a *statement of research activities and interests* to provide evidence of your suitability to carry out the proposed study. Box 7.5 shows an example of a suitable succinct statement that can be used as the basis for constructing your own.

BOX 7.5 Statement of research activities and interests

For the past four years I have been very interested in the financial measures used to evaluate the performance of managers. This interest originated with my MBA. My dissertation, which received a distinction, was entitled 'The behavioural aspects of a budgetary control system in a small engineering company'. From this I have developed three main areas of interest:

- Managerial performance measures in small manufacturing companies
- Managerial performance measures in financial services companies
- Managerial performance measures in charities.

My research into these issues has resulted in five conference papers and two refereed journal articles, as shown in my CV. In the past two years I have spent approximately 70% of my research time conducting studies in XYZ Charity. This is a national charity to which I have full access, as confirmed in the attached letter from their CEO. My proposed research would take my previous research further by . . .

7.6.8 REFERENCES

The Harvard system of referencing is the method most commonly used in business and management. It allows you to avoid plagiarism by acknowledging all ideas and sources of information you have used in your work with a *citation* in the text and providing full bibliographic details at the end under the heading of *references*. Do not number the heading of this section and do not number the items listed, but place them in alphabetical order by author's name. This will allow any reader to locate and consult the original source of information; you can support all your assertions with an authoritative published source; and you can also show your supervisor the extent of your reading. Remember that however flattering it may be to your lecturers to be cited, their lecture slides are not a publication and you need to refer to the original publications to which they refer.

A citation is made whether the information from your reading of a publication takes the form of a quotation or is summarized in your own words. If you are quoting, or reproducing a table or figure, your citation must include the page number(s) as well as the name(s) of the author(s) and the year of publication. You should bear in mind that your ability to apply the accepted system of referencing is one of the criteria against which your proposal will be assessed.

The more academic articles, reports, books and so on, you have read on your research topic or on research methods, the more citations you will have made and the longer your list of references will be. Therefore, you need to keep careful records of all the hard copy and internet sources you have used. Check that every citation in your proposal has a corresponding entry in your list of references and that you have not listed any items that you did not use and therefore did not cite. It is likely that your supervisor will do this when marking your proposal!

7.6.9 EVALUATING YOUR PROPOSAL

You will find that a considerable part of research involves reflecting on the work you have done. Designing your research is no exception. The most common reason for students failing at the proposal stage is because they have not been able to convert their general interest in a topic into the design of a study that will allow them to investigate a specific research problem. You must also ensure your design provides a good fit between your paradigm and the proposed research strategy and methods, and that the research process is logical. Your supervisor or sponsor will be looking at your research design from a practical point of view as well as an academic perspective, and will be assessing the feasibility of the design, given the resources available and the time constraints.

As you get involved in selecting a suitable research problem and developing an appropriate research design, it is easy to forget the big picture. Here are some words of general advice:

- Don't be too ambitious. It is much better to submit a modest research proposal which you can achieve than to come to grief on a project which sets out to remedy all the problems of the world
- Don't try to impress. The use of convoluted language and references to obscure articles does not help. Try to write simply and clearly so that any problems with your proposal can be identified and discussed with your supervisor
- Discuss your proposal with friends and family. Although they may not be familiar with the subject matter, they can often ask the awkward question which you have not spotted
- Be prepared to revise your proposal. It may be that you get part way through and realize that it is not possible to achieve all you set out to do. It is much better to correct this at the planning stage than to start the research and fail to complete it
- Remember that your proposal is a plan. You will have done a considerable amount of work preparing it; do not throw it all away. You should use your proposal to guide and manage the research. This does not mean that you cannot adapt your work as the research progresses, but the proposal is a map which should indicate your course and allow you to decide why and when to depart from it
- Try to allow time between completing your research proposal and submitting it so that you can reflect on it and improve it.

Once you have constructed your research proposal, you can use the checklist shown in Box 7.6 to evaluate it before you submit it to your supervisor and/or potential sponsor.

BOX 7.6   Project proposal checklist

1. Do you have, or can you acquire, the knowledge and skills to do the research?
2. Do you have the resources, such as computer facilities, travelling expenses?
3. Do you have access to the research data you need? If you need the co-operation of certain organizations or people, have you obtained their consent?
4. Does your title aptly describe your study?
5. Have you described the purpose and importance of your research?
6. Have you written a critical preliminary review of the literature and identified your main research question(s)?
7. Have you described and justified your methodology?
8. Is your timetable realistic?
9. Have you avoided plagiarism and checked that your work is correctly referenced?
10. Have you used the spelling and grammar check?

Just in case you are tempted to think that some of the items in the checklist are optional, Robson (1993) offers ten ways to get your proposal rejected. These are shown in Box 7.7.

BOX 7.7   Ten ways to get your proposal turned down

1. Don't follow the directions or guidelines given for your kind of proposal. Omit information that is asked for. Ignore word limits.
2. Ensure the title has little relationship to the stated objectives; and that neither title nor objectives link to the proposed methods or techniques.
3. Produce woolly, ill-defined objectives.
4. Have the statement of the central problem or research focus vague, or obscure it by other discussion.
5. Leave the design and methodology implicit; let them guess.
6. Have some mundane task, routine consultancy or poorly conceptualized data trawl masquerade as a research project.
7. Be unrealistic in what can be achieved with the time and resources you have available.
8. Be either very brief, or preferably, long-winded and repetitive in your proposal. Rely on weight rather than quality.
9. Make it clear what the findings of your research are going to be, and demonstrate how your ideological stance makes this inevitable.
10. Don't worry about a theoretical or conceptual framework for your research. You want to do a down-to-earth study so you can forget all that fancy stuff.

Source: Robson (1993, p. 468).

7.7 CONCLUSIONS

In this chapter we have built on your knowledge from studying the preceding chapters to explain how to design a research study and draw up a detailed plan for carrying out the study. We have explored ways in which you can identify a potential research problem by identifying gaps and deficiencies in the literature, and how the purpose of the research can be communicated succinctly through the use of a purpose statement. We have also discussed the role of the main research question(s), and the importance of determining your main research questions and a theoretical framework (the latter is not applicable if you are using a grounded theory methodology). We have looked at the role of hypotheses in a positivist study and the influence of your paradigm on your choice of methodology. Positivist and interpretivist studies will have different research designs. A positivist research design will incorporate a stronger theoretical basis and it will be necessary to develop hypotheses. There will be an emphasis on the proposed measurement and analysis of the research data. An interpretivist research design may incorporate a theoretical framework and set out various propositions, but the emphasis is more likely to be on the robustness of the methods that will be used to analyse the research data.

We have described how to write a research proposal, looked at a typical structure and suggested additional items that may need to be included, such as a statement of required resources, a budget or a statement of research activities and interests. Once your research proposal has been accepted, you can start collecting your research data. However, the acceptance of your proposal does not necessarily mean that your research project will be successful. A research proposal is merely a plan and the next step is to execute that plan. The following chapters explain how you can do this successfully.

Although every research proposal is unique, it is useful to look at other proposals. If you can obtain examples of successful proposals from your supervisor, these provide the best guide to what is acceptable at your own institution. The following examples are summaries of proposals submitted by MPhil and PhD candidates. For the purpose of this book they have been abbreviated and therefore do not capture the richness of a full proposal. However, they provide illustrations of the style and content of postgraduate and doctoral research proposals.

7.7.1 EXAMPLES OF BUSINESS RESEARCH PROPOSALS

Research area > ACCOUNTING DECISION MAKING

Evaluating investment decisions in advanced manufacturing systems: a fuzzy set theory approach

Research problem and literature overview

An important function of management accounting systems is providing managers with models that evaluate all relevant information needed for making investment decisions (Accola, 1994). Although Discounted Cash Flow Models (DCFM) have been widely accepted by both academicians and practitioners as a sound approach to investment decisions (Klammer *et al.*, 1991; Wilner *et al.*, 1992; Cheung, 1993), many authors have criticized applying them to evaluate the investment in Advanced Manufacturing Systems (AMS) (for example Mensah and Miranti, 1989; Medearis *et al.*, 1990) because these models are biased in favour of short-term investments whose benefits are more easily quantified than longer term projects. Consequently, these authors concluded that DCFM should not be applied to evaluate the investments in AMS. The most difficult task associated with applying DCFM in evaluating AMS investments lies in the existence of many variables which can hardly be measured and expressed in terms of cash flows, especially the benefits that the system will provide, such as greater manufacturing flexibility, learning effects, the effects on employee morale and decreased lead time.

Due to these criticisms some researchers (for example Medearis *et al.*, 1990; O'Brien and Smith, 1993) argue to ignore

processes in auditing focused on auditors' hypotheses formulation. These studies declared that auditors differ in their abilities to formulate correct or plausible hypotheses and these abilities are affected by various factors. Among these factors are expertise, source of hypotheses, hypotheses frame, professional scepticism, motivational factors and cognitive factors. The stated factors still need in-depth investigation, in addition to determining what other factors can trigger the use of confirmatory processes in auditing. A few studies also examined the process of hypotheses updating. Einhorn and Hogarth (1985) formulated a model called 'Contrast/Surprise Model' which investigates the effect of confirming and/or disconfirming evidence on hypotheses updating. Ashton and Ashton (1988) investigated the validity of the previous model. However, their study is insufficient for investigating the process of hypotheses updating because they concentrated only on evidence order.

Research objective

The main objective of the proposed research is determining the effect of using confirmatory processes on auditor's decision making, and investigating the process of hypotheses updating. The main research questions to be addressed are:

1. What factors trigger the use of confirmatory processes in auditing?
2. What is the process of hypotheses updating?
3. What theoretical models are relevant to the process of hypotheses updating?
4. What are the most appropriate circumstances for using confirmatory/disconfirmatory approaches?

Methodology and work plan

The research will be carried out through a theoretical and an empirical study. The empirical study will involve survey and experimental studies. The survey will be conducted through interviews with a number of auditors in auditing firms. It is intended to carry out 36 interviews in six auditing firms; two large, two medium and two small. Interviews will be held with two highly experienced, two medium experienced and two relatively inexperienced auditors in each firm. These interviews will help in determining factors affecting auditors' use of confirmatory processes. Following the analysis of this data, 18 experimental studies will be carried out to determine the validity of the proposed model. These experimental studies will be conducted in the same auditing firms as the interviews.

References

Ashton, A. H. and Ashton, R. H. (1988) 'Sequential belief revision in auditing', *Accounting Review*, October, pp. 623–41.

Bedard, J. C. and Biggs, S. F. (1991) 'Pattern recognition, hypotheses generation and auditor performance in an analytical task', *Accounting Review*, July, pp. 622–42.

Church, B. K. (1990) 'Auditors' use of confirmatory processes', *Journal of Accounting Literatures*, 9, pp. 81–112.

Einhorn, H. J. and Hogarth, R. M. (1985) *A Contrast/Surprise Model for Updating Beliefs*, Working Paper, University of Chicago, April.

McMillan, J. J. and White, R. A. (1993) 'Auditors' belief revisions and evidence search: The effect of hypothesis frame, confirmation bias and professional skepticism', *Accounting Review*, July, pp. 443–65.

Research area > **BUYER BEHAVIOUR**

The influence of children on the family purchase of environmentally friendly grocery products in South Wales

Previous studies of environmental consumerism have addressed the implications of the individual's buyer behaviour (Ottman 1989; Charter 1992) and changes in organizational management practices (Charter 1992; Smith 1993; Welford and Gouldson 1993). The majority of studies in the area of green consumerism focus on the greening of the individual's buying behaviour, the development of green consumerism and the reactions of management in a wide sphere of industries. This research will take family buying behaviour models and build in an environmental perspective. The conceptual framework is presented briefly in Figure A.1.

Research by Charter in 1992 revealed that environmental awareness is increasing in schools throughout Europe, with the introduction of environmental topics in range of school syllabuses, together with wide recognition of the importance of environmental issues as a cross-curricular subject. This has resulted in environmental awareness and concern diffusing among children, with the direct result of children acting as important catalysts in raising the environmental awareness of the family group by reporting back what has been learned about the environment at school.

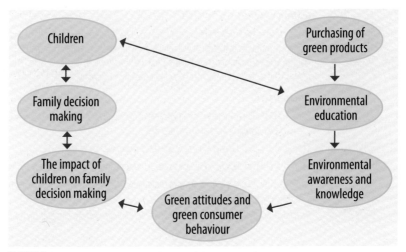

FIGURE A.1 Diagrammatic conceptual framework

As Buttle (1993) discovered, consumer decisions are influenced by systematic relationships of the family which have a variable and determined effect upon the actions of individuals. Most researchers in environmentally responsive buyer behaviour have employed what Buttle (1993) describes as individualistic concepts and constructs. This research intends to take the interactive phenomena of the family and the influence of children on the purchase of environmentally responsible grocery products.

Aims

To investigate the influence of children on the family purchase of environmentally friendly grocery products in South Wales.

The aims of this research centre on an understanding of the influence that children have on family purchase of environmentally friendly grocery products. Grocery products have been selected as the focus of this study because children have a major influence on product choice in this area, and are likely to be involved in product choice selection. The aim of this doctoral study is to determine children's attitudes to and awareness of environmental concerns and the family–child interaction process within the context of environmentally responsive family buying behaviour.

Methodology

The first stage of the research has been a review of the existing literature on green consumerism, environmental education and children, and family buying behaviour. The literature review concentrates on several areas – first, on the diffusion of environmentally responsive buying behaviour; second, on the issues surrounding the development of children's attitudes and awareness of environmental concerns; and third, on the family–child interaction process within the context of family buying behaviour, as Figure A.1. illustrates.

The primary methodology consists of three stages: The exploratory research which is underway, and consists of focus group sessions with primary school children in South Wales. The aims of the exploratory study are to determine the attitudes and behaviour of children towards environmental consumerism and how they believe they influence environmentally responsive family buying behaviour. The legal and ethical aspects of research with children will be adhered to.

Stage two will be an investigation of the family group through focus group sessions in South Wales, with the objective of establishing the actual interactive decision-making process within the sample families. This will be undertaken between September 1995 and March 1996.

The third stage of the research will consist of the development of case studies in order to investigate the holistic characteristics of the real-life situation. The case study sample will be developed from stage two of the research. The in-depth case study analysis will consist of semi-structured interviews and an observational study to be undertaken between March 1996 and March 1997.

Output

This doctoral research will contribute to family buyer behaviour knowledge and the understanding of environmentally responsive consumer behaviour; it will contribute to the understanding of the marketing implications of the influence of children in environmental decision making and the ways in which decision making is undertaken within the family group in the context of environmentally responsive buyer behaviour.

References

Buttle F. (1993) The co-ordinated management of meaning: A case exemplar of a new consumer research paradigm, *European Journal of Marketing*, 28, nos. 8/9.

Charter, M. I. (1992) *Greener Marketing*, Sheffield: Greenleaf Publishing.

Ottman, J. (1989) 'Industries' response to green consumerism', *Journal of Business Strategy*, 13, Part 4.

Smith, D. (1993) 'Purchasing department contributions to company environmental performance', *Purchasing Supply Management*, 20 (1).

Welford, R. and Gouldson, A. (1993) *Environmental Management Business Strategy*, London: Pitman Publishing.

Research area > ORGANIZATIONAL CHANGE

Changing the deal: The role of informal contracts in business transformation and organizational renewal

Introduction and literature review

In the last decade, the belief has grown amongst organizational theorists (Kanter, 1983; Handy, 1989; Pascale, 1990 and others) that in order to be successful in increasingly turbulent markets, organizations need to be able to assimilate – or better, instigate – dramatic shifts in their industries. Change is becoming more discontinuous (Handy, 1989) – or transformational – in nature. The management of discontinuous change demands a more 'holistic approach' (Hinings and Greenwood, 1988) and an ability to recognize – and if appropriate, act on – the limitations of the organization's existing paradigms (Morgan, 1986, 1993). It can also require organizations to build more flexibility into their structures and contractual arrangements (Atkinson, 1984). Roles may be restructured; jobs rescoped; new skills demanded; career paths obfuscated: in short, individuals are asked to undertake a radical rethink of their role, both within the organization and in a broader context. Formal contracts and cultures are being developed that aim to meet these challenges, but the informal side of organizational life cannot and should not be ignored.

A pilot project (in an operating company of a leading financial services group) conducted for this proposal, suggested that even when change is accepted at the 'rational' levels it may meet resistance if insufficient attention is paid to its broader implications (Jarvis, 1994). There is a growing need to understand the 'informal contract' between the employer and employee, if both parties' expectations are to be met.

A key output from the research will be a better understanding of the 'informal contract', and if and how it is evolving. At this stage, a working definition is being employed, as follows: 'the expectations – emotional and rational; conscious and unconscious – that employees bring to and take from their work and that are not covered by their job description and formal contract of employment'.

Research aim

The main aim of the MPhil project is to define the informal contract and establish its role in the implementation of major change programmes. PhD research will aim to uncover if and how the informal contract can be 'managed' to support employees through major change.

Research methodology and proposed timetable

Primary research will be qualitative, collaborative inquiry (Reason, 1988) built around 6–8 case studies, each being conducted over a period of 18–24 months. This approach has been selected for its ability to yield data at the unconscious, as well as conscious, level.

Hypotheses will be developed as the case study progresses and each case study will adopt four key research methods: interviews with senior management to provide an organizational context and an understanding of the aims and critical success factors for the change programme; depth interviews, with middle management grades and below, to provide context and a broad understanding of the individual meaning of the informal contract; individual diaries to provide a depth of information – 'felt' and rational – into the meaning of the informal contract to individuals; a series of inquiry groups to develop a shared meaning for the informal contract. Triangulation will be provided through this use of different methods and different sources, while an audit trail will ensure confirmability.

PhD research will test hypotheses for transferability. As well as the opportunities for comparison provided by multiple case studies, it is envisaged that a series of cross-organizational groups, comprising senior managers, will be set up to look at how these hypotheses transfer from theory into practice.

References

Atkinson, J. (1984) *Emerging UK Work Patterns*, IMS Paper No. 145.

Handy, C. (1989) *The Age of Unreason*, Business Books Ltd.

Hinings, C. R. and Greenwood, R. (1988) *The Dynamics of Strategic Change*, Basil Blackwell.

Jarvis, C. (1994) *The Introduction of a Self-Assessment Appraisal System in to FSG OpCo*, unpublished.

Kanter, R. M. (1983) *The Changemasters*, Unwin Hyman.

Morgan, G. (1986) *Images of Organisation*, Sage Publications.

Morgan, G. (1993) *Imaginization*, Penguin.

Pascale, R. (1990) *Managing on the Edge*, Penguin.

Reason, P. (1988) (ed.) *Human Inquiry in Action: Developments in New Paradigm Research*, Saga Publications.

Research area > ORGANIZATIONAL CHANGE

To evaluate input and effectiveness of culture change on individuals and organizations

Background

I have run and co-tutored personal, management and organizational development courses for the last ten years. Co-tutoring has given me the opportunity to observe others' training, receive feedback and reflect on my own practice. The dominant thought area that has emerged from this reflection is that the quality of relationship between tutor and learner, and learner and learner, is of critical importance if lasting change and development is to occur.

As a participant in a self-managed learning group at Lancaster University (MAML), I found the experience challenging and, at times, frustrating. I believe this was due to the developmental relationships within the group. While this subject has emerged from reflecting on my own personal experience, I believe it is relevant to tutors, learners and managers. Effective 'engaging' between individuals could be a basis for effective managerial relationships.

The project

The study will explore the nature of 'engaging' (that is, effective developmental relationships) between tutors and learners, and learners and learners. The aim is to define and develop a working model of effective developmental relationships.

Theoretical context

Rowland (1993) has proposed a spectrum of tutoring relationships from 'didactic' to 'exploratory', with the middle ground being occupied by an 'interpretative' model. In his 'exploratory' and 'didactic' models the learning process is seen as being 'a black box, a kind of private psychological process in which the tutor cannot engage' (1993, p. 27). In the 'interpretative' models the tutor deliberately attempts to become part of the learning process. He characterizes the relationship as being one in which there is a free flow of learning and the tutor becomes an important part of the students' learning process. The psycho-therapeutic work of Rogers (1961) clearly defines the characteristics of what he terms a 'helping relationship'. This relationship creates a 'psychological climate' that ultimately releases human potential. Combining the work of Rowland (1993) and Rogers (1961) suggests a definition of 'engaging' as a relationship that creates a developmental psychological climate and a culture of support in which individuals develop shared meanings and collectively become an integral part of each other's reflective processes.

Using Reason's (1988) post-positivist research methodology of co-operative enquiry, I will work with groups to establish how individuals successfully 'engage'. Reason provides many useful insights into establishing co-operative enquiry groups including creating the 'right' atmosphere for people to examine processes, freely challenge and support one another. He suggests this is not easy and needs to emerge from the group as it matures towards truly authentic collaboration. This is another factor within the process of 'engaging' but between researcher and researched. Thus, the theoretical context of the research methodology parodies the area under study.

Methodology and research process

The proposed study will use a form of co-operative enquiry, which is ontologically based on a belief in a participatory universe and attempts to undertake research with people rather than on them. Cunningham (1988) suggests a broad model of co-operative inquiry which he calls 'interactive holistic research'. This non-linear, or as he puts it 'omni-focussed', model (p. 167) has four elements:

a. Collaborative enquiry – that is with people and either of Type I – in which the group explores its internal processes together or Type II in which the group explores a process which happens outside the group.

b. Action research – research which is concerned with developing practical knowledge or praxis.

c. Experimental research – research which is concerned with how and what I experience.

d. Contextual locating – this represents the backdrop to the whole research study, either intellectually, socially or emotionally.

Within the MPhil phase, I propose to establish a collaborative enquiry group with fellow tutors and learners to explore experiences of 'engaging' (Type II according to Cunningham, 1988). The purpose of this phase is to define and develop a model of 'engaging' between tutors and learners. This will be elaborated in the PhD phase by exploring the nature of developmental relationships within the group (Type I according to Cunningham, 1988) and to look further at this relationship in the context of managing. In this phase the objective is to define 'engaging' between learners and to develop a model of collaborative learning or development. The group will be assembled by invitation and consist of fellow tutors with an interest in exploring developmental relationships. Initial research with learners will be confined to participant observation to enable a working hypothesis to be established and will be undertaken with the many groups that I currently co-tutor. This will be replaced with a more formal collaborative enquiry which attempts to elicit a learner's perspective on 'engaging', initially free of any hypothesis, but later to explore a hypothesis which is either given or developed.

Research with fellow tutors and with learners will take place concurrently. The synthesis of these views will take place through a critical examination of my own practice and experience, through observation and critical subjectivity. Ideas which are developed will then be available for scrutiny and development with the collaborative inquiry group. In each of the groups (that is, learners and tutors) I will be the primary researcher.

References

Cunningham, I. (1988) 'Interactive Holistic Research: Researching Self Managed Learning', in Reason, P. (1988) *Human Inquiry in Action – Developments in New Paradigm Research*, London: Sage Publications.

Rogers, C. (1961) *On Becoming a Person*, London: Constable.

Rowland, S. (1993) *The Enquiring Tutor: Exploring the Process of Professional Learning*, London: Falmer Press.

Research area > STRATEGIC MANAGEMENT

Tacit knowledge and sustainable competitive advantage

Introduction and literature review

An enduring problem for strategic management is the sustainability of competitive advantage (Porter, 1985; Barney, 1991; Black and Boal, 1994). The proposed research is concerned with competitive advantage and the link between a heterogeneous firm resource (in this instance tacit knowledge) and the use of relatively homogenous information technology (IT) assets. Much of the literature exploring the link between IT and competitive advantage, holds that innovatory systems are quickly and widely adopted and thus a source of enabling and not critical advantage (Banker and Kauffman, 1988; Ciborra, 1991). Contradictory research shows that this may not be the case as implementation of IT can produce unexpected outcomes (Ciborra, 1991). Other research (for example Cash and McFarlane, 1988; Kremar and Lucas, 1991; Lederer and Sethi, 1991) does not recognize the import of tacit knowledge and sees deviations in performance stemming from a lack of planning. However, recent additions to the literature question this logic, finding that intra-firm structural differences, the source of unexpected outcomes, can be combined with technology as complementary assets to confer a potential source of sustainable competitive advantage (Feeny and Ives, 1990; Clemons and Row, 1991; Heatley, Argarwal and Tanniru, 1995).

Inadequacy of current research

No empirical research has explored the role of tacit knowledge as a positive intra-firm structural differentiator in the implementation of IT. A priori observation seems to indicate that tacit knowledge is valuable, rare, imperfectly inimitable and non-transferable (Barney, 1991). Evaluating IT strategic successes, Ciborra (1991) identifies serendipity, trial and error, and bricolage as elements of a process of innovation in the use of systems. None of the literature explores the source, nor the effects of this process. Thus, while the literature has speculated as to the role of tacit knowledge in creating sustainable competitive advantage (Spender, 1993), the empirical question, 'Can tacit knowledge provide a source of sustainable competitive advantage?' has not been addressed.

Aims and objectives of research

The research aims to fill this gap in the literature by examining the proposition that tacit knowledge is a source of competitive advantage, and asking, if it is, what the conditions are that are required to support it. The research also aims to answer the question of how tacit knowledge can provide a source of sustainable competitive advantage. This requires an examination of pre-emption, dynamic economies of learning and continuing innovation effects from using IT and tacit knowledge as complementary assets. Thus, the research will test the proposition that combinations of tacit knowledge and IT create core competencies that lead to superior performance, and that these competencies are inimitable in the sense used by Barney (1991). Barriers to imitation can be created by combining tacit knowledge and technology.

Methodology and plan of work

At the highest level of abstraction, it is proposed to use the resource-based view of the firm as a framework to understand asset combinations that can be the source of differences among firms. It is proposed that the research will operationalize measures developed by Sethi and King (1994) which were devised to assess the extent to which IT applications provide competitive advantage. In this research competitive advantage is driven by system performance, and this is the dependent variable in this study. The sample will be taken from the population of firms who use SAP business process software. The sample will be stratified for external validity according to Collis and Ghemawat's (1994) resource-based industry typology: along the dimensions of key resources and the nature of the production task. Construct validity will be established using pilot research; in-depth interviews. The focus of the study will centre on deviations from expected performance of a tightly specified and robust business process oriented system which is widely used in a variety of industries. The unit of analysis is at the level of business processes. Deviations in performance between firms having the same IT system constitute differences in the dependent variable and this is a function of knowledge assets, their management and characteristics of the firm and system context. A research instrument will be designed which will be administered to collect cardinal and ordinal data on the dimensions of tacit knowledge, group dynamics, firm and system characteristics, including data collection on firm specific technology trajectories.

References

Banker, R. and Kauffman, R. (1988) 'Strategic contributions of IT', Proceedings of 9th Int. Conf. on IS, pp. 141–50.

Barney, J. (1991) 'Firm resources and sustained competitive advantage', Journal of Management, 17 (1), pp. 99–120.

Black, J. and Boal, K (1994) 'Strategic resources: Traits, configuration and paths to sustainable competitive advantage', Strat. Man. Jnl, 15, pp. 131–48.

Cash, J. and McFarlane, F. (1988) Competing Through Information Technology, Harvard Business School Press.

Ciborra, C. U. (1991) 'The limits of strategic information systems', International Journal of Information Resource Management, 2 (3), pp. 11–17.

Clemons, E. K. and Row, M. C. (1991) 'Sustaining IT: The role of structural differences', MIS Quarterly, September, pp. 275–92.

Collis, D. and Ghemawat, P. (1994) 'Industry Analysis: Understanding Industry Structure and Dynamics', in Fahey, L. and Randall, R. M. (eds) The Portable MBA, Wiley, pp. 171–93.

Feeny, D. and Ives, B. (1990) 'In search of sustainability: Reaping long-term advantage from investments in IT', Jnl Mgmt IS, 7 (1), pp. 27–45.

Heatley, J., Agarwal, R. and Tanniru, M. (1995) 'An evaluation of innovative information technology', Jnl Strat IS, 4 (3), pp. 255–77.

Kremar, H. and Lucas, H. (1991) 'Success factors for strategic IS', Information and Management, 21, pp. 137–45.

Lederer, A. and Sethi, V. (1991) 'Meeting the challenges of information systems planning', Long Range Planning, 25 (2), pp. 69–80.

8

Collecting qualitative data

Learning objectives

When you have studied this chapter, you should be able to:

- describe methods based on interviews

- describe methods based on diaries

- describe methods based on observation

- compare the strengths and weaknesses of methods

- choose a method that reflects your paradigm.

8.1 INTRODUCTION

In this chapter we focus on the main methods used to collect *qualitative data*. These methods will be of particular interest if you are designing a study under an interpretive paradigm. Many of the methods used to collect qualitative data have much in common with those used to collect quantitative data, as you will see when you move on to Chapter 10. However, there are important differences, which reflect the assumptions of the two main paradigms. Since positivists often collect some qualitative data that need to be quantified and because *methodological triangulation* may have been incorporated in the research design, this chapter will also be of interest to those designing a study under a positivist paradigm.

Some of the methods we describe in this chapter incorporate the collection and the analysis of the data simultaneously. This makes it hard to identify these elements in the process. Another problem is that some researchers refer to a classification based on 'quantitative methods' or 'qualitative methods'. This can be misleading, as it is the data rather than the means of collecting the data that are in numerical or non-numerical form! However, we agree that 'quantitative methods' is appropriate when referring to statistical methods.

It is essential you set out and justify your method(s) for collecting and analysing your data in your proposal. You would not want to be faced with the problem of having collected a vast amount of material, but not know how to analyse and interpret the data.

8.2 OVERVIEW OF QUALITATIVE DATA COLLECTION

Qualitative data are normally transient, understood only within context and are associated with an interpretive methodology that usually results in findings with a high degree of *validity*. It contrasts with *quantitative data*, which are normally precise, can be captured at various points in time and in different contexts, and are associated with a positivist methodology that usually results in findings with a high degree of *reliability*. The challenge for the researcher using an interpretive paradigm is to apply method(s) that will retain the integrity of the data.

> **KEY DEFINITIONS**
>
> Reliability refers to the absence of differences in the results if the research were repeated.
>
> Validity is the extent to which the research findings accurately reflect the phenomena under study.

Since qualitative data need to be understood within context, you need to collect some background information first. This is known as *contextualization*. Data about the context can relate to aspects such as time and location, or legal, social, political and economic influences. For example, a person working in a declining industry in a remote northern town in Canada, who is confronted with redundancy two weeks before the New Year starts, may have different views of the future than someone working in a booming high-tech industry in California. It is critical to your research that you establish and understand this contextual framework, as this will enhance your sensitivity to the qualitative research data you subsequently collect and aid your interpretation.

Much of the contextualizing data will be found in the literature. Do not ignore statistical data. Information such as the level of unemployment in an area, the economic performance of an industry or employment patterns in a particular company can contribute to setting the framework within which you will be doing your research. Local newspapers are also important, but quite often take a political stance. It is sometimes more revealing to read the readers' letters than the editorials. The former usually express the perceptions and feelings of people who are part of the phenomenon you are studying.

Having established the context, you need to collect data relating to the location of your study and any events taking place before you collect the data. Therefore, equipment such as a camera, video recorder, audio recorder and a notebook will be needed. The notes taken while collecting primary research data are sometimes referred to as *field notes*, a term borrowed from the natural sciences.

We will now examine some of the main methods for collecting data for qualitative analysis. It is important to remember that the methods associated with interpretive paradigms often allow the researcher to collect and analyse the research data in one process. This contrasts with methodologies associated with positivist paradigms, where statistical methods are used to analyse the data. If you are designing a study under an interpretive paradigm, you will need to read this chapter in conjunction with Chapter 9; if you are designing a study under a positivist paradigm, you will need to read this chapter in conjunction with Chapter 10 and the appropriate chapter(s) on statistical analysis.

8.3　INTERVIEWS

Interviews are a method for collecting data in which selected participants (the inter-viewees) are asked questions to find out what they do, think or feel. Prompts and probes may be required. Under an interpretive paradigm, interviews are concerned with exploring 'data on understandings, opinions, what people remember doing, attitudes, feelings and the like, that people have in common' (Arksey and Knight, 1999, p. 2) and will be unstructured. Under a positivist paradigm, interviews are structured, which means the questions are planned in advance (as in a questionnaire). All types of interviews can be conducted with individuals or groups, using face-to-face, telephone, email or video conferencing methods (see Chapter 10).

KEY DEFINITIONS

An interview is a method for collecting primary data in which a sample of interview-ees are asked questions to find out what they think, do or feel.

8.3.1　UNSTRUCTURED INTERVIEWS

An unstructured interview is one where the questions have not been prepared before-hand but evolve during the course of the interview. They are likely to be open-ended, with probes to explore the interviewee's answers in more depth. The most common form of interview is one-to-one, but some researchers find it useful to have two interviewers to help ensure that all the issues are fully explored and notes are kept of nuances, gestures, interruptions and so on. It is helpful to have a record of what occurred during the inter-view as it can be used to extract a more robust and comprehensive interpretation.

Unstructured interviews are very time-consuming and there may be problems with recording the questions and answers, controlling the range of topics and analysing the data. The questions raised and the matters explored change from one interview to the next as different aspects of the topic are revealed. This process of open discovery is the strength of such interviews, but it is important to recognize that the emphasis and balance of the emerging issues depend on the order in which your participants are interviewed.

Easterby-Smith, Thorpe and Lowe (1991) suggest that unstructured or semi-structured interviews are appropriate when:

- it is necessary to understand the construct that the interviewee uses as a basis for his or her opinions and beliefs about a particular matter or situation
- one aim of the interview is to develop an understanding of the respondent's 'world'

so that the researcher might influence it, either independently or collaboratively (as might be the case with action research)
- the step-by-step logic of a situation is not clear
- the subject matter is highly confidential or commercially sensitive
- the interviewee may be reluctant to be truthful about this issue other than confidentially in a one-to-one situation.

Table 8.1 shows examples of different types of interview question and their uses.

TABLE 8.1 Types of interview question		
Type of question	Useful for	Not useful for
Open question (e.g. Tell me what happened when …)	Most openings to explore and gather broad information	Very talkative people
Closed question (e.g. Who did you consult?)	Getting factual information	Getting broad information
Multiple questions (more than one in a sentence)	Never useful	Never useful
Probes (e.g. What happened next?)	Establishing sequence of events or gathering details	Exploring sensitive events
Hypothetical question (e.g. What might happen that could change your opinion?)	Encouraging broader thinking	Situations beyond the interviewee's scope
Comparison question (e.g. Do you prefer weekly or fortnightly team meetings?)	Exploring needs and values	Unrealistic alternatives
Summary question (e.g. So, am I right in thinking that the main issues are …?)	Avoiding ambiguity, validating data and linking answers	Premature or frequent use

To ensure that you gain maximum information, it is essential that you *probe* the interviewee by asking questions that require them to elaborate on their initial statement. There are a number of qualitative characteristics relating to the answers that you must establish and Table 8.2 shows examples of the probes you can use to elicit such data. Probes are questions you asked in response to what the interviewee has said. They are asked so that you can gain greater understanding of the issue under study and are the beginning of the data analysis stage. They are used in an unstructured or semi-structured interview. If you are thinking of asking prepared questions only, you would be using a structured interview, which is a method associated with a positivist paradigm.

You should bear in mind that recent events may affect the interviewee's responses. For example, he or she may have just received news of a promotion, a salary increase, a cut in hours, a reprimand or bad news about a member of the family. If time allows, you will find it useful to arrive at the interview venue 15 minutes beforehand to assimilate the atmosphere and the environment, and spend the first few minutes putting the interviewee at ease. It is difficult to predict or measure bias. Nevertheless, you should be alert to the fact that it can distort your data and hence your findings.

You should always ask the interviewee's permission to *record* the interview using some form of audio recorder and taking notes. After putting your interviewee at ease, you may find it useful to spend a little time establishing a rapport before starting to record. You can offer to switch the recorder off if he or she wants to discuss *confidential* information. You may find that this encourages a higher degree of frankness (see Chapter 3).

Characteristic	Probe
	Can you give me an example of this?
Clarity	What do you mean?
	Can you explain that again?
Relevance	How do you think that relates to the issue?
	Can you explain how these factors influence each other?
Depth	Can you explain that in more detail?
	Can you give me examples?
Dimension	Is it possible to look at this another way?
	Do you think that is a commonly held opinion?
	How much does this affect you?
Significance	What do you think is the most important?
	Would you change your opinion if X was to happen?
	Can you give me an example where this did not happen?
Comparison	Can you give me an example of a different situation?
	In what way does your opinion differ from the views of other people?
Bias	Why do you hold this opinion?
	What might happen that could change your opinion?

TABLE 8.2 Examples of probes

Lee (1993) offers the following advice if you are asking questions on *sensitive topics*:

- Use words that are non-threatening and familiar to the respondents. For example, when explaining the purpose of the interview, rather than saying you are conducting research into absenteeism in their workplace, say you are looking at working patterns.
- Lead up to any sensitive question slowly.
- You may find that participants will answer questions about past indiscretions more readily than questions about current behaviour. For example, they may admit to stealing from their employer at some time in the past, but be unwilling to disclose that they have done so recently.

These suggestions raise ethical issues and you must determine your own position on this. If you find your interviewee is showing signs of resisting some topics, the best advice is to drop those questions. However, this will alert you to the likelihood that these may be interesting and important issues and you may wish to find an alternative way of collecting the data, such as *diary methods* or *observation*.

You need to let the interviewee know that the interview is coming to an end. One way of doing so is to say that you have asked all the questions you had in mind and ask whether he or she has any final comments. You should then conclude by thanking them and reassuring them that you will be treating what they have told you as confidential. If you want to improve the validity of your findings, you should arrange to send a summary of your findings to the interviewee for feedback on your interpretation.

After you have left the interview, you should spend as much time as possible immediately afterwards adding to your notes. You will find it helpful if you can share your insights and reflections with your supervisor or fellow students.

8.3.2   POTENTIAL PROBLEMS

Sometimes the interviewee is accompanied by another person (often to ensure that all the questions you ask can be answered). You must be alert to the fact that if there is more than one interviewer or interviewee it will change the dynamics of the interview. Another situation that can arise is that your interviewee may be wearing 'two hats' (in other words, have multiple roles). For example, the finance director of a company you are interviewing may also be on an advisory group that influences EU company law; a factory employee may also be a trade union official. Therefore, when asking questions, you must determine whether he or she is giving a personal opinion or making a policy statement Another problem is that the interviewee may have certain expectations and give what he or she considers is the 'correct' or 'acceptable' answer to the question. Lee (1993) suggests that, to some extent, this can be overcome by increasing the depth of the interview.

When asking questions, you need to be aware of the potential for inadvertent class, race or sex *bias*. For example, a study that examined sex bias more than 40 years ago (Rosenthal, 1966) found that male and female researchers obtained significantly different data from their subjects. The following tendencies were observed:

*   Female subjects were treated more attentively and considerately than male subjects were.
*   Female researchers smiled more often than male researchers did.
*   Male researchers placed themselves closer to male subjects than female researchers did.
*   Male researchers showed higher levels of body activity than female researchers did. When the subject was male, both male and female researchers showed higher levels of body activity than they did with female subjects.
*   Female subjects rated male researchers as being friendlier than female researchers were, and as having more pleasant and expressive voices than female researchers had.
*   Both male and female researchers generally behaved more warmly towards female subjects than they did towards male subjects, with male researchers being the warmer of the two.

8.3.3   CRITICAL INCIDENT TECHNIQUE

Unstructured interviews are not merely idle conversations. It is your role to encourage the participant to tell his or her story in his or her own words, while keeping the interviewee to the relevant issues. You are trying to obtain in-depth and authentic knowledge of people's life experiences (Gubrium and Holstein, 2001). One way to do this is to use *critical incident technique*. This method is based on the participant's recollections of key facts and can be used to collect data about a specific activity or event. It was originally developed by Flanagan (1954) as a method to be used under a positivist paradigm, but principles can be modified and adapted according to the circumstances. This makes it very useful for designing interview questions in an interpretive methodology.

> **KEY DEFINITIONS**
>
> Critical incident technique is a method for collecting data about a defined activity or event based on the participant's recollections of key facts.

Flanagan intended the researcher to collect critical incidents using a form, but you can see from the example in Box 8.1 that his questions could form the basis of a semi-structured interview.

BOX 8.1   Example of how to collect effective critical incidents

'Think of the last time you saw one of your subordinates do something that was very helpful to your group in meeting your production schedule.' (Pause until he indicates that he has such an incident in mind.) 'Did his action result in increase in production of as much as one per cent for that day? – or some similar period?'

(If the answer is 'no', say) 'I wonder if you can think of the last time that someone did something that did have this much of an effect in increasing production.' (When he indicates he has such a situation in mind, say) 'What were the general circumstances leading up to this incident?'

....

....

'Tell me exactly what this person did that was so helpful at that time.' ....

....

'Why was this so helpful in getting your group's job done?' ....

....

'When did this incident happen?' ....

'What was this person's job?' ....

'How long has he been on this job?' ....

'How old is he?'...

Source: Flanagan (1954, p. 342).

Critical incident technique helps interviewees to talk about issues in the context of their own experience and discourages them from talking about hypothetical situations or other people's experiences. For example, if you are using interviews with owners of small businesses to investigate a research problem relating to access to finance, the critical incident might focus on their experiences at the start-up stage. You could follow this up by asking them to tell you about the next time they can remember needing capital and what happened, until you have covered all the occasions. If there are a great many of the type of critical incidents you are interested in, it is best to ask about the most recent or to ask the interviewee afterwards why he or she chose that particular event. One of the problems associated with methods based on memory is that the participant may have forgotten important facts. In addition, there is the problem of post-rationalization, where the interviewee recounts the events with a degree of logic and coherence that did not exist at the time.

8.4   PROTOCOL ANALYSIS

KEY DEFINITIONS

Protocol analysis is a method for collecting data used to identify a practitioner's mental processes in solving a problem in a particular situation, including the logic and methods used.

Protocol analysis is a data collection method used to identify the mental processes in problem solving, and is usually associated with an interpretive methodology. The aim of the method is to find out how people behave and think in a particular situation, particularly in solving a complex problem. Smagorinsky (1989, p. 475) describes protocol analysis as 'an expensive and meticulous research method that has had its share of growing pains'. However, the method offers a tool for the researcher who is interested in how individuals solve business problems.

The researcher gives some form of written problem to a practitioner who is experienced in that field. As the practitioner addresses the problem, he or she gives verbal explanations of how he or she is doing it and the researcher records the process. Sometimes the practitioner generates further questions, which form the basis of a subsequent stage in the research.

Protocol analysis studies tend to be small, involving fewer than a dozen participants. The process of constructing the problem that is given to the practitioners is difficult and is part of the research process. The researcher must seek to contrive a realistic problem and address the fundamental issues, and also define the scope of the study. Furthermore, the researcher must have sufficient knowledge to be able to understand and interpret the logic and methods the practitioner uses to address the problem (it cannot be assumed that a solution is always found).

8.4.1   GENERATING PROTOCOLS

There are a number of ways in which the verbal data can be generated. *Retrospective verbalization* takes place when the participant is asked to describe processes after they have occurred. *Concurrent verbalization* takes place when the participant is asked to describe and explain their thoughts as they undertake a task. There are two types of concurrent verbalization: directed reports and think-aloud protocol. The former result when participants are asked to describe only specific behaviours and the latter when they are asked to relay every thought that comes into their heads. Figure 8.1 summarizes the different types of protocol.

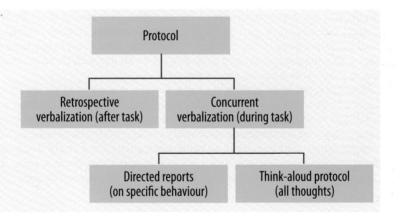

FIGURE 8.1 Types of protocol

Day (1986) identified the following advantages of using protocol analysis:

- It helps to reduce the problem of interviewer bias.
- The possibility of omitting potentially important areas or aspects is reduced.
- The technique is open-ended and provides considerable flexibility.

8.4.2   POTENTIAL PROBLEMS

Bolton (1991) used concurrent verbal protocols to test questionnaires and identify questions associated with information problems. However, he warns that it is 'time consuming and labour intensive' (Bolton, 1991, p. 565). Protocol analysis was used by

Smagorinsky (1994) to study writing, and by Clarkson (1962) to examine decisions made by a bank trust investment officer. Day (1986) used it to examine decisions made by investment analysts and points out that a major drawback of using retrospective verbalization is that it does not consider 'a real-time situation, but rather an action replay' (Day, 1986, p. 296). On the other hand, concurrent verbalization requires the researcher to maintain a continuous presence and is usually too time-consuming and disruptive to be considered a feasible choice.

8.5 REPERTORY GRID TECHNIQUE

Based on personal construct theory (Kelly, 1955), *repertory grid technique* is a form of structured interview during which a matrix (the grid) is developed that contains a mathematical representation of the perceptions and constructs a person uses to understand and manage his or her world. The technique 'allows the interviewer to get a mental map of how the interviewee views the world, and to write this map with the minimum of observer bias' (Stewart and Stewart, 1981, p. 5).

> **KEY DEFINITIONS**
>
> Repertory grid technique is a method based on personal construct theory that generates a mathematical representation of a participant's perceptions and constructs.

The underlying theory is that 'people strive to make sense of their world by developing a personal construct system: a network of hypotheses about how the world works' (Hankinson, 2004, p. 146). Our construct system changes as new experiences and knowledge alter the way we look at the world. Our current construct system helps us shape our perceptions about the world and our expectations about future events. It is reality as we know it. Others may share our reality, or part of it, where our construct systems overlap. There are internal inconsistencies in our construct system that may result in our behaviour being at odds with what others perceive as reality. As we all live with these internal inconsistencies, in most cases it causes few problems.

Although it has been used in positivist studies, it is argued that the foundations of personal construct theory lie within the interpretative paradigm (Reason and Rowan, 1981). If you want to use repertory grid technique to collect quantitative data for statistical purposes, you are designing your study under a positivist paradigm. We are going to treat repertory grid technique as being appropriate for a study designed under an interpretive paradigm, but you will need to remember that there is some debate over this when justifying your choice of method in your methodology chapter.

8.5.1 GENERATING ELEMENTS AND CONSTRUCTS

Repertory grid technique requires the identification of *elements* and *constructs*, and a procedure for enabling participants to relate the constructs to the elements. The elements on the grid are the objects or concepts under discussion, and constructs are the characteristics or attributes of the elements. Following Kelly's original approach, many studies have used people as elements, but other studies have used occupations and work activities (for example Easterby-Smith, 1981; Brook and Brook, 1989; Hunter, 1997) and organizations (for example Barton-Cunningham and Gerrard, 2000; Dackert, Brenner and Johanssen, 2003).

Elements can be generated in several ways:

• by eliciting a topic of interest through discussion with the participants and drawing up a list of elements (usually between 5 and 10, as more could be hard to manage)

- by describing a situation and allowing the participant to identify the elements
- by providing a pool of elements from which the participant selects a certain number of elements
- by providing predetermined elements.

A separate card is used to show the name of each element and these cards are used to elicit the constructs, using *triads* or *dyads*. The classical approach is to use triads, where the interviewer selects three cards at random to show the interviewee. He or she is first asked to decide which two are similar and what differentiates them from the third and then to think of a word or phrase for each similarity or difference between pairs in the triad. The process is repeated until a comprehensive list of personal constructs is obtained. The alternative approach is to use dyads, where pairs of cards are selected at random and the interviewee is asked to provide a word or phrase that describes each similarity or difference. Fransella and Bannister (1977) suggest the researcher adopts whichever method is the most appropriate for exploring the participant's view of the social world they inhabit. The main stages in repertory grid technique are summarized in Box 8.2.

BOX 8.2   Procedure for repertory grid technique

1. Determine the focus of the grid.
2. Determine the elements in advance or agree them with each interviewee (approximately 5–10).
3. Write each element on a separate card.
4. Decide whether to use triads or dyads.
5. Select the appropriate number of cards at random.
6. Ask the interviewee to provide a word or phrase that describes each similarity and difference between the pairs of elements.
7. Use these words or phrases as the constructs on the grid.
8. Explain the rating scale to the interviewee (for example 5 = high, 1 = low)
9. Ask the interviewee to indicate the number closest to his or her view and explain the reason.
10. Construct a grid for each interviewee based on his or her responses and scores.

In an *ideographic approach*, the grid is based on the unique elements and personal constructs elicited from the interviewee, and the scores he or she gives that measure relationships between each element and construct. These describe his or her world and the grid may have very little in common with the grids of other interviewees. In a *nomothetic approach*, predetermined elements and/or constructs are used, which facilitate comparison across cases and aggregation of the scores in the grids (Tan and Hunter, 2002). Table 8.3 shows an example of a repertory grid that represents an employee's constructs relating to a set of elements based on organizational systems. At a very simple level you can detect emerging patterns. However, it is also possible to take a statistical approach: Dunn and Ginsberg used the data to calculate three indices of cognitive content, thus allowing them to measure differences in the structure and content of reference frames.

TABLE 8.3   Example of a repertory grid

Constructs	Elements					
Rating scale 1–7	Inventory management system	Strategic planning system	Office automation	Decision support system	Quality working circle	Collateral organization
Technical quality	6	5	4	2	1	3
Cost	2	1	4	6	5	3
Challenge to status quo	6	1	2	4	5	3
Actionability	1	6	2	4	5	3
Evaluability	6	1	2	5	4	3

Source: Adapted from Dunn and Ginsberg (1986, p. 964).

8.5.2   POTENTIAL PROBLEMS

At one level a repertory grid 'is nothing more than a labelled set of numbers' (Taylor, 1990, p. 105), but it provides a structured way of assessing an individual's perceptions (Fransella and Bannister, 1977) and 'a framework for the patterning of subjective experiences that has the advantage of being available for statistical analysis' (Taylor, 1990, p. 117). However, the structure approach and a quantitative approach to the analysis is an essential part of the controversy surrounding repertory grid technique. If you are designing your study under an interpretive paradigm, it is essential to seek explanation of the constructs, elements and scores from the interviewee at the time. In all cases, we recommend that you use notes supported by an audio recording. As in any interview, you will need to ask for permission to record.

KEY DEFINITIONS

A diary is a method for collecting data where selected participants are asked to record relevant information in diary forms or booklets over a specified period of time.

8.6   DIARY METHODS

Diaries are a method for collecting written data that can be used under both an interpretive and a positivistic methodology. A diary is a record of events or thoughts and is typically used to capture and record what people do, think and feel. Participants are asked to record relevant information in diary forms or booklets over a specified period of time.

8.6.1   TYPES OF DIARY

Plummer (1983) distinguishes between three types of diary:

- A *log* is a detailed diary in which participants keep a record of the time they spend on their activities. This is a method of collecting quantitative data and is normally used in a positivist study.
- A *diary* is where participants keep descriptive records of their day-to-day lives. These are free-form and present the researcher with several challenges, but also tremendous insights. The diarist should be encouraged to write his or her thoughts as if the diary is secret and to be read by nobody else. This will encourage illuminating revelations but these can be difficult to interpret. It is also challenging to make comparisons if several participants are keeping diaries about the same phenome-

non. You may even question whether they are in fact observing the same events, as their perceptions can differ so much.

- A *diary-interview* has the advantage of allowing the researcher to progress to another level of enquiry. The participants are asked to keep a diary in a particular format for a short period. Detailed questions are subsequently developed from the diaries and form the basis of an in-depth interview with the diarist. The extent to which the researcher determines the format is a matter of judgment, but it is one that you must be able to defend. If there is time, we recommend that unstructured interviews are held to agree the format with the participants. Typical formats include those based on time (where the diarist records what they do, think or feel at specific times of the day), events (where the diarist makes the record whenever the activity, thought or feeling occurs) and random (where the diarist makes the choice).

Diary methods offer the advantage of allowing the perspectives of different diarists to be compared. They can be a useful means of gaining sensitive information or an alternative to using direct observation. In contrast to participant observation, where the researcher is involved in the research, in a diary study, data are collected and presented largely within the diarist's frame of reference. Stewart (1965) used diaries as part of a study of managers' jobs and cites the main advantages as:

- Diaries greatly increase the possible coverage of numbers and types of participants, and their geographical and industrial distribution.
- The data can be collected simultaneously, which is less time-consuming than observation.
- The classification of activities is made by the diarist rather than the observer, who may be unfamiliar with the technical aspects of the job.
- The diarist can record all activities, whereas an observer may be excluded from confidential discussions.

8.6.2 POTENTIAL PROBLEMS

Practical problems associated with diary studies include selecting participants who can express themselves well in writing, focusing the diary and providing encouragement over the record-keeping period. You will also find that setting up a diary study involves considerable time and effort. As with many other methods of data collection, there is also the issue of confidentiality. Stewart (1965) points out other disadvantages:

- There are severe limitations if the study is concerned with comparability, although these are reduced if the participants are a homogenous group.
- There may be difficulty in finding a suitable sample and the researcher may have to rely on volunteers.
- There will always be some unreliability in what is recorded.

This last point can be extended to the bias that can easily occur in the individual's recording. For example, the participants may misreport their activities or change their behaviour so that certain activities can be reported to put them in a favourable light. This can also happen when a researcher is using observation to collect data.

8.7 OBSERVATION

Observation can take place in a laboratory setting or in a natural setting. A natural setting is a 'research environment that would have existed had researchers never studied

KEY DEFINITIONS

Observation is a method for collecting data used in a laboratory or natural setting to observe and record people's actions and behaviour.

it' (Vogt, 1993, p. 150). A natural setting is preferred in a study designed under an interpretive paradigm because of the importance of context and its influence on the phenomenon being studied. This does not necessarily preclude the use of a laboratory setting, if that is an integral part of the research design.

8.7.1   TYPES OF OBSERVATION

The most common type of observation in business research is *non-participant observation* where the researcher observes and records what people say or do without being involved. The subjects of the research may not be aware that they are being observed, especially if they are being recorded on video or captured in photographs. As in all data collection methods, permission must be sought from the subjects in advance. These forms of data capture mean that if the observer is visible during the observation, he or she is not distracted by having to write notes, which could also influence the subjects' behaviour. If the focus of the research is dialogue, audio recordings can also be made. It is essential that reliable records are made.

Under an interpretive design, the themes relating to the actions and dialogue will emerge during the analysis of the recordings. However, in a study designed under a positivist paradigm, the observer may go on to measure the frequency of occurrence, time of duration or other quantitative data. Alternatively, a positivist observer may have prepared a schedule of phenomena of interest from the literature.

The second type of observation is *participant observation*. In this method, the researcher is fully involved with the participants and the phenomena being researched. The aim is to provide the means of obtaining a detailed understanding of values, motives and practices of those being observed. The main factors to be considered with this method of observation are the:

* purpose of the research
* cost of the research
* extent to which access can be gained
* extent to which the researcher would be comfortable in the role
* amount of time the researcher has available.

8.7.2   POTENTIAL PROBLEMS

There are a number of problems associated with observation techniques. One problem is that you cannot control variables in a natural setting, but by observing the behaviour in two different settings you can draw comparisons. Other problems are concerned with ethics, objectivity, visibility, technology for recording what people say and/or do, boredom, and the impact the researcher has on those observed. Problems of observer bias may arise, such as when one observer interprets an action differently from a colleague. Another problem can be that the observer fails to observe some activities because of distractions. In addition, the grid designed for recording observations may be deficient because it is ambiguous or incomplete.

Observing people in any setting is likely to make them wonder what you are doing. Knowing that they are being observed, may make them change their behaviour by becoming more productive than usual; more docile than usual; take more risks than usual, be less decisive than usual and so on. These are known as *demand characteristics*, because you are making demands on the individual, and this may affect the research. It may be possible to minimize the demand characteristics by not stating the exact purpose of the research. For example, instead of saying you are studying the effect of supervision on the level of productivity, you might say you are investigating the effect of different environments on job satisfaction.

Many years ago such an approach would be acceptable. After the observation you would state the true purpose of the research. However, under the ethical regulations for research now used by many countries and universities it is not acceptable to mislead the participants. It is usually necessary for you to explain beforehand the purpose of the research to the participants and to ensure that they understand it. In some universities it is necessary to obtain the signed consent of the participant. The ethics rules in most countries do not allow you to observe people without their prior permission and without explaining the purpose of your research.

8.8 FOCUS GROUPS

KEY DEFINITIONS

A focus group is a method for collecting data whereby selected participants discuss their reactions and feelings about a product, service, situation or concept, under the guidance of a group leader.

Focus groups are used to gather data relating to the feelings and opinions of a group of people who are involved in a common situation or discussing the same phenomenon. Focus groups combine interviewing and observation, but allow fresh data to be generated through the interaction of the group. They can be used in an interpretive methodology but are also used by positivists before or after conducting a survey. Focus groups have a long history and were used during the Second World War to examine the effectiveness of propaganda (Merton and Kendall, 1946). In business research, focus groups have long been popular in marketing research, but are increasingly being used in other disciplines.

Focus groups can be useful for a number of purposes, such as to:

- develop knowledge of a new phenomenon
- generate propositions from the issues that emerge
- develop questions for a survey
- obtain feedback on the findings of research in which the focus group members participated.

8.8.1 SETTING UP A FOCUS GROUP

Under the guidance of a group leader, selected participants are encouraged to discuss their opinions, reactions and feelings about a product, service, and type of situation or concept. For example, you might wish to get a group of employees from a company together to discuss what they feel about the profit-sharing scheme in operation, or a group of consumers to discuss their views on a particular brand of cell phone or a television programme. Listening to other group members' views stimulates participants to voice their own opinions. This helps produce 'data and insights that would be less accessible without the interaction found in a group' (Morgan, 1988, p. 12).

If you are planning to hold a focus group, you will need to enlist help. You will probably want to facilitate the meeting yourself, which means you will need someone else to take detailed notes and another person to manage the audio and/or video recording. Many researchers find it essential to make a video recording of the discussions as the visual cues can be even more revealing than the audio or written records. You will need to prepare a list of issues you want to cover and, if you are the facilitator, you will find it

technique difficult to classify but we include it in the section on quantitative approaches. The other methods we discuss in this chapter are non-quantifying methods and will be of particular interest to interpretivists.

9.3   QUANTIFYING METHODS

If you are designing a positivist study, you may collect most of your data in numerical form (via a self-completion questionnaire survey, for example) and you only have a small amount of qualitative data from the responses to open-ended questions that need to be quantified. If you are using *methodological triangulation*, you will not necessarily want to quantify certain qualitative data. Typical examples are where you collect data from exploratory interviews to help you identify variables for developing hypotheses, or conduct post-survey interviews with a small number of respondents to aid the interpretation and validity of the results. However, other studies require the quantification of very large amounts of data (for example the analysis of documents).

Many researchers quantifying small amounts of qualitative data adopt an informal method, while those faced with the challenge of quantifying large amounts tend to use a formal method known as content analysis.

9.3.1   INFORMAL METHODS

Positivist researchers often use *informal methods* to quantify qualitative data, such as counting the frequency of occurrence of the phenomena under study. This allows them to examine 'such things as repetitive or patterned behaviours' (Lindlof, 1995, p. 216).

If the action, event or other phenomenon occurs very frequently in the data, you might decide to omit some references to it to avoid repetition. This is not a shortcut because every occurrence must be counted to determine which data should be omitted. Frequency of occurrence can also be used to investigate whether an action, event or other phenomenon of interest is a common or rare occurrence. Another way of selecting data of interest is to designate items as 'important' and therefore retained in the analysis, or 'not important' and therefore ignored when counting the frequency of occurrence. You will need to be careful not to lose the richness and detail of the data in the process.

If you use informal methods to quantify your qualitative research data, it is essential that you explain the criteria for including and discarding data in your methodology chapter so that your supervisor and others can see that you have applied your methods systematically and rigorously. In addition, you must be clear about why the method is appropriate, as you will need to justify your choice. This will entail comparing its advantages and disadvantages with appropriate alternatives.

9.3.2   CONTENT ANALYSIS

Content analysis is a widely used method for quantifying qualitative data. It is usually associated with a positivist paradigm, although it has been described as 'the diagnostic tool of qualitative researchers, which they use when faced with a mass of open-ended material to make sense of' (Mostyn, 1985, p. 117). Content analysis is a method by which selected items of qualitative data are systematically converted to numerical data. Normally a document is examined, although the technique can be used to analyse other forms of communication, such as newspapers, broadcasts, audio recordings of interviews, and video recordings of non-participant observations and focus groups. Mostyn (1985) claims the technique was used to analyse communications as early as 1740.

If you have a large amount of data to analyse, the first step is to determine the basis for selecting a *sample*. However, if the amount of data is manageable and you have sufficient time, you can analyse all the data. The next step is to determine the *coding units*, such as a particular word, character, item or theme which is found in the material. Table 9.1 gives some examples of coding units.

TABLE 9.1 Examples of coding units

Coding unit	Example
Words/phrases	Examine minutes of company/union meetings for the word 'dispute'
	Examine circulars and press releases to shareholders for the phrase 'increased dividends'
Theme	Examine minutes of company/union meetings for examples where agreement was reached
	Examine circulars and press releases to shareholders for examples where increases in productivity are linked to increased profits
Item	Examine newspapers for articles focusing on small businesses
	Examine company reports for items dealing with environmental issues
Time	Measure the time allocated to business news items on the news bulletins of different television channels

Once you have determined the coding units, you can construct a *coding frame*, which lists the coding units in the first column, leaving room for the analysis of each communication to be added on the horizontal axis. The analysis can be based on the frequency of occurrence and/or other factors. For example, if you were examining the *Financial Times* for articles focusing on small businesses, you might want to analyse such things as the date of the paper, the page number, the length of the article, the author, the main issues in the article, names of firms, owners and so on. Under a positivist paradigm, the data could then be further analysed using statistics.

If you are planning to use content analysis, we advise you to read the following studies, which we have selected because the researchers explain their methods:

- Czepiec (1993) examined advertising traits by analysing 454 advertisements appearing in the *People's Daily* between 1980 and 1989 to determine which factors Chinese businessmen consider most important when promoting their industrial products. She analysed the text of the advertisements for mention of 21 advertising traits which had been generated from previous studies concerned with buying behaviour.
- Todd, McKeen and Gallupe (1995) examined changes in the knowledge and skill requirements in information systems (IS) by analysing recruitment advertisements placed in four major newspapers between 1970 and 1990. For each different type of IS job, the data were summarized over three main skills levels, then detailed over seven sub-categories. The data were also summarized to show the proportion of advertisements that referred to a main skill category at least once, and the average number of phrases per skill category was expressed as a percentage of the total

number of phrases. Their study demonstrates the volume of data that can be generated, the sophistication of analysis and the range of data displays that can be used.

- Pullman, McGuire and Cleveland (2005) analysed customers' comments from a hotel satisfaction survey. They provide a thorough guide to the methods used to count words and determine association between certain words. They also explain how they used linguistic analysis to explore the semantics, syntax and context of comments, which led to the identification of key ideas, evaluation of their relative importance and predictions of customer behaviour. The authors also provide worked examples of various software programs that support content analysis.

If you are analysing secondary data, content analysis offers a number of advantages to researchers over other methods because you need only select a population or sample and you have a permanent record which can be examined many times. You can avoid the time and expense associated with setting up and conducting questionnaire surveys, unstructured interviews, focus groups or observation. This leaves you free to spend more time on your analysis. It is also a non-obtrusive method, which means that the subjects of the study are not likely to be aware of or influenced by your interest. Finally, the systems and procedures for carrying out content analysis are very clear, so researchers who are concerned with the reliability and validity of their study will find the method highly acceptable.

If content analysis is appropriate for your paradigm, it can be a useful way of systematically analysing qualitative data by converting the material into quantitative data. However, it suffers from a number of problems. Silverman (1993, p. 59) contends that 'its theoretical basis is unclear and its conclusions can often be trite'. There is also the concern that if you select only the words or phrases you have determined are of interest, you may ignore large amounts of data that could help you understand the phenomena under study at a deeper level.

Another problem is concerned with the availability of published data. For example, perhaps you want to analyse quarterly data for the past five years, but subsequently find that one quarter's data are not available. You also need to remember that any documents you are analysing will have been written for another purpose and audience, and this influences their contents and wording. Finally, with large amounts of data, the method can be time-consuming and tedious, and requires a consistency of approach and high levels of concentration.

9.4   MAIN ISSUES IN NON-QUANTIFYING METHODS

New researchers have a tendency to design very ambitious studies. If you are designing your study under an interpretive paradigm, you are seeking depth and richness of data, so you should limit the *scope* of your study. This will provide more focus and help reduce the amount of qualitative data you collect. You can also reduce the amount of data you collect by conducting fewer interviews, focus groups, observations and so on. The breadth of scope of your study depends on the level of your course, what is normal in your discipline and what is acceptable to your supervisor, research committee and/ or sponsors.

9.4.1   REDUCING THE DATA

If you are designing a study under an interpretive paradigm, you will want to use *non-quantifying methods* to analyse your qualitative data. In an interpretive study, you will

KEY DEFINITIONS

Data reduction is 'a
form of data analysis
that sharpens, sorts,
focuses, discards and
reorganises data'
(Miles and Huberman,
1994, p. 11).

have collected a mass of qualitative data such as published documents, field
notes and interview transcripts that must be reviewed, analysed and interpreted. Whichever method(s) you decide to use to analyse your data, it will
involve reducing the data. *Data reduction* is 'a form of analysis that sharpens,
sorts, focuses, discards and reorganises data in such a way that "final" conclusions can be drawn and verified' (Miles and Huberman, 1994, p. 11).

Continuous data reduction involves discarding irrelevant data and collating data where relationships of interest exist. *Anticipatory data reduction*
occurs when the researcher uses a theoretical framework or highly structured
research instrument that leads to certain data being ignored. This is not usually a feature
of an interpretive study, as it restricts collection of rich data and limits any deep understanding of the phenomena under study.

You would be right in thinking that data reduction means that you will ignore some
of the data you have collected. This is because it is not until you are familiar with your
data that you can determine what is relevant and what is not. Consequently, *reflection* is
a key part of an interpretive methodology. Once again, imagine you are from another
planet and you are watching one of the events at the Olympic Games. Until you have
spent a considerable amount of time analysing and reflecting on what you observe, you
would find it very difficult to make sense of the behaviour of the participants.

9.4.2 RESTRUCTURING THE DATA

Data reduction can be achieved by *restructuring the data*. The data may have been
collected in a chronological form dictated by the method of collection (diary methods
and observation, for example) or because it is a convenient framework for asking questions (in interviews, for example). If you are using a theoretical framework, this will
provide categories into which the data can be fitted. If you are not using a theoretical
framework, a suitable structure may emerge during the data collection stage.

9.4.3 DETEXTUALIZING THE DATA

Data reduction of text can be achieved by *detextualizing the data*. This simply means
summarizing the data in the form of a diagram. For example, if a diarist or interviewee
gave you information about who he or she communicated with during the previous day
in the office, you could summarize these interactions by drawing a network diagram.

We can now summarize the main features of qualitative data analysis (see Box 9.1).
Although we have explained that data reduction is a key part of analysing qualitative
data, it is important that you keep all the data you have collected so that you can provide
your supervisor and/or sponsor with an audit trail showing the process you followed to
arrive at your conclusions. You will use some of the data to provide quotations or examples to illustrate your findings.

BOX 9.1 Main features of qualitative data analysis

- Reducing the data – finding a systematic way to select relevant data, often through the use of coding.
- Restructuring the data – using a pre-existing theoretical framework or one that emerges during the data collection stage to provide categories into which the data can be fitted.
- Detextualizing the data – summarizing data in the form of a diagram.

MAIN ELEMENTS IN THE PROCESS

Morse (1994) suggests that all the different approaches to analysing qualitative data are based on three key elements in the process, although the emphasis varies according to the methodology used:

- *Comprehending* is acquiring a full understanding of the setting, culture and study topic before the research commences. There is considerable debate in interpretive research on how much prior knowledge the researcher should have. There are those who believe that the researcher should not approach the study with pre-knowledge and the mind should be uncluttered by previous theories and concepts which might block out new perspectives and discoveries. Morse argues that the researcher does need to be familiar with the literature at the commencement of the study, but should remain distanced from it so that new discoveries can be made without being contaminated by preconceptions.
- *Synthesizing* is the drawing together of different themes and concepts from the research and forming them into new, integrated patterns. It is where items of data are reduced and sifted to give a general explanation of what is occurring.
- *Theorizing* is the 'constant development and manipulation of malleable theoretical schemes until the best theoretical scheme is developed' (Morse, 1994, p. 32). Theory gives qualitative data structure and application. It involves confronting the data with alternative explanations. Causal links or patterns can be hypothesized and 'tested' with selected informants who may refute or verify them. There are four ways of developing theory:
    - identify the beliefs and values in the data and attempt to make links with theory
    - use lateral thinking by examining and comparing the concepts and data from other settings
    - construct theory from the data by induction.
    - Recontextualize the data through the process of generalization, so that the theory emerging from the study can be applied to other settings and populations. In the process the researcher will return to existing theories to place the results in a context and establish new developments and models or new links.

This provides general guidance for researchers who are faced with the task of analysing qualitative data. However, you need to remember that these processes rely on the fact that you are very familiar with your data. This requires a systematic approach. We are now ready to examine some of the main methods.

USING QUALITATIVE DATA ANALYSIS SOFTWARE

In the past 20 years, the use of *qualitative data analysis* (QDA) software such as *NVivo* and *ATLAS.ti* has proliferated. This is not surprising, since the process of conducting an analysis on a manual basis is a formidable task when a large amount of data is involved. The widespread use of the internet and information communication technology (ICT), together with the availability of digital recording devices and voice recognition software, means that a substantial amount of data is in digital form or can be converted into digital format fairly easily. This has made the use of QDA software much more convenient than when the first programs were developed.

Dembowski and Hanmer-Lloyd (1995) identified the following ways in which QDA software can assist the interpretivist:

- importing text

- storing data
- coding the data
- searching and retrieving text segments
- stimulating interaction with the data
- relationship building within the data.

Wolfe, Gephardt and Johnson (1993) offer actual and potential applications of QDA software to management research and review the issues researchers should consider. They point to the practical issues of entering and preparing textual data for analysis, and emphasize that QDA software should be used to support the process, and interpretation is conducted by the researcher.

Critics argue that using QDA software distances the researcher from the data and the software encourages a mechanical approach to interpreting the data. This may be the case for new researchers. Gilbert (2002) identifies three stages that researchers experience in the use of software for analysing qualitative data:

1. The tactile–digital divide where the researcher must become familiar with working on a computer screen instead of the original documents.
2. The coding trap where researchers find that the software brings them too close to the detail of the data and much time can be spent in coding rather than taking a broader, more reflective view.
3. The meta-cognitive shift where researchers learn to reflect on and assess the software processes. It is at this stage that the researcher thinks on how and why they work in a particular way and the impact this may have on the analysis of the data.

If you have access to QDA software and are planning to use it for your research, you should remember that the software will not do the analysis for you, but it will help you with the process of structuring, coding (and often displaying data summaries), but the analysis and interpretation is up to you. You need to allow time to follow the on-line tutorials and become familiar with the software you are going to use. Johnston (2006, p. 387) advises students to keep a research journal inside the software program 'to rapidly and openly record their thoughts, questions, reflections and emergent theoretical ideas to a central executive point in the program'.

9.5   GENERAL APPROACHES

9.5.1   GENERAL ANALYTICAL PROCEDURE

Miles and Huberman (1994) describe a *general analytical procedure* for analysing qualitative data, which is not tied to a particular methodology. This can be used with any interpretive *methodology* and emphasizes the methodical rigour and systematic processes which are required. All qualitative data collection methods generate a considerable volume of material and the procedure shown in Box 9.2 offers a method by which it can be managed and controlled.

The extent to which your analysis is structured will depend on the extent to which you structured the collection of your data. A highly structured application of the above procedure is described in an evaluation conducted in an international business setting by Jinkerson, Cummings, Neisendorf and Schwandt (1992). The study was complex. It was concerned with the analysis of training needs in the tax practice of a firm of consultants and involved a number of researchers using personal interviews, telephone interviews and a postal questionnaire survey in 14 European countries.

BOX 9.2   General analytical procedure for qualitative data

1. Convert any rough field notes into a written record that you and your supervisors will still be able to understand later on. You may wish to add your own thoughts and reflections. This will be the start of your tentative analysis. You should distinguish your interpretation and speculations from your factual field notes.

2. Ensure that any material you have collected from interviews, observations or original documents is properly referenced. The reference should indicate who was involved, the date and time, the context, the circumstances leading to the data collection and the possible implications for the research. You may find it useful to record your references on a pro-forma summary sheet, which you can store in an indexed system for ease of retrieval.

3. Start coding the data as soon as possible. This will involve allocating a specific code to each variable, concept or theme that you wish to identify. The code can be allocated to a specific word or to a phrase. The use of exemplars is helpful when applying the code and explaining its significance in your dissertation or thesis. The code will allow you to store, retrieve and reorganize data in a variety of ways. You will find it easier if you start with as many codes as you feel necessary and later collapse them into a smaller number.

4. You can then start grouping the codes into small categories according to patterns or themes which emerge. This is not a mechanical task, but will require considerable reflection. If you are not using a theoretical framework, do not attempt to impose categories, but allow them to emerge from the data. Compare new items of data as they are collected with your existing codes and categories, and modify them as required.

5. At various stages, write summaries of your findings at that point. The discipline of putting your thoughts on paper will help with your analysis and highlight any deficiencies to be remedied.

6. Use your summaries to construct generalizations that you can use to confront existing theories or to construct a new theory.

7. Continue until you are satisfied that the generalizations are sufficiently robust to stand the analysis of existing theories or the construction of a new theory.

Two specific research instruments were used: a master questionnaire, which provided the conceptual framework for data collection, and a data checklist to track the collection of data from respondents. The questionnaire identified themes, key points and questions and each received a unique code, as did each country, office and participant. The data checklist was completed by the project researchers at the end of an interview or on receipt of data from respondents and showed the data collected. This permitted any missing data to be identified and subsequently collected. The researchers maintained six sets of files for the study and these are described in Table 9.2.

The process of research was conducted through the use of work papers which were contained in the first three files:

*   Work paper 1 contained the raw data from interview notes
*   Work paper 2 summarized the raw data in Workbook 1 for each of the main points for each of the offices in the study
*   Work paper 3 reconstructed the data in Workbook 2 to create a picture across all key points within a single theme for all offices in each country
*   Work paper 4 was a country summary where the researchers wrote an overall assessment of the tax practice and training situation in that country
*   Work paper 5 contained the findings of the research and the recommendations.

This may appear to be a very elaborate system, but it must be remembered that this was a particularly large and complex project. In addition to illustrating the use of systems and procedures to manage and analyse qualitative data, this example demonstrates the amount of planning and management required for a research project.

TABLE 9.2	Files documenting the study
File type	**Description of contents**
Raw data	Interview notes: documents describing existing training strategies etc: completed questionnaires: Work paper 1
Data summaries	Summaries of raw data: Workbook 2
Data reconstruction	Relationship with and across countries on key themes; notes about insights. Hunches, developing interpretations; drafts of reports including findings and conclusions; Workbooks 3, 4, and 5
Methodology	Descriptions of methodology and its limitations; description of instrument development processes and procedures for administration; correspondence with management about the study
Plans, proposal and budget	Work programme and timeliness, proposal, budget for personnel level, payroll and non-payroll
Instruments and tools	Data collection and analysis tools

Source: Jinkerson, Cummings, Neisendorf and Schwandt (1992, p. 278).

In this section we have focused on methods of analysing qualitative data through coding, summarizing, categorizing and identifying patterns or themes. Some qualitative researchers prefer a more intuitive approach to data analysis and 'assume that through continued readings of the source material and through vigilance over one's presuppositions, one can capture the essence of an account' (Miles and Huberman, 1994, p. 8). Although we have suggested ways in which you can analyse the qualitative data you have collected, the value of the analysis will depend on the quality of your interpretation.

9.5.2 DATA DISPLAYS

Miles and Huberman (1994) also provide a comprehensive guide to using *data displays*, such as a network, matrix (plural – matrices), chart or graphs, which are 'a visual format that presents information systematically, so the user can draw valid conclusions and take needed action' (Miles and Huberman, 1994, p. 91). Indeed, their approach not only spans the analysis of qualitative data, but the entire research design from the beginning to the writing of the final report. In this section we describe some of their suggestions for data displays for the analysis of qualitative data.

> **KEY DEFINITIONS**
>
> A data display is a summary of data in a diagrammatic form that allows the user to draw valid conclusions.

There are no limits to the types of displays which can be generated from qualitative data, but they fall into two major categories: networks and matrices:

- A *network* has a series of labelled nodes with links between them, which represent relationships.
- A *matrix* is a table with defined columns and rows and appropriate headings. If the matrix displays a chronological sequence of events, the headings of the columns show the dates and the row labels show the event, action or other phenomenon of interest. If time information is not relevant, another simple form of matrix might show partially ordered data that is little more than a checklist. A complex matrix may illustrate variables, periods of time and conditions, as well as the researcher's thoughts and evaluations. Whether a matrix is simple or complex, you will have to spend considerable time designing it and summarizing your raw data.

Miles and Huberman have developed variations within these two main display categories to deal with a number of situations which can confront the researcher. For a study in its early stages, they recommend some form of partially ordered display. However, if time is a crucial aspect of a study, they recommend a time-ordered display. If you are considering the reactions and relationships of people you may wish to prepare a role-ordered matrix where you are examining a clearly defined set of key variables. In this case, a conceptually oriented display would be appropriate. Box 9.3 shows Miles and Huberman's general advice for constructing data displays.

BOX 9.3   General advice for constructing data displays

- Consider what appropriate displays can be used to bring together qualitative data so that conclusions can be drawn.

- Be inventive in using displays; there are no limits on the types of diagrams and illustrations which can be used.

- Constructing displays is an iterative process where you construct an initial display and draw some tentative conclusions which will be modified, or even overturned, as new items of data become available and new displays are constructed.

- Be systematic in your approach to constructing displays and analysing data, but be aware that by becoming more formal in your approach there are the dangers of becoming narrow, obsessive or blind to new meaning which might emerge from the data.

- Use mixed models in your analysis and draw from different methodologies and approaches in your analysis.

- Remain self-aware of the entire research process and use supportive friends to act as critical voices on matters and issues you are taking for granted.

- Communicate what you learn with colleagues who are interested in qualitative studies. In particular share your analytical experiences.

Source: Miles and Huberman (1994, p. 310).

An *events flow network* is useful for displaying a complex sequence of events, in terms of both chronological order and relationships. It will also lay the foundation for a causal analysis: 'what events led to what further events and what mechanisms underlay those associations' (Miles and Huberman, 1994, p. 113). Figure 9.1 shows an example of an events flow network where the researcher had interviewed university students who had interrupted their studies. The students' experiences are presented in the boxes in the left-hand column, and the researcher's summary of the major forces moving the student to the next experience are shown on the right. The '+' signs indicate the strength of the various forces; the '–' signs, the strength of the students' dissatisfaction with the succeeding experiences.

An effects matrix is useful for selecting and displaying data which represents the changed state of individuals, relationships, groups or organizations. Table 9.3 shows an effects matrix which displays data on one or more outcomes where the researcher was examining organizational change in a school. The researcher has divided the outcome of change at the school into structural changes, procedural or operating changes and more general relational or social climate changes, where the conceptual sequence is from 'hard' to 'soft' change. In addition, these aspects are displayed separately for the early use period (the first and second years) and the later use period (the third year). The researcher also distinguishes between primary changes, which followed directly from the requirements of change, and 'spin-offs', some of which had not been fully anticipated. Thus, the matrix displays effects, time of use and primary as well as spin-off outcomes.

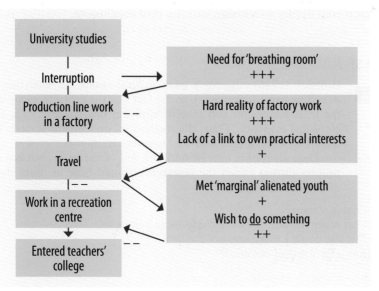

FIGURE 9.1 Events flow network: students' learning and work experience
Source: Miles and Huberman (1994, p. 114).

TABLE 9.3 Effects matrix: Organization changes after implementation of the ECRI Program

EFFECT TYPES	Early use 1st and 2nd yrs		Later use 3rd yr	
	PRIMARY CHANGES	SPIN-OFFS	PRIMARY CHANGES	SPIN-OFFS
Structural	Scheduling: ECRI all morning, rescheduling music, phys. ed. Helping teacher named: has dual status(teach/admin)	Cutting back on math, optional activities Two separate regimens in school Ambiguity of status and role	Integrated scheduling, cross-age grouping in grades 2–6	Less individual latitude: classroom problems become organizational problems
Procedural	No letter grades, no norms	Parents uneasy 2 regimens in class Teachers insecure Loosens age-grading system	ECRI evaluation sheets, tightening supervision	Teachers more visible, inspectable
	Institutionalizing assistance via helping teacher	In-house assistance mechanism implanted	More uniformity in work in all classes	Problems, solution more common, public
Relations/ Climate	Users are minority, band together	Cliques, friction between users, non-users	Tighter academic press	Reduction in 'fun activities', projects (eg Xmas)
			Perception by teachers of collective venture	More lateral help More 'public' distress

Source: Miles and Huberman (1994, p. 138).

Both the events flow network and the effects matrix are examples of simple diagrams and it is possible to construct far more complex displays. It is important to remember that constructing the display is only one aspect of the analytical process. The first step in constructing any type of display is to become familiar with your data; then construct your display and, finally, write up your conclusions.

9.6   QUASI-JUDICIAL METHOD

KEY DEFINITIONS

The quasi-judicial method is a method of analysis that involves the use of rational argument to interpret qualitative data.

Bromley (1986) suggests a *quasi-judicial method* for analysing qualitative data. The name is derived from the fact that the procedures are drawn from the legal profession and involve applying rational argument to interpret empirical evidence. Thus, the method focuses on the nature, source and quality of the evidence and the argument it supports.

Data analysis is not left until the end of the study, but is a continuous process during which the researcher should bear in mind the following questions:

- What is at issue?
- What other relevant evidence might there be?
- How else could I make sense of the data?
- How were the data obtained?

9.6.1   RULES

Bromley (1986) identifies six rules which must be applied when adopting a quasi-judicial method of analysis. Table 9.4 shows Bromley's rules and their legal equivalent. Brown and Canter (1985) illustrate how these rules can be used to analyse *interviews*. 'The researcher's task is to construct a multiperspective account of the particular event he or she is investigating, drawn from the explanations given by the primary participants' (Brown and Canter, 1985, p. 243).

TABLE 9.4 Rules for the quasi-judicial method and legal equivalents

Bromley's six rules	Legal equivalent
1. Investigator reports results truthfully	Testimony under oath
2. Aims and objectives of the investigation are stated explicitly	Formal charges are laid
3. Assessment of the achievement of aims and objectives	Presentation of evidence in court
4. Investigator is properly trained	Legal qualifications required to play formal role in court
5. The person is placed in his or her ecological (physical, cultural, social, symbolic) context	Extenuating/mitigating circumstances are considered
6. The account is written in good plain English	Case law/understandable to jury/as viewed by a reasonable person

Source: Brown and Canter (1985, p. 227).

9.6.2   PROCEDURE

Robson (1993) has adapted Bromley's rules to provide a procedure for analysing qualitative data in a *case study*. These are shown in Box 9.4.

BOX 9.4   Procedure for the quasi-judicial method

1.   State the initial problem and issues as clearly as possible.

2.   Collect background information to provide a context in terms of which the problems and issues are to be understood.

3.   Put forward prima facie explanations of the problems and issues.

4.   Use these explanations to guide the search for additional evidence. If they do not fit the available evidence, work out alternative explanations.

5.   Continue the search for sufficient evidence to eliminate as many of the suggested explanations as possible, in the hope that one will account for all of the available evidence and be contradicted by none of it. Evidence may be direct or indirect, but must be admissible, relevant and obtained from competent and credible sources.

6.   Closely examine the sources of evidence, as well as the evidence itself. All items should be checked for consistency and accuracy. This is analogous to legal cross-examination in the case of personal testimony.

7.   Enquire critically into the internal coherence, logic and external validity of the network of argument claiming to settle the issues and solve the problems.

8.   Select the most likely interpretation compatible with the evidence.

9.   Formulating the acceptable explanation usually carries an implication for action which has to be worked out.

10. Prepare an account in the form of a report. It should contribute to 'case law' by virtue of the general principles employed in explaining the specific case.

Source: Robson (1993, p. 376).

If you examine these procedures, you will see that they are underpinned by the main elements of an analysis identified by Morse (1994), which we described in Section 9.4.4. The emphasis is on the importance of examining and re-examining the data (the evidence) and seeking explanations which fit the data. For a substantial study you may find that the detailed procedures are difficult to apply, but the principles will be of help in assisting you to reflect on your data at various stages within the research. We have also found that the procedures, using the four questions set down by Bromley, are very helpful if you reach a sticking point in your analysis or are confronted by items of data that do not seem to fit.

9.7   METHODS BASED ON PERSONAL CONSTRUCT THEORY

9.7.1   REPERTORY GRID TECHNIQUE

We began our discussion of *repertory grid technique* in the previous chapter because the method combines the collection and analysis of data. You will remember that using personal construct theory (Kelly, 1955), a matrix is developed which contains a mathematical representation of the perceptions and constructs a person uses to understand and manage his or her world.

KEY DEFINITIONS

Repertory grid technique is a method based on personal construct theory that generates a mathematical representation of a participant's perceptions and constructs.

An example of business research using repertory grid technique is provided by a study in the workplace by Brook (1986). Using the technique in addition to interviews and questionnaires, she sought to measure the effectiveness of a management training programme. The grid was based on typical interpersonal situations encountered by managers in their daily work, together with two elements referring to performance before and after training, and two elements relating to examples of their best and worst performance. The situations she used to elicit the elements are shown in Box 9.5. The repertory grid provided 'rich and varied data on individual subjects which could then be validated against other information obtained from before-and-after interviews and questionnaires' (Brook, 1986, p. 495).

BOX 9.5   Example of situations used to elicit elements for repertory grid

1. A time when I delegated an important task to a co-worker.
2. The time when I actively opposed the ideas of my controlling officer (or someone in authority).
3. A time when I had to deal with a problem brought to me by a member of my staff.
4. A time when I had to make an important decision concerning my research or other work.
5. A time when I had a professional association with some outside organization.
6. The occasion when I made or proposed changes in the running and conduct of section meetings or other procedures of a similar nature.
7. An occasion when I felt most satisfied with my work performance.
8. An occasion when I felt least satisfied with my work performance.
9. My professional self now.
10. My professional self a year ago.

Source: Brook (1986, p. 495).

Interpretivists using the technique will be interested in gaining understanding of the scores on the grids from a qualitative analysis of the explanations given by the interviewees when they were completing the grid. Content analysis can be used to count the frequency of occurrence of elements and constructs (if the researcher has not used a standard set for all interviewees) with a view to identifying common trends. It is also possible to compare individuals' grids for cognitive content and structure. Although it is possible to examine a relatively small matrix for patterns and differences between constructs and elements, a larger matrix would require the use of software to generate the grid and analyse the data. A follow-up interview with the participant increases the validity of the statistical analysis, but you will need to bear in mind that the meaning given to events and experiences can change over time.

We mentioned in the previous chapter that part of the controversy surrounding repertory grid technique is that the scores on the grid can be analysed statistically. The particular statistics used should be appropriate for variables measured on an ordinal scale (see Chapters 11 and 12). If you have sufficient data, cluster analysis and factor analysis may be useful for aiding the interpretation of the data. If the hypotheses tested are not underpinned by theory or deductive reasoning, a mathematical 'relationship' may be found that is entirely spurious.

Potential problems are that it is very time-consuming and participants are not always able to compare and contrast the triads or dyads of elements or to describe constructs in the prescribed manner. There is also the difficulty of how to aggregate data from individual grids.

If you are thinking of using repertory grid technique, we advise you to read Stewart and Stewart (1981), Jankowicz (2004) and/or Tan and Hunter (2002).

9.7.2   COGNITIVE MAPPING

KEY DEFINITIONS

Cognitive mapping is a method based on personal construct theory that structures a participant's perceptions in the form of a diagram.

Cognitive mapping attempts to extend personal construct theory (Kelly, 1955) beyond the use of repertory grid technique and can be used to structure, analyse and make sense of written or verbal accounts of problems. It can also be used to summarize transcripts of interviews or other documentary data in a way that promotes analysis, questioning and understanding of the data. It also provides a powerful method for taking notes during an interview.

Box 9.6 shows the main stages in cognitive mapping.

BOX 9.6   Main stages in cognitive mapping

1. An account of the problem is broken into phrases of about ten words which retain the language of the person providing the account. These are treated as distinct concepts which are then reconnected to represent the account in a graphical format. This reveals the pattern of reasoning about a problem in a way that linear text cannot.

2. Pairs of phrases can be united in a single concept where one provides a meaningful contrast to the other. These phrases are Kelly's constructs where meaning is retained through contrast.

3. The distinct phrases are linked to form a hierarchy of means and ends; essentially explanations leading to consequences. This involves deciding on the status of one concept relative to another. There are a number of categories or levels defined in a notional hierarchy that help the user make these decisions. Meaning is retained through the context.

The technique is often used in projects concerned with the development of strategy and can be useful in action research studies. Box 9.7 shows a procedure for cognitive mapping that focuses on strategic issues.

BOX 9.7   Procedure for cognitive mapping

1. Attempt to construct your map on one sheet of A4 so that links can be made.
2. Start mapping about two-thirds of the way up the paper in the middle and try to keep concepts in small rectangles of text rather than as continuous lines.
3. Separate the sentences into phrases.
4. Build up a hierarchy.
5. Watch out for goals as the discussion unfolds and for potential strategic issues.
6. Hold on to opposite poles for additional clarification.
7. Add meaning to concepts by placing them in the imperative form; include actors and actions if possible.
8. Retain ownership by not abbreviating words and phrases used by the problem owner.
9. Identify the option and outcome within each pair of concepts.
10. Ensure that a generic concept is superordinate to specific items that contribute to it.
11. Code the first pole as that which the problem owner sees as the primary idea.
12. Tidying up can provide a more complete understanding of the problem.

Source: Adapted from Ackermann, Eden and Cropper (1990).

Cope is a software program that has been developed to aid cognitive mapping. There is no pre-set framework, other than the nodes and linkages convention. This means the researcher can impose any structuring convention that seems appropriate. The program can handle complex data, which are held in a database in a form that is amenable to analysis and presentation. As its name suggests, *Cope* aids the management of large amounts of data, but it also reduces the need for early data reduction and compels the researcher to be explicit about the assumptions he or she is using to structure and analyse the data. It can be used to build models that retain the meaning of the data and aid 'the development of theoretical accounts of phenomena' (Cropper, Eden and Ackermann, 1990, p. 347). This makes it a useful tool for researchers using a grounded theory methodology and the presentation of research findings satisfies the recommendations of Miles and Huberman (1994). Figure 9.2 shows an example of a cognitive map using *Cope*.

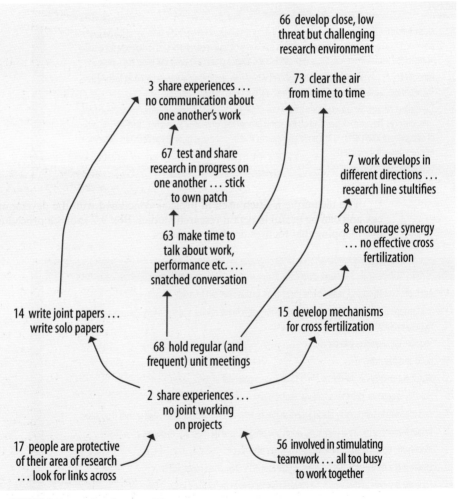

FIGURE 9.2 Example of a cognitive map

Source: Cropper, Eden and Ackermann (1990, p. 350).

KEY DEFINITIONS

Grounded theory is a methodology in which a systematic set of procedures is used to develop an inductively derived theory about phenomena.

9.8 GROUNDED THEORY

You will remember that *grounded theory* is 'a systematic set of procedures to develop an inductively derived grounded theory about a phenomenon. The findings of the research constitute a theoretical formulation of the reality under investigation, rather than consisting of a set of numbers, or a group of loosely related themes' (Strauss and Corbin, 1990, p. 24). We began our discussion of grounded theory in Chapter 5, when we were explaining the main methodologies that are used in business research, and continued our discussion in Chapter 8 in the context of data collection. Analysis occurs during the course of data collection and it is this aspect that we examine here.

9.8.1 CODING

The first stage of analysis under a grounded theory methodology is *coding*. The codes are labels which enable the qualitative data to be separated, compiled and organized. The codes are organized in a hierarchical framework:

- *Open coding* involves identifying, analysing and categorizing the raw data. It represents the basic level, where the codes are simple and topical.
- *Axial coding* involves connecting categories and sub-categories on a more conceptual level than was adopted at the open coding stage. The codes are more abstract.
- *Selective coding* involves selecting the core category and systematically relating it to other categories.

In practice, these three levels of coding are conducted simultaneously (particularly open coding and axial coding). It is important to emphasize that grounded theory requires the discovery and creation of codes from interpretation of the data. This contrasts with the approach under a positivist paradigm, where coding requires logically deduced, predetermined codes into which the data are placed. We will now examine the process in a little more detail.

Open coding of raw data involves a number of processes. First, the researcher breaks down and labels the individual elements of information, making the data more easily recognizable and less complicated to manage. These codes are then organized into a pattern of concepts and categories, together with their properties. This is accomplished by classifying the different elements into distinct ideas (the concepts) and grouping similar concepts into categories and sub-categories. The properties are those characteristics and attributes by which the concepts and categories can be recognized. The properties of each category of concepts must be defined along a continuum.

The labels by which the concepts and categories of concepts are known are entirely subjective (chosen by the researcher). However, the label should reflect their nature and content. As the concepts are grouped into more abstract categories, so too should the labels become more conceptual. The labels can come from a variety of sources; for example technical literature, interviewees and informants – *in vivo* codes (Glaser, 1978, p. 70; Strauss, 1987, p. 33) – or from the researcher's own imagination and vocabulary. However, the labels should be explained. Labels with technical content or unfamiliar jargon can cause problems of interpretation to readers outside the field. Other problems can arise when common terms are used as codes; sometimes readers can be biased by a prior knowledge or understanding of a term which conflicts with or does not reflect what is intended by the researcher. Therefore, it is important that the researcher's interpretation of the code labels is given.

Axial coding is an extension of open coding that involves connecting categories and sub-categories on a more conceptual level than was adopted at the open coding stage. Whereas the earlier stage of coding involved the breaking down and separation of individual elements, axial coding is the restructuring of the data and developing various patterns with the intention of revealing links and relationships. The process includes the development of the properties of concepts and categories of concepts, and linking them at the dimensional level. At this stage, the researcher will construct mini-theories about the relationships that might exist within the data and which need to be verified. Although the overall theoretical framework will not be discovered during axial coding, the mini-theories can be incorporated into and form part of the overall paradigm model that is being developed alongside the research. Box 9.8 shows the main stages of axial coding.

BOX 9.8   Main stages in axial coding

1. Identifying the phenomenon – The phenomenon should be defined in terms of the conditions that give rise to its existence, and what causes its presence. It should be characterized in terms of the context in which it is situated. The action and interactional strategies which are used to manage the phenomenon should be developed and linked to the phenomenon, as well as the consequences of those strategies. This will form a pattern showing the relationships between specific categories, as follows:

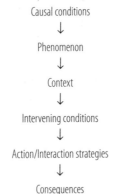

    Causal conditions

    ↓

    Phenomenon

    ↓

    Context

    ↓

    Intervening conditions

    ↓

    Action/Interaction strategies

    ↓

    Consequences

2. Linking and developing by means of the paradigm – This is achieved through rigorous questioning and reflection, and by continually making comparisons. By identifying and defining the phenomenon, the researcher has already asked questions about the possible relationship between certain categories and sub-categories and has linked them together in the sequence shown above. These statements which relate to categories and sub-categories must be verified against data. This is part of the inductive/deductive process of grounded theory. Where further data support the statements of relationships, the researcher can turn the statements into hypotheses.

3. Further development of categories and sub-categories in terms of properties and dimensions – This develops the ideas already generated within the identification of the phenomenon. It builds on the relationships discovered and purposefully tracks down other relationships, some of which will fall outside the paradigm model. The categories should be linked at the dimensional level. Within this further development is the recognition of the complexity of the real world. Although relationships are being discovered, not all the data will apply to the theory at all the times. These anomalies must not only be accepted, but must be incorporated into the research.

Selective coding is the process of selecting the core category, systematically relating it to other categories, validating these relationships and filling in categories that need further refinement. This process enables themes to be generated which can then be 'grounded' by referring back to the original data.

Grounded theory methodology is becoming increasingly popular in business research, but few studies provide full explanations of how the researcher analysed the data. Therefore, Box 9.9 shows an example of coded concepts in an interview transcript.

BOX 9.9   Example of coded concepts in an interview transcript

(A) Paragraphs from an interview relating to Hazardous Waste case-study

Interview S, 27 April

Paragraph 8

I don't think there is any doubt that on this job I readily accepted the advice of the civil engineering consultant, L, and didn't have the experience to question that advice adequately. I was not aware of the appropriate site investigation procedure, and was more than willing to be seduced by the idea that we could cut corners to save time and money.

Paragraph 9

But L's motives were entirely honorable in this respect. He had done a bit of prior work on a site nearby. And his whole approach was based upon the expectation that there would be fairly massive gravel beds lying over the clay valley bottom, and the fundamental question in that area was to establish what depth of piling was required for the factory foundations. He was assuming all along that piling was the problem. And he was not (and he knew he was not) experienced in looking for trouble for roads. His experience said that we merely needed a flight auger test to establish the pile depths.

Source: Architect S, a member of the design team involved in the incident, describing the decision of the civil engineering consultant, L, restricting the scope of the initial site investigation to the question of the need to have piled foundations for warehouse units.

(B) Significant concepts identified within paragraphs

Paragraph 8

Accepting professional advice

Criticizing other's work

Cutting corners

Experience

Paragraph 9

Knowledge of local conditions

Selective problem representation obscures wider view

Experience

Source: Pidgeon, Turner and Blockley (1991, p. 160).

9.8.2   DEVELOPING THEORIES

Although we have emphasized the coding procedures to demonstrate the analysis of qualitative data, this is only part of grounded theory methodology. Strauss and Corbin (1994, p. 277) complain that researchers 'often seem to concentrate on coding as this methodology's chief and almost exclusive feature, but do not do theoretical coding …

some researchers deliberately do not aim at developing theories'. If you intend to use the coding procedures only from grounded theory, you must justify your reasons for isolating this activity from the overall methodology. You should also explain why you have adopted this methodology and why other analytical procedures are not appropriate.

9.9 EVALUATING THE ANALYSIS

Once you have selected a method of analysis and applied it, you will want to know how to evaluate your analysis. A number of authors have suggested various criteria which can be used to evaluate an interpretive study in its entirety and these can be used to assess the quality of your analysis. Lincoln and Guba (1985) suggest that four criteria should be used:

- *Credibility* is concerned with whether the research was conducted in such a manner that the subject of the enquiry was correctly identified and described. Credibility can be improved by the researcher involving him or herself in the study for a prolonged period of time, by persistent observation of the subject under study to obtain depth of understanding, by triangulation by using different sources and collection methods of data, and by peer debriefing by colleagues on a continuous basis.
- *Transferability* is concerned with whether the findings can be applied to another situation that is sufficiently similar to permit *generalization*.
- *Dependability* focuses on whether the research processes are systematic, rigorous and well documented.
- *Confirmability* refers to whether the research process has been described fully and it is possible to assess whether the findings flow from the data.

Leininger (1994) has developed six criteria:
- Credibility
- Confirmability
- Transferability
- Saturation
- Meaning-in-context
- Recurrent patterning.

Although there are some differences between her definitions of the first three terms and those of Lincoln and Guba, the general thrust is similar. Saturation is concerned with the researcher being fully immersed and understanding the project. This is very similar to the recommendations used by Lincoln and Guba to enhance credibility. Meaning-in-context 'refers to data that have become understandable within holistic contexts or with special referent meanings to the informants or people studied in different or similar environmental contexts' (Leininger, 1994, p. 106). Recurrent patterning refers to the repetition of experiences, expressions and events that reflect identifiable patterns of sequenced behaviour, expressions or actions over time.

The above recommendations stress how important it is that you are highly familiar with the qualitative data you have collected. You will need to be systematic and rigorous in your approach to the analysis, which means you must be clear about your methodology, methods for collecting data and the techniques you use to analyse the data. One procedure adopted by a number of researchers at the analysis stage is concerned with obtaining respondent validity. This involves discussing your findings with participants to obtain their reactions and opinions. This can give you greater confidence in the validity of your conclusions.

9.10 CONCLUSIONS

In this chapter we have examined a number of different methods of analysing qualitative data. If you are conducting your research under an interpretive paradigm, the majority of the data you will have collected are likely to be in a qualitative form. Even if you have taken a positivist approach, some of the data you have collected may be qualitative. The main challenges when attempting to analyse qualitative data are how to reduce and restructure the data in a form other than extended text, both in the analysis and when presenting the findings. Unfortunately, few researchers describe their methods in enough detail to provide a comprehensive guide.

There are a number of methods and techniques which can be used to quantify the data. If that is not possible, or is philosophically unacceptable, you must devise some form of coding to represent the data to aid storage, retrievability and reconstruction. The synthesis and reorganization of data should lead to the development of themes and patterns which can be confronted by existing theories or used to construct new theories. Many researchers find that the use of displays is extremely valuable for part, if not all, of their data analysis. Others decide a particular technique is more appropriate. Whichever approach you adopt, it is essential that you establish systems and procedures to allow you to manage and organize the raw data you have collected.

You need to remember that your purpose, when analysing the data, is to find answers to your research questions. Therefore, you need to keep your research questions at the front of your mind while you are conducting the analysis. No matter how good the techniques and procedures you adopt are, the quality of your analysis will depend on the quality of the data you have collected and your interpretation.

ACTIVITIES

1. You intend to conduct research to examine the study habits of your fellow students. In the previous chapter you discussed the advantages and disadvantages of two data collection methods you could use. Build on this by discussing the advantages and disadvantages of any two methods you could use to analyse the data.

2. You are interested in environmental issues. Using content analysis, construct a coding frame and analyse the contents of a national newspaper that provides international news coverage (today's copy). Use a data display to summarize the data resulting from your content analysis.

3. Take the same coding frame and analyse the website for a television news channel with international coverage. Use a data display to summarize your findings. Are you surprised by the differences and how would you explain them?

4. Run the tutorial on the qualitative data analysis (QDA) software to which you have access (for example *NVivo*). Import an essay or paper you have written. Code the themes in each paragraph and indicate the relationships between themes. Generate a diagram. If you do not have access to QDA software, you can perform this task by hand. Print the paper in double spacing to allow room for codes and use different coloured highlighter pens to indicate themes. You can generate a diagram in *Word* using SmartArt, Shapes, Tables and so on from the Insert menu.

5. If you have done Activities 2–4, choose one of them and write notes on the transferability, dependability and confirmability of your analysis.

Learning objectives

When you have studied this chapter, you should be able to:

- classify variables according to their level of measurement

- describe the main methods for collecting data for statistical analysis

- discuss the strengths and weaknesses of different methods

- design questions for questionnaire and interview surveys

- select a random sample.

10.1   INTRODUCTION

You may be reading this chapter because you are designing a positivist study and you need to identify and discuss your intended method(s) of data collection to finalize your proposal. Alternatively, you may be reading this chapter because your proposal has been accepted, and you are now ready to start collecting original data for statistical analysis. In either case, this chapter will help guide you.

You will remember from Chapter 5 that the two main methodologies associated with positivism are experimental studies and surveys (which may be designed as cross-sectional or longitudinal studies). Since experimental studies are not widely used in business research for practical and ethical reasons, this chapter focuses on the methods used to collect original data when a survey methodology is adopted. The two main methods we discuss are self-completion questionnaires and interviews. We also describe critical incident technique, which can be incorporated in either method. This knowledge should build on what you have learned from studying Chapter 9 because methods are not necessarily identified as positivist or interpretivist by their labels, but by the type of data collected and how the data are analysed. Moreover, studies incorporating *triangulation* may use more than one method for collecting data.

The close relationship between collecting and analysing the research data means it is important to think ahead to the type of statistical analysis you will use when designing questions for self-completion questionnaires and interviews. Therefore, we examine the issues relating to designing questions separately. The final aspect of data collection we examine is concerned with finding a sampling frame and selecting a sample.

10.2   OVERVIEW OF DATA COLLECTION IN A POSITIVIST STUDY

Researchers are interested in collecting data about the phenomena they are studying. You will remember that in Chapter 1 we defined data as known facts or things used as a basis for inference or reckoning. Some authors distinguish between data and information, by defining information as the knowledge created by organizing data into a useful form. This obviously depends on how items of data are perceived and how they are used. For example, if you are a positivist, you may have collected data relating to the variables under study via a questionnaire survey, which you subsequently analysed using statistics. You probably consider that this process allowed you to turn data into information that makes a small contribution to knowledge. On the other hand, your respondents may consider that what they gave was information in the first place.

Data can be *quantitative* (in numerical form) or *qualitative* (in non-numerical form, such as text or images). Data can also be classified by source. Your literature review is an analysis of *secondary data* (data collected from an existing source), but your research data may be *primary data* (data you have generated by collecting it from an original source, such as an experiment or survey). Typical sources of secondary data include commercial databases, published books, articles, reports and statistics, or an organization's internal records and documents. Such data can be published in hard copy or in digital form, such as on the internet.

Figure 10.1 shows an overview of the data collection process. However, it is important to realize that this is purely illustrative and the process is not as linear as the diagram suggests. Moreover, research data can be generated or collected from different sources and more than one method can be used.

> ### KEY DEFINITIONS
>
> **Data** are known facts or things used as a basis for inference or reckoning.
>
> **Information** is the knowledge created by organizing data into a useful form.
>
> **Primary data** are generated from an original source, such as your own experiments, surveys, interviews or focus groups.
>
> **Secondary data** are collected from an existing source, such as publications, databases and internal records.

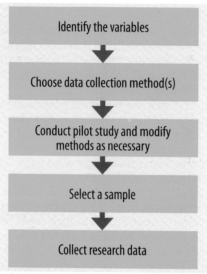

FIGURE 10.1 Overview of the data collection process

10.3 VARIABLES

KEY DEFINITIONS

Empirical evidence is data based on observation or experience.

A hypothesis is a proposition that can be tested for association or causality against empirical evidence.

A theory is a set of interrelated variables, definitions and propositions that specifies relationships among the variables.

A variable is a characteristic of a phenomenon that can be observed or measured.

Under positivism, research is deductive. Therefore, one of the purposes of the literature review is to identify a *theory* (or set of theories) to provide a theoretical framework for your study. A theory is a set of interrelated *variables*, definitions and propositions that specifies relationships among the variables. A variable is a characteristic of a phenomenon that can be observed or measured. Researchers collect data relating to each variable, which provide empirical evidence. Your theoretical framework forms the basis for constructing a *hypothesis* (plural *hypotheses*), which is an idea or proposition that can be tested for association or causality against the empirical evidence you collect.

Before you can collect any research data, you need to understand the properties of the variables relating to the phenomena you are studying. A *variable* is an attribute or characteristic of the phenomenon under study that can be observed and measured. You can see from this definition that variables are usually taken to be numerical and this is because any non-numerical observations can be quantified by allocating a numerical code (Upton and Cook, 2006). For example, the responses to open questions in a survey can be examined to identify the main themes and then a number given to each theme or category.

10.3.1 MEASUREMENT LEVELS

The level at which a variable is measured has important implications for your subsequent choice of statistical methods. 'A level of measurement is the scale that represents a hierarchy of precision on which a variable might be assessed' (Salkind, 2006, p. 100). There are four levels of measurement, which we will examine in decreasing order of precision:

- A *ratio* variable is a quantitative variable measured on a mathematical scale with equal intervals between points and a fixed zero point. The fixed zero point permits the highest level of precision in the measurement and allows us to say how much of the variable exists (it could be none) and compare one value with another. For example, using sea level as the fixed zero point, we can measure altitude in feet or metres. This means we can say that one aeroplane is flying at an altitude measured in metres that is twice as high as another aeroplane. If we use kilometres as the measurement scale, we can measure the distance by train from London to Brussels. If we use time as the measurement scale, we would designate the time of departure from London as the fixed zero point and compare the average time of the journey by high speed train with the time by air. This allows us to say that, the mean (average) train journey is only 10% longer than by air.

- An *interval* variable is a grouped quantitative variable measured on a mathematical scale that has equal intervals between points and an arbitrary zero point. This means you can place each data item precisely on the scale and compare the values. For example, the interval between an IQ score of 100 and 115 is the same as the interval between 110 and 125, but it is not possible to say that someone with an IQ of 120 is twice as intelligent as someone with an IQ of 60. Temperature is another example: If the temperature was $1°$ centigrade yesterday and $2°$ centigrade today, we know that today is warmer by an interval of $1°$, but we cannot say that today is twice as warm as yesterday because $0°$ centigrade does not mean there is no temperature! With only an arbitrary zero point, we cannot say that the difference between two points on the scale is a precise representation of the variable under study.

- An *ordinal* variable is measured using numerical codes to identify order (ranks). This allows you to see whether one observation is ranked more highly than another observation; for example, degree classifications of a candidate applying for a job (1, 2.1, 2.2 or 3) or their country of location preferences (1st, 2nd or 3rd). Ordinal variables fall between quantitative and categorical measures.

- A *nominal* variable is measured using numerical codes to identify named categories. For this reason, it is described as a 'categorical' variable. Each observation is placed in one of the categories. For example, you may have a variable for the gender of an applicant for a job (two categories), ethnicity (several categories) qualifications (several categories). If it is not possible to anticipate all the categories you can include a category named 'Other'. This is also used if you subsequently find some categories contain very few observations.

KEY DEFINITIONS

An interval variable is measured on a mathematical scale with equal intervals and an arbitrary zero point.

A nominal variable is measured using numerical codes to identify named categories.

An ordinal variable is measured using numerical codes to identify order or rank.

A ratio variable is measured on a mathematical scale with equal intervals and a fixed zero point.

One of the reasons why it is important to identify the level of measurement of variables is that it has implications for your statistical analysis. If you have collected data from ratio or interval variables, and the data meet certain distributional assumptions, you can use *parametric* statistic tests, which are based on the mean. On the other hand, if your data come from ordinal or nominal variables you will need to use the less powerful non-parametric methods. We examine this further in the next two chapters.

10.3.2 DISCRETE AND CONTINUOUS QUANTITATIVE VARIABLES

Quantitative variables measured on a ratio or interval scale can be *discrete* or *continuous*. A discrete variable can take only one value on the scale. For example, the number of sales assistants in a baker's shop on different days of the week might range from 1 to 5 and the variable can only take the values 0, 1, 2, 3, 4 or 5. Therefore, a value of 1.3 or 4.6 sales assistants is not possible.

On the other hand, a continuous variable can take any value between the start and end of a scale. For example, the amount of fruit and vegetables wasted in a hotel kitchen each day might vary from 0 kg to 10 kg and the variable can take any value between the start and end of the scale. Therefore, the data for Monday could be 3 kg exactly, but on Tuesday it could be 3.5 kg and on Wednesday 2.75 kg. In practice, there is considerable blurring of these definitions. For example, it can be argued that income is a discrete ratio variable, because income is a specific value within a range of values. However, because there are so many different possibilities when incomes are taken down to the last penny or cent, income is generally considered to be a continuous variable. Weight is certainly a continuous variable, but if the weighing scales are only accurate to the nearest tenth of a kilogram, the results will be from the distinct range of values, 0.1, 0.2, 0.3, 0.4 and so on.

10.3.3   DICHOTOMOUS AND DUMMY VARIABLES

A *dichotomous* variable is a variable that has only two possible categories, each with an assigned value. 'Gender' is an example of a natural dichotomous variable where the two groups are male and female and can be described as a categorical variable. Sometimes a variable that is not a natural dichotomy can be recoded into a new *dummy* variable. Perhaps you have collected data relating to the variable 'age', which measures the number of years since the business was started in five year periods (< 5 years, 6–10 years, 11–15 years, 16–20 years and so on). You could collapse this variable into a new variable called Maturity with two groups coded as 1 = Mature (≥ 5 years old) and 0 = Otherwise. If you do this, keep the original variable with its precise information in case you need it, because one of the disadvantages of recoding it into a dichotomous variable is that all this detail is lost.

Kervin (1992) suggests a number of arguments to support how you can treat a dichotomous variable in terms of the level of measurement. Using the above example of 'maturity', you might say that since the values represent a named category, it is a nominal variable with two groups named 'young' and 'mature'. Alternatively, you could argue that since the mature group has more of the original variable than the young group, it is an ordinal variable. Since there are only two values, you might decide to ignore the question of equal intervals and treat it as an interval variable. Finally, you might conclude that the 0 represents a natural zero point indicating that the business is not a mature business; in other words, the variable is a dummy variable where 0 = the characteristic of maturity is absent and 1 = the characteristic is present. Therefore, you treat it as a ratio variable. However, you are only likely to find support for the first of these arguments and we advise that you discuss the others with your supervisor before using them to justify your choice of statistical methods in your proposal.

10.3.4   HYPOTHETICAL CONSTRUCTS

Finding a measurement scale for variables such as the age of the businesses in your study or financial variables is not difficult, as there are widely accepted measures (the number of years since the business was started and monetary measures respectively). However, if your variables were abstract ideas such as intelligence or honesty, you will need to search the literature to find a suitable measurement scale or develop your own *hypothetical construct*. A *construct* is a set of concepts or general notions and ideas a person has in his or her mind about certain things. Because a construct is a mental image or abstract idea, it is difficult to observe and measure. Consequently, positivists develop a category or numerical scales to measure opinion and other abstract ideas. For example, intelligence has been measured by psychologists as a numerical hypothetical construct called intelligence quotient (IQ). This is a score that is derived from an individual taking a carefully designed test.

Apart from saving you time, the main advantages of finding an existing hypothetical construct, rather than developing your own, are that the validity of the measure is likely to have been tested (Kervin, 1992) and you can compare your results with others based on the same construct. Examples include social stratification categories, frequency categories, ranking and rating scales (see section 10.5.4).

10.3.5 DEPENDENT AND INDEPENDENT VARIABLES

In many statistical tests it is necessary to identify the *dependent variable (DV)* and the *independent variable (IV)*. A dependent variable is a variable whose values are influenced by one or more independent variables. Conversely, an independent variable is a variable that influences the values of a dependent variable. For example, in an experimental study, the intensity of lighting (IV) in the workplace might be manipulated to observe the effect on the productivity levels (DV), or a stressful situation might be created by generating random loud noises (IV) outside the workplace window to observe the effect on the completion of complex tasks (DV).

An *extraneous variable* is any variable other than the independent variable that might have an effect on the dependent variable. For example, if your study involves an investigation of the relationship between productivity and motivation, you may find it difficult to exclude the effect of other factors, such as a heatwave, a work-to-rule, a takeover or anxiety caused by personal problems. A *confounding variable* is one that obscures the effect of another variable. For example, employees' behaviour may be affected by the novelty of being the centre of the researcher's attention or by working in an unfamiliar place for the purposes of a controlled experiment.

10.4 DATA COLLECTION METHODS

The two main data collection methods we discuss in this section are self-completion questionnaires and interviews. We also describe critical incident technique, which can be incorporated in either method. These are widely used methods in positivist studies, but you should also explore other methods that you come across when studying previous research on your chosen topic.

10.4.1 QUESTIONNAIRES

A *questionnaire* is a list of carefully structured questions, which have been chosen after considerable testing with a view to eliciting reliable responses from a particular group of people. The aim is to find out what they think, do or feel because this will help you address your research questions. Of course, this raises the issue of *confidentiality*, which we examined in Chapter 3. When a questionnaire is used in an interview, many researchers call it an 'interview schedule'. You may also come across the term *research instrument*, which is a questionnaire or interview schedule that has been used and tested in a number of different studies. In a face-to-face or telephone interview, the answers to the questions are recorded by the interviewer. However, in a postal or on-line survey, the questionnaire is completed by the respondent. This is cheaper and less time-consuming, but there are a number of other factors that you should be aware of if you are conducting an interview survey and we discuss these in the next section.

Questionnaires or interview schedules are used in a *Delphi study*, where the aim is to gather opinions from a carefully selected group of experts. Once the responses have been summarized, the results are returned to the participants so that they can re-evaluate their original answers once they have seen the responses of the group. This process is repeated a number of times until there is consensus. Unlike a focus group, the experts do not meet or know the identities of the other group members.

Before you start designing your questionnaire or interview schedule, you need to have identified the variables about which you need data so that you can address your research questions. You also need to have found a list from which to choose a sample. In a large questionnaire or interview survey, many respondents or interviewees will be needed and you will need to decide on a method for selecting a suitable sample. We look at this important decision in section 10.7.

The main steps involved in designing a questionnaire or interview schedule are summarized in Figure 10.2.

> **KEY DEFINITIONS**
>
> A questionnaire is a method for collecting primary data in which a sample of respondents are asked a list of carefully structured questions chosen after considerable testing, with a view to eliciting reliable responses.

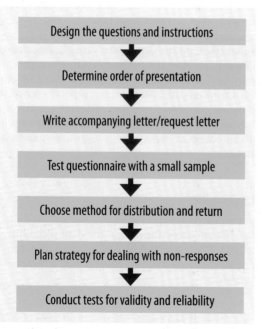

FIGURE 10.2 Designing a questionnaire or interview schedule

Question design is concerned with the type of questions, their wording, the order in which they are presented and the reliability and validity of the responses. We discuss this in detail in Section 10.5. You will need to explain the purpose of the study, since the respondents need to know the context in which the questions are being posed. This can be achieved by starting the questionnaire with an explanatory paragraph or attaching a covering letter.

It is essential that you *pilot* or test your questionnaire as fully as possible before distributing it. At the undergraduate level, you could ask your supervisor, friends and family to play the role of respondents. Even if they know little about the subject, they can still be very helpful in spotting a range of potential problems. However, the best advice is to try your questionnaire out on people who are similar to those in your sample. If you are a Master's or doctoral student, you may find it takes several drafts, with tests at every stage, until you are satisfied, so allow plenty of time for this important part of the process.

There are a number of *distribution* methods, each with different strengths and weaknesses. Cost is often an important factor and the best method for a particular study often depends on the size and location of the sample.

- *By post* – This is a commonly used method of distribution that is fairly easy to administer. The questionnaire and covering letter are posted to the population or the sample, usually with a prepaid envelope for returning the completed questionnaire. If you are conducting an internal survey in a particular company, it may be possible to use the internal mail. If it is a large survey, you will need to consider the cost of printing, postage and stationery. You should also leave plenty of time for getting the questionnaire printed, folding and inserting the contents, sealing the envelopes and franking or stamping them. However, one of the drawbacks is that response rates of 10% or less are not uncommon and this introduces the problem of sample bias because those who respond may not be representative of the population. Response rates can be increased by keeping the questionnaire as short as possible (for example two sides of A4) and using closed questions of a simple and non-sensitive nature.
- *By telephone* – This is also a widely used method to employ as it reduces the costs associated with face-to-face interviews, but still allows some aspect of personal contact. A relatively long questionnaire can be used and it can be helpful with sensitive and complex questions. However, achieving the desired number of responses may require a very large sampling frame and there is the cost of many calls to consider. Moreover, your results may be biased towards people who are available and willing to answer questions in this way.
- *On-line* – Web-based tools, such as SurveyMonkey, allow you to create your own survey for a fee and email it to potential respondents. You can view the preliminary results as they come in and the data file can be exported to *Excel*, *SPSS* and other software packages for analysis. Like the last two methods of distribution, on-line surveys are now so widely used that obtaining sufficient responses may take some time and the results may be biased.
- *Face-to-face* – The questionnaire can be presented to respondents in the street, at their homes, in the workplace or any convenient place. It is time-consuming and can be expensive if you have to travel to a particular location to meet an interviewee. However, this method offers the advantage that response rates can be fairly high and comprehensive data can be collected. It is often very useful if sensitive or complex questions need to be asked. Where the interview is conducted in the interviewee's home, it is possible to use a lengthy questionnaire. It is important that you

take precautions to ensure your personal safety when using the face-to-face method (see Chapter 3). We look at interviews in more detail in the next section.

- *Group distribution* – This method is only appropriate where the survey is being conducted in a small number of locations or a single location. You may be able to agree that the sample or sub-groups are assembled in the same room at the same time, such as the canteen during a quiet period in the afternoon. You can then explain the purpose of the survey and how to complete the questionnaire, while being available to answer any queries. This is a convenient, low-cost method for administering questionnaires and the number of usable questionnaires is likely to be high.

- *Individual distribution* – This is a variation of group distribution. If the sample is situated in one location, it may be possible to distribute, and collect, the questionnaires individually. As well as a place of work, this approach can be used in theatres, restaurants and even on trains and buses. It is normally necessary to supply pens or pencils for the completion of the questionnaires. You may encounter problems with sample bias if you use this method; for example, you may only capture patrons who visit a theatre on a Monday, or travel at a particular time. However, if properly designed, this method can be very precise in targeting the most appropriate sample.

There are two major problems associated with using questionnaires in a survey. The first is *questionnaire fatigue*. This refers to the reluctance of many people to respond to questionnaire surveys because they are inundated with unsolicited requests by post, email, telephone and in the street. The second problem is what to do about *non-response bias*, which can be present if some questionnaires are not returned. Non-response bias is crucial in a survey because your research design will be based on the fact that you are going to generalize from the sample to the population. If you have not collected responses from all the members of your sample, the data may not be representative of the population. Later on in this chapter, we will look at item non-response (non-response to particular questions) and the implications for the reliability and validity of the results.

Wallace and Mellor (1988) suggest three methods for testing for questionnaire non-response:

1. Compare responses by date of reply. One method of doing this is to send a follow-up request to non-respondents. If you intend to do this, you will need to keep a record of those who reply and when. In a postal questionnaire survey, you are advised to send a fresh copy of the questionnaire (perhaps printed on different coloured paper or with an identifying symbol in addition to the unique reference number). The questionnaires that result from the follow-up (late respondents) are then compared with those from the first request (early respondents).
2. Compare the characteristics of respondents with those of the population, assuming you know them.
3. Compare the characteristics of respondents with those of non-respondents in the sample, assuming you know them.

10.4.2   INTERVIEWS

Interviews are a method for collecting data in which selected participants (the interviewees) are asked questions to find out what they do, think or feel. Verbal or visual prompts may be required. Interviews can be conducted with individuals or groups using face-to-face, telephone or video conferencing methods (although video conferencing is not likely to be feasible for a large scale survey). A positivist approach suggests a *structured interview* based on a *questionnaire* or interview schedule.

In a *structured interview*, these questions are likely to be *closed questions*, each of which has a set of predetermined answers. There may be some *open questions*, which allow the respondent to answer in his or her own words. In a large structured or semi-structured face-to-face or telephone interview, a questionnaire is prepared in advance and is completed by the interviewer from the responses given by the interviewee (for example interviews used in market research surveys). In a *semi-structured interview*, some of the questions are pre-prepared, but the interviewer is able to add additional questions in order to obtain more detailed information about a particular answer or to explore new (but relevant) issues that arise from a particular answer. *Unstructured interviews* are associated with an interpretive paradigm.

In a large interview survey, many interviewees are needed and this gives rise to the problem of obtaining access to an appropriate sample. You will need to explain the purpose of the study, since the interviewees need to know the subject of the interview and the context in which you will ask your questions. Obtaining a sample and conducting the interviews can be very time-consuming and there may be travel and hospitality costs to consider. In some studies, a self-completion questionnaire may be more appropriate.

Structured interviews make it easy to compare answers because each interviewee is asked the same questions. However, in a semi-structured (or unstructured interview) the issues discussed, the questions raised and the matters explored change from one interview to the next as different aspects of the topic are revealed. This process of discovery is the strength of such interviews, but it is important to recognize that emphasis and balance of the emerging issues may depend on the order in which you interview the participants. In unstructured and semi-structured interviews, it may be difficult to keep a note of the questions and answers, controlling the range of topics and, later, analysing the data.

In all types of interview, you are advised to ask the interviewee's permission to record the interview using an audio recorder. After putting your interviewee at ease, you may find it useful to spend a little time establishing a rapport before starting to record. You can offer to switch the recorder off if your interviewee wants to discuss confidential or sensitive information; seek permission to continue to take notes. You may find that this encourages a higher degree of frankness. We discussed the issue of *confidentiality* in Chapter 3. Lee (1993) offers the following advice if you are asking questions on sensitive topics:

- Use words that are non-threatening and familiar to the respondents. For example, when explaining the purpose of the questionnaire, rather than saying you are conducting research into absenteeism in their workplace, say you are looking at working patterns.
- Lead up to any sensitive question slowly.
- You may find that participants will answer questions about past indiscretions more readily than questions about current behaviour. For example, they may admit to stealing from their employer at some time in the past, but be unwilling to disclose that they have done so recently.

These suggestions raise ethical issues and you must determine your own position on this. If you find your interviewee is showing signs of resisting some topics, the best advice is to drop those questions. However, this will alert you to the likelihood that these may be interesting and important issues and you may wish to find an alternative way of collecting the data, such as *diary methods* or *observation* (see Chapter 8).

In a positivist study, you will need to ensure that all the interviews are conducted in the same way to avoid *interviewer bias*. This means that not only should the same questions be asked, but also that they should be posed in the same way. Furthermore, you must ensure that each respondent will understand the question in the same way. This is known as *stimulus equivalence* and demands considerable thought and skill in question design. A checklist for keeping interviewer bias to the minimum is shown in Box 10.1.

BOX 10.1 Checklist for reducing interviewer bias

- Read each question exactly as worded in the questionnaire.
- Read each question slowly, using the same intonation and emphasis.
- Ask the questions in the same order.
- Ask every question that applies.
- Use the same response cards (if required as part of the design).
- Record exactly what the respondent says.
- Do not answer the question for the respondent.
- Show interest by paying attention when the respondent is answering, but do not show approval or disapproval.
- Make sure you have understood each answer and that the answer is adequate.

Source: Adapted from Brenner (1985).

There is also potential for inadvertent class, race or sex bias. Another problem is that the interviewee may have certain expectations about the interview and give what he or she considers is the 'correct' or 'acceptable' answer to the question. Lee (1993) suggests that, to some extent, this can be overcome by increasing the depth of the interview. You should bear in mind that recent events may also affect the interviewee's responses. For example, he or she may have just received news of a promotion, a salary increase, a cut in hours, a reprimand or bad news about a member of the family. If time allows, you will find it useful to arrive at the interview venue 15 minutes beforehand to assimilate the atmosphere and the environment, and spend the first few minutes putting the interviewee at ease. It is difficult to predict or measure bias. Nevertheless, you should be alert to the fact that it can distort your data and hence your findings.

The most common form of interview is one-to-one, but some researchers find it useful to have two interviewers to help ensure that all the issues are fully explored and notes are kept of nuances and relevant non-verbal factors. Sometimes the interviewee is accompanied by another person (often to ensure that all the questions you ask can be answered). You must be alert to the fact that more than one interviewer or interviewee will change the dynamics of the interview. Another problem is that an interviewee may be 'wearing two hats'. For example, the finance director of a company may also be a director of other companies or involved in other organizations; an employee may also be a trade unionist or a shareholder. When you are asking questions, you must determine which 'hat' the interviewee is wearing, and whether he or she is giving a personal opinion or making a policy statement.

As well as deciding on the structure and recording of an interview, you must also be able to bring it to a satisfactory conclusion and let the interviewee know that it is ending. One device is to say that you have asked all the questions you had in mind and ask whether the interviewee has any final comments. You should then conclude by thanking them and reassuring them that you will be treating what they have told you as confidential. After you have left the interview, it is beneficial to add further notes.

Despite some disadvantages, interviews permit the researcher to ask complex questions and ask follow-up questions, which is not possible in a self-completion questionnaire. Thus, further information can be obtained. An interview may permit a higher degree of confidence in the replies than responses to a self-completion questionnaire and can take account of non-verbal communications such as the attitude and behaviour of the interviewee. It is important to take precautions to ensure your personal safety when conducting face-to-face interviews.

10.4.3 CRITICAL INCIDENT TECHNIQUE

Critical incident technique is a method for collecting data about a defined activity or event based on the participant's recollections of key facts. Developed by Flanagan (1954), it allows important facts to be gathered about behaviour in defined situations 'in a rather objective fashion with only a minimum of inferences and interpretation of a more subjective nature' (Flanagan, 1954, p. 335). Although it is called a technique, it is not a set of rigid rules, but a flexible set of principles that can be modified and adapted according to the circumstances. In Chapter 8, we explained how it can be used as the basis for a semi-structured interview under an interpretive paradigm and we will now look at its use in interviews or surveys under a positivist paradigm.

> **KEY DEFINITIONS**
>
> Critical incident technique is a method for collecting data about a defined activity or event based on the participant's recollections of key facts.

Flanagan recommended that only simple types of judgements should be required of observers, who should be qualified. All observations should be evaluated by the observer in terms of an agreed statement of the purpose of the activity. The procedure for establishing the general aims of an activity, the training of the interviewers and the manner in which observations should be made are all predetermined. What is of prime interest to researchers is the way in which Flanagan concentrates on an observable activity (the incident), where the intended purpose seems to be clear and the effect appears to be logical; hence, the incident is critical.

We showed Flanagan's example of a form for collected effective critical incidents in Chapter 8. In this chapter we will look at an example taken from a questionnaire survey of householders (MacKinlay, 1986), which contained six open-ended questions. The questionnaire allowed a third of an A4 page per question for the reply, but some respondents added additional sheets. The questions were preceded by an explanation, as shown in Box 10.2.

BOX 10.2 Critical incident technique in a survey

These questions are open-ended and I have kept them to a few vital areas of interest. All will require you to reflect back on decisions and reasons for decisions you have made.

1. Please think about an occasion when you improved your home. What improvements did you make?
2. On that occasion what made you do it?
3. Did you receive any help? If 'yes', please explain what help you received.
4. Have you wanted to improve your home in any other way but could not?
5. What improvements did you wish to make?
6. What stopped you from doing it?

Source: MacKinlay (1986), cited in Easterby-Smith, Thorpe and Lowe (1991, p. 84).

It is likely that many researchers use this approach without realizing it. One of the benefits is that it allows the researcher to collect data about events chosen by the respondent because they are memorable, rather than general impressions of events or vicarious knowledge of events. In interviews, it can be of considerable value in generating data where there is a lack of focus or the interviewee has difficulty in expressing an opinion.

One of the problems associated with methods based on memory is that the participant may have forgotten important facts. In addition, there is the problem of post-rationalization, where the interviewee recounts the events with a degree of logic and coherence that did not exist at the time.

10.5   DESIGNING QUESTIONS

Many data collection methods rely on *questions* as the vehicle for gathering primary research data. In this section, we focus on designing questions for a positivist study, where the research data thus generated will be analysed using statistical methods. Before you can decide what the most appropriate questions will be, you must gain a considerable amount of knowledge about your subject to allow you to develop a theoretical or conceptual framework and formulate the hypotheses you will test. Your subject knowledge will come from your taught and/or independent studies; your theoretical framework (sometimes referred to as a conceptual framework) that underpins the hypotheses you will test will be drawn from your literature review. The statistical methods you will use will be described in your methodology chapter.

Questions should be presented in a logical order and it is often beneficial to move from general to specific topics. This is known as funnelling. In complex questionnaires, it may be necessary to use filter questions, where respondents who have given a certain answer are directed to skip a question or batch of questions. For example, 'Do you normally do the household shopping? *If YES, go to next question; if NO, go to Question 17.*'

In addition to designing the questions themselves, in a self-completion questionnaire you also give precise *instructions* (for example whether to tick one or more boxes, or whether a number or word should be circled to indicate the response). The clarity of the instructions and the ordering and presentation of the questions can do much to encourage and help respondents. These factors also make the subsequent analysis of the data easier.

Classification questions collect data about the characteristics of the unit of analysis, such as the respondent's job title, age or education; or the geographical region, industry, size or age of the business. If you wish to make comparisons with previous studies, government statistics or other publications, it is essential to use the same categories. Classification questions collect data that will enable you to describe your sample and examine relationships between subsets of your sample. Remember, you should only collect data about variables you will use in your analysis.

There is some debate over the best location for classification questions. Some authors believe that they are best placed at the beginning, so that respondents gain confidence in answering easy questions; others prefer to place them at the end, so that the respondent starts with the more interesting questions. If your questions are of a sensitive nature, it may be best to start with the non-threatening classification questions. If you have a large number of classification questions, it could be better to put them at the end, so that the respondent is not deterred at the start. Remember to allocate a unique reference number to each questionnaire. This will enable you to maintain control of the project and, if appropriate, you will be able to identify which respondents have replied and send follow-up letters to those who have not. If you are using *triangulation*, you will also be able to match data about the unit of analysis from different sources.

10.5.1   GENERAL RULES

It is essential to bear your target audience in mind when designing your questions. If your sample is composed of intelligent people, who are likely to be knowledgeable about the topic, you can aim for a fairly high level of complexity, but the general rule is to keep it simple. Box 10.3 summarizes the general rules for designing questions.

BOX 10.3   General rules for designing questions

- Provide a context by briefly explaining the purpose of the research
- Only ask questions that are needed for the analysis
- Keep each question as short and as simple as possible
- Only ask one question at a time
- Include questions that serve as cross-checks on answers to other questions
- Avoid jargon, ambiguity and negative questions
- Avoid leading questions and value-laden questions that suggest a 'correct' answer
- Avoid calculations and memory tests
- Avoid questions that could cause offence or embarrassment

These fundamental aspects of question design are important, because once you have asked the questions there is often little you can do to enhance the quality of the answers. It can be helpful to the respondent if you qualify your questions in some way, perhaps by referring to a specific time period, rather than requiring the respondent to search their memory for an answer. For example, instead of asking, 'Have you ever bought Fair Trade coffee?' you might ask, 'Have you bought Fair Trade coffee in the past three weeks?' A question can also be qualified by referring to a particular place. For example, 'What are your views on the choice of Fair Trade coffee in your local supermarket?'

If the issue addressed in the question is complex or rigid, we might wish to add some generality to it. For example, 'Do you travel to work in your own car?' might be taken to mean every day. This can be generalized by inserting the word 'normally' or 'usually', thus: 'Do you normally travel to work in your own car?' A question can also be made more general by inserting the word 'overall' or the term 'in general'. For example, 'In general, are you satisfied with the level of service you obtain from the company?' However, in some questions precision may be important and desirable.

Coolican (1992) identifies the following pitfalls to avoid when deciding on the order in which questions should be asked:

- To address the tendency for participants to agree rather than disagree (known as response acquiescence), you should mix positive and negative questions to keep them thinking of their answers.
- The participant may try to interpret the aim of the question or questionnaire, or set

---

BOX 10.9 Intensity rating scale

4. What are your views on the following statements regarding the audit? *(Circle number closest to your view)*

	Agree			Disagree	
(a) Provides a check on accounting records and systems	5	4	3	2	1
(b) Improves the quality of the financial information	5	4	3	2	1
(c) Improves the credibility of the financial information	5	4	3	2	1
(d) Has a positive effect on company's credit rating score	5	4	3	2	1

Source: Adapted from Collis (2003).

An advantage of using ranking and rating scales is that a number of different statements can be provided in a list, which makes economical use of the space and is easy for the respondent to complete. Moreover, these ordinal variables are measured at a higher level than a nominal variable requiring a simple 'Yes' or 'No' answer, which has implications for the type of statistic tests that can be used in your analysis. Box 10.10 gives examples of commonly used scales.

10.5.5 RELIABILITY AND VALIDITY

If you decide to use rating scales or attitude scales in the questions you ask, you will want to be sure that they will measure the respondents' views consistently. The *reliability* of the responses you receive to all your questions is an important issue in a positivist study. Reliability is concerned with the findings of the research. The findings can be said to be reliable if you or someone else repeats the research and obtains the same results. *Validity* is also important and this is concerned with the extent to which the research findings accurately represent what is happening in the situation; in other words, whether the data collected represent a true picture of what is being studied.

The reason why there may be doubt lies in the problem that our questions may contain errors (perhaps they are worded ambiguously), the respondent may become bored or there may be antagonism between the researcher and the participants leading to *item non-response*. Typical examples include failing to answer questions that apply or not following instructions by ticking more than one box when only one choice was allowed. There are a number of ways of dealing with such problems, ranging from making an educated guess based on the respondent's other answers to statistical methods. If you have a large number of non-responses to a particular question across the sample, it usually means the question design was at fault and the data from that question should not be used in your analysis. If a respondent returns an incomplete questionnaire or one where questions that are crucial to your analysis are not answered, you will have to discard it.

There are three common ways of estimating the reliability of the responses to questions in questionnaires or interviews:

- *Test re-test method* – The questions are asked of the same people, but on two separate occasions. Responses for the two occasions are correlated and the *correlation co-efficient* of the two sets of data computed (see Chapter 12), thus providing an index of reliability. However, this method suffers from the considerable disadvantage that it is often difficult to persuade respondents to answer questions a second time and, if they do, they may think more deeply about the questions on the second occasion and give different answers.

BOX 10.10 Examples of intensity, frequency and evaluation rating scales

General adjectives (unipolar)

5 Very/Extremely/Strongly satisfied, important, agree, etc.

4 Fairly/Quite/Moderately

3 Slightly/Weakly

2 Not very/Hardly

1 Not at all

Directional general adjectives (bipolar)

5 Very/Extremely/Strongly satisfied, important, agree, etc.

4 Moderately/Fairly/Mostly

3 Neutral/Undecided/Unsure

2 Moderately/Fairly/Mostly

1 Very/Extremely/Strongly dissatisfied, unimportant, disagree, etc.

Directional comparisons (bipolar)

5 Much better

4 Better

3 About the same

2 Worse

1 Much worse

Frequency (unipolar)

5 All the time

4 Most of the time

3 Sometimes

2 Seldom/Rarely

1 Never/Not at all

Evaluation (unipolar)

5 Excellent

4 Very good

3 Average

2 Poor

1 Very poor

Source: Adapted from Kervin (1992, p. 319).

- *Split-halves method* – The questionnaires or interview record sheets are divided into two equal halves, perhaps by putting the responses to the odd numbered questions in one pile and the responses to the even numbered questions in another. Alternatively, the responses to the first half of the questions are put in a separate pile from the answers to the remainder. The two piles are then correlated and the *correlation co-efficient* of the two sets of data computed as above.

- *Internal consistency method* – Every item is correlated with every other item across the sample and the average inter-item correlation is taken as the index of reliability. Although this is a popular method of computing the reliability of the results where questions have been used as the basis of the data collection method, it requires substantial computing facilities and software that uses a special formula called *Kuder-Richardson (KR20)*.

The responses to your questions may turn out to be highly reliable, but the results will be worthless if your questions do not measure what you intended them to measure; in other words *validity* is low. Therefore, it is important that the questions you ask correspond with the explanation you give respondents regarding the purpose of your study; otherwise, they may lose interest in answering the questions, as these will appear to be irrelevant.

10.5.6 ELIMINATING QUESTIONS

Having decided on the questions you wish to ask, it is common to find that you have far too many. Use the checklist given in Box 10.11 to determine which questions you should retain and which you should drop when designing questions for interviews or questionnaires.

BOX 10.11 Checklist for eliminating questions

1. Does the question measure some aspect of one of the research questions?
2. Does the question provide information needed in conjunction with some other variable?
   (If NO to both 1 and 2, drop the question; if YES to one or both, retain)
3. Will most respondents understand the question and in the same way?
   (If NO, revise or drop; if YES, retain)
4. Will most respondents have the information to answer it?
   (If NO, drop; if YES, retain)
5. Will most respondents be willing to answer it?
   (If NO, drop; if YES, retain)
6. Is other information needed to analyse this question?
   (If NO, retain; if YES, retain only if the other information is available or can be obtained)
7. Should this question be asked of all respondents or only a subset?
   (If ALL, retain; if ONLY A SUBSET, retain only if the subset is identifiable beforehand or through questions in the interview)

Source: Adapted from Czaja and Blair (1996, p. 61).

You must be alert to the possibility that some of the issues you wish to investigate may be offensive or embarrassing to the respondents. We do not recommend you ask any *sensitive questions* in a self-completion questionnaire. Not only is it likely to deter respondents from answering the sensitive question, but it may discourage them from participating at all.

10.6 CODING QUESTIONS

* *SPSS* is an abbreviation for Statistical Product and Service Solutions (formerly Statistical Package for the Social Sciences).

Although *coding* is more closely related to data analysis than to data collection, it is important to consider at this stage how you will analyse your research data and what software is available to help you with this task (for example *Excel, Minitab* and *SPSS for Windows*).* *SPSS* is widely used in business research because it can process large amounts of data and we will be introducing the principles of data entry and analysis using *SPSS* in the next chapter.

10.6.1 CODING CLOSED QUESTIONS

Pre-coding questions for statistical analysis as part of the questionnaire design makes the subsequent data entry easier and less prone to error. Where this is not possible, it is important to remember to keep a record of the codes used for each question and what they signify. This is essential should you decide to use a third party to input your data, and also for when you start to interpret the analysed data.

It is usual to reserve certain code numbers for particular purposes. For nominal variables where only one can be selected, allocate a different code to each so that the answer can be identified. For nominal variables where more than one answer may apply, each variable is treated independently: use 1 to indicate the box has been ticked (the characteristic is present) and leave blank if it has not been ticked. This will be interpreted by *SPSS* as a 'missing' data, which means a non-response. Depending on your planned analysis, you may wish to use 0 if the box has not been ticked (the characteristic is not present). Similarly, it is usual to code the answer 'yes' as 1 and the answer 'no' as 0. There is no need to pre-code ordinal variables because they use a numerical rating scale.

You may have noticed that the examples of questions we used in this chapter were pre-coded. Box 10.12 shows an example of a pre-coded questionnaire. Look carefully at the way in which the potential answers have been coded. Each code is discretely shown in brackets next to the relevant box. There are no hard and fast rules about where to place the codes and you may find that it makes more sense to put the codes at the top of a column of boxes for some sets of variables. You simply need to adopt a location that improves the accuracy and efficiency of processing the data, while not confusing the respondent. In this example, a smaller, lighter font has been used to reduce the likelihood of the respondent becoming distracted by codes.

Earlier in this chapter, we suggested that you should pilot your questions before commencing your data collection in earnest. We also recommend that once you have your test data, you also pilot your coding. Amending coding errors now will save you valuable time and effort later when errors can only be painstakingly corrected by hand on every record sheet or questionnaire.

BOX 10.12 A pre-coded questionnaire

URN 42

1. Is the company a family-owned business? *(Tick one box only)*

Wholly family-owned (or only 1 owner) ☐ (1)

Partly family-owned ☐ (2)

None of the shareholders are related ☐ (0)

2. How many shareholders (owners) does the company have?

(a) Total number of shareholders ☐

Breakdown:

(b) Number of shareholders with access to internal financial information ☐

(c) Number of shareholders *without* access to internal financial information ☐

3. Would you have the accounts audited if not legally required to do so? *(Tick one box only)*

Yes, the accounts are already audited voluntarily ☐ (1)

Yes, the accounts would be audited voluntarily ☐ (2)

No ☐ (0)

Please give reasons for either answer

....

....

4. What are your views on the following statements regarding the audit? *(Circle number closest to your view)*

	Agree				Disagree
(a) Provides a check on accounting records and systems	5	4	3	2	1
(b) Improves the quality of the financial information	5	4	3	2	1
(c) Improves the credibility of the financial information	5	4	3	2	1
(d) Has a positive effect on company's credit rating score	5	4	3	2	1

5. Apart from Companies House, who normally receives a copy of the company's statutory accounts?
(Tick as many boxes as apply)

(a) Shareholders ☐

(b) Bank and other providers of finance ☐

(c) Employees who are *not* shareholders ☐

(d) Major suppliers and trade creditors ☐

(e) Major customers ☐

(f) Tax authorities ☐

(g) Other *(Please state)* .... ☐

6. Do you have any of the following qualifications/training? *(Tick as many boxes as apply)*

(a) Undergraduate or postgraduate degree ☐

(b) Professional/vocational qualification ☐

(c) Study/training in business/management subjects ☐

Source: Adapted from Collis (2003).

10.6.2 CODING OPEN QUESTIONS

Statistical analysis can only be conducted on quantitative data. *Open questions* where the answer takes a numerical value do not need to be coded (for example dates or financial data). However, open questions where you are unable to anticipate the response (including those where you provide an 'Other' category) will result in qualitative data that cannot be coded until all the replies have been received. The task of recording and counting frequencies accurately and methodically can be helped by using *tallies*. A tally is just a simple stroke used to count the frequency of occurrence of a value or category in a variable. You jot down one upright stroke for each occurrence until you have four; the fifth is drawn horizontally across the group, like a five bar gate. You can then count in fives until you get to the single tallies. Box 10.13 shows tallies being used to help record the frequencies for the second part of question 3, which was designed as an open question to capture the respondents' reasons for a particular action.

BOX 10.13 Using tallies to count frequencies

3. Would you have the accounts audited if not legally required to do so? *(Tick one box only)*

Yes, the accounts are already audited voluntarily	☐	(1)
Yes, the accounts would be audited voluntarily	☐	(2)
No	☐	(0)

Please give reasons for either answer

Voluntary audit

Assurance for third party   ῂ ῂ ῂ ῂ ῂ ῂ ῂ   35

Good practice   ῂ ῂ ‖‖‖   14

No audit

No benefit/no need   ῂ ῂ ῂ ῂ ῂ ῂ ῂ ‖   36

Cost savings   ῂ ῂ ῂ ῂ ῂ ῂ ‖   32

10.7 SAMPLING METHODS

10.7.1 SAMPLING FRAMES

A *sampling frame* is a record of the population from which a sample can be drawn. A sample is an unbiased subset that represents the population and a *population* is a body of people or collection of items under consideration for statistical purposes. If the population is relatively small, you can select the whole population; otherwise, you will need to select a random sample. 'In a positivist study, it is vital to obtain a random sample to get some idea of variation ... To build general conclusions on ... limited data is a bit like a lazy evolutionist biologist finding a few mutant finches ... in a population on day one of a field outing, then returning home to claim that all finches of this species display the same properties' (Alexander, 2006, p. 20).

A random sample is one where every member of the population has a chance of being chosen. Therefore, the sample is an unbiased subset of the population, which allows the results obtained for the sample to be taken to be

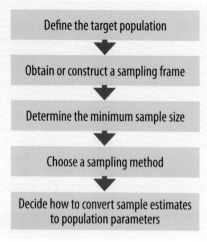

Define the target population

Obtain or construct a sampling frame

Determine the minimum sample size

Choose a sampling method

Decide how to convert sample estimates to population parameters

FIGURE 10.3 Main steps in selecting a random sample

true for the whole population; in other words, the results from the sample are generalizable to the population.

To find out how many items there are in the population, you need to find a suitable sampling frame. For example, if you were conducting research where employees are the unit of analysis, the Human Resources department of the business may be willing to supply a staff list. However, if businesses are your unit of analysis, you will need to look for a suitable database, such as FAME, Dun & Bradstreet or DataStream. For example, perhaps your research focuses on the financial structure of small companies in the paper recycling industry in the London postal area. Your *unit of analysis* is a small company, which you decide to define as a private limited company with up to 50 employees. You decide to use the FAME database to identify companies that fit your criteria and your investigations show that there are 32 such companies. Obviously, your research findings will relate only to paper recycling companies in London of this size and you will not be able to generalize the results of your study to other companies.

On the other hand, perhaps you are investigating the performance of all small companies in all industries throughout the UK. In this case, your unit of analysis is still a small company and you can still use the FAME database as the sampling frame, but this time you find that there are thousands of companies that fit your criteria. To save the expense and inconvenience of investigating all these companies, it is acceptable to reduce the number to a manageable size by selecting a random sample. Figure 10.3 shows the main steps in selecting a random sample.

10.7.2   SAMPLE SIZE

For a Bachelor's or taught Master's dissertation or thesis, it is common to accept a degree of uncertainty in the conclusions you draw, so selecting a sufficiently large random sample to allow your results to be generalized to the population may not be vital to your study. Nevertheless, you still need a large enough sample to address your research questions because if your sample is too small, it may preclude some important statistical tests among the subsets in the sample (for example looking for differences between industry sectors). Therefore, the greater the expected variation within the sample, the larger the sample required.

The larger the sample, the better it will represent the population. Therefore, if you want to generalize from your results, you must also determine the minimum sample size to reflect the size of the population. In a questionnaire survey, you will also need to take account of your expected *response rate*, which may be 10% or less. Recent surveys in your field or your own pilot survey will give you a guide.

The minimum sample size to allow results from a random sample to be generalized to the population is much higher for a small population than it is for a large population. 'As the population increases, the sample size increases at a diminishing rate and remains relatively constant at slightly more than 380 cases' (Krejcie and Morgan, 1970, p. 610). This is illustrated in Table 10.1.

TABLE 10.1 Determining sample size from a given population	
Population	**Sample size**
10	10
100	80
200	132
300	169
400	196
500	217
700	248
1,000	278
2,000	322
3,000	341
4,000	351
5,000	357
7,000	364
10,000	370
20,000	377
50,000	381
75,000	382
≥1,000,000	384

Source: Adapted from Krejcie and Morgan (1970, p. 608).

Clegg (1990) suggests the three main considerations are:

- the statistical analysis planned
- the expected variability within subsets in the sample
- the tradition in your research area regarding what constitutes an appropriate sample size.

The factors that must be considered when determining the appropriate number of subjects to include in a sample are discussed in detail by Czaja and Blair (1996); essentially, it is a question of deciding how accurate you want your results to be and how confident you want to be in that answer.

10.7.3 METHODS FOR SELECTING A RANDOM SAMPLE

One way to select a random sample is to allocate a number to every member of the population and select a sample based on the numbers given in a random number table (see Appendix at the end of this chapter) or random numbers created by a computer. This is the equivalent of a lottery, where every number has a chance of being drawn. An unbiased sample is one that represents every section of a population in the same proportion as the population. However, the sample will be biased if the researcher chooses members of the population, asks for volunteers or offers financial inducements to attract participants. Such methods are likely to produce a biased sample because the volunteers may possess certain characteristics that others in the population do not possess.

In *systematic sampling*, the population is divided by the required sample size (n) and the sample chosen by taking every 'nth' subject, as illustrated in Box 10.14.

BOX 10.14 Systematic sampling

Example

Population: 10,000

Sample size: 370

Divide the population by the required sample size:

$$\frac{10,000}{370} = 27$$

Select a randomly chosen number between 1 and the required sample size of 27 (we have chosen 3); then choose every 27th number thereafter until 370 numbers have been selected:

30, 57, 84, 111, 138, 165 and so on

KEY DEFINITIONS

Inferential statistics are a group of statistical methods and models used to draw conclusions about a population from quantitative data relating to a random sample.

'statistical tests that lead to conclusions about a target population based on a random sample and the concept of sampling distribution' (Kervin, 1992, p. 727).

In an undergraduate dissertation, the research may be designed as a small, descriptive study. Therefore, the use of descriptive statistics to explore the data from individual variables (hence the term *univariate analysis*) may be sufficient to address the research questions. However, at postgraduate level, you are likely to design an analytical study. Therefore, you are more likely to use descriptive statistics at the exploratory stage and then go on to use inferential statistics (or other techniques) in a bivariate and/or multivariate analysis. We will examine the statistics used in *bivariate analysis* (two variables) and *multivariate analysis* (more than two variables) in the next chapter.

11.3 GETTING STARTED WITH *SPSS*

11.3.1 THE RESEARCH DATA

We are going to use real business data collected for a postal questionnaire survey of the directors of small private companies. You have already seen some of the questions asked, as they were used as examples in the previous chapter. The companies were selected on the basis that they were likely to qualify for exemption from the statutory requirement to have their accounts audited. Do not worry if you know nothing about this topic, as no prior knowledge is required. The Collis Report (2003) was commissioned by the government as part of the consultation on raising the turnover threshold for audit exemption in UK company law from £1 million to £4.8 million, which would extend this regulatory relaxation to a greater number of small companies. The literature showed that although some of the companies that already qualified for audit exemption made use of it, others apparently chose to continue having their accounts audited. This led to the following research question: What are the factors that have a significant influence on the directors' decision to have a voluntary audit?

Very briefly, the theoretical framework for the study was that the emphasis on turnover in company law at that time implied a relationship between size and whether the cost of audit exceeded the benefits. Agency theory (Jenson and Meckling, 1976) suggests that audit would be required where there was information asymmetry between 'agent' and 'principal' (for example the directors managing the company and external owners, or between the directors and the company's lenders and creditors).

Based on this framework, a number of *hypotheses* were formulated. Each hypothesis is a statement about a relationship between two variables and starts with the Latin phrase *ceteris paribus*, which means 'all things being equal'. The *null hypothesis* (H_0) states that the two variables are independent of one another (there is no relationship) and the *alternative hypothesis* (H_1) states that the two variables are associated with one another (there is a relationship). Using inferential statistics, the hypotheses are tested against the empirical data and the alternative hypothesis is accepted if there is statistically significant evidence to reject the null hypothesis (in other words, the null hypothesis is the default). Here is the first hypothesis in the null and the alternative form:

- H_0 *Ceteris paribus*, the likelihood of the directors choosing a voluntary audit does not increase with company size, as measured by turnover.
- H_1 *Ceteris paribus*, the likelihood of the directors choosing a voluntary audit increases with company size as measured by turnover.

Box 11.1 lists the nine hypotheses tested in the null form. You should check with your supervisor which form is acceptable.

BOX 11.1 Hypotheses to be tested

H1 *Ceteris paribus*, the likelihood of the directors choosing a voluntary audit does not increase with company size, as measured by turnover.

H2 *Ceteris paribus*, the likelihood of the directors choosing a voluntary audit does not increase with perceptions that the audit provides a check on accounting records and systems.

H3 *Ceteris paribus*, the likelihood of the directors choosing a voluntary audit does not increase with perceptions that the audit improves the quality of the financial information.

H4 *Ceteris paribus*, the likelihood of the directors choosing a voluntary audit does not increase with perceptions that the audit improves the credibility of the financial information.

H5 *Ceteris paribus*, the likelihood of the directors choosing a voluntary audit does not increase with perceptions that the audit has a positive effect on the company's credit score.

H6 *Ceteris paribus*, the likelihood of the directors choosing a voluntary audit does not increase if the company is not family owned.

H7 *Ceteris paribus*, the likelihood of the directors choosing a voluntary audit does not increase if there are shareholders without access to internal financial information.

H8 *Ceteris paribus*, the likelihood of the directors choosing a voluntary audit does not increase if the statutory accounts are given to the bank and other providers of finance.

H9 *Ceteris paribus*, the likelihood of the directors choosing a voluntary audit does not increase if they have a degree, a professional/vocational qualification or have studied/trained in business or management subjects.

The sampling frame used was FAME. This is a database containing data from the annual report and accounts of 2.8 million companies in the UK and Ireland. At any one moment in time, some of these companies are dormant, some are in the process of liquidation, some have not yet registered their accounts for the latest year and some do not qualify for audit exemption on the grounds of the public interest (for example listed companies and those in the financial services sector). A search of the database identified a population of 2,633 active companies within the scope of the study (likely to qualify for audit exemption if the turnover threshold were raised), and which had registered their accounts for 2002. The questionnaire was sent to the principal director of each company with an accompanying letter explaining the purpose of the research and that it had been commissioned by the Department for Trade and Industry which was subsequently restructured as the Department for Business, Enterprise and Regulatory Reform. After one reminder, 790 completed questionnaires were received, giving a response rate of 30%. This unexpectedly high rate was undoubtedly due to the use of the government logo on the questionnaire, since response rates from small businesses are usually considerably lower.

We are going to use this survey data to illustrate some of the key features of *SPSS*. The identity of the respondents will not be revealed as they were assured anonymity. This was achieved through the use of a unique reference number (URN) known only to the researcher. Box 11.2 shows the responses given by respondent 42.

BOX 11.2 Questionnaire completed by respondent 42

URN 42

1. Is the company a family-owned business? *(Tick one box only)*

Wholly family-owned (or only 1 owner)	P	(1)
Partly family-owned	☐	(2)
None of the shareholders are related	☐	(0)

2. How many shareholders (owners) does the company have?

(a) Total number of shareholders — 2

Breakdown:

(b) Number of shareholders with access to internal financial information — 2

(c) Number of shareholders <u>without</u> access to internal financial information — 0

3. Would you have the accounts audited if not legally required to do so? *(Tick one box only)*

Yes, the accounts are already audited voluntarily	☐	(1)
Yes, the accounts would be audited voluntarily	☐	(2)
No	P	(0)

Please give reasons for either answer

....

....

4. What are your views on the following statements regarding the audit? *(Circle number closest to your view)*

	Agree			Disagree	
(a) Provides a check on accounting records and systems	5	4	(3)	2	1
(b) Improves the quality of the financial information	5	4	3	(2)	(1)
(c) Improves the credibility of the financial information	5	4	3	(2)	1
(d) Has a positive effect on company's credit rating score	5	4	3	(2)	1

5. Apart from Companies House, who normally receives a copy of the company's statutory accounts?
(Tick as many boxes as apply)

(a) Shareholders — P

(b) Bank and other providers of finance — ☐

(Other variables omitted in this example)

6. Do you have any of the following qualifications/training? *(Tick as many boxes as apply)*

(a) Undergraduate or postgraduate degree — ☐

(b) Professional/vocational qualification — ☐

(c) Study/training in business/management subjects — ☐

Turnover data taken from 2002 accounts on FAME: £74,411k

Source: Adapted from Collis (2003).

11.3.2   LABELLING VARIABLES AND ENTERING THE DATA

Our illustrations are based on *SPSS 16.0*. You run the program in the same way as any other software. For example, *start* ⇒ All Programs ⇒ SPSS16 (or whatever version is available to you). If your programs are on a local area network, *SPSS* may be located within a folder for mathematical and statistics packages. The program usually opens with a screen inviting you to choose what you would like to do. Select Type in data and *SPSS* Data Editor will then open a new data file in Data View (see Figure 11.1), in which each row of cells represents a different case (for example a respondent to a questionnaire survey) and each column represents a different variable. If you are using secondary research data that you have exported to an *Excel* spreadsheet, you can simply copy and paste it into *SPSS* Data Editor.

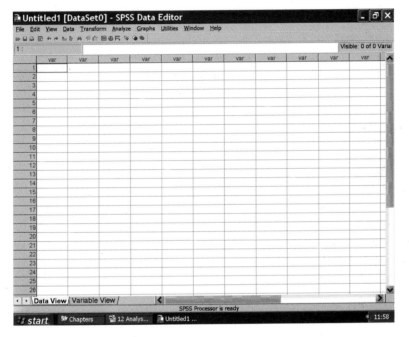

FIGURE 11.1 *SPSS* Data Editor

Now switch from Data View to Variable View by clicking on the tab at the bottom left of the screen and you can start naming and labelling your variables:

- Under Name, type a short word to identify the variable. In this survey, each respondent was given a unique reference number (URN) so that primary data from the questionnaire survey could be matched to secondary data from FAME. Therefore, you might decide to type URN as the name for the first variable. The second variable relates to the first question, so you might want to name it Q1. You will find that *SPSS* prevents you from using a number as the first character or any spaces. Initially you will find this a quick and easy way to name your variables.
- Under Decimals, amend the default to reflect the number of decimal places in the data for that variable. For example, for Q1 you will select 0 decimal places, whereas for turnover you will need to select 3 decimal places.

- Under **Labels**, type a word or two that adds information to the name of the variable. For example, **Family ownership** for Q1; **Total owners** for Q2a; **With internal info** for Q2b; **Without internal info** for Q2c. For Q4, you might decide to use a key word, such as **Check** for Q4a; **Quality** for Q4b; **Credibility** for Q4c; **Credit score** for Q4d.
- Under **Values**, enter the codes and what they signify. For example, in Q4, 1 = Disagree and 5 = Agree (once you have entered this information, you can copy and paste it to other variables using the same codes); for Q6, 1 = Yes and 0 = Otherwise. Turnover does not need any codes entered because it is a ratio variable.
- *SPSS* provides a default measure for missing data (or no response), so unless you have a particular reason to enter a code for a non-response, move on to **Measurement**. *SPSS* gives you a choice of **Scale** (use for *ratio* or *interval* variables) **Ordinal** or **Nominal**. If you need to jog your memory to make these decisions, refer to Chapter 10, section 10.3.1).

At this point, save the file (**File, Save As**) and name it **Data for URN 42.sav** (Figure 11.2 shows the screen at this stage in the process).

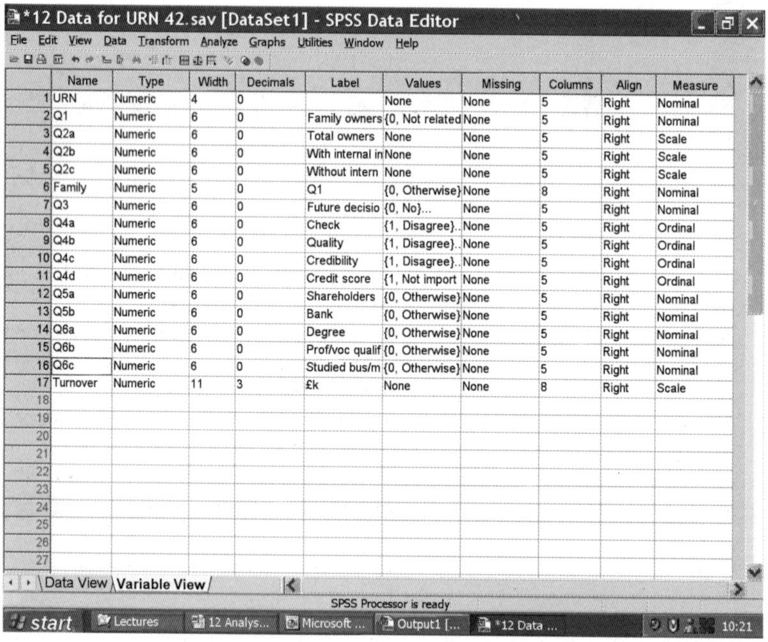

	Name	Type	Width	Decimals	Label	Values	Missing	Columns	Align	Measure
1	URN	Numeric	4	0		None	None	5	Right	Nominal
2	Q1	Numeric	6	0	Family owners	{0, Not related}	None	5	Right	Nominal
3	Q2a	Numeric	6	0	Total owners	None	None	5	Right	Scale
4	Q2b	Numeric	6	0	With internal in	None	None	5	Right	Scale
5	Q2c	Numeric	6	0	Without intern	None	None	5	Right	Scale
6	Family	Numeric	5	0	Q1	{0, Otherwise}	None	8	Right	Nominal
7	Q3	Numeric	6	0	Future decisio	{0, No}...	None	5	Right	Nominal
8	Q4a	Numeric	6	0	Check	{1, Disagree}..	None	5	Right	Ordinal
9	Q4b	Numeric	6	0	Quality	{1, Disagree}..	None	5	Right	Ordinal
10	Q4c	Numeric	6	0	Credibility	{1, Disagree}..	None	5	Right	Ordinal
11	Q4d	Numeric	6	0	Credit score	{1, Not import	None	5	Right	Ordinal
12	Q5a	Numeric	6	0	Shareholders	{0, Otherwise}	None	5	Right	Nominal
13	Q5b	Numeric	6	0	Bank	{0, Otherwise}	None	5	Right	Nominal
14	Q6a	Numeric	6	0	Degree	{0, Otherwise}	None	5	Right	Nominal
15	Q6b	Numeric	6	0	Prof/voc qualif	{0, Otherwise}	None	5	Right	Nominal
16	Q6c	Numeric	6	0	Studied bus/m	{0, Otherwise}	None	5	Right	Nominal
17	Turnover	Numeric	11	3	£k	None	None	8	Right	Scale

FIGURE 11.2 Variable View of Data for URN 42.sav

Next return to **Data View** and enter the data values (the observations) for respondent 42, including the data for turnover, which for the convenience of this exercise is shown as a note at the end of the questionnaire. If you place your cursor over the name of a variable, *SPSS* will reveal the label you added in **Variable View**. For example, Figure 11.3 shows that by placing the cursor on the variable Q4a, the label **Check** is displayed, which was used to remind us that this variable relates to the role of the audit as a check on accounting records and systems. This is a very useful feature that helps ensure you enter the data in the appropriate column.

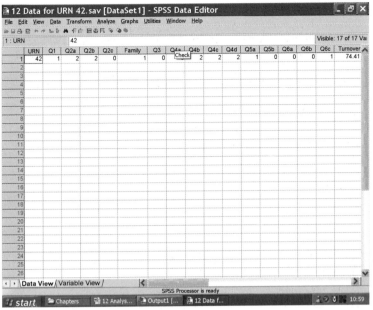

FIGURE 11.3 Data View of Data for URN 42.sav

11.3.3   RECODING VARIABLES

In the previous chapter, we mentioned situations where you might have collected data in a particular form for one purpose, but want to recode it into a different variable in a new, simpler form called a *dummy variable*. This is a dichotomous variable containing only two categories, where 1 = the characteristic is present and 0 = the characteristic is absent. It is important to keep the original variable in case you need the more detailed and precise information for another purpose. We will illustrate how to recode a variable with Q1, which collected data about the extent to which the company is family-owned. We are going to recode it into a new variable called **Family**, which will have two groups: companies that are wholly-family owned (or have only one owner) and those that are not.

In **Variable View** select the whole of row 6 to position the new variable above it:

-   From the menu, select Edit ⇒ Insert Variable.
-   Name the new variable Family and label it as Q1.
-   Under Values, enter the details for the two groups: 1 = Wholly family-owned, 0 = Otherwise.
-   Change the measurement level to nominal.

From the menu, select Transform ⇒ Recode into Different Variable:

-   From the list of variables on the left, select Q1 and use the arrow button ➡ to move it into the Input Variable --> Output Variable box.
-   Type Family in the Output Variable Name box and click Old and New Values.
-   Under Old value, click System-missing and under New value click System-missing and then click Add.

- Under Old value, type 1 and under New value, type 1 and click <u>A</u>dd.
- Under Old value, click All <u>o</u>ther values and under New value, type 0 and click Add ⇒ Continue ⇒ Change and OK. Figure 11.4 illustrates this process.

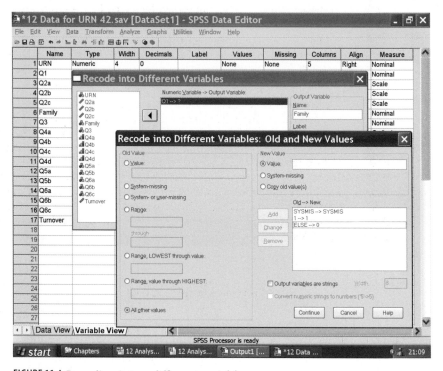

FIGURE 11.4 Recoding into a different variable

When you have finished, return to Data View and carry out a visual check that the value 1 in the new dummy variable coincides with the value 1 in the original variable. This is just an exercise, but when you enter your own research data, you will not start recoding any variables until you have finished entering all the observations for your sample. Remember that it is essential to verify the accuracy of your recoding instructions by checking the outcome. With a large number of cases, it is not practical to use a visual check and we suggest you compare the total frequencies for each category in the old and new variables instead. We will show you how to generate frequency tables in the next section. If you find you have made a mistake, simply go through the steps for recoding the variable again.

You can reinforce and extend your knowledge of recoding by creating three more dummy variables:

- Recode Q2c into Exowners, where 1 = External owners, 0 = Otherwise. Do this by recoding SYSMIS --> SYSMIS, 0 --> 0, ELSE --> 1.
- Recode Q3 into Volaudit, where 1 = Yes, 0 = No. Do this by recoding SYSMIS --> SYSMIS, 0 --> 0, ELSE --> 1.
- Recode Q6a, Q6b and Q6c into Education, where 1 = Degree, qualifications or

training, 0 = Otherwise. This is a bit more complicated. As each variable will make a contribution to the new variable, recode 1 --> 1 for each variable in turn. Then check **Data View** to see the new variable accurately reflects your instructions. If so, from the menu select **Transform ⇒ Recode ⇒ Into same variable** and after selecting **Education**, recode 1 --> 1, **ELSE** --> 0. Then in **Data View** carry out a last visual check on the accuracy of the outcome. As already mentioned, this is essential when working with your own data, as you will not do any recoding until you have finished entering the data for your entire sample.

At this point, you may have begun to think that it would be more convenient if the names we used for the four variables in **Q4** were more informative, like the names of the new variables you have created. Renaming them is easy. Go into **Variable View** and under **Name**, type **Check** instead of Q4a and under **Label**, type Q4a instead of Check. Carry out a similar reversal for **Q4b, Q4c** and **Q4d**. Although using the question numbers was useful at the data entry stage, this small change will aid the next stage, which involves analysing the variables and interpreting the results. When you have finished, save the file and exit. Table 11.1 now summarizes the variables in the analysis, where for some tests we will be describing **Volaudit** as the dependent variable (DV) and the others as the independent variables (IVs).

TABLE 11.1 Variables in the analysis

Hypothesis	Variable	Description
	Volaudit	Whether company would have a voluntary audit (1, 0)
H1	Turnover	Turnover in 2002 accounts (£k)
H2	Check	Audit provides a check on accounting records and systems (5 = Agree, 1 = Disagree)
H3	Quality	Audit improves the quality of the financial information (5 = Agree, 1 = Disagree)
H4	Credibility	Audit improves the credibility of the financial information (5 = Agree, 1 = Disagree)
H5	Creditscore	Audit has a positive effect on the credit rating score (5 = Agree, 1 = Disagree)
H6	Family	Whether company is wholly family-owned (1, 0)
H7	Exowners	Whether company has external shareholders (1, 0)
H8	Bank	Whether statutory accounts are given to the bank/lenders (1, 0)
H9	Education	Whether respondent has degree/qualifications/training (1, 0)

We are now ready to examine some of the *descriptive statistics* used to explore data in a *univariate analysis*. The methods we are going to use are simple statistical models, which not only help us describe the data, but also help determine whether parametric or non-parametric methods will be appropriate in any bivariate or multivariate analysis. Box 11.3 summarizes the statistics we are going to generate.

BOX 11.3   Univariate analysis

Descriptive statistics
Frequency distribution
    Percentage frequency
Measures of central tendency
    Mean
    Median
    Mode
Measures of dispersion
    Range
    Standard deviation
Measures of normality
    Skewness
    Kurtosis

11.4   FREQUENCY DISTRIBUTIONS

In statistics, the term *frequency* refers to the number of observations for a particular data value in a variable (the frequency of occurrence of a quantity in a ratio or interval variable and a category in an ordinal or nominal variable). A *frequency distribution* is an array that summarizes the frequencies for all the data values in a particular variable (Upton and Cook, 2006). For example, the data values in the survey for the variable **Turnover** were the figures reported in the companies' 2006 annual accounts. If no company had precisely the same figure for turnover as another, the number of observations for each data value would be 1. If the variable is measured on an ordinal scale (for example, **Check**, which is coded 1–5) or a nominal scale (for example, **Family**, which is coded 1 or 0), the data values are the codes and the number of observations are the number of companies in each category.

A frequency distribution can be presented for one variable (*univariate* analysis) or two variables (*bivariate* analysis) in a table, chart or other type of diagram. Even with a very small data set (say, 20 data values or less), an examination of how the values are distributed will aid your interpretation of the data.

11.4.1   PERCENTAGE FREQUENCIES

A *percentage frequency* is a familiar statistical model, which summarizes frequencies as a proportion of 100. It is calculated by dividing the frequency by the sum of the frequencies and then multiplying the answer by 100. This can be expressed as a formula:

$$\text{Percentage frequency} = \frac{f}{\Sigma f} \times 100$$

where

f = the frequency
Σ = the sum of

> **Example**
> The survey found that 633 companies out of 790 in the sample had a
> turnover of less than £1 million. Putting these figures into the formula:
>
> $$\frac{633}{790} \times 100 = 80\%$$

The formula we have used is not difficult to understand, but if you are not a statistician, you may find the mathematical notation somewhat mysterious. However, it is merely a kind of shorthand that speeds up the process of writing the formulae and, once you know what the symbols represent, you can decipher the message. As we are going to show you how to use *SPSS* to generate the statistics you require, we will not examine the mathematical side.

11.4.2 CREATING INTERVAL VARIABLES

In a large sample, you may find it useful to recode ratio variables into non-overlapping groups and create a new variable measured on an equal-interval scale. This allows the overall pattern in the frequencies and percentage frequencies to be discerned. However, much of the detail is lost in the process, so it is important to recode into a different variable (rather than the same variable) and keep the original precise information in case you need it for another purpose later on.

KEY DEFINITIONS

A frequency is the number of observations for a particular data value in a variable.

A frequency distribution is an array that summarizes the frequencies for all the data values in a particular variable.

A percentage frequency is a descriptive statistic that summarizes a frequency as a proportion of 100.

When deciding how many groups to create, you need to bear in mind that too few might obscure essential features while too many could emphasize minor or random features. A rule of thumb might be 5 to 10, depending on the range of values in the data. You need to take care that you can allocate each item of data to the appropriate group without ambiguity. For example, the original variable **Turnover** was recoded into a different variable named **Turnovercat** with five groups containing equal intervals of £1m. However, we should not use intervals of £0–£1m, £1m–£2m, £2m–£3m and so on, because a value of £1m could be placed in either the first or the second group and a value of £2m could be placed in the second or the third group. The correct intervals would be £0–£0.99m, £1m–£1.99m, £2m–£2.99m and so on.

11.4.3 GENERATING FREQUENCY TABLES

Although a *frequency table* can be generated for a ratio variable, it is more usually associated with variables that contain groups or categories, such as interval, ordinal or nominal variables. To generate a frequency table in *SPSS*, start the program in the usual way and open the file named **Data for 790 cos.sav**.

- From the menu, select **Analyze** ⇒ **Descriptive Statistics** ⇒ **Frequencies** ...
- From the list of variables on the left, select **Turnovercat** and use the arrow button ➡ to move it into the **Variable(s)** box on the right (see Figure 11.5). If you also wanted to generate frequency tables for other variables, you would simply move them into the box on the right at this point.
- The default is to display the frequency tables, so click **OK** to see the output (see Table 11.2).

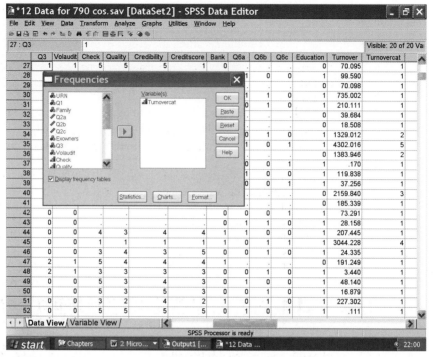

FIGURE 11.5 Generating a frequency table

TABLE 11.2 Frequency table for Turnovercat

Statistics

Turnovercat

N	Valid	790
	Missing	0

Turnovercat

		Frequency	Percent	Valid Percent	Cumulative Percent
Valid	1 Under £1m	633	80.1	80.1	80.1
	2 £1m–£1.99m	55	7.0	7.0	87.1
	3 £2m–£2.99m	37	4.7	4.7	91.8
	4 £3m–£3.99m	40	5.1	5.1	96.8
	5 £4m–£4.9m	25	3.2	3.2	100.0
	Total	790	100.0	100.0	

To copy a table from the *SPSS* output file into a *Word* document, left click with your mouse on the table to select it, and from the menu at the top of the screen, select <u>E</u>dit then <u>C</u>opy and you will then be able to paste the table into your document. You need to remember that every table should be accompanied by one or more paragraphs of explanation.

Table 11.2 shows the presentation of *univariate* data for a variable containing grouped data, but if you want to analyse data from two such variables, you need to generate a *cross-tabulation*. We will demonstrate this with the grouped data from the interval variable **Turnovercat** and the categorical data from the dummy variable **Volaudit**. You can generate a cross-tabulation in *SPSS* using these two variables using the following procedure:

- From the menu at the top, select <u>A</u>nalyze ⇒ <u>D</u>escriptive Statistics... ⇒ <u>C</u>rosstabs and use the arrow button to move **Volaudit** into <u>C</u>olumn(s) and **Turnovercat** into Row(s).
- The default is to show the count of the observations, but it is often more useful to show the percentages. Be wary of showing too much data in a table (generally no more than 20 items of data) as this can detract from the main message. As we have put the dependent variable in the column(s), it makes sense to show the column percentages rather than the row percentages. To do this, select **Cells** and under **Percentages** select **Column** (see Figure 11.6).
- Then click **Continue** and **OK** to see the output (see Table 11.3).

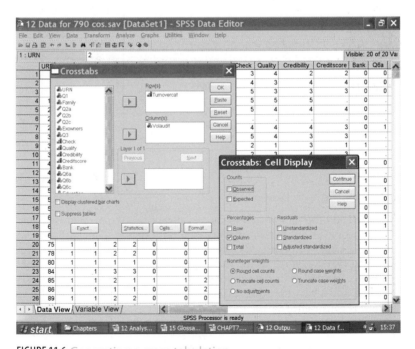

FIGURE 11.6 Generating a cross-tabulation

Once copied into a *Word* document, a table can be edited in the usual way. In this example, both groups in the dependent variable **Volaudit** follow more or less the same size order. If your data do not conveniently coincide in this way, base the order on the group that contains the larger frequencies and let the other group follow that order.

TABLE 11.3 Cross-tabulation for Volaudit and Turnovercat

Case Processing Summary

	Cases					
	Valid		Missing		Total	
	N	Percent	N	Percent	N	Percent
Turnovercat * Volaudit	772	97.7%	18	2.3%	790	100.0%

Turnovercat * Volaudit Crosstabulation

			Volaudit		
			0 Otherwise	1 Yes	Total
Turnovercat	1 Under £1m	Count	406	214	620
		% within Volaudit	92.7%	64.1%	80.3%
	2 £1m–£1.99m	Count	12	42	54
		% within Volaudit	2.7%	12.6%	7.0%
	3 £2m–£2.99m	Count	10	26	36
		% within Volaudit	2.3%	7.8%	4.7%
	4 £3m–£3.99m	Count	5	33	38
		% within Volaudit	1.1%	9.9%	4.9%
	5 £4m–£4.9m	Count	5	19	24
		% within Volaudit	1.1%	5.7%	3.1%
Total		Count	438	334	772
		% within Volaudit	100.0%	100.0%	

11.4.4 GENERATING CHARTS

Charts (and other graphical forms) can also be used to present frequency information. Some people prefer to read summarized information in a chart and detailed information in a table. In both cases, there must also be a written explanation. You need to consider the level at which the variable is measured when choosing the type of chart. If you have entered your data into a spreadsheet or into a specialist statistical program, you will find it easy to produce a variety of different charts. Table 11.4 shows how your choice is constrained by the measurement level of the research data.

TABLE 11.4 Charts for different types of data

Measurement level	Bar chart	Pie chart	Histogram
Nominal	✓	✓	
Ordinal	✓		
Interval			✓
Ratio			✓

The advantages of using a chart are:

- it is a good way to communicate general points
- it is attractive to look at
- it appeals to a more general audience
- it makes it easier to compare data sets
- relationships can be seen more clearly.

The disadvantages of using a chart are:

- it is not a good way to communicate specific details
- it can be misinterpreted
- the design may detract from the message
- designing a non-standard chart can be time-consuming
- it can be designed to be deliberately misleading.

You can create a chart in *SPSS* at the same time as generating a frequency table.

- From the menu, select <u>A</u>nalyze ⇒ D<u>e</u>scriptive Statistics... ⇒ <u>F</u>requencies.
- From the list of variables on the left, move **Turnovercat** into the <u>V</u>ariable(s) box on the right and click **Charts**.
- Under **Chart Type**, select **Bar charts**, and under **Chart Values**, select **Percentages** and click **Continue** (see Figure 11.7).
- Click **OK** to see the output (see Figure 11.8).

Go through the same procedure again, to select a pie chart or a histogram (not surprisingly, *SPSS* does not anticipate that you might want all three, so you can only select one at a time).

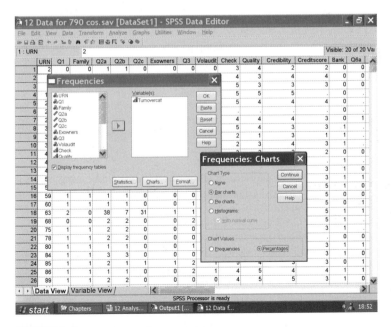

FIGURE 11.7 Generating a chart

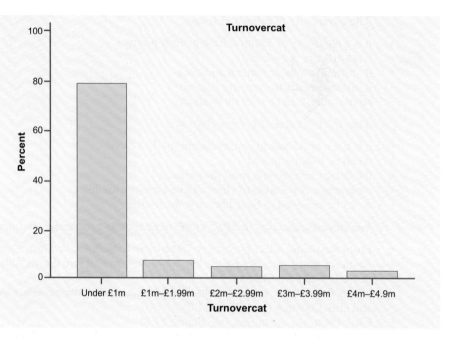

FIGURE 11.8 Bar chart for Turnovercat

In a *bar chart*, the frequency or percentage frequency for each ordinal or nominal category is displayed in a separate vertical (or horizontal) bar. The frequencies are indicated by the height (or length) of the bars, which permits a visual comparison. In a *component bar chart*, the bars are divided into segments. However, these are not recommended, as the segments lack a common axis or base line, which makes them difficult to interpret visually. The alternative is a *multiple bar chart* in which the segments are adjoined and each starts at the base line. This allows the reader to compare several component parts, but the comparison of the total is lost.

In a *pie chart*, the percentage frequency for each value or category is displayed as a segment of a circular diagram. Each segment represents an area that is proportional to the whole 'pie'. Figure 11.9 shows a pie chart representing the percentage frequencies for each category in **Turnovercat**.

A *histogram* is a refinement of a bar chart, but the adjoining bars touch, indicating that the variable is measured on an interval or ratio scale. If you have data measured on an interval scale based on equal intervals, the width of the bars will be constant and the height of each bar will represent the frequency because Area = Width $\square$ Height. Thus, a histogram shows the approximate shape of the distribution. We will illustrate this with the original variable **Turnover**, which is measured on a ratio scale and the chart is shown in Figure 11.10.

We suggest you run the tutorial on creating and editing charts. To amend the appearance of the chart, double click on the chart to open the **Chart Editor**. For example, in the bar chart and pie chart we have illustrated, it would be useful to add value labels to the segments, but specify 0 decimal places to reduce unwanted 'noise' in the communication. In the histogram for **Turnover**, you might want to use a scaling factor of 1,000, which would allow you to label the values in millions as shown in the bar and pie charts

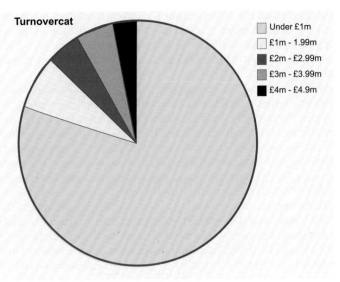

FIGURE 11.9 Pie chart for Turnovercat

for **Turnovercat**. For future reference, note that the histogram can also show the distribution curve and the default is to show some descriptive statistics that summarize the data. We will examine these in the next section.

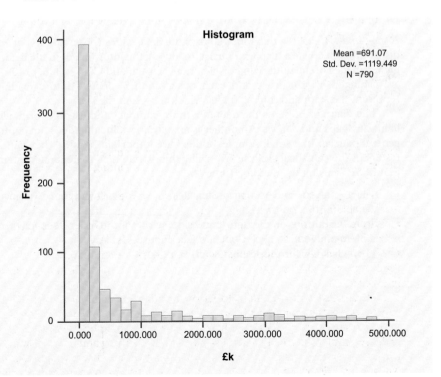

FIGURE 11.10 Histogram for Turnover

To copy a chart from the *SPSS* output file into a *Word* document, left click with your mouse on the chart to select it, and from the menu at the top of the screen, select Edit then Copy and you will then be able to paste the table into your document. You need to remember that every chart should be accompanied by one or more paragraphs of explanation.

The Chart Editor allows you to generate a *line graph* to present continuous data (such as Turnover) across a number of categories. It is not appropriate to use a line graph to represent discrete data, such as number of employees. This is because you can represent turnover as a line by dividing it into fractional denominations (such as £1.01, £1.02, £1.03 and so on) but you cannot have 1.1, 1.2 or 1.3 employees. Line graphs are often used to present data collected at different points in time. For example, if you have turnover data for the past five years, you could use a line chart to illustrate any volatility, stability or trend over the period and compare companies with external share-holders with those that are owner-managed. The frequencies are always shown on the vertical axis (the Y axis) and data values for the categories on the horizontal axis (the X axis). In this example, Turnover would be shown on the Y axis (in £k or £m) and the years would be shown along the X axis. You might want to use Exowners as the variable to define the lines by. If you did this, the two groups in Exowners would be described as 'External owners' and 'Otherwise' in the legend.

You can see from this brief description that one advantage of line graphs over other charts is that, providing they share the same scale and unit of measurement, a number of variables can be represented on the same graph (a multiple line graph). This greatly facilitates visual comparison of the data.

11.4.5   GENERATING A STEM-AND-LEAF PLOT

A *stem-and-leaf plot* is a diagram that uses the data values (observations) in a frequency distribution to create a display. Thus, it 'retains all the information in the data, while also giving an idea of the underlying distribution' (Upton and Cook, 2006, p. 409). The data are arranged in size order and each observation is divided into a leading digit to represent the stem and trailing digits, which represent the leaf.

The diagram presents the data in a more compact and useable form, which high-lights any gaps and *outliers*. An outlier is an extreme value that does not conform to the general pattern. In a small sample, outliers are important because they can distort the results of the statistical analysis. We will demonstrate how to generate a stem-and-leaf plot in *SPSS* using the data for Turnover.

- Select Analyze ⇒ Descriptive Statistics… ⇒ Explore and move Turnover into the Variable(s) box on the right.
- From the buttons on the right-hand side, select Plots. Under Descriptive, the default is Stem-and-leaf, so click Continue (see Figure 11.11).
- Then click OK for the results (see Box 11.4).

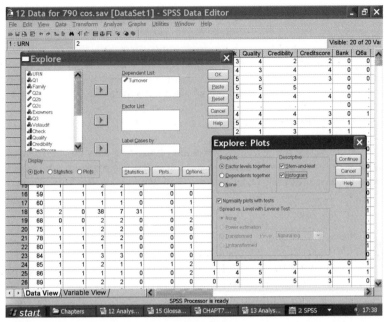

FIGURE 11.11 Generating a stem-and-leaf plot

Box 11.4 illustrates the stem-and-leaf plot for the **Turnover**.

BOX 11.4 Stem-and-leaf plot for Turnover

```
Turnover £k
Frequency      Stem & Leaf
 321.00          0 . 00000011111222223334444555566677788899 9
 104.00          1 . 0111223456788&
  65.00          2 . 0123469&
  39.00          3 . 0123&&
  25.00          4 . &&&
  18.00          5 . &&
  18.00          6 . &&
   6.00          7 . &
  18.00          8 . &&
  19.00          9 . &&
   5.00         10 . &
   5.00         11 . &
   8.00         12 . &
   9.00         13 . &
   2.00         14 . &
   6.00         15 . &
  11.00         16 . 1&
   3.00         17 . &
 108.00       Extremes  >=1795)

Stem width: 100.000
Each leaf: 8 case(s)

& denotes fractional leaves
```

11.5   MEASURING CENTRAL TENDENCY

We are now going to look at a group of statistical models that are concerned with measuring the *central tendency* of a frequency distribution. Measures of central tendency provide a convenient way of summarizing a large frequency distribution by describing it with a single statistic. The three measures are the mean, the median and the mode.

11.5.1   THE MEAN

The *mean* ($\bar{x}$) is the arithmetic average of a set of data in a sample and can only be calculated for ratio or interval variables. It is found by dividing the sum of the observations by the number of observations, as shown in the following formula:

$$\text{Mean} = \frac{\Sigma x}{n}$$

where

x = each observation
n = the total number of observations
Σ = the sum of

Example
A student's exam marks were as follows:

Module 1	Module 2	Module 3	Module 4	Module 5	Module 6
82%	78%	80%	64%	70%	64%

Inserting the data into the formula:

$$\frac{82 + 78 + 80 + 64 + 70 + 64}{6} = \frac{438}{6} = 73\%$$

The advantages of the mean are:

*   it can be calculated exactly
*   it takes account of all the data
*   it can be used as the basis of other statistical models.

The disadvantages of the mean are:

*   it is greatly affected by outliers (extreme values that are very high or very low)
*   it is a hypothetical value and may not be one of the actual values
*   it can give an impossible figure for discrete data (for example the average number of owners in the sample of small companies was 5.8)
*   it cannot be calculated for ordinal or nominal data.

11.5.2   THE MEDIAN

The *median* (M) is the mid-value of a set of data that has been arranged in size order (in other words, it has been ranked). It can be calculated for variables measured on a ratio, interval or ordinal scale and is found by adding 1 to the number of observations and dividing by 2. The formula is:

$$\text{Median} = \frac{n + 1}{2}$$

where

n = number of observations

This is very straightforward if you have an even number of observations because the formula will take you directly to the observation at the mid-point. The following example shows what you need to do if you have an uneven number of observations.

Example
The student's exam marks in chronological order were:

Module 1	Module 2	Module 3	Module 4	Module 5	Module 6
82%	78%	80%	64%	70%	64%

The marks arranged in size order are:

64%	64%	70%	78%	80%	82%

Inserting the data into the formula:

$$\frac{6 + 1}{2} = 3.5$$

Therefore, the median is half-way between the third and the fourth of the ranked marks. A simple calculation will tell us the exact value:

$$\frac{70 + 78}{2} = 74\%$$

The advantages of the median are:

- it is not affected by outliers or open-ended values at the extremities
- it is not affected by unequal class intervals
- it can represent an actual value in the data.

The disadvantages of the median are:

- it cannot be measured precisely for distributions reflecting grouped data
- it cannot be used as the basis for other statistical models
- it may not be useful if the data set does not have normal distribution (we will be looking at this in section 11.7)
- it cannot be calculated for nominal data.

11.5.3   THE MODE

The *mode* (m) is the most frequently occurring value in a data set and can be used for all variables, irrespective of the measurement scale.

Example
The student's exam marks were:

Module 1	Module 2	Module 3	Module 4	Module 5	Module 6
82%	78%	80%	64%	70%	64%

The mode is 64%

The advantages of the mode are:

- it is not affected by outliers
- it is easy to identify in a small data set
- it can be calculated for any variable, irrespective of the measurement scale.

The disadvantages of the mode are:

- it is a dynamic measure that can change as other values are added
- it cannot be measured precisely for distributions reflecting grouped data
- there may be multiple modes
- it cannot be used as the basis for other statistical models.

One of the things you will have noticed from the analysis in this section is that the mean, the median and the mode each use a different definition of central tendency. Our analysis of the student's marks has produced a different result under each method. The reason for this will become apparent when we look at the importance of examining the spread of data values in section 11.6.

11.5.4   GENERATING MEASURES OF CENTRAL TENDENCY

With a large data set, you will need some help in calculating measures of central tendency, but *SPSS* allows you to do this at the same time as generating frequency distributions in tables and/or charts. The procedure is as follows:

- From the menu, select Analyze ⇒ Descriptive Statistics… ⇒ Frequencies.
- We will use the original ratio variable to measure turnover, so use the arrow button to return Turnovercat to the list on the left and move Turnover into the Variable(s) box on the right. If you also wanted to generate frequency tables for other variables, you would simply move them into the box on the right at this point.
- Now click on Statistics and under Central Tendency, select Mean, Median and Mode and click Continue (see Figure 11.12).
- Then click OK to see the results table (see Table 11.5).

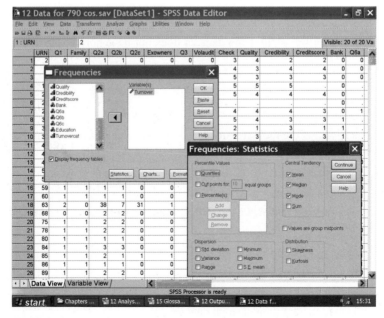

FIGURE 11.12 Generating measures of central tendency

TABLE 11.5 Measures of central tendency for Turnover

Turnover £k

N	Valid	790
	Missing	0
Mean		691.07062
Median		158.06450
Mode		8.000

Interpreting the results, you can see that despite being called measures of central tendency, the 'centre' differs for each statistic. The reasons for this will become apparent in the next section. For the time being, we can simply say that the different results arise from the different definitions we used for each measure.

Before moving on to the next subject, we are going to demonstrate the importance of retaining the detailed data in the original variable **Turnover** by comparing the precise mean we have obtained for that variable with the mean we can calculate for the five classes of grouped data in **Turnovercat**. To determine the mean for grouped data, we need to take the mid-points of each class and multiply by the frequency, as shown in the following formula:

$$\text{Mean for grouped data} = \frac{\Sigma fx}{\Sigma f}$$

where

f = the frequency
x = each observation
Σ = the sum of

The calculations are as follows:

Turnover	Frequency (f)	Mid-point (x)	(fx)
Under £1m	633	0.5	316.5
£1m–£1.99m	55	1.5	82.5
£2m–£2.99m	37	2.5	92.5
£3m–£3.99m	40	3.5	140.0
£4m–£4.9m	25	4.5	112.5
Total	790		744.0

We can now substitute the figures we have calculated in the formula:

$$\frac{744}{790} = 0.94$$

The results show that the mean for the grouped data in the interval variable **Turnovercat** is £0.94m compared to the mean of £0.69m that we calculated earlier using the precise data contained in the ratio variable **Turnover**. The grouped data can only give an approximation of this important statistic. Moreover, this approximation is larger than the actual mean because it is based on the median in each category rather than every data value (observation). This helps demonstrate the superiority of ratio data over interval or ordinal data when it comes to measuring the mean, which lies at the heart of the most powerful statistical models used in inferential statistics. We will discuss this further in Chapter 12.

11.6   MEASURING DISPERSION

Measures of central tendency are useful for providing statistics that summarize the location of the 'middle' of the data, but they do not tell us anything about the spread of the data values. Therefore, we are now going to look at *measures of dispersion*, which should only be calculated for variables measured on a ratio or interval scale. The two measures are the range and the standard deviation.

KEY DEFINITIONS

The interquartile range is a measure of dispersion that represents the difference between the upper quartile and the lower quartile (the middle 50%) of a frequency distribution arranged in size order.

The range is a measure of dispersion that represents the difference between the maximum value and the minimum value in a frequency distribution arranged in size order.

11.6.1   RANGE

The range is a simple measure of dispersion that describes the difference between the maximum value (the upper extreme or E_U) and the minimum value (the lower extreme or E_L) in a frequency distribution arranged in size order. You will remember from the previous section that the median is the mid-point, but in a large set of data (say, 30 observations or more) it can be useful to divide the frequency distribution into quartiles, each containing 25% of the data values. This allows us to measure the interquartile range, which is the difference between the upper quartile (Q_3) and the lower quartile (Q_1), and the spread of the middle 50% of the data values. When comparing two distributions, the interquartile range is often preferred to the range, because the latter is more easily affected by outliers (extreme values). The formulae are:

$$\text{Range} = E_U - E_L$$
$$\text{Interquartile range} = Q_3 - Q_1$$

Example
Inserting the data for Turnover (£k) into the formulae:

$$\text{Range} = 4{,}738.271 - 0.054 = 4{,}738.217$$
$$\text{Interquartile range} = 742.76625 - 52.74525 = 690.021$$

Unfortunately, the drawback of using the range is that it only takes account of two items of data and the drawback of the interquartile range is that it only takes account of half the values. What we really want is a measure of dispersion that will take account of all the values and we discuss such an alternative next.

11.6.2   STANDARD DEVIATION

The *standard deviation* (sd) should only be calculated for ratio or interval variables, but it overcomes the deficiencies of the range and the interquartile range discussed in the previous section by using all the data. The standard deviation is related to the normal distribution and the term was introduced by Karl Pearson in 1893 (Upton and Cook, 2006). It is based on the *error* and the *variance*, which are two statistical models used to measure how well the *mean* represents the data (Field, 2000).

In this context, the error is the difference between the mean and the data value (the observation). It is called an error because it measures the deviation of the observation from the mean (which is a hypothetical value that summarizes the data). We then add up the errors and make some adjustments. These are necessary because the difference between the mean and each value below the mean produces a negative figure while the difference between the mean and each value above the mean produces a positive figure. Unfortunately, when these are added together, the answer is zero. To resolve this problem, the errors are squared (in mathematics, squaring a positive or a negative number always produces a positive figure).

This allows us to calculate the variance, which is the mean of the squared errors. However, this is very difficult to interpret because it is measured in squared units (for example our turnover data would be in square £). To de-square the units, we calculate the square root of the variance. This gives us the standard deviation, which we can now define as the square root of the variance. A small standard deviation relative to the mean suggests the mean represents the data well; conversely, a large standard deviation relative to the mean, suggests the mean does not represent the data well because the data values are widely dispersed.

In case you only have a small data set and want to calculate the standard deviation unaided, the formula for individual data is:

$$sd = \sqrt{\frac{\Sigma(x - \bar{x})^2}{n}}$$

where

x = an observation
$\bar{x}$ the mean
n = the total number of observations
$\sqrt{}$ = the square root
Σ = the sum of

The formula for grouped data is:

$$sd = \sqrt{\frac{\Sigma x^2 f}{\Sigma f} - \frac{(\Sigma xf)^2}{\Sigma f}}$$

where

x = the mid-point of each data class
f = the frequency of each class
$\sqrt{}$ = the square root
Σ = the sum of

The advantages of the standard deviation are:

* it uses every value
* it is in the same units as the original data
* it is easy to interpret.

The disadvantages are:

* the calculations are complex without the aid of suitable software
* it can only be used for variables measured on a ratio or interval scale.

The final term we are going to introduce is the *standard error* (se), which is calculated by 'taking the difference between each sample mean and the overall mean, squaring the differences, adding them up and dividing by the number of samples' (Field, 2000, p. 9). A small standard error relative to the overall sample mean suggests the sample is representative of the population, whereas a large standard error relative to the overall sample mean suggests the sample might not be representative of the population.

11.6.3   GENERATING MEASURES OF DISPERSION

By now you will have realized that *SPSS* allows you to generate frequency tables, measures of central tendency and measures of dispersion for one or more variables in one set of instructions under the Analyze ⇒ Descriptive Statistics menu. We will now show you how to add the measures of dispersion we have been discussing:

- From the menu, select Analyze ⇒ Descriptive Statistics... ⇒ Frequencies and move Turnover into the Variable(s) box on the right. If you also wanted to generate frequency tables for other variables, you would simply move them into the box on the right at this point.
- Deselect the default to display frequency tables, as you already have them.
- Now click on Statistics and deselect any options under Central Tendency, as you have them already. Under Percentile Values, select Quartiles and under Dispersion click all the options and then click Continue (see Figure 11.13).
- Click OK to see the output (see Table 11.6).

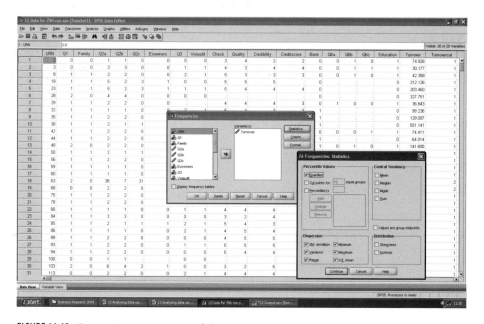

FIGURE 11.13 Generating measures of dispersion

TABLE 11.6 Measures of dispersion for Turnover

Statistics

Turnover

N	Valid	790
	Missing	0
Std. Error of Mean		39.828205
Std. Deviation		1119.448910
Variance		1253165.862
Range		4738.217
Minimum		.054
Maximum		4738.271
Percentiles	25	52.74525
	50	158.06450
	75	742.76625

11.7 NORMAL DISTRIBUTION

We mentioned in the previous section that the standard deviation is related to the *normal distribution*. This term was introduced in the late 19th century by Sir Francis Galton, cousin of Charles Darwin who published *The Origin of Species* in 1859 (Upton and Cook, 2006), and refers to a theoretical frequency distribution that is bell-shaped and symmetrical, with tails extending indefinitely either side of the centre. In a normal distribution, the *mean*, the *median* and the *mode* coincide at the centre (see Figure 11.14). It is described as a theoretical frequency distribution because it is a mathematical model representing perfect symmetry, against which empirical data can be compared.

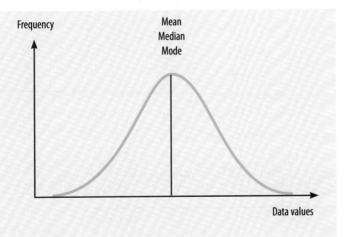

FIGURE 11.14 A normal frequency distribution

11.7.1 SKEWNESS AND KURTOSIS

When the frequency distribution does not have a symmetrical distribution, it is described as skewed. Thus, *skewness* is a measure of the extent to which a frequency distribution is asymmetric. In a skewed distribution, the mean, the median and the mode have different values. Indeed, we found that the mean turnover for the sample companies was £691,071, the median was £158,065 and the mode was £8,000. The skewness of a normal distribution is 0 (the distribution is symmetrical). When a distribution has a positive skewness value, the tail is on the right (the positive side of the centre) and most of the observations are at the lower end of the range (see Figure 11.15). When the distribution has a negative skewness value, the tail is on the left (the negative side of the centre) and most of the observations are at the upper end of the range (see Figure 11.16). A skewness value that is more than twice the standard error of the skewness suggests the distribution is not symmetrical.

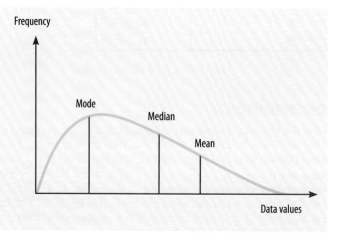

FIGURE 11.15 A positively skewed frequency distribution

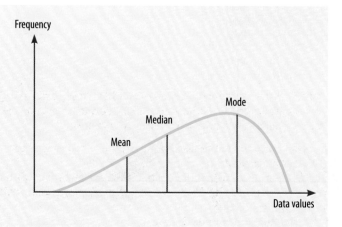

FIGURE 11.16 A negatively skewed frequency distribution

Kurtosis is a measure of the extent to which a frequency distribution is flatter or more peaked than a normal distribution (a normal distribution has a kurtosis of 0).

A normal distribution is a theoretical frequency distribution that is bell-shaped and symmetrical, with tails extending indefinitely either side of the centre. The mean, median and mode coincide at the centre.

A second important measure is *kurtosis*, which measures the extent to which a frequency distribution is flatter or more peaked than a normal distribution (Upton and Cook, 2006). The kurtosis value of a normal distribution is 0, which indicates the bell-shaped distribution with most of the observations clustered in the centre. A distribution with positive kurtosis is more peaked than a normal distribution because it has more observations in the centre and longer tails on either side. A distribution with negative kurtosis is flatter than a normal distribution because there are fewer observations in the centre and the tails on either side are shorter.

Both the mean and the standard deviation are related to the normal distribution. While the mean represents the centre of the frequency distribution, the standard deviation measures the spread or dispersion of the data values around the mean. If the data set has a normal distribution, 68% of the data values will be within 1 standard deviation of the mean, 95% will fall within 2 standard deviations of the mean and 99.7% will fall within 3 standard deviations of the mean. This is illustrated in Figure 11.17.

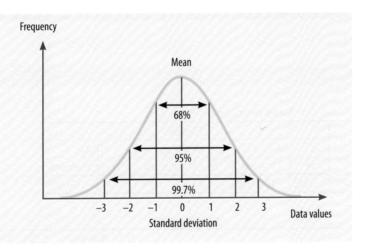

FIGURE 11.17 Proportion of a normal distribution under 1 standard deviation

11.7.2 TESTING FOR NORMALITY

Although you can obtain measures of skewness and kurtosis under the Frequencies menu we have been using so far, if you want to run normality tests at the same time, you need to use the Explore menu. The procedure is as follows:

- Select Analyze ⇒ Descriptive Statistics... ⇒ Explore and move Turnover into the Variable(s) box on the right.
- The default is for both statistics and plots. Under Statistics, accept the default of Descriptives. However, under Plots, select Normality plots with tests and click Continue (see Figure 11.18).
- Click OK for the output (see Table 11.7).

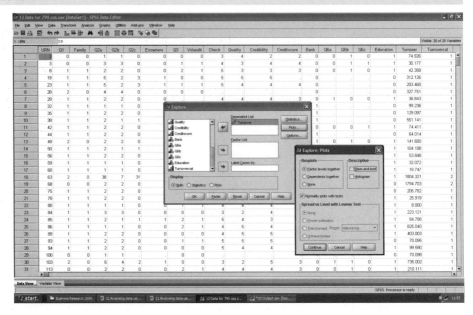

FIGURE 11.18 Generating descriptive statistics and testing for normality

TABLE 11.7 Descriptive statistics and normality tests for Turnover

Case Processing Summary

	Cases					
	Valid		Missing		Total	
	N	Percent	N	Percent	N	Percent
Turnover	790	100.0%	0	.0%	790	100.0%

Descriptives

		Statistic	Std. Error
Turnover	Mean	691.07062	39.828205
	95% Confidence Interval for Mean — Lower Bound	612.88884	
	95% Confidence Interval for Mean — Upper Bound	769.25240	
	5% Trimmed Mean	537.33076	
	Median	158.06450	
	Variance	1253165.862	
	Std. Deviation	1119.448910	
	Minimum	.054	
	Maximum	4738.271	
	Range	4738.217	
	Interquartile Range	690.021	
	Skewness	2.042	.087
	Kurtosis	3.170	.174

Tests of Normality

	Kolmogorov-Smirnov[a]			Shapiro-Wilk		
	Statistic	df	Sig.	Statistic	df	Sig.
Turnover	.276	790	.000	.643	790	.000

a. Lilliefors Significance Correction

These results confirm what we could see from the general shape of the data in the histogram and from the measures of central tendency: Turnover does not have a normal distribution. The positive value for skewness confirms the spread of the data is skewed with more observations on the right of the mean; the positive value for kurtosis indicates a more peaked distribution than expected in a normal distribution with a higher degree of clustering of observations around the mean and longer tail(s).

The tests of normality compare the frequency distribution of the sample with a normal distribution with the same mean and standard deviation (Field, 2000). The test statistic is a function of the observations in our random sample. If the actual value is too far from the expected value, the test result is significant and this evidence leads us to reject the null hypothesis. Conversely, if the actual value is close to the expected value, the test result is not significant, and we do not reject the null hypothesis. There are two cases when a test result leads to a correct result (Upton and Cook, 2006):

- H_0 is true and the test leads to its acceptance
- H_1 is true and the test leads to the rejection of H_0.

However, there are also two cases when a test leads to an incorrect result (an error):
- H_0 is true, but the test leads to its rejection (referred to as a *Type 1 error*)
- H_1 is true, but the test leads to the acceptance of H_0 (referred to as a *Type II error*).

We need to specify the size of the critical region that determines whether the test result is significant by setting the *significance level*. If you are conducting research into issues relating to health or safety you would want this critical region to be less than 1%, but in most business and management research, a 5% probability of a Type I or II error is usually acceptable. This is reflected in the default on *SPSS*, where the significance level is set at 0.05, which is 5%. Therefore, you will interpret the result of any test as being significant if the probability statistic (which we refer to as p) is significant at 5% or less (in other words, $p \leq 0.05$).

Looking at the tests of normality in the second part of Table 11.7, you can see the results are significant (the value under Sig. is ≤ 0.05). This means we can reject the null hypothesis and we accept that the frequency distribution for Turnover differs significantly from a normal distribution. If a result showed $p > 0.05$, it would indicate that the size of the deviation from normality in the sample was not large enough to be significant. In this case, a significant result is not surprising, since small and medium-sized businesses account for 99.9% of all enterprises in the UK (BERR, 2008, p. 1), thus size is positively skewed in the population. When you have finished, save your files and exit from *SPSS*.

The tests you choose for your study will depend on your hypotheses and your research questions. A typical analysis might start with bivariate analysis to explore differences between independent or related samples and to test for relationships between variables and measure the strength of those relationships. This might lead to multivariate analysis where a regression model is developed from one or more predictor variables. Table 12.2 summarizes the parametric and non-parametric methods we are going to examine. We will demonstrate the non-parametric methods using the data from the Collis Report (2003) first and then explain the equivalent parametric method. If you have longitudinal data, you will also need to refer to the final sections of the chapter where we discuss indexation methods and time series analysis.

TABLE 12.2 Bivariate and multivariate analysis		
Purpose	For parametric data	For non-parametric data
Tests of difference for independent or dependent samples	*t*-test	Mann-Whitney test
Tests of association between two nominal variables	Not applicable	Chi-square test
Tests of association between two quantitative variables	Pearson's correlation	Spearman's correlation
Predicting an outcome from one or more variables	Linear regression	Logistic regression

12.3 TESTS OF DIFFERENCE

12.3.1 MANN-WHITNEY TEST

If you have non-parametric data for an IV measured on a quantitative scale (a non-normal ratio or interval scale, or an ordinal scale) and a DV containing two independent samples, you can use the *Mann-Whitney test* to establish whether there is a difference between the two samples. In the Collis Report, Volaudit is the DV. This is a dummy variable relating to whether the company would have a voluntary audit, and is coded 1 = Yes, 0 = No. This gives us our two independent samples or groups of subjects. We are going to use the Mann-Whitney test for each of the following IVs: Turnover, which is measured on a non-parametric ratio scale; Check, Quality, Credibility and Creditscore, which are measured on an ordinal scale where 1 = Disagree and 5 = Agree. The null hypothesis (H_0) is that there is no difference between the two groups.

Start *SPSS* in the usual way and open the file named Data for 790 cos.sav. Although we are going to run five tests, we can instruct *SPSS* to do this in one procedure as follows:

- From the menu, select Analyze ⇒ Nonparametric tests ⇒ 2 Independent samples.
- Move Turnover, Check, Quality, Credibility and Creditscore to Test Variable List. The order does not matter, but our principle is to list them in the order of the hypotheses shown in Table 12.1 (which coincides with the level of measurement).
- Move Volaudit to Grouping Variable and click Define groups.
- The two groups in Volaudit are labelled 1 and 0, so in Group 1 type 1 and in Group 2 type 0 (see Figure 12.1).
- We want the default test, Mann-Whitney U, so click OK to see the output (see Table 12.3).

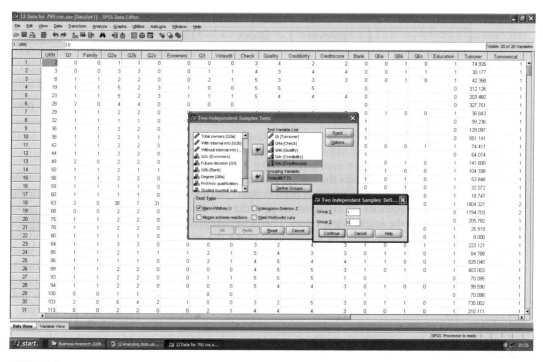

FIGURE 12.1 Running a Mann-Whitney test

TABLE 12.3 Mann-Whitney test for Turnover, Check, Quality, Credibility and Creditscore

Ranks

	Volaudit	N	Mean Rank	Sum of Ranks
Turnover	0 No	438	311.29	136344.50
	1 Yes	334	485.13	162033.50
	Total	772		
Check	0 No	362	285.45	103332.00
	1 Yes	320	404.91	129571.00
	Total	682		
Quality	0 No	356	268.62	95629.00
	1 Yes	316	412.97	130499.00
	Total	672		
Credibility	0 No	358	278.17	99584.00
	1 Yes	315	403.86	127217.00
	Total	673		
Creditscore	0 No	355	273.52	97100.00
	1 Yes	312	402.81	125678.00
	Total	667		

S

ence of one numerical random variable on another' (Upton and Cook, 2006, p. 101). The two variables are not referred to as the DV and the IV because 'they are measured simultaneously and so no cause-and-effect relationship can be established' (Field, 2000, p. 78).

The correlation coefficient is measured within the range –1 to +1. The direction of the correlation is positive if both variables increase together, but it is negative if one variable increases as the other decreases. The strength of the correlation is measured by the size of the correlation coefficient:

1 represents a perfect positive linear association
0 represents no linear association
–1 represents a perfect negative linear association

Therefore, values in between can be graded roughly as:

0.90 to   0.99 (very high positive correlation)
0.70 to   0.89 (high positive correlation)
0.40 to   0.69 (medium positive correlation)
  0 to   0.39 (low positive correlation)
  0 to –0.39 (low negative correlation)
–0.40 to –0.69 (medium negative correlation)
–0.70 to –0.89 (high negative correlation)
–0.90 to –0.99 (very high negative correlation)

You need to take care when interpreting correlation coefficients, since correlation between two variables does not prove the existence of a causal link between them; two causally unrelated variables can be correlated because they both relate to a third variable. For example, the sales of ice-cream and suntan lotion may be correlated because they both relate to higher temperatures.

12.5.1   BIVARIATE SCATTERPLOT

If you have parametric data, a preliminary step is to generate a display of the relationship between the two quantitative variables using a simple *scatterplot*. One variable is plotted against the other on a graph as a pattern of points, which indicates the direction and strength of any linear correlation. The more the points cluster around a straight line, the stronger the correlation.

- If the points tend to cluster around a line that runs from the lower left to the upper right of the graph, the correlation is *positive*, as shown in Figure 12.3. Positive correlation occurs when an increase in the value of one variable is associated with an increase in the value of the other. For example, an increase in the volume of orders from customers may be associated with increased calls to customers by the sales representatives.
- If points tend to cluster around a line that runs from the upper left to the lower right of the graph, the correlation is *negative*, as shown in Figure 12.4. Negative correlation occurs when an increase in the value of one variable is associated with a decrease in the value of the other. For example, higher interest rates for borrowing may be associated with lower house sales.
- If the points are scattered randomly throughout the graph, there is no correlation between the two variables as shown in Figure 12.5. Alternatively, the pattern may show non-linear correlation as illustrated in Figure 12.6.

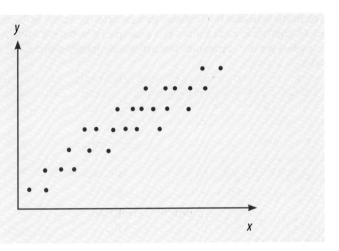

FIGURE 12.3 Scatterplot showing positive linear correlation

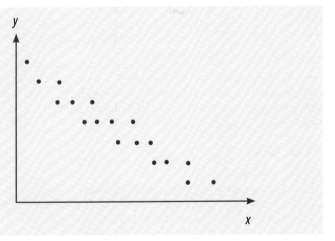

FIGURE 12.4 Scatterplot showing negative linear correlation

Using *SPSS*, the general procedure is as follows:

- From the menu at the top, select <u>G</u>raphs ⇒ <u>L</u>egacy Dialogs ⇒ <u>S</u>catter/Dot.
- The default is a Simple Scatterplot, but you will see that you have other choices.
- Move one variable into the <u>Y</u> Axis box and the other into the <u>X</u> Axis box.
- If you want different symbols or different coloured dots for different groups in the sample, move a third variable into the <u>S</u>et Markers by box. For example, if you used **Bank**, companies giving their accounts to the bank could be shown with a currency symbol and the default dot could be retained for the others.
- With a small data set, you can move a variable into the Label <u>C</u>ases by box to use the value labels to label the points on the plot. For example, if you used **ID**, the points would be labelled with the case numbers; alternatively, you could use the case numbers to label any outliers.

- Move one or more variables that contain groups into the **Panel by** boxes to generate a matrix of charts for each group. For example, if you used **Family**, you could generate one chart for the companies that are wholly family-owned and another for the remainder.

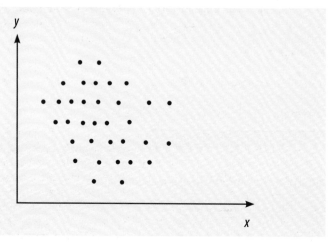

FIGURE 12.5 Scatterplot showing no correlation

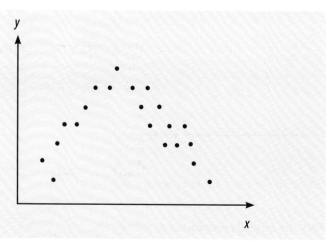

FIGURE 12.6 Scatterplot showing non-linear correlation

12.5.2   SPEARMAN'S CORRELATION

If you have non-parametric data for two variables measured on a ratio, interval or ordinal scale, you can use a correlation coefficient called *Spearman's rho* (or r_s) to measure the linear association between the variables. This overcomes the problem that the data are non-parametric by placing the data values in order of size and then examining differences in the rankings of one variable compared to the other.

We are going to use Spearman's *rho* to measure the correlation between **Check**,

Quality, Credibility, Creditscore and Turnover. The null hypothesis (H_0) we are testing is that there is no correlation between any two variables and we can instruct *SPSS* to do this in one procedure as follows:

- From the menu at the top, select <u>A</u>nalyze ⇒ <u>C</u>orrelate ⇒ <u>B</u>ivariate…
- Move Turnover, Check, Quality, Credibility and Creditscore into <u>V</u>ariables.
- Under Correlation Coefficients, deselect Pearson and then select Spearman.
- Under Test of Significance, click One-tailed and accept the default to Flag significant correlations.
- Under <u>O</u>ptions, you will see that the default for missing values is to Exclude cases <u>p</u>airwise, which we will accept, so you can now click Continue (see Figure 12.7).
- Then click OK to see the output (see Table 12.5).

The results in Table 12.5 are somewhat confusing because the statistics are shown for every possible pairing and this means some information is repeated. For convenience, we have added a shaded background to the duplicated information you can ignore. We will now examine the results in the cells without shading. A correlation coefficient of 1 (shown as 1.000) indicates perfect positive correlation. You can see this in the results where a variable is paired with itself. In all the other bivariate tests, you can see that the probability statistic (Sig. 1-tailed) tells us that the results are significant at the 1% level ($p = \leq 0.01$). Therefore, we can conclude that there is evidence to reject the null hypothesis of no correlation, but you need to remember that this does not mean we have established causality because there may be several explanatory variables.

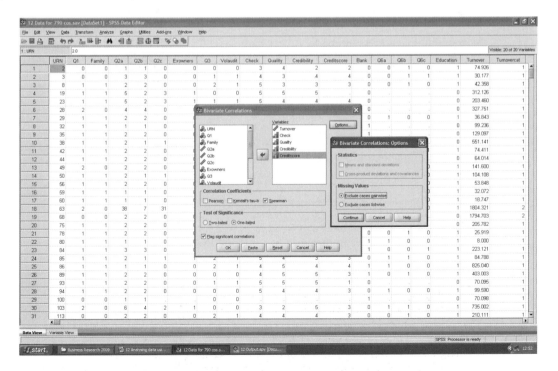

FIGURE 12.7 Running Spearman's correlation

TABLE 12.5 Spearman's rho for Turnover, Check, Quality, Credibility and Creditscore

Correlations

			Turnover	Check	Quality	Credibility	Creditscore
Spearman's rho	Turnover	Correlation Coefficient	1.000	.106**	.112**	.180**	.179**
		Sig. (1-tailed)	.	.003	.002	.000	.000
		N	790	697	687	688	681
	Check	Correlation Coefficient	.106**	1.000	.606**	.609**	.467**
		Sig. (1-tailed)	.003	.	.000	.000	.000
		N	697	697	681	682	674
	Quality	Correlation Coefficient	.112**	.606**	1.000	.651**	.529**
		Sig. (1-tailed)	.002	.000	.	.000	.000
		N	687	681	687	681	671
	Credibility	Correlation Coefficient	.180**	.609**	.651**	1.000	.532**
		Sig. (1-tailed)	.000	.000	.000	.	.000
		N	688	682	681	688	670
	Creditscore	Correlation Coefficient	.179**	.467**	.529**	.532**	1.000
		Sig. (1-tailed)	.000	.000	.000	.000	.
		N	681	674	671	670	681

**. Correlation is significant at the 0.01 level (1-tailed)

One of the reasons for conducting this analysis is to check for potential *multicollinearity*. This occurs when the correlation between independent (predictor) variables in a multiple regression model is very high (≥ 0.90), which can give rise to unreliable estimates of the standard errors (Kervin, 1992, p. 608). Multicollinearity can make it hard to identify the separate effects of the independent variables (Judge, Griffiths, Hill, Lutkepol and Lee, 1985, p. 896) and therefore it is essential to establish that there is no major 'overlap' in the predictive power of the variables. Kervin (1992) advises that if two predictor variables are highly related, the one with less theoretical importance to the research should be excluded from the analysis.

If you look at the correlation coefficients in our results, none of them are higher than 0.7, which means that the strength of the correlation is not likely to be a problem at the next stage of our analysis where we will be using multiple regression.

12.5.3 PEARSON'S CORRELATION

If you have parametric data for two continuous variables, you can use *Pearson's product-moment correlation coefficient* (or *r*) to measure the linear association between the variables. You will remember that a continuous variable is a ratio or interval variable measured on a scale where the data can take any value within a given range (for example turnover or assets but not number of employees). The null hypothesis (H_0) is that there is no correlation between the two variables and the procedure in *SPSS* is as follows:

- From the menu at the top, select <u>A</u>nalyze $\Rightarrow$ <u>C</u>orrelate $\Rightarrow$ <u>B</u>ivariate...
- Move the appropriate variables into the <u>V</u>ariables box.
- Under Correlation Coefficients, accept the default, which is Pearson.

- Under **Test of Significance**, select **One-tailed** if your hypotheses specify the direction of the correlation and accept the default to **Flag significant correlations**.
- Under **Options**, accept the default for missing values, which is to **Exclude cases pairwise**, so you can click **Continue** and **OK**.

12.6 LINEAR REGRESSION

We commented earlier that correlation offers additional information about an association between two variables because it measures the direction and strength of any linear relationship between them. *Linear regression* goes further by giving an indication of the ability of an independent variable to predict an outcome in a dependent variable where there is a linear relationship between them. The term *regression* was introduced in the late 19th century by Sir Francis Galton and refers to statistical models where 'the expected value of one variable Y is presumed to be dependent on one or more other variables $(x_1, x_2, ...)$' (Upton and Cook, 2006, p. 364). Linear regression is based on an algebraic equation that allows a straight line to be drawn on a graph from information about the slope (the gradient of the line in relation to the horizontal axis of the graph) and the intercept (the point at which the line crosses the vertical axis of a graph) (Field, 2000). The equation states the relationship between a dependent (outcome) variable Y and an independent (predictor) variable x (Upton and Cook, 2006, p. 243):

$$Y = \alpha + \beta x + \varepsilon$$

where

α (alpha) = the parameter corresponding to the intercept
β (beta) = the parameter corresponding to the slope
ε (epsilon) = a random error

In a linear regression model, an *error* (ε) is the difference between the observed (actual) values and the expected (theoretical) values in the model and therefore can be described as a *residual*. Drawing on Field (2000), the assumptions underpinning the linear equation can be summarized as follows:

- The dependent (outcome) variable is a continuous quantitative variable (measured on a ratio or interval scale), but an independent (predictor) variable can be continuous or a dummy variable (categorical variables can be used if they are first recoded as dummy variables).
- There is some variation in the data values of the independent variable(s) (in other words, none have a variance of 0).
- There is no perfect multicollinearity between the independent variables.
- None of the independent variables correlates with another variable that is not included in the analysis.
- The errors are uncorrelated and have a normal distribution with a mean of 0 and constant variance.
- The data values in the dependent variable are independent (in other words, they come from different cases).
- The relationship between the dependent variable and each independent variable is linear.

12.6.1 SIMPLE OR MULTIPLE LINEAR REGRESSION

In a *simple regression* model, the outcome in the dependent variable is predicted by a single independent variable, while in a *multiple regression* model it is predicted by more than one independent variable. If your data meet the assumptions of the linear equation we have just described, you can use the following procedure in *SPSS*:

- From the menu at the top, select <u>A</u>nalyze ⇒ <u>R</u>egression ⇒ Linear...
- Move your dependent (outcome) variable into **Dependent** and your independent (predictor) variable(s) into **Independent**.
- If you have theoretical reasons for choosing the predictor variables (in other words, your hypothesis is based on theory), accept the default method, **Enter**, which means the variables will be entered simultaneously as one block.
- Click on the **Options** button and under **Statistics and Plots** select any additional statistics you want to help you assess the fit of the model to the data and click **Continue**.
- Then click **OK** for the results.

> **KEY DEFINITIONS**
>
> Linear regression is a measure of the ability of an independent variable to predict an outcome in a dependent variable where there is a linear relationship between them.

It is useful at this point to summarize the results of the bivariate analysis for the data from the Collis Report (2003) in which we have tested the variables suggested by the theoretical framework that would influence the demand for the audit. This was represented by the dummy variable, Volaudit. The bivariate analysis found a significant difference between the two groups in Volaudit and Turnover, Check, Quality, Credibility and Creditscore and significant association between Volaudit when paired with Family, Exowners and Bank. The association with Education was not significant and we have accepted the null hypothesis represented by H9 in Box 12.1.

The next step is to run a multiple regression analysis with Volaudit as the dependent (outcome) variable and the remaining eight variables as the independent (predictor) variables. However, if the dependent variable is a dummy variable, the relationship with an independent variable is non-linear, which means the assumptions of the linear equation are not met. To overcome this problem, the dependent variable can be transformed into a logit, which allows a non-linear relationship to be expressed in a linear form (Field, 2000). If the dependent variable is a dummy variable and one or more of the independent variables are continuous quantitative variables, a *logistic regression* model can be used. If none of the independent variables is a continuous quantitative variable, a *logit* model is appropriate (Upton and Cook, 2006).

Since our dependent variable (Volaudit) is a dummy variable and one of our independent variables (Turnover) is a continuous quantitative variable, we should choose a logistic regression model.

12.6.2 LOGISTIC REGRESSION

As explained above, *logistic regression* is a form of multiple regression that is used where the dependent variable is a dummy variable and one or more of the independent variables are continuous quantitative variables. Any other independent variables can be ordinal or dummy variables. Nominal variables can be used if they are first recoded as dummy variables, as described in Chapter 11. There is also an opportunity to do this automatically under the logistic regression options in *SPSS*. The procedure for logistic regression is as follows:

- From the menu at the top, select Analyze ⇒ Regression ⇒ Binary logistic…
- Move Volaudit into Dependent.
- Move Turnover, Check, Quality, Credibility, Creditscore, Family, Exowners and Bank into Covariates (the term used by *SPSS* for the independent variable). As we have mentioned before, the order does not matter, but it seems logical to list them in the order of the hypotheses shown in Table 12.1.
- We have theoretical reasons for choosing the independent variables, so accept the default method, Enter, which means they will be entered simultaneously as one block.
- If you have any nominal predictor variables that are not dummy variables, you can click on the Categorical button and move them into the Categorical Covariates box. You would highlight each variable in turn and under Change Contrast select First or Last to indicate which of these categories represents the characteristic is present and click Change. For example, if you did this for Family, the variable would then be shown as Family(Indicator(first)), as illustrated in Figure 12.8. Click Cancel to leave that dialogue box.
- Now click on the Options button and under Statistics and Plots select Hosmer-Lemeshow goodness-of-fit to help you assess the fit of the model to the data and click Continue.
- Then click OK for the results (see Table 12.6).

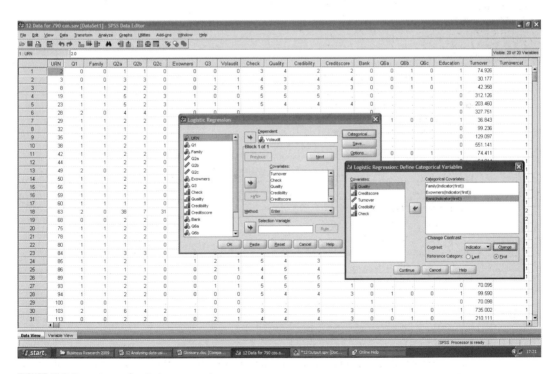

FIGURE 12.8 Running a logistic regression

TABLE 12.6 Logistic regression for Volaudit

Case Processing Summary

Unweighted Cases[a]		N	Percent
Selected Cases	Included in Analysis	588	74.4
	Missing Cases	202	25.6
	Total	790	100.0
	Unselected Cases	0	.0
	Total	790	100.0

a. If weight is in effect, see classification table for the total number of cases

Dependent Variable Encoding

Original Value	Internal Value
0 No	0
1 Yes	1

Block 0: Beginning Block

Classification Table[a,b]

			Predicted		
			Q3		
Observed			0 No	1 Yes	Percentage Correct
Step 0	Q3	0 No	306	0	100.0
		1 Yes	282	0	.0
		Overall Percentage			52.0

a. Constant is included in the model
b. The cut value is .500

Variables in the Equation

		B	S.E.	Wald	Df	Sig.	Exp(B)
Step 0	Constant	-.082	.083	.979	1	.322	.922

Variables not in the Equation

			Score	Df	Sig.
Step 0	Variables	Turnover	67.579	1	.000
		Check	58.876	1	.000
		Quality	82.641	1	.000
		Credibility	73.669	1	.000
		Creditscore	65.224	1	.000
		Family	25.419	1	.000
		Exowners	14.612	1	.000
		Bank	39.666	1	.000
		Overall Statistics	173.140	8	.000

Block 1: Method = Enter

Omnibus Tests of Model Coefficients

		Chi-square	df	Sig.
Step 1	Step	205.031	8	.000
	Block	205.031	8	.000
	Model	205.031	8	.000

Model Summary

Step	-2 Log likelihood	Cox & Snell R Square	Nagelkerke R Square
1	609.130[a]	.294	.393

a. Estimation terminated at iteration number 5 because parameter estimates changed by less than .001

Hosmer and Lemeshow Test

Step	Chi-square	Df	Sig.
1	8.306	8	.404

Contingency Table for Hosmer and Lemeshow Test

		Volaudit = 0 No		Volaudit = 1 Yes		Total
		Observed	Expected	Observed	Expected	
Step 1	1	55	55.356	4	3.644	59
	2	50	49.934	9	9.066	59
	3	43	45.181	16	13.819	59
	4	46	40.020	13	18.980	59
	5	31	33.309	28	25.691	59
	6	27	27.177	32	31.823	59
	7	21	23.189	38	35.811	59
	8	14	17.345	45	41.655	59
	9	16	10.681	43	48.319	59
	10	3	3.809	54	53.191	57

Classification Table[a]

		Observed	Predicted		
			Q3		
			0 No	1 Yes	Percentage Correct
Step 1	Q3	0 No	225	81	73.5
		1 Yes	71	211	74.8
		Overall Percentage			74.1

a. The cut value is .500

Variables in the Equation

		B	S.E.	Wald	df	Sig.	Exp(B)
Step 1	Turnover	.001	.000	21.810	1	.000	1.001
	Check	.246	.124	3.932	1	.047	1.278
	Quality	.403	.104	15.086	1	.000	1.496
	Credibility	.124	.128	.939	1	.333	1.132
	Creditscore	.256	.097	7.026	1	.008	1.292
	Family	-.794	.214	13.767	1	.000	.452
	Exowners	.644	.268	5.796	1	.016	1.905
	Bank	.448	.218	4.212	1	.040	1.565
	Constant	-4.116	.551	55.779	1	.000	.016

This is another situation where there is no need to be alarmed by the volume of output. The first table to check is the **Case Processing Summary** at the beginning, which shows that 588 cases in the sample of 790 were included in the analysis. In multi-variate analysis, a case is omitted if there is missing data for any one of the variables and this can be a problem with small samples. However, it is not a matter of concern here.

We can skip the tables in Block 0 where no variables have been entered in the model and concentrate on Block 1, starting with the **Model Summary**. In this table, the **Nagelkerke R Square** indicates that the model including our predictor variables explains .393 or 39% of the variance in the two groups in the outcome variable (whether the directors would have a voluntary audit). The hypothesis for the Hosmer and Lemeshow test is that the observed frequencies (actual counts) are not associated with the expected frequencies (theoretical counts). The probability statistic (**Sig.**) is .404), which is not significant. This means we can reject the null hypothesis and conclude that there is a good fit between the actual data and the model. The Hosmer and Lemeshow test is 'more robust than the traditional goodness-of-fit statistic used in logistic regression, particularly for models with continuous covariates and studies with small sample sizes … [This is achieved by] group-ing cases into deciles of risk and comparing the observed probability with the expected probability within each decile' (*SPSS*, version 16).

The final table shows the results for the **Variables in the Equation** which we entered in one block:

- The probability statistics (**Sig.**) show that the results for all the predictor variables are significant ($p \leq 0.05$), apart from **Credibility**.
- The factor coefficient (**B**) for **Family** indicates the expected negative relationship with **Volaudit** (demand for voluntary audit comes from companies that are <u>not</u> wholly family-owned).
- The higher values of the Wald statistic and the lower values of the probability statis-tics for **Turnover, Quality, Creditscore, Family** and **Exowners** indicate that these are the most influential factors.

We now have evidence to reject the null hypotheses for **Turnover, Check, Quality, Family, Exowners** and **Bank** (H1–H3 and H5–H8), but not for **Credibility** (H4). This concludes our interpretation of the statistics, but in a dissertation or thesis would lead on to a narrative discussion with links to previous studies, limitations and theoretical and practical implications arising from the results. You will find further guidance in Chapter 13.

12.7 TIME SERIES ANALYSIS

If you have collected *longitudinal data* for a random variable, you can use *time series analysis* to forecast future values. A *time series* is a sequence of measurements of a variable taken at regular intervals over time. The purpose of a time series analysis is to examine the *trend* and any *seasonal variation*. Both can be further analysed using linear regression (Moore *et al.*, 2009). However, before the analysis can commence, it is usually necessary to remove the effects of inflation or seasonal fluctuations. You can do this in *Excel* or *SPSS*. We will explain the methods in sufficient detail to allow you to calculate the statistics in *Excel*.

12.7.1 INDEXATION

An *index number* is a statistical measure which shows the percentage change in a variable, such as costs or prices, from some fixed point in the past. The base period of an index is the period against which all other periods are compared. A simple index shows each item in a series relative to some chosen base period value. For example, you may have collected data about a variable whose value changes over time, such as property prices, the cost of a certain component used in manufacturing, the average pay of employees in a particular industry, or consumers' annual expenditure on durable goods.

For a clearer indication of the pattern of movement of the value of such a variable over time, it is customary to choose an appropriate point in time as a base; for example a particular year for a variable that is observed annually. The base time-point should be chosen to reflect a time when values of the variable are relatively stable. The value of the variable at other points in time can then be expressed as a percentage of the value at the base time-point. The general formula is:

$$\text{Index number} = \frac{\text{Current value}}{\text{Value at base time-point}} \times 100$$

The resulting figure (known as the *relative*) is the simplest form of index number. The value of the index number at the base time-point is always 100. The following example shows how to construct a simple index.

Example

You have obtained the following historical data relating to the average price of a house in the UK over six years in the 1970s. You will use the first year in the series as the base year (thus, 1971 = 100) and then apply the following formula:

$$\text{Index} = \frac{\text{Current year price}}{\text{Base year price}} \times 100$$

This generates the index shown in the final column of Table 12.7.

TABLE 12.7	House price index 1971–6		
Year	Price	Formula	Index (1971 = 100)
1971	£5,632	$\frac{£5,632}{£5,632} \times 100$	100.0
1972	£7,374	$\frac{£7,374}{£5,632} \times 100$	130.9
1973	£9,942	$\frac{£9,942}{£5,632} \times 100$	176.5
1974	£11,073	$\frac{£11,073}{£5,632} \times 100$	196.6
1975	£12,144	$\frac{£12,144}{£5,632} \times 100$	215.6
1976	£13,006	$\frac{£13,006}{£5,632} \times 100$	230.9

Index figures are very useful for transforming multiple sets of data so that they can be compared in a table or a graph. The following example illustrates how to do this.

Example

You want to analyse the following production data from a factory in your study.

Year	Production units (m)	Number of employees	Units per employee shift
2003	184	602	1.40
2004	180	571	1.45
2005	188	551	1.56
2006	188	524	1.65
2007	185	498	1.72
2008	179	466	1.80

You start by constructing a simple index for each variable, as previously demonstrated, where 2003 = 100. The results are shown in Table 12.8. When these are plotted on a multiple line graph (see Figure 12.9), you can see that the overall production has remained stable despite a steady reduction in the number of employees. This is because the number of units produced per employee shift has increased.

TABLE 12.8	Production indices 2003–8		
Year	Production units index	Number of employees index	Units per employee shift index
2003	100.0	100.0	100.0
2004	97.8	94.9	103.6
2005	102.2	91.5	111.4
2006	102.2	87.0	117.9
2007	100.5	82.7	122.9
2008	97.3	77.4	128.6

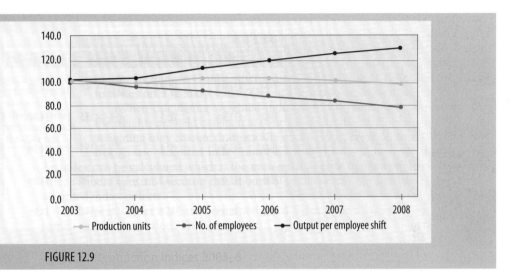

FIGURE 12.9

12.7.2   DEFLATING DATA

If you have collected financial data over a period when there has been inflation in the economy, this will obscure the underlying trend in the data. However, you can use indexation to *deflate* the data and thus remove the effect of inflation. The resulting data will then reflect the value of money as it was in the base year of the index you use. It is convenient to use an index such as the Retail Price Index (RPI) as it is known in the UK or the Consumer Price Index (CPI) in the USA and some other countries. A price index is the weighted mean of the prices paid by consumers for a set of standard household goods and services. The following example illustrates how to deflate your research data using such a price index.

Example

You have obtained the following historical data relating to a company's profit over a five-year period in the 1980s and the RPI for each year. You find out that the base year for the RPI at that time was 1974 (thus, 1974 = 100). You then apply the following formula:

$$\text{Deflated profit} = \frac{\text{Base year RPI}}{\text{Current year RPI}} \times \text{Profit}$$

This generates the deflated profit figures shown in the last column of Table 12.9.

- It can only be compared against the base year as the weights for each year change.
- It tends to underestimate price increases.
- It requires new weights each period which can be both costly and time-consuming to collect.

12.7.4　CALCULATING THE DE-SEASONALIZED TREND

We have already mentioned that the main use of time series analysis is to predict *trends*. A trend is a consistently upward or downward movement in the data values over the time period. A *seasonal variation* is where a pattern in the movements repeats itself at regular intervals. The two main statistical models for analysing time series data are the *additive model* and the *multiplicative model*. The formulae are as follows:

$$Y = T + S + C + I \text{ (additive model)}$$
$$Y = T \times S \times C \times I \text{ (multiplicative model)}$$

where

Y = the observation
T = trend
S = seasonal variation
C = cyclical component
I = irregular component

Although the additive model is simpler to analyse, the multiplicative model is generally considered to be more realistic. The adequacy of the multiplicative model may be tested by analysing the irregular component. If this is not random, the suitability of the model must be questioned. Any component may be absent from a particular time series (for example annual data cannot include the seasonal variation component).

Example
Perhaps you have collected quarterly data relating to the number of ice-creams sold (the sales volume) by a particular business over a five-year period.

- First calculate the 4 quarter moving total by adding the sales volume in groups of four.
- Then calculate the 8 quarter moving total by adding the 4 quarter moving totals in groups of two.
- Next, divide the 8 quarter moving totals by 8 to obtain the trend.
- Before you can eliminate any seasonal variations, you will need to calculate the de-trended series by dividing your original quarterly data (Y) by the trend (T).

These calculations are quickly computed on an *Excel* work sheet and Table 12.10 illustrates this stage of the analysis. If you use a calculator, discrepancies may occur due to rounding.

You are now ready to calculate the seasonal variation (S) which you do by averaging the de-trended series you calculated in Table 12.10. These data have been transferred to Table 12.11 to demonstrate how the seasonal index is calculated. The averages should add up to 4 for quarterly data and 12 for monthly data.

The mean for each quarter represents the seasonal variation (S), which we need in order to calculate the de-seasonalized data ($Y \div S$). Table 12.12 illustrates this and summarizes the key statistics we have calculated.

TABLE 12.10 De-trended series for ice-cream sales (m) 2004–8

Year	Quarter	Sales (m) (Y)	4 quarter moving total	8 quarter moving total	Trend (T)	De-trended series (Y ÷ T)
2004	Q1	106		–	–	–
			–			
	Q2	192		–	–	–
			726			
	Q3	278		1,463	183	1.52
			737			
	Q4	150		1,481	185	0.81
2005			744			
	Q1	117		1,488	186	0.63
			744			
	Q2	199		1,492	187	1.07
			748			
	Q3	278		1,518	190	1.47
			770			
	Q4	154		1,541	193	0.80
2006			771			
	Q1	139		1,575	197	0.71
			804			
	Q2	200		1,631	204	0.98
			827			
	Q3	311		1,652	207	1.51
			825			
	Q4	177		1,670	209	0.85
2007			845			
	Q1	137		1,692	212	0.65
			847			
	Q2	220		1,694	212	1.04
			847			
	Q3	313		1,701	213	1.47
			854			
	Q4	177		1,672	209	0.85
2008			818			
	Q1	144		1,591	199	0.72
			773			
	Q2	184		1,551	194	0.95
			778			
	Q3	268		1,412	177	1.52
			634			
	Q4	182		–	–	–

TABLE 12.11 Seasonal index for ice-cream sales (m) 2004–8

Year	De-trended series			
	Q1	Q2	Q3	Q4
2004	–	–	1.52	0.81
2005	0.63	1.07	1.47	0.8
2006	0.71	0.98	1.51	0.85
2007	0.65	1.04	1.47	0.85
2008	0.72	0.95	–	–
Total	2.71	4.04	5.97	3.31
Mean (seasonal variation)	0.68	1.01	1.48	0.83
Seasonal index	68	101	148	83

TABLE 12.12 De-seasonalized data for ice-cream sales (m) 2004–8

Year	Quarter	Sales (m) (Y)	Trend (T)	De-trended series (Y ÷ T)	Seasonal variation (S)	De-seasonalized data (Y ÷ S)
2004	Q1	106	–	–	0.68	156
	Q2	192	–	–	1.01	190
	Q3	278	183	1.52	1.48	187
	Q4	150	185	0.81	0.83	180
2005	Q1	117	186	0.63	0.68	173
	Q2	199	187	1.07	1.01	197
	Q3	278	190	1.47	1.48	187
	Q4	154	193	0.80	0.83	185
2006	Q1	139	197	0.71	0.68	205
	Q2	200	204	0.98	1.01	198
	Q3	311	207	1.51	1.48	210
	Q4	177	209	0.85	0.83	212
2007	Q1	137	212	0.65	0.68	202
	Q2	220	212	1.04	1.01	218
	Q3	313	213	1.47	1.48	211
	Q4	177	209	0.85	0.83	212
2008	Q1	144	199	0.72	0.68	213
	Q2	184	194	0.95	1.01	182
	Q3	268	177	1.52	1.48	181
	Q4	182	–	–	0.83	218

If you have tried this for yourself on a spreadsheet, you can now plot the trend for ice-cream sales over the period on a graph and use the seasonal index to forecast the data for the next year in the series.

12.7.5 EVALUATING THE CYCLICAL AND IRREGULAR VARIATION

In order to evaluate the cyclical variation (C) you need to obtain the de-trended, de-seasonalized series:

$$\frac{Y}{T \times S} = C \times I$$

Next, smooth out the irregular component (I) by means of a moving average performed on the $\frac{Y}{T \times S}$ series.

Since the aim is to smooth and not to remove the cycle, a three-point moving average could be used. The irregular component (I) is obtained from:

$$\frac{Y}{T \times S \times C}$$

This should be random in nature; otherwise the adequacy of the proposed model must be questioned. Therefore, evaluation of the irregular component yields a measure of method suitability. For multiplicative models, the irregular component should be random about unity ($\pm$ 1). If the irregular component is evaluated and shown to be random, it can be removed from the series, producing an error-free series:

$$\frac{Y}{I} = T \times S \times C$$

In order to be reasonably certain that components exist in a time series, there should be sufficient data to establish the reality of these components or complementary information to suggest their presence. In a short span of data, random phenomena can appear to be systematic and, conversely, systematic effects can be masked by random variation.

12.8 CONCLUSIONS

Apart from the important matter of whether your data meet the four basic assumptions that determine whether you can use parametric tests, you need to consider time constraints and your skills. The data used to illustrate the inferential statistics in this chapter relate to a study that was designed to address a set of hypotheses underpinned by theory. Although the research data was non-parametric, we have also explained the equivalent parametric models.

In the previous sections we have showed how comparison of longitudinal data can be aided through indexation and time series analysis can be used to examine the trend and any seasonal variation. If the latter is present, the de-seasonalized trend can be

Learning objectives

When you have studied this chapter, you should be able to:

- plan a strategy for writing up your research

- structure the chapters and content of your dissertation or thesis

- decide how to present qualitative and quantitative data

- understand the general standards for a dissertation or thesis

- develop a strategy for getting published.

13.1 INTRODUCTION

By the time you get to the final writing-up stage in your research, you should have collected and analysed a significant amount of literature and research data. During the course of your study, you should have been writing draft material for the chapters in your dissertation or thesis, discussing them with your supervisor(s) and making amendments. Therefore, you should now be ready to write the first complete draft of your research report. This chapter offers guidance on this important final stage in a research project.

At the undergraduate and taught Master's level you are likely to find that your time is fully taken up with your studies and doing your research, whereas MPhil students and doctoral students may have written and presented papers at conferences or had articles published. Once you have successfully completed your dissertation or thesis, all students should consider writing conference papers and articles. This will improve your academic reputation and enhance your employability. This chapter also gives guidance on getting published.

13.2 PLANNING THE RESEARCH REPORT

Writing up often presents the greatest challenge to research students, but it is made somewhat easier if you have been writing notes and rough drafts throughout the period of your research. If you are a doctoral student and you have put off writing until your final year, you are likely to encounter major difficulties or even failure (Torrance, Thomas and Robinson, 1992). In our experience, this applies to all researchers. You need to start developing the sections in your proposal into the sections of your final research report as you proceed with your research.

13.2.1 PLANNING STRATEGIES

There are a number of strategies you can adopt when it comes to writing up your final research report. In a survey of 110 social science research students at British universities, Torrance *et al.* (1992) found that 104 reported using the specified planning and writing strategies when producing their last substantial piece of academic text. These are shown in Table 13.1.

TABLE 13.1 Planning and writing strategies adopted by students

Strategy	% reporting
Brainstorming or writing down a checklist of ideas which might be included in the final document but which does not specify the order in which they might be presented	80
Taking verbatim notes from the relevant literature	78
Putting notes into some kind of order	63
Constructing a 'mind map' which gives a spatial representation of the links between particular ideas	54
Constructing a plan that details not only the content of the finished piece, but also the order in which it will be presented	84
Writing out full drafts in continuous prose but not necessarily in polished English	94
Revising full drafts	94

Source: Torrance, Thomas and Robinson (1992, p. 159).

We can use advice from the general literature to expand these strategies into activities you can pursue. Most authors emphasize the importance of getting your thoughts committed to paper in one way or another. Phillips and Pugh (1994) advocate using a brainstorming approach and putting down all the main points that come to mind. By generating all the main points in a random order, some students claim it frees the mind. Moreover, a point from the literature or methodology can generate points concerned with the research results and analysis.

Creswell (1994) suggests that visual maps can be helpful. He recommends that once you have constructed a mind map in the most appropriate structure, you can then proceed to construct the points into grammatical paragraphs made up of well-balanced sentences. We prefer to do this a chapter at a time, organizing the points into each of the sections in the chapter, and then concentrating on writing the paragraphs.

However, it is important to remember that you do not have to start the process of writing the chapters in your research report in any particular order. Some researchers prefer to write in the same order as the research report is structured. However, it is not advisable to finalize your introductory chapter, or even your title, until the end. Therefore, an appropriate chapter to work on at an early stage is your literature review, as in many cases it forms part of the research proposal. This would lead you on to your methodology chapter, which can be finalized once you have enough information to describe the more detailed aspects of the methods of data collection and analysis you have used. Doctoral students may have written conference papers or articles on parts of their research, which can be used to form the basis of different chapters in the final research report. It does not matter what strategy you adopt; the important thing is to start developing your draft chapters at an early stage in your research and getting timely feedback from your supervisor.

> **KEY DEFINITIONS**
>
> A mind map is an informal diagram of a person's idea of key elements of a subject and the links between the elements.

Some students put off writing up because they are still updating their literature or collecting more data because there has been a change. You must be strong willed and decide to impose a definite cut-off point on your research. Your dissertation or thesis will be an account of your research up to the chosen date and you need not worry about events after that time. Your supervisor(s) and examiners appreciate that you are not writing a newspaper which must contain the latest news!

13.2.2   SETTING A TIMETABLE

While determining the structure of your thesis, it is also useful to draw up a timetable showing the critical dates when different sections will be completed. You will have a deadline for submission of your dissertation or thesis, and it is easy to think of this as coinciding with when you have finished writing up. However, finishing writing is not the final stage; you will also need time for editing, proofreading and binding the finished report.

It is difficult to estimate exactly how long the writing up and final tasks will take, as there are so many factors to be considered, but, even when you are an experienced researcher, it can take a good deal longer than you think. We recommend that you build in additional time for contingency factors, such as illness and domestic interruptions (both in your life and those of your supervisors), computer problems, lost documents and so on. In Table 13.2 we give an indicative breakdown of the main tasks and approximately how long they take for a full-time PhD candidate. This schedule assumes that some preliminary work has been done. By this we mean that the literature review and methodology chapters are in draft form, the analysis has been completed, some of the figures and/or tables have been prepared and a list of references has been kept. Even so, you can see that six months is given to the final writing-up stage for such a doctoral thesis of about 80,000 words.

TABLE 13.2 Indicative time for writing a PhD thesis

Chapter or task	Weeks
Introduction	2
Literature review	4
Methodology	2
Findings and discussion	8
Conclusions	2
Tables, figures, references, appendices and so on	1
Consultation with supervisor/others and revisions	4
Editing, proofreading and binding	3
Total	26

Editing is a process which involves re-reading and identifying errors and omissions in the content and structure of your work, and consequently amending it. There are no short cuts, but if your supervisor, colleagues and family will read and comment on your early drafts it will make your job easier. Before you start editing try to have a break of a week or two, so that you can return to it with a fresh eye and, possibly, a more open perspective. When you have finished editing your research report, you are ready to begin reading it for errors in spelling, grammar, chapter and section numbering, table and figure numbering, page numbering and so on.

13.2.3   WRITING STYLE

Your written communication skills are clearly very important at this stage and it is essential that the meaning is clear, even if the content is technically or conceptually complex. Some students adopt a long-winded and complicated style of writing in the mistaken belief that it is more academic. Try to resist this temptation. Your dissertation or thesis is a unique piece of research (even if it is a replication study) and you want your supervisors and examiners to understand every aspect of it, so that you have the greatest chance of gaining high marks. Think about attracting and keeping the examiner's attention in the way you present your report. By using certain techniques, such as dividing the text up into digestible chunks, interspersing it with graphical and other illustrations, using headings, subheadings, different fonts and typefaces, providing wide margins and a clear layout, 'a reader can be virtually "forced" to read' (Martin, 1989, p. 49). Chall (1958) identifies three key, interrelated elements of the readability of text which we advise you to take into account:

*   interest (the ability to hold the reader's attention)
*   legibility (the impact of factors such as typography and layout on the reader)
*   ease of understanding (reading comprehension).

In Box 13.1 we offer some general guidance on the presentation of text. We recommend you use up-to-date reference books, such as an authoritative dictionary, thesaurus and grammar guide. Use the *spelling* and *grammar checker* on your software, but be aware that it cannot take account of the sense in which the words are used or whether they represent an interesting or dull form of expression. However, the dictionary used by the spelling checker can be set to take account of cultural differences between English-speaking nations which give rise to differences in spelling. Before using an *abbreviation*, you should show the term in full the first time you use it, with the abbreviation in brackets next to it; subsequently you can simply use the abbreviation.

BOX 13.1　Guide to the presentation of text

Writing style

- Text should be written as lucidly and clearly as possible.
- The language and style should be appropriate for your paradigm and your intended audience.
- Sentences should be kept short; preferably no longer than 20 words.
- A new paragraph should be started for each new idea.

Grammar and semantics

- The grammar, punctuation and spelling (especially of names) should be checked. Computerized spelling and grammar checkers should be used judiciously.
- Precise words, rather than general or abstract words, should be used.
- The meaning of words and phrases should be checked for correct usage.
- Jargon should be avoided and a glossary provided for any technical terms.
- The document should be carefully proofread for typographical mistakes, repetition, clichés, colloquialism, errors and omissions.

Although spelling, grammar and punctuation play an important role, writing is more than a matter of correct usage; it involves a careful choice of words to create a lucid, flowing style, which both attracts and maintains the interest of the reader. Therefore, it is important not to become pedantic over rules. This should allow a personal style of writing to develop. If you already have a good writing style, the above principles will be relatively easy to apply. Unfortunately, most of us are not so blessed, but we can, at least, aim to be competent.

One way to improve your style is to look at how the academic authors you admire express themselves. In addition you should get others to comment on your work. Your supervisor can do this, but is more likely to be concerned with the way that you conducted the research and the results. Therefore, you may find it more useful if you can agree to exchange your written work with fellow students for comment. This kind of mutual support can be very encouraging and may also help you keep ahead of the various deadlines you set yourself.

13.2.4　DESIGNING THE REPORT

In this section we consider the overall report design. When planning your research report, it is useful to bear in mind the concept of synergy: your dissertation or thesis should be greater than the sum of its parts. To achieve this, you must remember that the chapters which comprise your report do not exist in isolation from one another; they are interrelated and need to be integrated to form a cohesive whole. In Box 13.2 we offer a logical and structured approach to report design.

BOX 13.2   Guide to report design

Structure

- The information should be presented in a logical sequence. Each section should have a logical progression and support a central message. Each item should lead to the next.

- A standard hierarchy of headings and subheadings should be adopted to structure the report.

- The chapters, main sections and subsections should be numbered sequentially. Thus Section 3.5.5 refers to the fifth subsection in section 5 of Chapter 3. Three is normally considered to be the maximum number of subdivisions. Therefore it is usual to divide the report into chapters which contain a number of main sections and, in turn, these are divided into subsections. As a general rule, paragraphs should not be numbered.

- Titles and headings used for tables, graphs and other illustrations should also be standardized and numbered sequentially. The first digit should refer to the chapter number and the second digit to the table/chart number. Thus, Table 3.5 refers to the fifth table in Chapter 3.

Format

- There should be consistency of style in terms of margins, page numbers, paragraphs, bulleted lists, numbered lists, fonts used in hierarchical headings and so on.

- A reasonable sized font, say 10 or 12 point, should be used to ensure legibility.

- The layout should aid communication.

- Colour or space should be used to attract the reader's attention to key information.

- Use dark colours for text and figures since light colours are less legible.

- Do not distract the reader by using more than four or five colours in any diagrams or charts you generate. Avoid the combination of red and green for adjacent data, which is a problem for readers who are colour-deficient.

Presentational forms

- Tables, graphs and other illustrations should relate to the text so that the information is supported by the different representations.

- To maintain the interest of the reader, a variety of presentations should be used, as dictated by the type of data (for example interval or continuous) and the purpose (for example for comparison).

- It is usual to divide the research report into numbered chapters which contain several numbered main sections, which in turn can be divided into subsections if required. For example section 3.5.2 refers to the second subsection in section 5 of Chapter 3. Three is normally considered to be the maximum number of divisions (chapter, main section and subsection).

- It is not usual to number the paragraphs in a dissertation or thesis. However, this may be required if you are designing a report for a non-academic sponsor, such as a government department or professional body. In such cases, we advise that you seek guidance on your sponsor's preferred style.

- Titles and headings used for tables, graphs and other illustrations should also be standardized and numbered sequentially. The first digit should refer to the chapter number and the second digit to the table/figure number. Thus, Table 3.5 refers to the fifth table in Chapter 3. It is helpful to the reader if the title is shown above or below the table or figure and the source of the data is shown below.

- The pages should be numbered sequentially. It is usual to show the page number in the footer.

Style and layout

- Throughout the document there should be consistency of style in terms of page size, layout, headings, fonts, colour, justification and so on.

- A reasonable sized font, say 10 or 12 point, should be used to ensure legibility.

- The design and layout should be attractive; colour and/or white space should be used to complement the layout.

- If available, colour should be used to attract the reader's attention to key information.

- Different colours may be useful for highlighting key variables throughout a report.
- Avoid the combination of red and green for adjacent data, which we have already mentioned is a problem for people who are colour-deficient.
- Do not distract the reader by using more than four or five colours (except for illustrations and photographs).
- Use dark colours for text and figures, since light colours are less legible.

Presentational forms

- Tables, graphs and other illustrations should relate to the text so that the information is supported by the different representations.
- To maintain the interest of the reader, a variety of presentations should be used, as appropriate to level of measurement and purpose (for example comparison).

Even at the first draft stage, it is valuable to put the material in the format required by your institution. This will save you considerable time later on when you are trying to refine and improve the content of the document. You will need to ascertain from your university or college what the requirements are with regard to style, length and structure of your research report. You will be expected to submit your work in double spacing (or 1.5 lines), printed on only one side of the page. There are also likely to be requirements to meet regarding page numbering, font size and margin widths. For example, a left-hand margin of at least 1.25 inches leaves room for the document to be bound; a right-hand margin of 1 inch allows examiners to write comments. You must ensure that your document complies with your institution's regulations.

You will be restricted in the maximum length of your research report, and this is likely to be measured by the number of words it contains. Table 13.3 gives a general indication of the typical word count for a dissertation or thesis. The references and appendices are not usually included in the word count. You should bear in mind that supervisors and examiners are aware of students' ploys in placing information in an appendix rather than write in a more succinct style to keep within the maximum length. At any level, a research report accompanied by a voluminous set of appendices is likely to give a poor impression.

TABLE 13.3   Typical length of a dissertation or thesis

Level	Research report	Word count
Undergraduate	Dissertation	10,000–15,000
Taught Master's	Dissertation	20,000
Master's by research	Thesis	40,000
Taught doctorate	Thesis	50,000
Doctorate by research	Thesis	80,000

13.3   STRUCTURE AND CONTENT

13.3.1   STRUCTURE

The overall structure of your dissertation or thesis should be logical and clear to the reader, and you should bear this in mind when deciding on the wording of your headings for each section, table or figure. Table 13.4 shows a generic structure, with an indication of the approximate size of the chapters in relation to the whole report. It is important to note that this structure is only a guide; you will need to modify it to reflect your own research project after discussions with your supervisor. In practice, the size of each chapter will vary according to the nature of the research problem, the methodology adopted and the use of tables, charts and diagrams. In an undergraduate or taught Master's dissertation, there is often less scope for primary research and therefore the literature review will form a more substantial part of the report. On the other hand at the doctoral level, particularly where the research is designed under an interpretive paradigm, the methodology chapter plays a very significant role.

TABLE 13.4 Indicative structure of a research report

	% of report
1. Introduction	10
– The research problem or issue and the purpose of the study	
– Background to the study and why it is important or of interest	
– Structure of the remainder of the report	
2. Review of the literature	30
– Evaluation of the existing body of knowledge on the topic	
– Theoretical framework (if applicable)	
– Where your research fits in and the research question(s) and propositions or hypotheses (if applicable)	
3. Methodology	20
– Identification of paradigm (doctoral students will need to discuss)	
– Justification for choice of methodology and methods	
– Limitations of the research design	
4. Findings/results *(more than one chapter if appropriate)*	30
– Presentation and discussion of the analysis of your research data/ statistical tests and their results	
5. Conclusions	10
– Summary of what you found out in relation to each research question you investigated	
– Your contribution to knowledge	
– Limitations of your research and suggestions for future research	
– Implications of your findings (for practice, policy and so on)	
	<u>100</u>
References *(do not number this section)*	
– A detailed, alphabetical (numerical, if appropriate) list of all the sources cited in the text	
Appendices *(if required)*	
– Detailed data referred to in the text, but not shown elsewhere	

It is useful if the chapter titles you use reflect the contents, but do not be over-imaginative; the examiner will have certain expectations about the content and the order in which it will appear. Therefore, it is best not to depart too far from a traditional structure, unless you have good reasons. There are no hard and fast rules about how individual chapters should be structured, but some form of numbering is common. You will have noted that in this chapter we have numbered the main sections 13.1, 13.2, 13.3 and so on. Where we have decided that there is a need for subsections they are numbered 13.2.1, 13.2.2, 13.2.3 and so on. Think carefully about the wording of the headings and subheadings you use, as these give important signals to the reader about content and sequence of different aspects of your discourse in your table of contents. You should consider carefully before dividing your subsections any further, as this may lead to a fragmented appearance.

The more logical you can make your structure, the easier it will be for you to write the report and for the examiner to read it. The ordering of the sections in the chapters is very much a matter of choice, influenced by the nature of the research and the arguments you are trying to make. Howard and Sharp (1994) suggest a number of different ways that the sections can be ordered:

- chronologically, where you describe events in the order in which they occurred. This is clearly most appropriate when you are trying to give a historical perspective or describe developments
- categorically, where you group the issues into various categories or groups, a good example of which is a geographical classification, although in business research you may choose to group matters by activity (for example production, administration, sales and so on)
- sequentially, where you describe the events in the sequence in which they occur. This is useful when explaining or analysing the events in a process, and is similar to chronological ordering but not so closely time related
- by perceived importance, where you present the information starting with the least important and move to the most important, or vice versa. The direction in which you move will depend on the nature of the argument you are making.

13.3.2 PRELIMINARY PAGES

The preliminary pages precede the first chapter. The page numbers for these pages are normally small Roman numerals (i, ii, iii and so on). This allows the pages of the chapters to be numbered in Arabic numerals (1, 2, 3 and so on). The preliminary pages are typically as follows, but you should check the regulations at your institution:

- *Title page* (no page number) – Your research project will have been registered with a particular title, but you may wish to amend it to ensure that it clearly indicates the topic and focus of your study. Keep the title as short as possible and eliminate unnecessary words. Choose your words carefully and do not include general phrases such as 'A study of …' or 'An investigation into …' as they are superfluous. Sometimes a colon is used in the title, as in 'Demand for voluntary audit: The UK and Denmark compared'.
- *Copyright notice* (no page number) – Only include if appropriate.
- *Abstract* (start numbering the pages here) – If you are required to include an abstract, remember that it is not an introduction, but a brief summary of the purpose of the research, the methodology and the key findings.
- *Declaration* – Use the wording required by your institution, such as: 'I declare that

this dissertation is all my own work and the sources of information and material I have used (including the internet) have been fully identified and properly acknowledged as required.'

- *Table of contents* – If you designate styles to your hierarchy of headings in your software, you can automatically generate this list of the chapters and sections within them, together with their associated page numbers.
- *List of tables* and *list of figures* – As appropriate.
- *List of abbreviations* – If required, you can list the acronyms in alphabetical order with the full term providing the explanation.
- The *acknowledgements* – If appropriate, these consist of one or two sentences thanking those who have helped you with your research; for example participants (while being careful to write in general terms to preserve their anonymity), your supervisor(s), colleagues and family.

Having described the preliminary pages, we are now ready to look at the chapters, which form the main body of the research report. You will need to divide each chapter into several numbered sections. All your chapters should have an introductory section and a concluding section, which allows you to provide links between the chapters, but it will not always be appropriate to head them 'Introduction' and 'Conclusions'. We will comment on this in the next section.

13.3.3   INTRODUCTORY CHAPTER

It may surprise you to know that once your supervisor(s) and examiner(s) have glanced at your contents page, the first two chapters they are likely to read are the first and the last. This is because your introduction and your conclusions chapters give overviews rather than the detailed information contained in the chapters sandwiched between them. Therefore, it is very important that you do not neglect these smaller chapters. Nevertheless, we suggest you do not finalize your introductory chapter until after you have completed your conclusions chapter to ensure they are complementary.

The introductory chapter will probably have four or five sections. As in all chapters, your first section will be an introduction to the chapter. This may cause you a problem if you've decided to call your first chapter '1. Introduction to the study'. A simple way round this is to call the chapter '1. Background to the study' or '1. Overview of … [name of the research topic]', which will allow you to call your first section in the chapter '1.1 Introduction'.

The first few sentences of the introduction are crucial, as these will attract the reader's attention and set the tone for the entire document. Winkler and McCuen-Metherell (2007) offer three strategies for beginning a research paper which we believe can be used as a guide to the opening of the introduction in any research report:

- Use an appropriate quotation that is directly relevant to the research problem or issue and leads you on to develop an argument to support or refute the quotation.
- Pose a question that draws the reader into your discussion. This allows you to word the question to fit the arguments you wish to present.
- Use a carefully chosen illustration that is directly relevant to the research problem or issue that can capture the reader's interest immediately.

In the early sections you must explain the research problem or issue and the purpose of the study. You can then go on to provide the background to the study, which is a broad view of the topic that gradually narrows down to explain why your study is important or of interest. There is no need to go into great detail, as subsequent chapters will do this. Do not make the mistake of mentioning any of your findings or conclusions in this chapter. Remember that you will need to review and amend any material you wrote for your proposal. The final part of your introduction will give a brief guide to the subsequent chapters of your research report. Therefore, this chapter does not need conclusions.

13.3.4 LITERATURE REVIEW CHAPTER(S)

In Chapter 6 we defined a literature search as a critical evaluation of the existing body of knowledge on a topic, which guides the research and demonstrates that relevant literature has been located and analysed. Thus, the main task is to evaluate the existing body of knowledge on the research problem or issue you have studied. If you are a positivist, you will draw out your theoretical framework and hypotheses. Your literature review will reflect your method of analysis and will be structured thematically, rather than a descriptive list of publications you have read. The concluding sections will draw attention to the gaps and deficiencies in our knowledge, and identify which of these your study addresses. This will lead to a statement of the main research question(s).

By now you should be familiar with the methodologies and findings of the seminal studies in your topic area, and the names of the authors. These citations and others from the leading journals for your topic will play a key role in your literature review. If you have published an exploratory study or a paper on a related topic, or presented it at a conference, you should also cite that. This will demonstrate to your supervisors and examiners that your work has been exposed to a certain level of peer review.

On the subject of citations, we have a few tips to offer. If you are referring to an author whose work you think is important or whose argument you consider supports yours, you should start the sentence with his or her name. For example, 'Smith (1994) found evidence of a link with motivation that may explain …' On the other hand, if you want to place more emphasis on the idea than the author, cite the name within the sentence. For example, 'Although a link with motivation has been suggested as an explanation (Smith, 1994) …'. Remember that it is your research and you are setting out to be the authority in this specialized area, so do not be afraid to criticize their work, regardless of their status. However, it is essential that you justify your criticisms. If your supervisors or examiners have published on your topic, ensure that you fully understand their work and take note of any limitations they point out themselves in their papers.

Cooper (1988, p. 107) provides a useful definition which covers all styles of literature review. 'First, a literature review uses as its database reports or primary or original scholarship, and does not report new primary scholarship itself. The primary reports used in the literature may be verbal, but in the vast majority of cases reports are written documents. The types of scholarship may be empirical, theoretical, critical/analytic, or methodological in nature. Second, a literature review seeks to describe, summarize, evaluate, clarify and/or integrate the content of primary reports.' While perusing the literature, you will read other authors' literature reviews. These should offer you an additional guide to what is required. The main point to remember is that your literature review should show a competent exploration of the background to the work and a comprehensive review of the relevant literature, including the most recent publications. It is a written discussion of the literature and forms a significant part of your dissertation or thesis.

If you are concerned that your literature review is too long, you may need to go through it summarizing where you have become too verbose. If you feel inclined to delete some of the less important items, pick out references to newspapers, commercial magazines and unpublished academic work, rather than articles in refereed academic journals. Only delete references to articles in the latter if they are not relevant. There is much more detailed guidance in Chapter 6, but we will conclude this section by looking at some of the common faults made by students when reviewing the literature.

BOX 13.3   Common faults when reviewing the literature

- Making assertions without stating where the evidence is
  - You must support all assertions with references to the literature, even if your claims are accepted wisdom, otherwise you will be guilty of plagiarism
- Failing to state the country, time, objectives, respondents, methodology of previous studies
- Listing the literature rather than providing a synthesis and a critical evaluation
- Poor structure, writing style, spelling and grammar
  - Use section headings within the chapter to signal themes and link ideas
  - Adopt a style that reflects your rhetorical assumptions
  - Avoid colloquial phrases in your own writing
  - Use the spelling and grammar checker
- Literature review fails to show relevance to the study
  - Identify the theoretical framework or context for your study
  - Conclude with the research question(s) addressed by your study

---

13.3.5   METHODOLOGY CHAPTER

The methodology chapter is a critical part of the report in both a positivist and an interpretive study, but will vary according to which paradigm you have adopted. From a general point of view, both approaches require a section which 'explains how the problem was investigated and why particular methods and techniques were used' (Bell, 1993, p. 155). Both will start with an introductory paragraph which briefly describes the main features of the methodology and the organization of the chapter. In a positivist study, this will be followed by a statement of the procedures adopted, description of the sampling methods, formulation of hypotheses and the statistical techniques of analysis employed. In an interpretive study, the structure is more flexible and will be closely related to the methodology employed.

In a positivist study, the methodology section 'describes the exact steps that will be undertaken to address your hypotheses and/or research questions' (Rudestam and Newton, 1992, p. 60). If you are using well-known procedures and tests, there is no need to describe them in detail; you need only refer to them. You will also need to describe any little known techniques, or those you have devised or modified, in detail. In a positivist study, the methodology chapter can usually be divided into the main sections as shown in Box 13.4.

BOX 13.4   Main sections in the methodology chapter of a positivist study

- Description of the sampling method, the sampling frame, size of the population, number of responses, and the response rate compared with previous studies.
- Explanation of the appropriateness of the methodology in the context of your paradigm.
- Description of the methods used to collect data for the literature review and the research data. Discussion of their strengths and weaknesses in the context of alternatives to justify your choice. If the research data were collected over a long period of time, include a timetable showing when specific activities took place and any critical events.
- Description of the methods used to analyse the literature and the research data. Discussion of their strengths and weaknesses in the context of alternatives to justify your choice.
- Description of the variables in the analysis, level of measurement, unit of measurement and codes used.
- Discussion of the limitations in the research design, making reference to generalizability, reliability and validity.

In an interpretive study, the methodology chapter should stress the nature and rationale for the chosen methodology, before leading on to discuss the method(s) of data collection and analysis. You may consider that the philosophy and assumptions underpinning the methodology, and their appropriateness to the research problem, are so important that you devote a separate chapter to their discussion. Box 13.5 gives guidance on writing the methodology chapter(s) in an interpretive study.

BOX 13.5   Main sections in the methodology chapter of an interpretive study

- Description of the sampling method, focusing on how cases were located and selected.
- Explanation of the appropriateness of the methodology in the context of your paradigm. As there are many variations within an interpretive approach, quote a number of definitions of your methodology, explain the main features and refer to studies that have used it.
- Description of the methods used to collect data for the literature review and the research data. Discussion of their strengths and weaknesses in the context of alternatives to justify your choice. If the research data were collected over a long period of time, include a timetable showing when specific activities took place and any critical events.
- Description of the methods used to analyse the literature and the research data. Keep this general and do not start discussing your findings.
- Discussion of the limitations in the research design, making reference to generalizability, reliability and validity.

The philosophical assumptions of your paradigm must be woven into the way you write. Merriam (1988) identifies the following assumptions which provide a platform for interpretivists:

- You are concerned primarily with process, rather than outcomes or products.
- You are interested not in frequency, but in meaning; that is, how people make sense of their experiences and the world around them.

- You are the primary research instrument. It is by and through you that data are collected, analysed and interpreted.
- Your research is placed in a natural, rather than an artificial, setting. It is conducted in the field by you visiting the places where the activity takes place so that you can observe and record it.
- The research is descriptive and seeks to capture process, meaning and understanding.
- The process of research is mainly inductive because you are attempting to construct abstractions, concepts, hypotheses and theories from abstractions.

13.3.6   FINDINGS/RESULTS CHAPTER(S)

While positivists usually refer to their *results* because their analysis is based on statistical tests, interpretivists are more likely to use the term *findings*. More than one chapter may be necessary to present and discuss your analysis.

You should start by restating the purpose of the research and the research questions from your first chapter, since these should direct your analysis and discussions. You can then move on to a description of your sample or cases (positivists will provide descriptive statistics). This sets the scene for you to present the analysis of your research data, which you should structure in a logical order that allows the reader to relate your evidence to the research questions. Positivists will need to discuss their results in the context of their hypotheses and make reference to existing theory; interpretivists are more likely to be drawing out theory that emerges from the analysis.

Positivists will find it relatively easy to present the results of their analysis in tables and figures, whereas interpretivists will need to spend some time reflecting on diagrammatic forms to support their narrative findings. We will be looking at this more closely later on in this chapter.

13.3.7   CONCLUSIONS CHAPTER

It is very important that this final chapter in your dissertation or thesis complements your first chapter, because many examiners turn immediately to it after reading the introductory chapter. While your introductory chapter should start broadly and then become focused, your conclusions chapter should do the opposite.

Start by restating the purpose of the research and then summarize what you found out in relation to each research question. Do not introduce new information. This is a good time to check that you have used the same terms when describing the purpose of your research and your research questions throughout your dissertation or thesis.

You should then widen your discussion by explaining your contribution to knowledge, without being too ambitious in your claims. This will include making reference to the gaps and deficiencies in the literature that your study has addressed. Look at the aims of your research in the introductory chapter and ensure that your conclusions show that they have been achieved or explain why they have not. Of course, you must also summarize the limitations of your research, which you discussed in your methodology chapter, and this will lead you to make suggestions for future research. Do not be reluctant to be self-critical and demonstrate what you have learned from your experience.

To end your dissertation or thesis on a strong, positive note, you might conclude by discussing the implication of your results/findings for practice, policy and so on. Remember that the theme of the whole of this chapter is the conclusions that can be drawn from your study, so you will not head your final section of this chapter 'conclusions'. In the same way that you spent quite a bit of time choosing the opening of the introductory chapter, you should spend a long time on the last sentence. Aim for a convincing ending.

If your dissertation or thesis is going to be examined orally at a *viva voce*, this chapter often receives the greatest attention. Therefore, be careful not to make any sweeping statements or exaggerated claims. If you have found out something which is interesting and worthwhile, and we hope you have, discuss it fully and with enthusiasm. However, remember to acknowledge the contribution made by previous studies, which underpins your work.

13.3.8 APPENDICES

The place for information that is too detailed or not sufficiently relevant to be included in the main part of your dissertation or thesis is an *appendix*. Typically, the appendices (one for each group of items) will contain material such as background information on the industry or cases, regulations and published statistics.

Each appendix should be numbered sequentially and given a title. The numbering should relate to the order in which each appendix is first mentioned in your dissertation or thesis. If you have not mentioned an appendix in your report, perhaps the information in the appendix is superfluous and can be excluded. Most examiners are not impressed by large quantities of data in appendices and you should not make the appendices a dustbin for all those bits and pieces you could not fit into the main part of the document or a way of reducing your word count!

13.4 PRESENTING QUALITATIVE AND QUANTITATIVE DATA

The use of analytical software for analysing quantitative data and qualitative data greatly assists the generation of tables and figures, and the drawing facilities on *Word* and other word processing programs help you develop your own diagrams using ready-made shapes, arrows, lines, flow chart symbols and callout balloons. We will start by looking at the presentation of qualitative data.

13.4.1 QUALITATIVE DATA

Presenting qualitative data you have collected can pose a number of difficulties. The process involves taking field notes and other documentation and making an initial draft before writing a working, interpretative document which 'contains the writer's initial attempts to make sense of what has been learned' (Denzin, 1994, p. 501). Note that this is only a working document which you will wish to reflect on and discuss with your supervisor(s) and colleagues. You may make a number of drafts before you arrive at the final document which 'embodies the writer's self-understandings, which are now inscribed in the experiences of those studied' (Denzin, 1994, p. 502).

If your data are mainly qualitative, it is essential that you intersperse your text with quotations. This will give your text authenticity and vibrancy, and will enable the reader to share the world you are analysing. However, you must be careful that any illustrations or quotations you give are relevant and part of the fabric of the study. 'Provided they are supported by other forms of data and tie in clearly with other aspects of the analysis, using individual episodes can provide a powerful means of getting a hold on the problems of presenting complex qualitative data' (Allan, 1991, p. 187).

The data displays you used for analysing your research of the data can be used to great effect when presenting your qualitative data, although your main discussions will be in the text. You may also want to create your own diagrams. In an article reporting an ethnographic study conducted in a retail gift store, McGrath (1989) used data from participant observation, in-depth interviews and photographs to provide description and interpretative insights into the consumer gift selection and retailer socialization process.

13.4.2 QUANTITATIVE DATA

The general rule for writing numbers in the text is to use words for the numbers one to nine, and numerals for 10 onwards. For example, 'Only five of the respondents answered this question', as opposed to 'There were 52 respondents in this category'. There are many exceptions to this rule. For example when numbers below 10 are grouped together for comparison with numbers 10 and above in the same paragraph, they should all appear as numerals. For example, 'Only 5 of the 52 respondents in this category answered this question'. Other exceptions are described by Rudestam and Newton (1992).

In the sections which follow, we have drawn together a number of principles to form guidelines for different forms of presentation. This is not intended to be a rigid set of rules and you may discover other principles.

Tables

The data in a table are tabulated or classified by arranging the data items in a framework of columns and rows. Research shows that some people prefer data presented in tabular form, although 'even quite sophisticated people need time to get the main points from a table (often much more time than they would need with a bar chart or pictorial chart)' (Macdonald-Ross, 1977, p. 379). However, tables offer the advantage of being compact and exact, and 'usually outperform graphics in reporting on small data sets of 20 numbers or less' (Tufte, 1983, p. 56).

Iselin (1972) suggests that the way in which a table is constructed can aid the reader's comprehension. Construction signalling allows items which are grouped together to be identified, as well as differentiating names of items from names of groups. Iselin uses three different methods of construction signalling:

* lower and upper case letters
* the indentation of items under a group heading
* spacing between groups of items.

Although Iselin's experiments were confined to students and some of his findings require further research, he shows that effective construction signalling has a significant effect on the speed and accuracy of the extraction of information.

Drawing from the literature and our own experience, in Box 13.6 we offer guidance on the construction of tables in your research report.

BOX 13.6 Guide to constructing tables

General advice

- Use a tabular presentation for an educated audience.

- Use columns rather than rows to compare figures. If comparison is the main purpose of the presentation, consider using a comparative bar chart.

- Restrict the size to 20 numbers or less. This can be done by dividing a large table into two or more small tables. Consider a graph for large data sets.

- Minimize the number of words used, but spell words out rather than using abbreviations or codes.

Structure and layout

- Place the table number and title at the top to allow the reader to identify and understand the purpose of the presentation before proceeding to the body of the table.

- Use different fonts and styles to distinguish the table title, headings and subheadings.

- In pairs or sequences of tables, use identical labels for common headings and labels.

- Indent items under a group variable label.

- Set columns compactly so that the eye does not have to travel too far between labels and each column of figures.

- Add grid lines to facilitate the reading of columns and rows.

The quantitative data

- Round numbers to two significant digits, unless precision of data is important.

- Where possible, order columns/rows by size of numbers. Place any miscellaneous variable last, regardless of size.

- Provide column/row averages or totals where appropriate.

- Draw attention to key figures with colour, shading or bold typeface.

Charts and graphs

When using a graphical presentation for quantitative data, it is important to remember that you must endeavour at all times to present the information 'in a manner that is clear and concise, simple and effective, uncluttered and understandable' (Martin, 1989, p. 46). Research shows that some people prefer data presented in graphics, such as charts and graphs. Playfair, the 18th-century political economist, developed nearly all the basic graphical designs when looking for ways in which to communicate substantial amounts of quantitative data. He preferred graphics to tables because they show the shape of the data in a comparative perspective (Playfair, 1786). 'Often the most effective way to describe, explore, and summarise a set of numbers – even a very large set – is to look at pictures of those numbers' (Tufte, 1983, p. 9).

Graphics, especially when colour is used, can attract and hold the reader's attention and help identify trends in the data. Therefore, quantitative information displayed in a graph 'has the potential to be both read and understood. But effective communication does not follow automatically from graph use; the graph must comply with certain principles of graph design and construction' (Beattie and Jones, 1992, p. 30).

Although most commentators promote the graphical presentation of comparative data, there appears to be some conflict over acceptable levels of complexity. Ehrenberg (1975; 1976) advises that a graph should communicate a simple story, since many readers concentrate on the visual patterns, rather than reading the actual data. Tufte (1983) and Martin (1989) suggest that both colour and monochrome presentations require careful handling to avoid detracting from the message or misleading the reader. In Box 13.7 we offer general guidance on constructing charts and graphs.

BOX 13.7   Guide to constructing charts and graphs

General advice

- Do not mix different types of data (for example percentage and absolute figures) on the same chart, but draw up separate charts.
- Items should only be compared on the same chart if they have the same basic data structure and a clear relationship.
- Label the axes.
- Label data elements directly and include the unit of measurement. If there is insufficient room to label the elements directly, provide a key.
- Minimize the number of words used but, if possible, spell words out, rather than using abbreviations or codes. The majority of ink used to produce the graph should present the quantitative data. Delete anything which does not present fresh information, since this represents a barrier to communication.

Structure and layout

- Place the chart number and title at the top to allow the reader to identify and understand the purpose of the presentation before proceeding to the body of the graph.
- Use different fonts and styles to distinguish the chart title, axes and data element labels.
- Select an unobtrusive background.

The quantitative data

- Select colours for the data elements with high contrast from adjacent items.
- Avoid the combination of red and green on adjacent elements, which is one of the commonest problems for people who are colour-deficient.

Bar charts

Macdonald-Ross (1977) suggests that the elements of bars should be labelled directly; horizontal bars give room for labels and figures near the elements. However, for time sequences, he recommends vertical bar charts. Thibadoux, Cooper and Greenberg (1986) advise that bars should be of uniform width and evenly spaced; they are easier to read and interpret if a space of half the width of the bar is left as the distance between the bars. The scale should begin with zero and normally should remain unbroken. The number of intervals should assist with measuring distances and generally should be in round numbers, marked off with lines or ticks. They recommend that in general graphics which use horizontal and vertical scale, lines should be proportioned so that the horizontal scale is greater than the height. This view is shared by Tufte (1983) who proposes that if the nature of the data suggests the shape of the graphic, follow that suggestion; otherwise move towards a horizontal graphical presentation about 50 per cent wider than tall.

With regard to shading, Thibadoux *et al.* (1986) suggest that black is appropriate if the bars are not extremely wide, when diagonal line shading or cross-hatching may be used. However, horizontal and vertical shadings should not be used in segmented bars because they may affect the perceived width and shape of the bar. Care must also be taken with cross-hatching not to create optical illusions. Box 13.8 shows additional principles that apply to bar charts.

BOX 13.8 Additional principles for bar charts

General advice

- Use a bar chart for comparing data.
- In a bar chart the bars represent different categories of data. The frequency should be shown by the length (horizontal bar chart) or height (vertical bar chart) of each bar. In a histogram, the frequency is indicated by the area of the bar.
- Use a vertical bar chart for time sequences with the scale on the left. The time elements should move from left to right on the horizontal axis.
- Use a multiple bar chart, rather than a segmented bar chart, since the former provides a common base for the segments.
- Use a histogram for continuous, ratio or interval data where the class widths are unequal.

The bars

- In a bar chart, the bars should be of uniform width and evenly spaced.
- The bar end should be straight.
- Horizontal bars give room for labels and figures near the elements. Values should only be given if the result is legible and does not look cluttered.
- When using three-dimensional bars, clearly label the reading dimension.
- In multiple bar charts, do not use more than four elements.
- In histograms, the ordering of the bars should be sequential.
- If you are using pictograms, take care that the dimensions (length, area or volume) correctly reflect the changing value of the variable.
- Avoid pictograms with undefined reading points, such as piles of coins.
- Black is appropriate if the bars are not extremely wide; alternatively use shades of grey.
- Horizontal, vertical and diagonal lines should be avoided, as they can create optical illusions.

The scale

- Commence the scale at zero.
- If a break in the scale is unavoidable, it must be clearly indicated.
- Proportion the horizontal scale so that it is about 50% greater than the vertical scale.

Pie charts

Pie charts are useful for presenting proportional data. Morris (1993) recommends that labels and figures should be placed nearby to facilitate comparison of the different segments. Thibadoux *et al.* (1986) suggest that the largest segment is placed at the central point of the upper right half of the circle, followed in a clockwise direction by the remaining segments in decreasing order, with any miscellaneous segment placed last.

There appears to be agreement that a pie chart should contain no more than six categories and should not be used to compare different sets of data. Research by Flannery (1971) shows that if quantity is related to area, readers tend to underestimate differences. Box 13.9 shows the additional principles that apply to pie charts.

BOX 13.9   Additional principles for pie charts

General advice

- Use a pie chart to present proportional data only.
- Use the angle at the centre to divide the circle into segments; the area of each segment should be proportional to the segment represented.
- Do not use pie charts to compare different sets of data; instead, consider a bar chart.

The segments

- Use no more than six segments.
- Place the largest segment at the central point of the upper right half of the circle, followed in a clockwise direction by the remaining segments in decreasing order.
- Place any miscellaneous variable last, regardless of size.
- Each segment should be labelled and its value given as a percentage of the whole.

Line graphs

In a line graph the independent variable is shown on the horizontal axis and the dependent variable on the vertical axis. Although it is usual to place the scale figures on the left-hand side of the graph, in wide graphs it may be helpful if they appear on both sides (Thibadoux *et al.*, 1986). One advantage of line graphs over other forms is that a number of graphs can be superimposed on the same axes. This enables comparisons to be made very clearly. Thibadoux *et al.* recommend that if the curves are close together or cross, colour coding may be used to differentiate them or different patterns, such as solid, dash, dotted or dot-dash lines. However, Bergwerk (1970) found that experts on the communication of financial data preferred one- or two-element charts. Box 13.10 shows the additional principles that apply to line charts.

BOX 13.10   Additional principles for line charts

- The component categories should be represented by a series of points joined by a line.
- The axes must represent continuous scales with the independent variable shown on the horizontal axis and the dependent variable on the vertical axis.
- Place the scale figures for the vertical axis on the left. In a wide graph show the scale on both sides.
- Use no more than two elements.

As with tabular presentations, it is important to remember that however clearly presented your graphs and charts are, it is still necessary to offer some interpretation and, if possible, further analysis of the data. This should be given immediately after the graphical presentation.

student responding. These may be clarification questions or a question centred on some weakness the examiner considers is present. In either case, he or she is testing your knowledge. As the examination progresses, it is likely to become a discussion, with the student taking the lead in explaining the research. The examiners are not trying to trip you up, but they will want to explore any weaknesses in your dissertation or thesis. They will expect you to know your subject. This means you need to be very familiar with your research, even though it may have been several weeks or months since you submitted it to the examiners. Phillips and Pugh (1994) give detailed instructions on how to prepare for this by summarizing every page into a few words which capture the main idea and the page number. You can then use the summaries for revision before the examination and take them in with you so that you can refer the examiners to particular pages. Ask your supervisors if they can arrange a mock viva voce. If not, persuade colleagues, family and friends to help you. At the MPhil and PhD levels, it is imperative that you have practised presenting your research and this is why attending conferences, seminars and workshops is so valuable. These activities should have alerted you to potential weaknesses and the sort of questions which might arise in your viva voce.

Be careful not to argue with the examiners, but where you have strong opinions and you can support them, do not hesitate to voice them strongly. Play to your strengths and not your weaknesses. Some of the questions put to you may appear to be on the edge of the scope of your study, so attempt to place them in a context where you are certain of the facts. You need to accept that there may be defects in your study and explain to the examiners how they arose and how you would set about remedying them. If you do not understand a question ask for clarification. This is far better than giving an inept response. Do not rush into giving replies. Many of the questions will be complex and you should take time to reflect on the question and your answer. Your responses should be balanced, with a review of the advantages and disadvantages, and conclude with your own opinions. The major advantage you have is that you conducted the research, not the external examiners. Therefore, you will certainly know more about the details than they do. Try to keep the discussions in this area and explain any interesting factors or aspects. Even an amusing anecdote of an event while you were conducting the research would not go amiss, provided it is not too long.

Increasingly students and supervisors are permitted to use their laptops to refer to the research report. Check before your viva voce before making this assumption. If permission is granted, make sure that you and your supervisors have the version of your research report that you submitted to the examiners. You also need to be certain that you are fully conversant with its location on your laptop and the functions of your laptop. Examiners are likely to become irritated if they have to wait while the student searches through endless files for some interesting data 'that is on there somewhere'.

The outcome of a viva voce depends on the nature of the qualification. For an undergraduate or taught Master's degree, the research project is only one element that earns you credits towards your degree. With an MPhil and PhD, the degree rests solely on the thesis and viva voce and the following outcomes are possible:

- The award is made immediately after the viva voce and you have nothing else to do except receive the congratulations of friends and family.
- The award is made, subject to minor amendments to be made within a specified period. These are usually modest changes and should cause you no problems. You will not be subjected to another viva voce and your internal examiner will be responsible for making certain that the final, bound thesis incorporates the amendments.

- The award is not made and you are asked to make substantial revisions. You have not failed and have the opportunity to resubmit and be re-examined. In this case the changes will be major and will take you a number of months to complete. However, you will have the benefit of having received guidance from the examiners on what is expected, and as long as you can meet these requirements you will receive the award.
- An outright fail with no possibility of being able to resubmit. This is a disaster.
- With a PhD, the examiners may decide that although the work is of some merit, it does not meet the standard required for a doctorate. If appropriate, they may recommend that an MPhil is awarded instead.

13.6 GETTING PUBLISHED

Much of what we have suggested in this chapter also applies to writing for conferences and journals, but with some important differences. A research report as part of a programme of study is solely an academic document. You may decide to use your research to present papers at conferences or to write for journals and magazines. You will be communicating to different audiences in a different medium and in this section we will consider some of the issues.

13.6.1 CONFERENCE PAPERS

Conferences can be divided into commercial and academic conferences. Commercial conferences are well advertised and the business people attending them often have to pay a sizeable fee. Usually there are a number of speakers who are regarded as experts in their fields. If you are fortunate enough to be regarded as an expert, you can expect a substantial fee, but you must be articulate and know your subject. The audience will not be interested in your research design, literature review or methodology, but in your research results and the implications for their businesses.

Academic conferences are less lavish affairs and can range from small regional conferences, with only a dozen participants, to large international conferences with an audience of thousands. Despite differences of size and location, both audiences will be interested in and critical of your research. The call for papers usually goes out several months before the conference and you are usually expected to submit a paper for consideration of approximately 5,000 words, together with an abstract. If the conference organizers consider it is worthy, they will allocate a certain length of time for you to present it. With some conferences this can be as short as 20 minutes; with others you may be allocated an hour. You should devise a presentation based on your paper, bearing in mind the time available and allowing time at the end for questions.

If you are looking for an academic career, you must present papers at academic conferences. You may find that this also leads to a publication, as some organizers publish a collection of selected papers presented at the conference. You will find out details of academic conferences from your supervisor(s), departmental notice boards and journals. The costs are usually fairly low, often involving little more than accommodation, meals, travel and hire of rooms. Once you have attended one or two conferences, you will find a network of other researchers.

13.6.2 · ARTICLES

There are three main types of publication which may be interested in receiving an article about your research; each with its own style and word length. Table 13.7 gives details.

TABLE 13.7 Indicative lengths of articles	
Type of article	**Approximate length**
Newspapers and magazines	800–1,500 words
Professional journals	1,200–2,000 words
Academic journals	2,500–5,000 words

Popular publications include the local and national press, as well as commercially focused and other magazines. With these types of publication, it is likely that the editor will only commission an article if you have something to write from your research that is controversial and/or highly topical. Therefore, a study of the hardships suffered by textile workers in the 19th century is unlikely to be commissioned, but if you can use your research to illuminate and explain current events you may find an outlet for it. However, if your research is not topical but focuses on local industry or events, you may find that your local press is interested. Before you submit an article, read past copies of the publication so that you are familiar with the style and the topics they cover. At the local level you may not receive any payment, but at the national level you will normally receive a modest payment based on the length of the article.

The associations and societies of professional bodies, such as accountants, lawyers and engineers produce their own professional journals, usually on a monthly basis. These concentrate on topical issues and other matters that are relevant to their members, including those that are of historical importance. You might find that your research contains something that will entice the editor to commission an article, but he or she may want you to put a certain slant on your story. You can expect payment, but again this is likely to be modest.

The editors of academic journals will require you to submit several copies of your article that does not reveal the name of the author(s), together with a fee. The editor decides whether the subject of the article is appropriate to the journal and, if so, will send it to members of the editorial board (other academics) to be reviewed. In most cases, this is a 'double blind' review because the reviewers do not know the name of the author(s) or the name of the other reviewer(s). The outcome of the review can be to recommend to the editor that the article is:

- published as it is
- resubmit once reviewers' comments have been addressed
- reject.

The fee for reviewing the work is payable even if the article is rejected and there is no financial reward from the publisher. The reward is simply getting published, because it is highly competitive with many academics trying to get their work published by the most prestigious journals to advance their careers. There is guidance in the literature to help you achieve success and we have distilled these recommendations into the following tips:

- Know what the journals publish – You need to do your market research and identify the journals which accept articles of the type you are trying to get published. Your own literature search should have identified those journals which may be interested in your offering. You will also find articles which have surveyed the types of articles published by specific journals (for example Beattie and Goodacre, 2004; Prather-Kinsey and Rueschoff, 2004) or identified topics which are hot in certain business disciplines (for example Piotrowski and Armstrong, 2005).

•   Be realistic about your contribution – Your article must make a contribution to knowledge and the best way to do this is to demonstrate how it fits into the existing literature.
•   Read the guide to authors – Follow the instructions exactly. They vary from one journal to another. Go through copies of the past five years or so of the journal looking for articles in the same general area and making certain that you cite them.
•   Try not to become disillusioned by the reviewers' comments and recommendations.

The number of rejections by journals is high and for an inexperienced author there is considerable merit in writing the article jointly with someone with greater experience, such as your supervisor. If you are a PhD student, your supervisors will expect to co-author articles with you, even if at that stage they do little more than provide advice and editing. It is one of the ways in which you show appreciation for their contribution to the development of your research.

Your initial submission may be rejected but the editor, on the advice of the referees, may ask you to make revisions and resubmit. This will often require considerable work on your part but it is normally worthwhile. If you address the criticisms of the referees successfully you should achieve publication. You may find, however, that the demand of the referees is such that you have to alter your contribution significantly to gain publication (Frey, 2003).

There is some disparity among the different business disciplines regarding the number of articles published in the top academic journals (Swanson, 2004) and it is extremely difficult to get articles accepted in such journals in many disciplines. When targeting journals, you should be aware that despite the increasingly international orientation of business, many journals are nationally orientated in the articles that they accept (Jones and Roberts, 2005). Despite this challenge, you must persist if you are seeking an academic career.

13.6.3   MEASURES OF QUALITY

Unfortunately, it can be difficult to measure the quality of your publications, but this can be critical if you are applying for an academic position or wanting to move up the scale. There are three main methods of measurement:

•   The number of publications you have, regardless of the reputation of the journal
•   The quality of the journal in which you have published
•   The impact of your publications, as measured by the number of citations it has received from other authors since it was published.

Volume is by far the easiest and, in the early stages of your career, your academic institution may only expect that you publish and, if possible, in a refereed journal. Credit is given for the number of articles published and you should ensure that you obtain the maximum output of articles from your research.

Quality of journals may be less easy to determine or, at least, to agree upon. Quality, in academic terms, does not mean the most read journals but those where it is most difficult to get an article accepted. There are several lists that have been compiled and there tends to be agreement as to which journals have particular merit. In addition many universities and colleges will construct their own rankings, drawn from published sources but amended to fit their own particular needs.

The impact of your publications becomes more important as your career progresses. What you are hoping is that other researchers will refer to your work in their own articles. Citation counts also include self-citations, that is, where an author cites his or her own work. This would seem to be more common in some disciplines than in others (Hyland, 2003). Your research has therefore had an impact on what others are doing and thinking. There are several sources of information on citation impact, including *Google Scholar*.

13.7   CONCLUSIONS

In this chapter we have looked at the planning and the practical side of writing, from designing the report to developing a suitable writing style and presenting the data. Writing up your research can be a highly rewarding process once you get started. The secret to completing on time is to write notes and draft sections of your dissertation or thesis from the outset, rather than leave it until the last minute. If, for one reason or another, you have not managed to start writing early enough, you will face major problems and we give advice in the next chapter on how these might be resolved.

If you are a serious researcher or wish to have an academic career, conferences and academic journals are highly important. We have offered advice on achieving publication in academic journals, but we will not pretend that it is easy. The best personal quality you can have is persistence – somewhere there is a journal that will publish your article even if it takes several revisions.

ACTIVITIES

Writing skills improve by practice and attempting different styles of expression. It is best if you can wait a few weeks before comparing the writing exercises you do in this section.

1. Take a piece text that you have written recently (about 500 words). Identify the key words you have used most frequently. Using a hard copy thesaurus or the facility on your word processing software, substitute synonyms as appropriate. Compare the two pieces of text and reflect on which is better and why.

2. Select a short section of text from a book (no more than one or two pages) and read it. Without referring to it again, write a letter to a friend explaining what the section is about. Put the original text and the letter aside for about two weeks and then try to reconstruct the text from the letter. Compare the two pieces identifying where there are significant differences in context and style.

3. Use a well-known proverb, phrase or verse and write a short narrative using the passive voice and the personal voice to reflect the two main paradigms. In addition, write it again in a colloquial style as if you were talking informally to a friend. This exercise will improve the flexibility of your style.

Example:

The mouse ran up the clock. The clock struck one, the mouse ran down.

Passive voice

It was observed that the mouse ascended the case of the grand-father clock in a rapid manner. When the chiming mechanism of the clock struck one o'clock, the rodent descended speedily. As this behaviour was only observed on one occasion, it is not possible to generalize from it. However, it is hypothesized that the rapid descent was associated with fright. This requires further investigation with a large sample of rodents in a controlled environment.

4. Conduct a literature search for articles that discuss the ranking of journals in your discipline. Compare the rankings across the articles and identify potential journals for articles you will write from your research.

5. Select four target journals as above and analyse the articles published over the past five years by methodology, topic, sample size, country and the affiliation of the author (university, college or other institution). Identify any pattern and determine how any article you might write fits into this pattern.

14

Troubleshooting

14.1 INTRODUCTION

As we explained in Chapter 1, business research is not a simple linear process and even though you may have studied all the chapters in this book very carefully, you may encounter difficulties of one type or another. Regardless of how much support and guidance you receive from your supervisors, colleagues, friends and family, you are bound to make some mistakes, and this is true for researchers at all levels. In addition, things beyond your control may create problems. If the research you designed in your proposal does not come to fruition exactly as planned, you will need to explain what the problems were and, irrespective of whether you decide to take action to remedy the situation or decide to do nothing, you will need to justify your strategy by weighing up the alternatives.

In this chapter we examine typical challenges associated with the main stages of the research process. The solutions to these problems refer you to different chapters in the book where you will be able to obtain the appropriate guidance. You can also use the index and look up terms in the glossary. The problems we cover are:

- Getting started
- Managing the process
- Identifying a topic and/or a research problem or issue
- Making a preliminary plan of action
- Finding a theoretical framework
- Writing the proposal
- Deciding the methodology
- Searching and reviewing the literature
- Collecting research data
- Organizing qualitative research data
- Analysing the research data
- Structuring the dissertation or thesis
- Writing the dissertation or thesis
- Dealing with writer's block
- Achieving the standards
- Eleventh-hour strategies for writing up.

14.2 GETTING STARTED

Problem
You are unable to start because you are totally confused over what research is all about and what you are expected to do.

Before you can start your research, you will find it useful to gain an understanding of what business research entails by implementing the following plan of action:

1. Start with the basics and read about the nature and purpose of research, focusing on the definitions of research and the different types of research (see Chapter 1).
2. The next steps are to:
   - Identify a research topic (see Chapters 3 and 6)
   - Define a research problem (see Chapters 3 and 6)
   - Design the project (see Chapter 7)

- Collect the data (see Chapters 8 and 10)
- Analyse the data (see Chapters 9, 11 and 12)
- Write up the research (see Chapter 13).

14.3 MANAGING THE PROCESS

Problem
You are ready to get started, but you are worried about how you will manage your research project.

To manage your research efficiently and in the time available, you should try the following:

1. Find out when you will have to submit your dissertation or thesis.
2. Read about the research process, set yourself a timetable for each stage (some will overlap) and agree it with your supervisor (see Chapter 2).
3. To ensure that your time is spent efficiently, you must use your knowledge, skills and personal qualities to manage the process of the research (see Chapter 3).

14.4 IDENTIFYING A TOPIC AND/OR A RESEARCH PROBLEM OR ISSUE

Problem
You are unable to find a suitable topic and/or research problem or issue to investigate.

If you are unable to identify a suitable topic and/or a research problem or issue to investigate (or you have to abandon your choice because it was not feasible, you should take the following steps:

1. Try techniques such as brainstorming, analogy, mind mapping, morphological analysis and relevance trees to generate a research topic that is relevant to your degree (see Chapter 3).
2. Consider issues such as your skills, potential costs, access to data and ethics (see Chapter 3).
3. Arrange to meet your supervisor to discuss your ideas (see Chapter 2).
4. Once you have identified a research topic, conduct a literature search to identify gaps and deficiencies that suggest a specific research problem or issue to investigate (see Chapter 6).

14.5 MAKING A PRELIMINARY PLAN OF ACTION

Problem
You know the research topic you want to investigate but you do not know how to plan the first stages of the research.

The research proposal is going to be your detailed research plan, but you have to carry out some preliminary investigations before you can write it. Your preliminary plan of action should be as follows:

1. Carry out a literature search using key words related to your research topic to find the most important academic articles and other publications on this topic (see Chapter 6).
2. Identify a research problem or issue to investigate and conduct a focused search to find the key articles and other publications (see Chapter 6).
3. Write a preliminary review of this literature for your research proposal that leads the reader to the research question(s) your study will address (see Chapter 6).
4. Make a decision on the appropriate method(s) for collecting the data (see Chapters 8 and 10) and analysing them (see Chapters 9, 11 and 12). Describe and justify your choices in the methodology section of your proposal (see Chapter 7).

14.6   FINDING A THEORETICAL FRAMEWORK

Problem
You cannot write a research proposal because you have difficulty in applying an appropriate theoretical framework.

If a theoretical framework is appropriate under your research paradigm, you should take the following steps:

1. Ensure that you have clearly specified the purpose of the research (see Chapter 7) and that you have conducted a literature search (see Chapter 6).
2. You should then be able to identify the theories and models used by other researchers studying the same or similar issues, and develop a theoretical framework (see Chapter 7).
3. You can then define the unit of analysis and construct the hypotheses you will test, which are the propositions you will investigate to answer your research questions (see Chapter 7).

14.7   WRITING THE PROPOSAL

Problem
You are uncertain about how to write a research proposal that will be acceptable to your supervisor(s).

If you are worried about how to write your research proposal, you should implement the following plan:

1. Start by looking at the indicative structure of a research proposal and read about what is usually contained in each section (see Chapter 7).

2. Your preliminary review of the literature forms a major part of your research proposal. It focuses on the most influential articles and other publications in the literature and should lead the reader to the research question(s) your study will address (see Chapter 6).

3. You must mention how you will solve any problems relating to covering costs, gaining access to data and issues concerning ethics (see Chapter 3).

4. Identify a research problem or issue to investigate and conduct a focused search to find the key articles and other publications (see Chapter 6).

5. Write a preliminary review of this literature (see Chapter 6) for your research proposal that leads to your research question(s).

6. Make a decision on the appropriate method(s) for collecting the data (see Chapters 8 and 10) and analysing them (see Chapters 9, 11 and 12). Describe your methodology and methods and justify your choices in the methodology section of your proposal, commenting on the limitations of your research design.

7. Conclude with remarks about the expected outcomes of the research (related to the purpose) and a timetable for completing the various stages (see Chapter 7).

14.8 DECIDING THE METHODOLOGY

Problem
You are unable to decide which methodology to use.

Deciding which methodology to use is made easier when you realize that your choice is limited by a number of factors. Your action plan should be as follows:

1. Start by considering the constraints placed by the research problem or issue your study will address (see Chapter 7) and your research paradigm (see Chapter 4).

2. Identify which methodologies are usually associated with your research paradigm (see Chapter 5).

3. Consider whether triangulation is appropriate and/or feasible (see Chapter 5).

14.9 SEARCHING AND REVIEWING THE LITERATURE

Problem
You are unable to find articles and other publications on your research topic or you are unable to write the literature review.

Planning is the key to an efficient and successful literature search and a critical review of the relevant literature. We advise you to adopt the following strategy:

1. Before you begin your search, you need to define your terms and determine the scope of your research (see Chapter 6).

2. Then you should start a systematic search (see Chapter 6).

3. You must be certain to record the references (see Chapter 6) and avoid plagiarism when writing your literature review (see Chapters 6 and 13).

4. You should take an analytical approach to reviewing the literature rather than writing a descriptive list of items you have read (see Chapter 6). By pointing out the gaps and deficiencies in the literature, you will be able to lead the reader to the research question(s) your study will address.

14.10   COLLECTING RESEARCH DATA

Problem
You are unable to decide how to collect your research data.

Deciding which data collection method to use is made easier when you realize that your choice is limited.

1. Start by considering the nature of the research problem or issue your study will address (see Chapter 6) and any access to data that will be needed.

2. Then consider your research paradigm (see Chapter 4) and your methodology (see Chapter 5).

3. This should enable you to select appropriate methods for collecting the data (see Chapters 8 and 10). You must make this choice in the context of the methods you plan to use to analyse the data (see Chapters 9, 11 and 12).

14.11   ORGANIZING QUALITATIVE RESEARCH DATA

Problem
You plan to collect qualitative research data, but you do not know when to start the analysis.

In an interpretive study, it is difficult *not* to start the process of analysing qualitative data during the collection stage. Therefore, this is not usually a problem once you get started. Your plan of action should be as follows:

1. As you collect the research data, you need to be clear about your choice of methodology (see Chapter 5) and issues relating to reliability and validity (Chapters 4, 8 and 9).

2. You need to ensure that your methods for capturing primary data (using equipment such as a camera, video or audio recorder) are supported by notes taken at the time (see Chapter 8).

3. If you are collecting secondary research data, you need to ensure that you have followed a systematic method (see Chapter 9).

4. While you are collecting the qualitative data, use methods for reducing the amount of material data by restructuring or detextualizing the data (see Chapter 9).

14.12 ANALYSING THE RESEARCH DATA

Problem
You are unable to decide how to analyse the data you have collected.

Deciding which method of data analysis to use is made easier when you realize that your choice is limited:

1. The first step is to consider whether you have designed your study under a positivist or an interpretive paradigm (see Chapters 4 and 5).
2. If you are a positivist, you want your research data to be in numerical form so that you can use statistical methods of analysis (see Chapters 11 and 12). You may first need to quantify any qualitative data (see Chapter 10).
3. All positivists will conduct an exploratory analysis of their data using descriptive statistics (see Chapter 11). However, postgraduate and doctoral students will need to go on to use inferential statistics (see Chapter 12).
4. Depending on their philosophical assumptions, interpretivists who have collected qualitative data can use either quantifying methods or non-quantifying methods for analysing their research data (see Chapter 9).

14.13 STRUCTURING THE DISSERTATION OR THESIS

Problem
You are uncertain about how to structure your dissertation or thesis.

If you are uncertain about how to structure your dissertation or thesis, the following plan of action should help:

1. Adopt or adapt the indicative structure that shows the main chapters in a research report (see Chapter 13).
2. Read about what needs to be included in each chapter and add names for the main sections within each chapter (see Chapter 13). Remember that each chapter will need to have some kind of introduction and a conclusion section that will help provide links between chapters.
3. Based on the indicative proportion of the whole report that each chapter represents, allocate an approximate number of words to each of your chapters (see Chapter 13).
4. The last step is to decide what form any tabular or diagrammatic summaries of your results/findings will take (see Chapters 10–13).

14.14 WRITING THE DISSERTATION OR THESIS

Problem
You are worried about writing up the research.

If you have followed the guidance in this book, you will have decided on the main structure of your dissertation or thesis at an early stage and will have used the sections in your proposal as the basis of some of the chapters. You will have added further draft material as you embarked on different stages in the research. You should now adopt the following plan of action:

1. You will need to draw up a plan and give some thought to the overall design of the report (see Chapter 13).
2. You will then be in a position to finalize your literature review, methodology and analysis. Once you have drafted your conclusions chapter, develop the introductory section you wrote for your proposal as the first chapter in your dissertation. Then check all chapters to ensure that you use the same terms and wording every time you mention the purpose of the research and the research questions.
3. As you write, add the bibliographic references for all the sources you cite. It is essential to follow the referencing system recommended on your course and avoid plagiarism (see Chapters 6 and 13).
4. If you have run out of time, use our eleventh-hour strategies at the end of this chapter.

14.15   DEALING WITH WRITER'S BLOCK

Problem
You are part way through writing up your research, but suffering from writer's block.

Make sure you are having regular, balanced meals and drinking enough liquid to stop you becoming dehydrated. All this helps your brain process information efficiently. Take a short break to give your mind a rest and relieve the aches and pains of spending hours at the computer. Even though you may be feeling weary, do something aerobic during the break as it will increase your sense of well-being in general and improve your circulation. In addition, try the following tips:

1. Stop trying to write the particular section that is proving to be problematic and turn to a different part of your report.
2. Alternatively, start a totally different task, such as checking your references, preparing tables and diagrams, running the spelling and grammar check or improving your writing by looking up synonyms.
3. Try to find a way round the impasse you are experiencing with the problematic section by generating a mind map or other diagram to help structure your thoughts. Alternatively, reflect on what you have written in that section so far and draw up a list of its strengths and weaknesses. You can also do this by making an audio recording of your thoughts and reviewing them.
4. Have a brainstorming session with your supervisor or a fellow student.
5. Sometimes a good moan to a sympathetic member of the family or a friend is enough to clear the tension and clarify your thoughts.

14.16 ACHIEVING THE STANDARDS

Problem
You are worried about whether your work will be up to the standards required.

Apart from the advice that you should always do your best, the following suggestions should help:

1. The most important source of guidance on standards is the handbook or other source of information provided by your institution.
2. You can discuss these criteria with your supervisor (see Chapter 2), who provides feedback in the form of comments on your proposal and draft chapters (see Chapters 7 and 13).
3. There are a number of general characteristics of a good research project (see Chapter 1) and indicative assessment criteria that will give you an idea of what is expected at different degree levels (see Chapter 13).

14.17 ELEVENTH-HOUR STRATEGIES FOR WRITING UP

If you have left all or most of the writing up until the eleventh hour, you will be feeling very worried indeed. The submission date is looming and you have little to show for the work you have done. If this applies to you, we suggest the following strategy:

1. Decide on a structure of chapters and main sections within each chapter, but do not take too long over it; no more than half a day, even for a doctoral thesis. Use the sample structures given in Chapter 13 and put in as many of the subsections as you can. Work out the approximate word count you are aiming for with each chapter.
2. On your computer, open a document for each chapter and name it. Set up the page layout to the required size, margins, pagination, font, line spacing and so on. Type in the number and name of the chapter and the number and heading for each main section within the chapter.
3. Now aim for volume. Do not worry unduly about grammar, punctuation or references. You must get as many words down as possible in each of the chapters. Leave the introductory chapter and concentrate on those sections you know well. You should find that the act of writing one part will spark off other aspects which you want to include. This will entail switching from chapter to chapter. In your hurry, you may put things in the wrong places, but that does not matter.
4. When you have written approximately two-thirds of your target word count, stop and print each chapter. This will use up a lot of paper, but you are in a crisis situation and cost must come second to speed now. Put your printout in a ring binder file, using dividers to separate the chapters.
5. Read all the chapters, marking any changes on the hard copy in a bright colour as you go, adding text wherever possible as well as references and quotations from other authors. Now make these corrections and additions to the computer files and open a new file for the references/bibliography. You should find that you are now within 10% to 15% of your target number of words.
6. Print two copies and persuade a friend or member of the family to read through one and mark down any comments. We imagine that you have missed the deadline

Abstract	A brief summary of the purpose of the research, the methodology and the key findings.
Action research	A methodology used in applied research to find an effective way of bringing about a conscious change in a partly controlled environment.
Analogy	A means of designing a study in one subject by importing ideas and procedures from another area where there are similarities.
Analytical research	A study where the aim is to understand phenomena by discovering and measuring causal relations among them.
Anonymity	The provision of protection to participants by ensuring that their names are not identified with the information they give.
Applied research	Describes a study that is designed to apply its findings to solving a specific, existing problem.
Axiological assumption	A philosophical assumption about the role of values.
Bar chart	A graphical presentation of a frequency distribution of an ordinal or nominal variable in which the data are represented by a series of separate vertical or horizontal bars. The frequencies are indicated by the height (or length) of the bars.
Basic (or pure) research	Describes a study that is designed to make a contribution to general knowledge and theoretical understanding, rather than solve a specific problem.
Bibliography	A list of publications relating to a topic.
Bivariate analysis	Analysis of data from two variables.
Brainstorming	A technique that can be used to generate research topics by listing spontaneous ideas with one or more interested people.
Case study	A methodology that is used to explore a single phenomenon (the case) in a natural setting using a variety of methods to obtain in-depth knowledge.
Categorical variable	A nominal variable measured using numerical codes to identify categories.
Chi squared (χ^2) test	A non-parametric test of association for two variables measured on a nominal scale.
Citation	An acknowledgement in the text of the original source from which information was obtained.
Closed question	A question where respondents select the answer from a number of predetermined alternatives.
Coding frame	A list of coding units against which the analysed material is classified.

Coding unit	A particular word, character, item, theme or concept identified in the data and allocated a specific code.
Cognitive mapping	A method based on personal construct theory that structures a participant's perceptions in the form of a diagram.
Confidence interval	A parametric technique for estimating a range of values of a sample statistic that is likely to contain an unknown population parameter at a given level of probability; the wider the confidence interval, the higher the confidence level.
Confidentiality	The provision of protection to participants by ensuring that sensitive information is not disclosed and the research data cannot be traced to the individual or organization providing it.
Confounding variable	A variable that obscures the effects of another.
Content analysis	A method by which selected items of qualitative data are systematically converted to numerical data for analysis.
Continuous variable	A ratio or interval variable measured on a scale where the data can take any value within a given range, such as time or length.
Correlation	A measure of the direction and strength of association between two quantitative variables. Correlation may be linear or non-linear, positive or negative.
Critical incident technique	A method for collecting data about a defined activity or event based on the participant's recollections of key facts.
Cross-sectional study	A methodology designed to investigate variables or a group of subjects in different contexts over the same period of time.
Cross-tabulation	A bivariate analysis of frequency distributions (usually relating to ordinal or nominal variables) in the form of a table.
Data (singular is datum)	Known facts or things used as a basis for inference or reckoning.
Data display	A summary of data in diagrammatic form that allows the user to draw valid conclusions.
Data integrity	Characteristics of the research that affect error and bias in the results.
Data reduction	'A form of data analysis that sorts, focuses, discards and reorganizes data' (Miles and Huberman, 1994, p. 11).
Deductive research	A study in which a conceptual and theoretical structure is developed which is then tested by empirical observation; thus particular instances are deducted from general inferences.
Delimitation	Establishes the scope of the research.

Dependent variable (DV)	A variable whose values are influenced by one or more independent variables.
Descriptive research	A study where the aim is to describe the characteristics of phenomena.
Descriptive statistics	A group of statistical methods used to summarize, describe or display quantitative data.
Diary	A method for collecting data where selected participants are asked to record relevant information in diary forms or booklets over a specified period of time.
Dichotomous variable	A variable that has two categories, such as gender.
Discrete variable	A ratio or interval variable measured on a scale that can take only one of a range of distinct values, such as number of employees.
Dissertation	'A detailed discourse, esp. as submitted for [an] academic degree'. A discourse is 'a lengthy treatment of a theme' (*Oxford Dictionary & Thesaurus*, 1997, pp. 216 and 211).
Dummy variable	A dichotomous quantitative variable coded 1 if the characteristic is present and 0 if the characteristic is absent.
Empirical evidence	Data based on observation or experience.
Epistemological assumption	A philosophical assumption about what constitutes valid knowledge in the context of the relationship of the researcher to that being researched.
Error	The difference between the mean and the data value (observation).
Ethnography	A methodology in which the researcher uses socially acquired and shared knowledge to understand the observed patterns of human activity.
Evaluation	The ability to make qualitative or quantitative judgements; to set out a reasoned argument through a series of steps, usually of gradually increasing difficulty; to criticize constructively.
Experimental study	A methodology used to investigate the relationship between two variables, where the independent variable is deliberately manipulated to observe the effect on the dependent variable.
Exploratory research	A study where the aim is to investigate phenomena where there is little or no information, with a view to finding patterns or developing propositions, rather than testing them. The focus is on gaining insights prior to a more rigorous investigation.
Extraneous variable	Any variable other than the independent variable which might have an effect on the dependent variable.

Feminist studies	A methodology used to investigate and seek understanding of phenomena from a feminist perspective.
Field experiment	An experimental study conducted in a natural location.
Focus group	A method for collecting data whereby selected participants discuss their reactions and feelings about a product, service, situation or concept, under the guidance of a group leader.
Frequency	The number of observations for a particular data value in a variable.
Frequency distribution	An array that summarizes the frequencies for all the data values in a particular variable.
Generalizability	The extent to which the research findings (often based on a sample) can be extended to other cases (often a population) or to other settings.
Grounded theory	A methodology in which a systematic set of procedures is used to develop an inductively derived theory about phenomena.
Harvard system of referencing	A system where citations are shown as author and date (and page number if quoting) in the text and the references are listed in alphabetical order by author at the end of the document.
Hermeneutics	A methodology that focuses on the interpretation and understanding of text in the context of the underlying historical and social forces.
Histogram	A refinement of a bar chart where adjoining bars touch, indicating continuous interval or ratio data. Frequency is represented by area, with the width of each bar indicating the class interval and the height indicating the frequency of the class.
Hypothesis (plural is hypotheses)	A proposition that can be tested for association or causality against empirical evidence.
Hypothetical construct	A rating scale used to measure opinion and other abstract ideas.
Independent variable (IV)	A variable that influences the values of a dependent variable.
Index number	A statistical measure that shows the percentage change in a variable from a fixed point in the past.
Inductive research	A study in which theory is developed from the observation of empirical reality; thus general inferences are induced from particular instances.
Inferential statistics	A group of statistical methods and models used to draw conclusions about a population from quantitative data relating to a random sample.

Information	The knowledge created by organizing data into a useful form.
Interpretivism	A paradigm that emerged in response to criticisms of positivism. It rests on the assumption that social reality is in our minds, and is subjective and multiple. Therefore, social reality is affected by the act of investigating it. The research involves an inductive process with a view to providing interpretive understanding of social phenomena within a particular context.
Interquartile range	A measure of dispersion that represents the difference between the upper quartile and the lower quartile (the middle 50%) of a frequency distribution arranged in size order.
Interval variable	A variable measured on a mathematical scale with equal intervals and an arbitrary zero point.
Interview	A method for collecting primary data in which a sample of interviewees are asked questions to find out what they think, do or feel.
Kurtosis	A measure of the extent to which a frequency distribution is flatter or more peaked than a normal distribution (a normal distribution has a kurtosis of 0).
Laboratory experiment	An experimental study conducted in an artificial setting.
Limitation	A weaknesses or deficiency in the research.
Line graph	A graphical presentation of a frequency distribution in which the data are represented by a series of points joined by a line; only suitable for continuous data.
Linear regression	A measure of the ability of an independent variable to predict an outcome in a dependent variable where there is a linear relationship between them.
Literature	All sources of published data on a particular topic.
Literature review	A critical evaluation of the existing body of knowledge on a topic, which guides the research and demonstrates that the relevant literature has been located and analysed.
Literature search	A systematic process with a view to identifying the existing body of knowledge on a particular topic.
Location	The setting in which the research is conducted.
Logistic regression	A form of multiple regression that is used where the dependent variable is a dummy variable and one or more of the independent variables are continuous quantitative variables. Any other independent variables can be ordinal or dummy variables.

Longitudinal study	A methodology used to investigate variables or a group of subjects over a long period of time.
Mann-Whitney test	A non-parametric test of difference for two independent or dependent samples for ratio, interval or ordinal variables.
Mean ($\bar{x}$)	A measure of central tendency based on the arithmetic average of a set of data values.
Median (M)	A measure of central tendency based on the mid-value of a set of data arranged in size order.
Method	A technique for collecting and/or analysing data.
Methodological assumption	A philosophical assumption about the process of research.
Methodological rigour	The appropriateness and intellectual soundness of the research design and the systematic application of the research methods.
Methodology	An approach to the process of the research encompassing a body of methods.
Mind map	An informal diagram of a person's idea of the key elements of a subject that shows connections and relationships.
Mode (m)	A measure of central tendency based on the most frequently occurring value in set of data (there may be multiple modes).
Morphological analysis	A technique for generating research topics whereby the subject is analysed into its key attributes and a 'mix and match' approach is adopted.
Multivariate analysis	Analysis of data more than two variables.
Natural setting	A research environment that would have existed had researchers never studied it.
Nominal variable	A variable measured using numerical codes to identify named categories.
Non-participant observation	A method of observation in which the observer is not involved in the activities taking place and the phenomena studied.
Normal distribution	A theoretical frequency distribution that is bell-shaped and symmetrical with tails extending indefinitely either side of the centre. The mean, median and mode coincide at the centre.
Observation	A method for collecting data used in the laboratory or in a natural setting to observe and record people's actions and behaviour.
Ontological assumption	A philosophical assumption about the nature of reality.

Open question	A question where respondents can give a response in their own words.
Ordinal variable	A variable measured using numerical codes to identify order or rank.
Paradigm	A framework that guides how research should be conducted based on people's philosophies and their assumptions about the world and the nature of knowledge.
Parameter	A number that describes a population.
Participant observation	A method of observation in which the observer is involved in the activities taking place and the phenomena studied.
Participative enquiry	A methodology that involves the participants as fully as possible in the study, which is conducted in their own group or organization.
Pearson's correlation coefficient (r)	A parametric test that measures linear association between two continuous variables measured on a ratio or interval scale.
Percentage frequency	A descriptive statistic that summarizes a frequency as a proportion of 100.
Phenomenon (plural phenomena)	An observed or apparent object, fact or occurrence, especially one where the cause is uncertain.
Pie chart	A circular diagram showing the percentage frequency distribution of a nominal variable in which the data are represented by a series of segments. Each segment represents an area that is proportional to the whole 'pie'.
Plagiarism	The act of taking someone's words, ideas or other information and passing them off as your own because you fail to acknowledge the original source.
Population	A precisely defined body of people or objects under consideration for statistical purposes.
Positivism	A paradigm that originated in the natural sciences. It rests on the assumption that social reality is singular and objective, and is not affected by the act of investigating it. The research involves a deductive process with a view to providing explanatory theories to understand social phenomena.
Predictive research	A study where the aim is to generalize from an analysis of phenomena by making predictions based on hypothesized general relationships.
Primary data	Data generated from an original source, such as your own experiments, surveys, interviews or focus groups.

Problem statement	A short statement (usually one sentence) describing the research problem.
Protocol analysis	A method for collecting data used to identify a practitioner's mental processes in solving a problem in a particular situation, including the logic and methods used.
Purpose statement	A statement (usually two or three sentences long) that describes the overall purpose of the research study.
Qualitative data	Data in a nominal form.
Quantifying methods	Methods used to analyse qualitative data by converting it into quantitative data.
Quantitative data	Data in a numerical form.
Quantitative variable	A ratio, interval or dummy variable.
Quasi-judicial method	A method of analysis that involves the use of rational argument to interpret qualitative data.
Questionnaire	A method for collecting primary data in which a sample of respondents are asked a list of carefully structured questions chosen after considerable testing, with a view to eliciting reliable responses.
Random sample	A sample that is representative of the population because every member had an equal chance of being selected.
Range	A measure of dispersion that represents the difference between the maximum value and the minimum value in a frequency distribution arranged in size order.
Ranked data	Quantitative data arranged in size order so that statistical tests can be performed on the ranks.
Rating scale	A hypothetical construct for obtaining ordinal data, such as the Likert scale.
Ratio variable	A variable measured on a mathematical scale with equal intervals and a fixed zero point.
Recontextualizing data	A process of generalization so that the theory emerging from a study can be applied to other settings and populations.
References	A list containing bibliographic details of the sources cited in the text.
Relevance tree	A diagram that can be used as a device for generating research topics and develop clusters of related ideas from a fairly broad starting concept.
Reliability	The absence of differences in the results if the research were repeated.

Repertory grid technique	A method based on personal construct theory that generates a mathematical representation of a participant's perceptions and constructs.
Replication	Repeating a research study to test the reliability of the results.
Research	A systematic and methodical process of enquiry and investigation with a view to increasing knowledge.
Research design	The detailed plan for conducting a research study.
Research instrument	A means of collecting data, such as a questionnaire, that has been used in a number of studies and can be adopted by any researcher.
Research problem	The specific problem or issue that is the focus of the research.
Research proposal	The document which sets out the research design for a study.
Research question	The specific question the research is designed to investigate and attempt to answer.
Research topic	The general area of research interest.
Results currency	The generalizability of the research results.
Rhetorical assumption	A philosophical assumption about the language of research.
Sample	A subset of a population. In a positivist study, a random sample is chosen to provide an unbiased subset of the population.
Sampling frame	A record of the population from which a sample can be drawn.
Scatter plot	A diagram for presenting data where one variable is plotted against another on a graph as a pattern of points, which indicates the direction and strength of any linear correlation. The more the points cluster around a straight line, the stronger the correlation.
Seasonal variation	Where a pattern in the movements of time series data repeats itself at regular intervals.
Secondary data	Data collected from an existing source, such as publications, databases and internal records.
Significance level	Level of confidence that the results of a statistical analysis are not due to chance. It is usually expressed as the probability that the results of the statistical analysis are due to chance (usually 5% or less).
Skewness	A measure of the extent to which a frequency distribution is asymmetric (a normal distribution has a skewness of 0).
Spearman's correlation coefficient (rho)	A non-parametric test that measures linear association between two variables measured on a ratio, interval or ordinal scale.

Standard deviation (sd)	A measure of dispersion that is the square root of the variance. A large standard deviation relative to the mean suggests the mean does not represent the data well.
Standard error (se)	The standard deviation between the means of different samples. A large standard error relative to the overall sample mean suggests the sample might not be representative of the population.
Statistic	A number that describes a sample.
Statistics	A body of methods and theory that is applied to quantitative data.
Stem-and-leaf plot	A diagram that uses the data values in a frequency distribution to create a display. The data values are arranged in size order and each is divided into the leading digit (the stem) and trailing digits (the leaves).
Stratified sample	A random sample chosen by selecting an appropriate proportion from each strata of the population.
Structuring data	Reorganizing data into suitable categories or sequences.
Supervisor	The person responsible for overseeing and guiding a student's research.
Survey	A methodology designed to collect primary or secondary data from a sample, with a view to generalizing the results to a population.
Synthesis/creativity	The ability to build up information from other information.
Systematic sample	A random sample chosen by dividing the population by the required sample size (n) and selecting every nth subject.
Tally	A simple stroke used to count the frequency of occurrence of a value or category in a variable.
Theoretical framework	A collection of theories and models from the literature which underpins a positivist study. Theory can be generated from some interpretivist studies.
Theory	A set of interrelated variables, definitions and propositions that specifies relationships among the variables.
Thesis	'A dissertation, esp. by [a] candidate for a higher degree' (*Oxford Dictionary & Thesaurus*, 1997, p. 801).
Time series	A sequence of measurements of a variable taken at regular intervals over time.
Time series analysis	A statistical technique for forecasting future events from time series data.

Trend	A consistently upward or downward movement in time series data.
Triangulation	The use of multiple sources of data, different research methods and/or more than one researcher to investigate the same phenomenon in a study.
t-test	A parametric test of difference for two independent or dependent samples for ratio or interval variables.
Type I error	An error that occurs when H_0 is true, but the test leads to its rejection.
Type II error	An error that occurs when H_1 is true, but the test leads to the acceptance of H_0.
Unit of analysis	The phenomenon under study, about which data are collected and analysed.
Univariate analysis	Analysis of data from one variable.
Validity	The extent to which the research findings accurately reflect the phenomena under study.
Vancouver system	A system of referencing where citations are shown as an in-text number each time the source is cited and the references are listed in numerical order at the end of the document.
Variable	A characteristic of a phenomenon that can be observed or measured.
Variance	The mean of the squared errors.
Viva voce	A defence of a dissertation or thesis by oral examination.
Weighted index number	An index number constructed by calculating a weighted average of some set of values, where the weights show the relative importance of each item in the data set.

References

Ackermann, F., Eden, C. and Cropper, S. (1990) 'Cognitive Mapping: A User Guide', Working Paper No. 12, Glasgow, Strathclyde University, Department of Management Science.

Adams, G. and Schvaneveldt, J. (1991) *Understanding Research Methods*, 2nd edition, New York: Longman.

Agnew, N. M. and Pyke, S. W. (1969) *The Science Game: An Introduction to Research in Behavioral Sciences*, Englewood Cliffs, NJ: Prentice-Hall.

Alexander, D. (2006) 'The devil with Dawkins', *Times Higher Education*, London: TSL Education, 3 February, p. 20.

Allan, G. (1991) 'Qualitative Research' in Allan, G. and Skinner, C., *Handbook for Research Students in the Social Sciences*, London: The Falmer Press, pp. 177–89.

Arksey, H. and Knight, P. (1999) *Interviewing for Social Scientists*, London: Sage.

Barber, T. X. (1976) *Pitfalls in Human Research*, Oxford: Pergamon.

Barker, R. G. (1998) 'The market for information: Evidence from finance directors, analysts and fund managers', *Accounting and Business Research*, 29 (1) pp. 3–20.

Barton-Cunningham, J., and Gerrard, P. (2000) 'Characteristics of well-performing organisations in Singapore', *Singapore Management Review*, 22 (1), pp. 35–65.

Beattie, V., Fearnley, S. and Brandt, R. (2004) 'A grounded theory model of auditor–client negotiations', *International Journal of Auditing* 8 (1), pp. 1–19.

Beattie, V. and Goodacre, A. (2004) 'Publishing patterns within the UK accounting and finance academic community', *British Accounting Review*, 36 (1), pp. 7–44.

Beattie, V., and Jones, M. (1992) 'Graphic accounts', *Certified Accountant*, November, pp. 30–5.

Bell, J. (1993) *Doing Your Research Project*, Buckingham: Open University Press.

Bergwerk, R. J. (1970) 'Effective communication of financial data', *The Journal of Accountancy*, February, pp. 47–54.

BERR (Department for Business, Enterprise & Regulatory Reform) (2008) *Small and Medium-Sized Enterprise (SME) Statistics for the UK and Regions 2007*, URN 08/92. [Accessed 22 August 2008]. Available from http://stats.berr.gov.uk/ed/sme.

Black, T. R. (1993) *Evaluating Social Science Research*, London: Sage.

Blaikie, N. (2000) *Designing Social Research*, Cambridge: Polity

Blumberg, B., Cooper, D. R. and Schindler, P. S. (2005) *Business Research Methods*, Maidenhead: McGraw-Hill Education.

Blumer, H. (1980) 'Social behaviourism and symbolic interactionism', *American Sociological Review*, 45, pp. 405–19.

Bogdan, R. and Taylor, S. (1975) *Introduction to Qualitative Research Methods*, New York: John Wiley.

Bolton, R. N. (1991) 'An exploratory investigation of questionnaire pretesting with verbal protocol analysis', *Advances in Consumer Research*, 18, pp. 558–65.

Bonoma, T. V. (1985) 'Case research in marketing: Opportunities, problems, and a process', *Journal of Marketing Research*, XXII, May, pp. 199–208.

Borg, W. R. and Gall, M. D. (1989) *Educational Research: An Introduction*, 5th edition, New York: Longman.

Boyle, J. S. (1994) 'Styles of Ethnography' in Morse, J. M. (ed.) *Critical Issues on Qualitative Methods*, Thousand Oaks, CA: Sage, pp. 159–85.

Brenner, M. (1985) 'Survey Interviewing' in Brenner, M., Brown, J. and Canter, D. (eds) *The Research Interview: Uses and Approaches*, New York: Academic Press, pp. 9–36.

Bromley, D. B. (1986) *The Case Study Methodology in Psychology and Related Disciplines*, Chichester: Wiley.

Brook, J. A. (1986) 'Research applications of the repertory grid technique', *International Review of Applied Psychology*, 35, pp. 489–500.

Brook, J. A. and Brook, J. R. (1989) 'Exploring the meaning of work and non work', *Journal of Organizational Behaviour*, 20, pp. 169–78.

Brown, J. and Canter, D. (1985) 'The Uses of Explanation in the Research Interview', in Brenner, M., Brown, J. and Canter, D. (eds) *The Research Interview: Uses and Approaches*, New York: Academic Press, pp. 217–45.

Bruce, C. S. (1994) 'Research students' early experiences of the dissertation literature review', *Studies in Higher Education*, 9 (2), pp. 217–29.

Bryman, A. (1988) *Quantity and Quality in Social Research*, London: Unwin Hyman.

Burrell, G. and Morgan, G. (1979) *Sociological Paradigms and Organisational Analysis*, London: Heinemann.

Chall, J. S. (1958) *Readability – An Appraisal of Research and Application*, Columbus, OH: Ohio State University Press.

Clarkson, G. P. E. (1962) *Portfolio Selection: A Simulation of Trust Investment*, Englewood Cliffs, NJ: Prentice Hall.

Clegg, F. G. (1990) *Simple Statistics*, Cambridge: Cambridge University Press.

Collis, J. (2003) *Directors' Views on Exemption from the Statutory Audit*, URN 03/1342, London: DTI, October. Available from http://www.berr.gov.uk/files/file25971.pdf.

Coolican, H. (1992) *Research Methods and Statistics in Psychology*, London: Hodder & Stoughton.

Cooper, H. M. (1988) 'The structure of knowledge synthesis', *Knowledge in* Society, 1, pp. 104–26.

Couch, C. J. (1987) *Researching Social Processes in the Laboratory*, Greenwich, CT: JAI Press.

Creedy, J. (2001) 'Starting research', *The Australian Economic Review*, 34 (1), p. 116.

Creswell, J. W. (1994) *Research Design: Qualitative and Quantitative Approaches*, Thousand Oaks, CA: Sage.

Creswell, J. W. (1998) *Qualitative Inquiry and Research Design: Choosing Among Five Approaches*, Thousand Oaks, CA: Sage.

Creswell, J. W. (2003) *Research Design: Qualitative, Quantitative, and Mixed Methods Approaches*, 2nd edition, Thousand Oaks, CA: Sage.

Cropper, S., Eden, C. and Ackermann, F. (1990) 'Keeping sense of accounts using computer-based cognitive maps', *Social Science Computer Review*, 8 (3), Fall, pp. 345–66.

Cryer, P. (1997) 'Handling common dilemmas in supervision', *Issues in Postgraduate Supervision, Teaching and Management No. 2*, November, London: Society for Research into Higher Education and the Times Higher Education Supplement.

Curran, J. and Blackburn, R. A. (2001) *Researching the Small Enterprise*, London: Sage.

Czaja, R. and Blair, J. (1996) *Designing Surveys: A Guide to Decisions and Procedures*, Thousand Oaks, CA: Pine Forge Press.

Czepiec, H. (1993) 'Promoting industrial goods in China: Identifying the key appeals', *International Journal of Advertising*, 13, pp. 257–64.

Dackert, I., Jackson P. R., Brenner, S. O. and Johansson, C. R. (2003) 'Eliciting and analyzing employees' expectations of a merger', *Human Relations*, 56 (6), pp. 705–13.

Day, J. (1986) 'The use of annual reports by UK investment analysts', *Accounting & Business Research*, Autumn, pp. 295–307.

De Venney-Tiernan, M., Goldband, A., Rackham, L. and Reilly, N. (1994) 'Creating Collaborative Relationships in a Co-operative Inquiry Group' in Reason, P. (ed.) *Participation in Human Inquiry*, London: Sage, pp. 120–37.

Dembowski, S. and Hanmer-Lloyd, S. (1995) 'Computer applications – a new road to qualitative data analysis', *European Journal of Marketing*, 29 (11), pp. 50–62.

Denzin, N. K. (1978) *The Research Act: A Theoretical Introduction to Sociological Methods*, 2nd edition, New York: McGraw-Hill.

Denzin, N. K. (1994) 'The Arts and Politics of Interpretation', in Denzin, N. K. and Lincoln, Y. S. (eds) *Handbook of Qualitative Research*, Thousand Oaks, CA: Sage, pp. 500–15.

Denzin, N. K. and Lincoln, Y. S. (eds) (1994) *Handbook of Qualitative Research*, Thousand Oaks, CA: Sage.

DeVault, M. L. (1990) 'Talking and listening from women's standpoint: Feminist strategies for interviewing and analysis', *Social Problems*, 31 (1), February, pp. 96–116.

Dilthey, W. (1976) *Selected Writings*, (ed. and trans. H. P. Rickman) Cambridge: Cambridge University Press.

Dobbins, G. H., Lane, I. M. and Steiner, D. D. (1988) 'A note on the role of laboratory methodologies in applied behavioural research: Don't throw out the baby with the bath water', *Journal of Organisational Behaviour*, 9, pp. 281–6.

Dunn, W. and Ginsberg, A. (1986) 'A sociocognitive network approach to organisational analysis', *Human Relations*, 40 (11), pp. 955–76.

Easterby-Smith, M. (1981) 'The Analysis and Interpretation of Repertory Grids', in M. L. Shaw (ed.) *Recent Advances in Personal Construct Theory*, London: Academic Press, pp. 9–30.

Easterby-Smith, M., Thorpe, R. and Lowe, A. (1991) *Management Research: An Introduction*, London: Sage.

Ehrenberg, A. S. C. (1975) *Data Reduction*, New York: Wiley.

Ehrenberg, A. S. C. (1976) 'Annual reports don't have to be obscure', *The Journal of Accountancy*, August, pp. 88–91.

Eisenhardt, K. M. (1989) 'Building theories from case study research' *Academy of Management Review*, 14 (4), pp. 532–50.

Fiedler, F. E. (1964) 'A contingency model of leadership effectiveness', *Advances in Experimental Social Psychology*, 1, pp. 149–90.

Field, A. (2000) *Discovering Statistics Using SPSS for Windows*, London: Sage.

Fineman, S. (1983) *White Collar Unemployment: Impact and Stress*, Chichester: Wiley.

Flanagan, J. C. (1954) 'The critical incident technique', *Psychological Bulletin*, 51 (4), July, pp. 327–58.

Flannery, J. J. (1971) 'The relative effectiveness of some common graduated point symbols in the presentation of quantitative data', *Canadian Cartographer*, pp. 96–109.

Fransella, F. and Bannister, D. (1977) *The Manual for Repertory Grid Technique*, New York: Academic Press.

Frey, B. S. (2003) 'Publishing as prostitution? – Choosing between one's own ideas and academic success', *Public Choice*, 116 (1–2), pp. 205–23.

Gilbert, L. S. (2002) 'Going the distance: 'Closeness' in qualitative data analysis software', *International Journal of Social Research Methodology*, 5 (3), pp. 215–28.

Gill, J. and Johnson, P. (1991) *Research Methods for Managers*, London: Paul Chapman.

Glaser, B. (1978) *Theoretical Sensitivity*, Mill Valley, CA: Sociology Press.

Glaser, B. and Strauss, A. (1967) *The Discovery of Grounded Theory*, Chicago, IL: Aldine.

Gregg, R. (1994) 'Explorations of Pregnancy and Choice in a High-Tech Age', in Riessman, C. K. (ed.) *Qualitative Studies in Social Work Research*, Thousand Oaks, CA: Sage, pp. 49–66.

Gubrium, J. and Holstein, J. (eds) (2001) *Handbook of Interview Research*, London, Sage.

Gummesson, E. (1991) *Qualitative Methods in Management Research*, Newbury Park: Sage.

Hankinson, G. (2004) 'Repertory grid analysis: An application to the measurement of distant images', *International Journal of Nonprofit and Voluntary Sector Marketing*, 9 (2), pp. 145–54.

Howard, K. and Sharp, J. A. (1994) *The Management of a Student Research Project*, Aldershot: Gower.

Hunter, M. G. (1997) 'The use of RepGrids to gather interview data about information system analysts', *Information Systems Journal*, 7, pp. 67–81.

Hussey, R. (2007) 'The application of personal construct theory in international accounting research,' *Journal of Theoretical Accounting Research*, 2 (2), pp. 34–51.

Hussey, R. and Ong, A. (2005) 'A substantive model of the annual financial reporting exercise in a non-market corporate', *Qualitative Research in Accounting and Management*, 2 (2) pp. 152–70.

Hyde, C. (1994) 'Reflections on a Journey: A Research Story', in Riessman, C. K. (ed.) *Qualitative Studies in Social Work Research*, Thousand Oaks, CA: Sage, pp. 169–89.

Hyland, K. (2003) 'Self-citation and self-reference: Credibilty and promotion in academic publication', *Journal of the American Society for Information Science and Technology*, 54 (3), pp. 251–9.

Innes, J. (2001) 'Social Performance Measures and Management Control: A Grounded Theory Case Study', Discussion Paper, Dundee: University of Dundee.

Iselin, E. R. (1972) 'Accounting and communication theory', *The Singapore Accountant*, 7, pp. 31–7.

Jankowicz, A. D. (1991) *Business Research Projects for Students*, London: Chapman & Hall.

Jankowicz, D. (2004) *The Easy Guide to Repertory Grids*, London: Wiley.

Jensen, M. C. and Meckling, W. H. (1976) 'Theory of the firm: Managerial behavior, agency costs and the ownership structure', *Journal of Financial Economics*, 3, pp. 305–60.

Jick, T. D. (1979) 'Mixing qualitative and quantitative methods: Triangulation in action', *Administrative Science Quarterly*, December, 24, pp. 602–11.

Jinkerson, D. L., Cummings, O. W., Neisendorf, B. J. and Schwandt, T. A. (1992) 'A case study of methodological issues in cross-cultural evaluation', *Evaluation and Program Planning*, 15, pp. 273–85.

Johnston, L. (2006) 'Software and method: Reflections on teaching and using QSR NVivo in doctoral research', *International Journal of Social Research Methodology*, 9 (5), pp. 379–91.

Johnston, S. (1995) 'Building a sense of community in a research Master's course', *Studies in Higher Education*, 20 (3), pp. 279–303.

Jones, M. J. and Roberts, R. A. (2005) 'International publishing patterns: An investigation of leading UK and US accounting and finance journals', *Journal of Business Finance and Accounting*, 32 (5–6), pp. 1107–40.

Judge, G. G., Griffiths, W. E., Hill, R. C., Lutkepol, H. and Lee, T. C. (1985) *The Theory and Practice of Econometrics*. Chichester: John Wiley & Sons.

Kelly, G. A. (1955) *The Psychology of Personal Constructs: A Theory of Personality*, New York: Norton.

Kerlinger, F. N. (1979) *Behavioural Research: A Conceptual Approach*, New York: Holt, Rinehart & Winston.

Kerlinger, F. N. (1986) *Foundations of Behavioral Research* (3rd edn), New York: Holt, Rinehart & Winston.

Kervin, J. B. (1992) *Methods for Business Research*, New York: HarperCollins.

Krejcie, R. V. and Morgan, D. W. (1970) 'Determining sample size for research activities', *Educational and Psychological Measurement*, 30, pp. 607–10.

Kuhn, T. (1970) *The Structure of Scientific Revolutions*, Chicago, IL: Chicago University Press.

Kuhn, T. S. (1962) *The Structure of Scientific Revolutions*, Chicago, IL: University of Chicago Press.

Laughlin, R. (1995) 'Methodological themes – empirical research in accounting: Alternative approaches and a case for "middle-range" thinking', *Accounting, Auditing and Accountability Journal*, 8 (1), pp. 63–87.

Lee, R. M. (1993) *Doing Research on Sensitive Topics*, London: Sage.

Leininger, M. (1994) 'Evaluation Criteria and Critique of Qualitative Research Studies' in Morse, J. M. (ed.) *Critical Issues in Qualitative Research Methods*, Thousand Oaks, CA: Sage, pp. 95–115.

Lewin, K. (1946) 'Action research and minority problems', *Journal of Social Issues*, 2, pp. 34–6.

Lincoln, Y. S. and Guba, E. G. (1985) *Naturalistic Enquiry*, Newbury Park, CA: Sage.

Lindlof, T. R. (1995) *Qualitative Communication Research Methods*, Thousand Oaks, CA: Sage.

Lovie, P. (1986) 'Identifying Outliers' in Lovie, A. D. (ed.) *New Developments in Statistics for Psychology and the Social Sciences* 1, London: Methuen.

Macdonald-Ross, M. (1977), 'How numbers are shown – A review of research on the presentation of quantitative data in texts', *AV Communication Review*, 25 (4), Winter, pp. 359–409.

MacKinlay, T. (1986) *The Development of a Personal Strategy of Management*, M.Sc. thesis, Manchester Polytechnic, Department of Management.

Martin, D. M. (1989) *How to Prepare the Annual Report*, Cambridge: Director Books.

McGrath, M. A. (1989) 'An ethnography of a gift store: Trappings, wrappings, and rapture', *Journal of Retailing*, 65 (4), Winter, pp. 421–49.

Merriam, S. B. (1988) *Case Study Research in Education: A Qualitative Approach*, San Francisco, CA: Jossey-Bass.

Merton, R. K. and Kendall, P. L. (1946) 'The focussed interview', *American Journal of Sociology*, 51, pp. 541–57.

Miles, M. B. and Huberman, A. M. (1994) *Qualitative Data Analysis*, Thousand Oaks, CA: Sage.

Mingers, J. (2001) 'Combining IS research methods: Towards a pluralist methodology', *Information Systems Research*, September, 12 (3) p. 240. Available from: http://proquest.umi.com.

Moore, D., McCabe, G. P., Duckworth, W. M. and Alwan, L. C. (2009) *The Practice of Business Statistics* , 2nd edition, New York: W.H. Freeman and Company.

Morgan, D. L. (1988) *Focus Groups as Qualitative Research*, Newbury Park, CA: Sage.

Morgan, G. (1979) 'Response to Mintzberg', *Administrative Science Quarterly*, 24 (1), pp. 137–9.

Morgan, G. and Smircich, L. (1980) 'The case of qualitative research', *Academy of Management Review*, 5, pp. 491–500.

Morris, C. (1993) *Quantitative Approaches in Business Studies*, London: Pitman.

Morse, J. M. (1994) 'Emerging from the data: The cognitive processes of analysis in qualitative inquiry' in Morse, J. M. (ed.) *Critical Issues in Qualitative Research Methods*, Thousand Oaks, CA: Sage, pp. 23–43.

Mostyn, B. (1985) 'The Content Analysis of Qualitative Research Data: A Dynamic Approach', in Brenner, M., Brown, J. and Canter, D. (eds) *The Research Interview, Uses and Approaches*, London: Academic Press, pp. 115–46.

Normann, R. (1970) *A Personal Quest for Methodology*, Stockholm: Scandinavian Institute for Administrative Research.

Oakshott, L. (1994) *Essential Elements of Business Statistics*, London: DP Publications.

Otley, D. and Berry, A. (1994) 'Case study research in management accounting and control', *Management Accounting Research*, 5, pp. 45–65.

Oxford Compact Dictionary & Thesaurus (1997), Oxford: Oxford University Press.

Oxford Dictionary of Accounting (2005), Oxford: Oxford University Press.

Parker, D. (1994) *Tackling Coursework*, London: DP Publications.

Parker, L. D. and Roffey, B. H. (1996) 'Back to the drawing board: Revisiting grounded theory and the everyday accountant's and manager's reality', *Accounting, Auditing and Accountability Journal'*, 10 (2) pp. 212–347.

Patton, M. (1990) *Qualitative Evaluation and Research Methods*, Newbury Park, CA: Sage.

Phillips, E. M. (1984) 'Learning to do research', *Graduate Management Research*, Autumn, pp. 6–18.

Phillips, E. M. and Pugh, D. S. (1994) *How to Get a Ph.D.*, Buckingham: Open University Press.

Pidgeon, N. F., Turner, B. A. and Blockley, D. I. (1991) 'The use of grounded theory for conceptual analysis in knowledge elicitation', *International Journal of Man–Machine Studies*, 35, pp. 151–73.

Piotrowski, C. and Armstrong, T. R. (2005) 'Major research areas in organization development: An analysis of ABI/INFORM', *Organization Development Journal*, 23 (4) pp. 86–92.

Playfair, W. (1786) *The Commercial and Political Atlas*, London.

Plummer, K. (1983) *Documents of Life: An Introduction to the Problems and Literature of a Humanistic Method*, London: Allen & Unwin.

Prather-Kinsey, J. and Rueschoff, N. (2004) 'An analysis of international accounting research in US and non-US based academic accounting journals', *Journal of International Accounting Research*, 3, pp. 63–82.

Pullman, M., McGuire, K. and Cleveland, C. (2005) 'Let me count the words: Quantifying open-ended interactions with guests', *Cornell Hotel & Restaurant Administration Quarterly*, 46 (3), pp. 323–45

Raimond, P. (1993) *Management Projects: Design, Research and Presentation*, London: Chapman & Hall.

Reason, P. (1994a) (ed.) *Participation in Human Inquiry*, London: Sage.

Reason, P. (1994b) 'Three Approaches to Participative Inquiry', in Denzin, N. K. and Lincoln, Y. S. (eds) *Handbook of Qualitative Research*, Thousand Oaks, CA: Sage, pp. 324–39.

Reason, P. and Rowan, J. (1981) *Human Enquiry: A Sourcebook of New Paradigm Research*, Chichester: John Wiley.

Ricoeur, P. (1977) 'The Model of the Text: Meaningful Action Considered as a Text', in Dallmayr, F. R. and McCarthy, T. A. (eds) *Understanding and Social Enquiry*, Notre Dame, IN: University of Notre Dame Press, pp. 316–34.

Ricoeur, P. (1981) *Hermeneutics and the Human Sciences*, (trans. J. B. Thompson) Cambridge: Cambridge University Press.

Robson, C. (1993) *Real World Research: A Resource for Social Scientists and Practitioner Researchers*, Oxford: Blackwell.

Rosenthal, R. (1966) *Experimenter Effects in Behavioural Research*, New York: Appleton-Century-Crofts.

Rowntree, D. (1991) *Statistics Without Tears: A Primer for Non-mathematicians*, Harmondsworth: Penguin.

Rudestam, K. E. and Newton, R. R. (1992) *Surviving Your Dissertation*, Newbury Park, CA: Sage.

Ryan, B., Scapens, R. W. and Theobald, M. (2002) *Research Method and Methodology in Finance and Accounting*, 2nd edition, London: Thomson Learning.

Salkind, N. J. (2006) *Exploring Research*, Upper Saddle River, NJ: Pearson International.

Saunders, M., Lewis, P. and Thornhill, A. (2007) *Research Methods for Business Students*, 4th edition, Harlow: Pearson Education.

Scapens, R. W. (1990) 'Researching management accounting practice: The role of case study methods', *British Accounting Review*, 22, pp. 259–81.

Sekaran, U. (2003) *Research Methods for Business*, 4th edition, New York: John Wiley.

Silverman, D. (1993) *Interpreting Qualitative Data: Methods for Analysing Talk, Text and Interaction*, London: Sage.

Slife, B. D. and Williams, R. N. (1995) *What's Behind the Research: Discovering Hidden Assumptions in the Behavioural Sciences*, Thousand Oaks, CA: Sage.

Smagorinsky, P. (1989) 'The reliability and validity of protocol analysis', *Written Communication*, 6 (4), October, pp. 463–79.

Smagorinsky, P. (1994*) Speaking about Writing: Reflections on Research Methodology*, Thousand Oaks, CA: Sage.

Smith, J. K. (1983) 'Quantitative v qualitative research: An attempt to classify the issue', *Educational Research*, March, pp. 6–13.

Stebbins, R. A. (1992) 'Concatenated exploration: Notes on a neglected type of longitudinal research', *Quality and Quantity*, 26, pp. 435–42.

Stern, P. N. (1994) 'Eroding Grounded Theory' in Morse, J. M. (ed.) *Qualitative Research Methods*, Thousand Oaks, CA: Sage, pp. 212–23.

Stewart, R. (1965) 'The use of diaries to study managers' jobs', *Journal of Management Studies*, 2, pp. 228–35.

Stewart, V. and Stewart, A. (1981) *Business Applications of Repertory Grid*, Maidenhead: McGraw-Hill.

Strauss, A. (1987) *Qualitative Analysis for Social Scientists*, New York: Cambridge University Press.

Strauss, A. and Corbin, J. (1990) *Basics of Qualitative Research: Grounded Theory Procedures and Techniques*, Newbury Park, CA: Sage.

Strauss, A. and Corbin, J. (1994) 'Grounded Theory Methodology: An Overview', in Denzin, N. K. and Lincoln, Y. S. (eds) *Handbook of Qualitative Research*, Thousand Oaks, CA: Sage.

Swanson, E. P. (2004) Publishing in the majors: A comparison of accounting, finance, management and marketing. *Contemporary Accounting Research*, 21(1), pp. 223–52.

Tan, F. and Hunter, M. G. (2002) 'The repertory grid technique: A method for the study of cognition in information systems', *MIS Quarterly*, 26 (1), pp. 39–57.

Taylor, D. S. (1990) 'Making the most of your matrices: Hermeneutics, statistics and the repertory grid', *International Journal of Personal Construct Psychology*, 3, pp. 105–19.

Thibadoux, G., Cooper, W. D. and Greenberg, I. S. (1986) 'Flowcharts and graphics: Part II', *CPA Journal*, March, pp. 17–23.

Todd, P. A., McKeen, J. D. and Gallupe, R. B. (1995) 'The evolution of IS job skills: A content analysis of IS job advertisements from 1970 to 1990', *MIS Quarterly*, March, pp. 1–24.

Torrance, M., Thomas, G. V. and Robinson, E. J. (1992) 'The writing experiences of social science research students', *Studies in Higher Education*, 17 (2) pp. 155–67.

Traylen, H. (1994) 'Confronting hidden agendas: Co-operative inquiry with health visitors' in Reason, P. (ed.) *Participation in Human Inquiry*, London: Sage, pp. 59–81.

Treleaven, L., (1994) 'Making a space: A collaborative inquiry with women as staff development', in Reason, P. (ed.) *Participation in Human Inquiry*, London: Sage, pp. 138–62.

Tufte, E. R. (1983) *The Visual Display of Quantitative Information*, Cheshire: Graphic Press.

Turner, B. A. (1981) 'Some practical aspects of qualitative data analysis: One way of organizing the cognitive processes associated with the generation of grounded theory', *Quality and Quantity*, 15 (3), pp. 225–47.

Upton, G. and Cook, I. (2006) *Oxford Dictionary of Statistics*, 2nd edition, Oxford: Oxford University Press.

Van Maanen, J. (1983) *Qualitative Methodology*, London: Sage.

Vogt, W. P. (1993) *Dictionary of Statistics and Methodology*, Newbury Park, CA: Sage.

Wallace, R. S. O. and Mellor, C. J. (1988) 'Non-response bias in mail accounting surveys: A pedagogical note', *British Accounting Review*, 20, pp. 131–9.

Walliman, N. (2001) *Your Research Project*, Sage: London.

Werner, O. and Schoepfle, G. (1987) *Systematic Fieldwork: Foundations of Ethnography and Interviewing*, Newbury Park, CA: Sage.

Wilkinson, A. M. (1991) *The Scientist's Handbook for Writing Papers and Dissertations*, Englewood Cliffs, NJ: Prentice Hall.

Winkler, A. C. and McCuen-Metherell, J. R. (2007) *Writing the Research Paper: A Handbook*, 7th edition, New York: Harcourt Brace Jovanovitch.

Wolfe, R. A., Gephardt, R. P. and Johnson, T. E. (1993) 'Computer-facilitated data analysis: Potential contributions to management research', *Journal of Management*, 19 (3), pp. 637–60.

Yin, R. K. (2003) *Case Study Research: Design and Methods*, 3rd edition, Thousand Oaks, CA: Sage.

Name index

Subject index

A

abstract,
    journal articles, 93
    writing, 300
academic institutions, 26
access to data, 43, 114
action research, 81
additive model in time series
    analysis, 284
administration and planning, 47
alternative hypothesis, 22
analogy, 41
analysing data,
    evaluating methods, 182
    qualitative data, 161–84
    quantitative data, 219–90
analytical procedures,
    for qualitative research data,
      169
    for reviewing the literature, 100
analytical research, 4–6
analytical survey, 77
anonymity, 45
anticipatory data reduction, 167
applied research, 4, 7, 8
articles,
    searching for, 91
    writing, 315
association measures
    chi-square test, 263
assumptions,
    linear regression models, 273
    parametric tests, 259
average *see* mean
axial coding in grounded theory,
    179
axiological assumption, 59

B

Bachelor's level research, 3, 9, 21
    choosing an institution, 26
    supervision, 29
bar charts, 234, 236
basic research, 4, 7, 8
bibliographic software, 95
bivariate analysis, 222, 230, 260,
    268, 274
Boolean operators, 94
brainstorming, 40

C

case study, 82
central tendency measures, 240
charts and graphs, 234, 308
chi squared (χ^2) test, 263
citations and references, 96, 126
    Harvard system, 96
    Vancouver system, 98
classifying research, 4
closed questions, 200
cluster sampling, 212
coding
    content analysis, 165
    grounded theory, 179
    questionnaires, 207
cognitive mapping, 177
collecting data *see* methods
composite index number *see*
    weighted index number
concurrent verbalization, 150
conference papers,
    searching for, 93
    writing, 315
confidentiality, 46, 192, 195
confirmability, 182
confounding variable, 74
construct 150
    hypothetical, 190
    validity, 191
content analysis, 164
continuous data reduction, 167
continuous quantitative variable, 189
correlation measures, 267
    Pearson's correlation (r), 272
    Spearman's correlation
      coefficient (*rho* or r_s), 270
credibility, 182
critical incident technique, 147, 197
cross-sectional study, 77
cross tabulations, 233,
cyclical variation in a trend, 287

D

data, 114
    access, 43, 114
    discrete and continuous, 189
    primary or secondary, 23, 73,
      163
    qualitative, 163

quantitative, 187
data analysis, *see* methods
data collection, *see* methods
data displays, 171
data integrity, 64
deconstruction, 124
deductive research, 8, 188
deflating data, 281
delimitations, 124
Delphi study, 192
dependability, 182
dependent variable, 74, 191
descriptive case study, 82
descriptive research, 4–6
descriptive statistics, 219–54
descriptive survey, 77
de-seasonalized trend, 284
designing
    dissertation or thesis, 296
    questions, 193, 198, 206, 208
    research, 111
detextualizing qualitative data, 167
diagrams,
    mind map, 42, 294
    relevance tree, 43
    scatter plot, 268
    stem-and-leaf plot, 239
diary methods, 152, 196
dichotomous variable, 190
difference measures,
    t-test, 262
discourse, 4, 21
discrete quantitative variable, 198
dispersion measures, 244
dissertation, 4, 9, 11, 12, 21
distribution of frequency data, 230
distribution methods for
    questionnaires, 193
doctoral level research, 4, 9, 21–5
    choosing an institution, 26–9
    supervision, 29–32
dummy variable, 227

E

effects matrix, 172
empirical evidence, 6, 63
employability, 28
entry requirements for degree
    programmes, 21
epistemological assumption, 59